PROPORTIONALITY OF CRIMINAL PENALTIES IN EU LAW

This book develops a systematic analysis of the principle of proportionality of penalties in EU law.

Until now, the principle has been mainly assessed from a criminological point of view. By departing from existing literature, the book advances an original EU law perspective on proportionality of penalties, which underlies the analysis of its theorisation, place and influence on domestic criminal systems. Building upon this approach, scholarly contributions in the book systematically delve into the various implications of the principle in EU law, while paying particular attention to its profound interaction with criminal law concepts.

Volume 21 in the series Hart Studies in European Criminal Law

Hart Studies in European Criminal Law

Series Editors: Professor Valsamis Mitsilegas, Queen Mary University of London; Professor Katalin Ligeti, University of Luxembourg; Professor Anne Weyembergh, Brussels Free University

Since the Lisbon Treaty, European criminal law has become an increasingly important field of research and debate. Working with the European Criminal Law Academic Network (ECLAN), the series will publish works of the highest intellectual rigour and cutting edge scholarship which will be required reading for all European criminal lawyers.

The series is happy to consider both edited and single authored titles. The series defines 'European' and 'criminal law' in the broadest sense so books on the European criminal law, justice and policy will be considered. The series also welcomes books which offer different methodological approaches.

Volume 1: *EU Criminal Law after Lisbon: Rights, Trust and the Transformation of Justice in Europe*
Valsamis Mitsilegas

Volume 2: *Challenges in the Field of Economic and Financial Crime in Europe and the US*
Edited by Vanessa Franssen and Katalin Ligeti

Volume 3: *Chasing Criminal Money: Challenges and Perspectives On Asset Recovery in the EU*
Edited by Katalin Ligeti and Michele Simonato

Volume 4: *Limits to EU Powers: A Case Study of EU Regulatory Criminal Law*
Jacob Öberg

Volume 5: *The Needed Balances in EU Criminal Law: Past, Present and Future*
Edited by Chloé Brière and Anne Weyembergh

Volume 6: *Redefining Organised Crime: A Challenge for the European Union?*
Edited by Stefania Carnevale, Serena Forlati and Orsetta Giolo

Volume 7: *White Collar Crime: A Comparative Perspective*
Edited by Katalin Ligeti and Stanislaw Tosza

Volume 8: *Criminal Liability of Managers in Europe: Punishing Excessive Risk*
Stanisław Tosza

Volume 9: *The European Union and Deprivation of Liberty: A Legislative and Judicial Analysis from the Perspective of the Individual*
Leandro Mancano

Volume 10: *The Legitimacy of EU Criminal Law*
Irene Wieczorek

Volume 11: *The Fight Against Impunity in EU Law*
Edited by Luisa Marin and Stefano Montaldo

Volume 12: *Controlling Immigration Through Criminal Law: European and Comparative Perspectives on 'Crimmigration'*
Edited by Gian Luigi Gatta, Valsamis Mitsilegas, and Stefano Zirulia

Volume 13: *The Principle of Mutual Trust in EU Criminal Law*
Auke Willems

Volume 14: *Surveillance and Privacy in the Digital Age: European, Transatlantic and Global Perspectives*
Edited by Valsamis Mitsilegas and Niovi Vavoula

Volume 15: *The External Dimension of the EU's Policy against Trafficking in Human Beings*
Chloé Brière

Volume 16: *Criminal and Quasi-criminal Enforcement Mechanisms in Europe: Origins, Concepts, Future*
Edited by Vanessa Franssen and Christopher Harding

Volume 17: *Data protection, Migration and Border Control: The GDPR, the Law Enforcement Directive and Beyond*
Teresa Quintel

Volume 18: *Corporations and the Privilege against Self-Incrimination*
Stijn Lamberigts

Volume 19: *EU Enforcement Authorities: Punitive Law Enforcement in a Composite Legal Order*
Edited by Michiel Luchtman, Katalin Ligeti and John Vervaele

Volume 20: *Admissibility of Evidence in EU Cross-Border Criminal Proceedings: Electronic Evidence, Efficiency and Fair Trial Rights*
Edited by Lorena Bachmaier Winter and Farsam Salimi

Volume 21: *Proportionality of Criminal Penalties in EU Law*
Edited by Lorenzo Grossio, Stefano Montaldo and Valsamis Mitsilegas

Volume 11: *The Fight Against Impunity in EU Law*
Edited by Luisa Marin and Stefano Montaldo

Volume 12: *Controlling Immigration Through Criminal Law: European and Comparative Perspectives on 'Crimmigration'*
Edited by Gian Luigi Gatta, Valsamis Mitsilegas, and Stefano Zirulia

Volume 13: *The Principle of Mutual Trust in EU Criminal Law*
Auke Willems

Volume 14: *Surveillance and Privacy in the Digital Age: European, Transatlantic and Global Perspectives*
Edited by Valsamis Mitsilegas and Niovi Vavoula

Volume 15: *The External Dimension of the EU's Policy against Trafficking in Human Beings*
Chloé Brière

Volume 16: *Criminal and Quasi-criminal Enforcement Mechanisms in Europe: Origins, Concepts, Future*
Edited by Vanessa Franssen and Christopher Harding

Volume 17: *Data protection, Migration and Border Control: The GDPR, the Law Enforcement Directive and Beyond*
Teresa Quintel

Volume 18: *Corporations and the Privilege against Self-Incrimination*
Stijn Lamberigts

Volume 19: *EU Enforcement Authorities: Punitive Law Enforcement in a Composite Legal Order*
Edited by Michiel Luchtman, Katalin Ligeti and John Vervaele

Volume 20: *Admissibility of Evidence in EU Cross-Border Criminal Proceedings: Electronic Evidence, Efficiency and Fair Trial Rights*
Edited by Lorena Bachmaier Winter and Farsam Salimi

Volume 21: *Proportionality of Criminal Penalties in EU Law*
Edited by Lorenzo Grossio, Stefano Montaldo and Valsamis Mitsilegas

Proportionality of Criminal Penalties in EU Law

Edited by
Lorenzo Grossio
Stefano Montaldo
and
Valsamis Mitsilegas

•HART•
OXFORD • LONDON • NEW YORK • NEW DELHI • SYDNEY

HART PUBLISHING

Bloomsbury Publishing Plc

Kemp House, Chawley Park, Cumnor Hill, Oxford, OX2 9PH, UK

1385 Broadway, New York, NY 10018, USA

Bloomsbury Publishing Ireland Limited, 29 Earlsfort Terrace, Dublin 2, D02 AY28, Ireland

HART PUBLISHING, the Hart/Stag logo, BLOOMSBURY and the Diana logo are trademarks of Bloomsbury Publishing Plc

First published in Great Britain 2025

A catalogue record for this book is available from the British Library.

A catalogue record for this book is available from the Library of Congress.

Library of Congress Control Number: 2024946860

ISBN: HB: 978-1-50997-415-3
ePDF: 978-1-50997-417-7
ePub: 978-1-50997-416-0

Typeset by Compuscript Ltd, Shannon

For product safety related questions contact productsafety@bloomsbury.com

To find out more about our authors and books visit www.hartpublishing.co.uk. Here you will find extracts, author information, details of forthcoming events and the option to sign up for our newsletters.

ACKNOWLEDGEMENTS

This volume was prepared in the context of the research project 'Proportionality of Criminal Penalties in EU law', funded by the University of Turin under the Grant for Internationalisation 2023 initiative, within the framework of the *UNITA – Universitas Montium* network.

UNIVERSITÀ DI TORINO

UNITA universitas montium

dg Università di Torino Dipartimento di Giurisprudenza

2023 - 2027 DIPARTIMENTO DI ECCELLENZA Ministero dell'Università e della Ricerca

TABLE OF CONTENTS

LIST OF CONTRIBUTORS

Lorenzo Bernardini

Postdoctoral Research Fellow in Criminal Law
Faculty of Law, Economics and Finance (FDEF), Department of Law, University of Luxembourg, Luxembourg

Chloé Brière

Professor of EU Law
Centre for European Law, Institute of European Studies, Université libre de Bruxelles, Belgium

Pedro Caeiro

Associate Professor and Integrated Researcher
Faculty of Law, UCILeR, University of Coimbra, Portugal

Vittorio Cama

Ph.D. Candidate in Criminal Law
Doctoral Programme in European and Comparative Legal Studies, University of Trento, Italy

Chloé Fauchon

Associate Professor
Department of European and International Studies, University of Pau, France

Francesca Finelli

Ph.D. Candidate in International and EU Law
Faculty of Law, Economics and Finance (FDEF), Department of Law, University of Luxembourg, Luxembourg in joint supervision with the University of Pisa, Italy

Lorenzo Grossio

Postdoctoral Research Fellow in EU Law
Department of Law, University of Turin, Italy

Valsamis Mitsilegas

Professor of European and Global Law – Dean of the School of Law and Social Justice
School of Law and Social Justice, University of Liverpool, UK

Adriano Martufi

Assistant Professor of Criminal Law
Department of Law, University of Pavia, Italy

Stefano Montaldo

Associate Professor of EU Law
Department of Law, University of Turin, Italy

Jacob Öberg

Full Professor of European Law
Department of Law, University of Southern Denmark, Denmark

Marco Pelissero

Full Professor of Criminal Law
Department of Law, University of Turin, Italy

Emanuela Pistoia

Full Professor of EU Law
Department of Law, University of Teramo, Italy

Stefano Maria Ronco

Assistant Professor of Tax Law
Department of Law, University of Turin, Italy

Alessandro Rosanò

Assistant Professor of EU Law
Department of Law, Politics and International Studies, University of Parma, Italy

Araceli Turmo

Associate Professor
Department of Public Law, University of Nantes, France

Gniewomir Wycichowski-Kuchta

Ph.D. Candidate in Law
Doctoral School of Social Sciences, University of Warsaw, Poland

1

Introduction

LORENZO GROSSIO, STEFANO MONTALDO
AND VALSAMIS MITSILEGAS

As a general principle of the EU legal order, proportionality is inherently multidimensional. It encompasses distinct declinations that range from the exercise of EU powers to fundamental rights adjudication and the compatibility of domestic measures *vis-à-vis* internal market freedoms. Against this background, the principle has a clear theoretical identity in the EU legal order. Proportionality is traditionally conceptualised as a threefold prospective requirement: any measure shall be suitable and necessary to attain a given objective and must ensure that its negative consequences are not disproportionate in that respect.

Proportionality is also a key principle of EU criminal law, as its role is not limited to guiding the exercise of EU harmonisation powers under Article 83 TFEU. Since the early stages of the integration process, the European Court of Justice (ECJ) has consistently referred to the principle of proportionality to assess the compatibility of domestic criminal penalties with the Treaties. The Lisbon Treaty itself gave autonomous significance to the principle of proportionality of penalties, now enshrined in Article 49(3) of the Charter: 'the severity of penalties must not be disproportionate to the criminal offence'.

Over the last decades, the proportionality of sanctions has generated outstanding scholarly reflections in the criminal law discourse. Conversely, the EU criminal law dimension of proportionality of penalties still needs to be explored in full. From a conceptual viewpoint, the wording of the Charter falls short of depicting the whole spectrum of the principle of proportionality of criminal penalties in EU law. In fact, it postulates a retrospective understanding of the principle, which differs from the inherently prospective theorisation of the EU concept of proportionality previously recalled.

Moreover, Article 49(3) of the Charter has long been a silent provision, as the ECJ abstained from granting it any actual role. The Court has traditionally reviewed the severity of domestic sanctions by relying, instead, on other facets of the principle of proportionality, such as the Treaty provisions on derogations to free movement law, Article 52(1) of the Charter, or the 'effective, proportionate and dissuasive' *Greek Maize* paradigm, derived from the Court's case-law and frequently enshrined in EU secondary law.

However, the most recent case-law provides evidence of a structural paradigm shift. The Court has acknowledged that these declinations of proportionality reiterate the principle enshrined in Article 49(3) of the Charter. What is more, in *NE* (C-205/20 *Bezirkshauptmannschaft Hartberg-Fürstenfeld (Effet direct)*) the ECJ has also recognised that the principle of proportionality of penalties is directly enforceable at the domestic level. This evolution marks the emergence of a distinct theoretical identity for the principle of proportionality of penalties in the EU legal order. But this contention is far from conclusive, as it raises an array of systemic questions concerning the principle's conceptualisation, place and influence on domestic criminal systems.

With a view to fostering deeper reflection on the topic, the Law Department of the University of Turin, the School of Law and Social Justice of the University of Liverpool and the School of Law of the University of Milano-Bicocca gathered key experts on the field at an international conference, held in Turin on 11–12 May 2023. This book represents the outcome of that collective discussion. The collection explores three complementary streams of analysis.

The first part (Part A) delves into the conceptualisation of proportionality of criminal penalties in EU law. On the one hand, the emergence of a distinct dimension for the principle questions its relationship with the general principle of proportionality that underpins the EU legal order. On the other hand, proportionality of criminal penalties urges an interdisciplinary approach, as it entails an interaction between the EU concept of proportionality and the criminal law one.

To address these issues, Jacob Öberg frames the three possible theoretical understandings of proportionality of criminal sanctions in EU law: respectively, as a principle of free movement law, as a competence principle and as a retrospective requirement derived from criminal law. The author contends that only the latter dimension is theoretically intended to provide a guarantee for individuals against excessive penalisation. Building upon these theoretical premises, Gniewomir Wycichowski-Kuchta argues that the three dimensions of proportionality may be combined in the exercise of harmonisation powers by the EU legislator under Article 83 TFEU. From this perspective, proportionality of criminal penalties can be construed as a criminalisation principle under EU law.

The following chapter shifts the focus of the analysis to the intersection between proportionality of penalties and the functions of criminal punishments. In particular, Adriano Martufi shows that the principle's conceptualisation is deeply influenced by the penological purposes underlying the imposition of sanctions. While general prevention entails benchmarking the severity of penalties to the attainment of a sufficient deterrent effect, a retributive account of sanctions calls retrospective proportionality into question. The choice between the latter scheme and prospective proportionality is therefore not neutral, as it discloses a clear choice between different penological understandings of punishment.

What is more, the principle of proportionality of penalties may amount to a gateway for grounding other criminal law doctrines in the EU legal order. That is the case of the harm principle, which, as Vittorio Cama argues, may be read as complementary to the proportionality of criminal penalties.

Lastly, Lorenzo Grossio concludes the theoretical assessment by broadening the analysis to the European Convention on Human Rights (ECHR) dimension of proportionality of criminal penalties. While the law of both the EU and ECHR adheres to the same theoretical understanding of the principle, the practice shows remarkable differences between the two legal systems. The author explains these divergencies in the light of the distinct institutional characteristics of the EU legal order and the ECHR. These differences make a convergence of standards on proportionality of penalties tendentially unattainable.

Having explored the principle's uneasy conceptualisation, the second part of the book (Part B) zooms in on the multifaceted role of proportionality of criminal penalties in EU criminal law. In particular, the chapters address topical issues related to three domains: the harmonisation of criminal penalties, judicial cooperation in criminal matters, and *ne bis in idem*.

Building upon an extensive analysis of EU instruments in substantive criminal law, Chloé Brière advances a critical account of the legislator's approach towards proportionality of criminal penalties towards both natural and legal persons. Indeed, the practice discloses noteworthy inconsistencies between different instruments, stemming from a variety of factors. In line with this perspective, Francesca Finelli and Lorenzo Bernardini provide an in-depth critical assessment of the recent EU initiatives aimed to criminalise the violation of restrictive measures. By taking into account both the Council Decision to add this area of crime to the list enshrined in Article 83(1) TFEU and the subsequent Commission Proposal for a Directive, the authors contend that EU institutions have not appropriately justified the proportionality of harmonised penalties in this domain. In the following chapter, Pedro Caeiro looks at the same Proposal for a Directive from a different viewpoint. He stresses that this legislative initiative marks a new development in the EU approach to sanctions against legal entities, as it compels Member States to introduce turnover-based criminal fines. Having traced the origins of this sanctioning scheme to competition law, the author argues that extending this regime to criminal law raises proportionality concerns. Pedro Caeiro dedicates this chapter to John AE Vervaele, a decision that the Editors of this book are deeply pleased to welcome.

The two subsequent chapters address the role of proportionality of criminal penalties in judicial cooperation in criminal matters. On the one hand, Emanuela Pistoia advances some fresh reflections on proportionality under the European Arrest Warrant system. As it is well-known, the Commission has repeatedly affirmed that it is for issuing judicial authorities to assess whether or not recourse to surrender under the EAW system is proportionate. However, the author contends that only executing authorities would be in the position to effectively review if the penalties for which surrender have been requested comply with Article 49(3) of the Charter. On the other hand, Alessandro Rosanò delves into the surrender mechanism between EU Member States and the UK established by the Trade and Cooperation Agreement. As this instrument expressly provides for the possibility to refuse surrender for lack of proportionality, the author argues that EU institutions' practice and domestic case-law may provide guidance on how the assessment should be conducted.

In the concluding chapter of the book's second part, Araceli Turmo discusses the uneasy relationship between proportionality and the *ne bis in idem* principle enshrined in Article 50 of the Charter. As the author underlines, the two principles are complementary as both aim to protect individuals against excessive penalisation. However, the lack of consistency in case-law does not allow to easily distinguish in which circumstances Article 49(3) of the Charter is invoked as a fundamental right *per se* or as a condition for the legitimacy of limitations to *ne bis in idem*.

Finally, Part C considers the influence of the EU principle of proportionality of criminal penalties on domestic criminal legislation and sentencing. While proportionate sentencing represents a pressing issue in Member States' criminal systems, the direct effect of proportionality of criminal sanctions adds further complexity. Two chapters in this section address this issue specifically. Firstly, Stefano Montaldo explores the implications of the direct enforceability of the proportionality requirement enshrined in the *Greek Maize* paradigm by emphasising the crucial role it entails for domestic courts. The latter are now empowered not only to assess the proportionality of sanctions in given cases, but also to determine the scope of the remedy of disapplication. Secondly, Marco Pelissero further emphasises the uneasy impact of the principle on domestic criminal systems, by taking a closer look at the Italian experience. In particular, the author contends that the disapplication of domestic sanctioning scales may put into question the added value of minimum penalty thresholds in domestic criminal systems.

The two final chapters take a narrower perspective on the topic; they focus on, respectively, tax punitive sanctions and confiscation measures. Stefano Maria Ronco sheds light on shortcomings for tax sanctioning systems that may derive from the ECJ case-by-case approach in the proportionality review of penalties. The chapter considers the development of a set of minimum standards and guidelines as a potential way for chiselling the application of proportionality of penalties in the realm of punitive tax sanctions. Lastly, Chloé Fauchon establishes a combined assessment of the French and Spanish experiences on confiscation through the prism of the EU principle of proportionality of penalties. Notwithstanding the diversified judicial practice between the two Member States concerned, the approach of some domestic courts may pave the way for refining the proportionality review of confiscation measures.

To conclude, the Editors take this opportunity to warmly thank all authors for their contributions, as well as the University of Turin and the UNITA – Universitas Montium Network for the financial support to this research initiative. This publication covers several research streams on the principle of proportionality of criminal penalties in the EU legal order, but the analysis is far from exhaustive or conclusive. The book should be conceived, conversely, as a step towards a more in-depth understanding of proportionality of penalties, a principle that is expected to acquire an ever-increasing importance in EU criminal law in the coming years.

PART A

Proportionality of Penalties in EU Criminal Law: A Theoretical Appraisal

2

Conceptualising Proportionality and Criminal Sanctions in EU Law: Three Different Visions

JACOB ÖBERG

I. Introduction

The principle of proportionality is a key principle in EU law; however, it has distinctive meanings in different contexts. In the field of free movement, proportionality constrains the Member States' possibilities to diverge from EU law on the basis of the requirement of suitability and necessity.[1] In the area of EU competences it is a principle that guides the relationship between the EU and Member States and requires the EU legislator to use the least intrusive means of regulation/legislation to protect state sovereignty.[2] There is also a third approach to proportionality in the field of EU sanctions and the Court of Justice's case-law, which entails that the sanction imposed must be commensurate to the gravity of the offence.[3] This more conventional criminal law 'retrospective' version of proportionality has now been enshrined in the Charter of Fundamental Rights and suggests that 'the severity of penalties must not be disproportionate to the criminal offence'.[4]

The chapter intends to briefly illustrate the different ways in which proportionality constrains and shapes the imposition of EU (criminal law) sanctions and penalties. In this area, it should be noted that Dougan has written extensively on sanctions for enforcing EU law.[5] Asp has also examined proportionality in a stricter criminal law sense and its implications for EU law on a more abstract

[1] P Craig, *EU Administrative Law* (Oxford, Oxford University Press, 2012, 2nd edn) ch 19.

[2] Art 5(4) of the Consolidated Version of the Treaty on European Union [2010] OJ C 83/13.

[3] Craig (n 1) ch 20.

[4] Art 49 of the Charter of Fundamental Rights of the European Union [2012] OJ C 326/91.

[5] M Dougan, 'From the Velvet Glove to the Iron Fist: Criminal Sanctions for the Enforcement of Union Law' in M Cremona (ed), *Compliance and the Enforcement of EU Law* (Oxford, Oxford University Press, 2012).

level.[6] This chapter wishes to contribute to the literature by discussing – in particular from the perspective of the individual – how proportionality can constrain the imposition of sanctions that are too draconian. The key proposition of the chapter is that the criminal law retrospective version of proportionality is best suited for this purpose.

II. Proportionality and Sanctions in the Field of EU Free Movement Law

The first instance where the application of the principle of proportionality is relevant concerns the situation in which the Member States derogate from the Treaties by hindering the exercise of the fundamental freedoms.[7] The key premise here is that whilst criminal law is outside the scope of EU competences, national criminal laws cannot be such that they hinder the exercise of individual's free movement rights.

Where a national measure is held to be incompatible with a primary Treaty provision, such as the free movement of goods,[8] or the free movement of workers,[9] any sanction intended to enforce that national measure is automatically prohibited by EU law, without the need to conduct an self-standing analysis of whether the sanction itself complies with the principle of proportionality.[10] Even where a domestic rule is found to be compatible with the free movement provisions, sanctions for implementing that domestic rule must itself be in line with the principle of proportionality.[11]

In the second place, there is support in the case-law for the proposition that certain national penalties and particularly the decision to impose criminal liability can hinder the exercise of EU citizens' free movement rights. Under Article 36 TFEU, the Member States can be justified in having rules that constitute a restriction of free movement but those national rules need to be proportionate to the aim pursued.[12] By way of example, if the right to stay in other Member States is conditioned on the individual notifying the authorities in that Member State within a certain period, the sanction for non-compliance with those rules must not be

[6] P Asp, The Substantive Criminal Law Competence of the EU – Towards an Area of Freedom, Security & Justice – Part 1 (Stockholm, Jure, 2013) 188–206.

[7] Dougan (n 5).

[8] Art. 34 of the Consolidated Version of the Treaty on the Functioning of the European Union [2010] OJ C 83/47 ('TFEU').

[9] Art 45 TFEU.

[10] Case 88/77 *Schonenberg* ECLI:EU:C:1978:30; Case 179/78 *Rivoira* ECLI:EU:C:1979:73; Case C-13/01 *Safalero* ECLI:EU:C:2003:447; Case C-167/01 *Inspire Art* ECLI:EU:C:2003:512; Case C-12/02 *Grilli* ECLI:EU:C:2003:288; Cases C-338, 359 and 360/04 *Placanica* ECLI:EU:C:2007:133.

[11] Case 8/77 *Salgulo* ECLI:EU:C:1977:131; Case C-265/88 *Messner* ECLI:EU:C:1989:632; Case C-378/97 *Wijsenbeek* ECLI:EU:C:1999:439.

[12] Case C-189/95 *Franzén* ECLI:EU:C:1997:504.

disproportionate to the gravity of this infringement. The reason behind such a requirement is that sanctions that are too draconian can make it less attractive for citizens to exercise their rights under EU law.[13]

In *Skanavi*, the Court held that it would be incompatible with Article 49 TFEU to impose certain criminal sanctions on drivers of motor vehicles lacking a licence to drive in the host state. In the absence of EU rules governing the matter, the Member States remain competent to impose penalties for breaches of such an obligation. However, the Court stated that Member States may not impose a penalty so disproportionate to the gravity of the infringement that this becomes an obstacle to the free movement of persons.[14] Treating a person who has failed to have a licence exchanged as if they were a person driving without a licence, thereby applying criminal penalties, would be disproportionate to the gravity of that infringement in view of the ensuing consequences. A criminal conviction may have consequences for the exercise of a profession by an employed or self-employed person in respect of access to certain activities or certain offices which would constitute a lasting restriction on freedom of movement.[15]

Following this logic, it could be argued that any criminal offence that results in an imprisonment sentence creates such a disruption to the claimant's professional activities that it would infringe the free movement provisions and thus would be subject to scrutiny under Union law.[16] The ruling in *Carpenter* – in which the Court scrutinised national rules on the basis of a remote link to EU law – might support the proposition that a deprivation of liberty is indeed capable of acting as a barrier to movement, which must then always be objectively justified and be in conformity with the principle of proportionality.[17]

There is, however, an argument to be made that the *Skanavi* ruling should be read more carefully, since the obligation to exchange driving licences at issue in *Skanavi* would be indirectly discriminatory against foreign migrants. Reference to the professional difficulties that might be encountered by migrant EU citizens due to the imposition of criminal penalties was primarily intended to reinforce the need to undertake a careful proportionality review.[18] This reading would restrict an autonomous scrutiny of national criminal sanctions to their compatibility with the principle of non-discrimination within the scope of EU law, avoiding the categorisation of domestic criminal law as a barrier to movement simply through its alleged severity.

[13] Asp (n 6) 192.

[14] Case C-265/88 *Messner*, para 14.

[15] Case C-193/94 *Skanavi* ECLI:EU:C:1996:70, paras 49–52; Case C-156/04 *Commission v Greece* ECLI:EU:C:2007:316.

[16] In a manner reminiscent of the problems which arose in ascertaining the appropriate boundaries of Article 34 TFEU before the ECJ delivered the *Keck and Mithouard* ruling: Case C-299/95 *Kremzow* ECLI:EU:C:1997:254, para 15; Case 145/88 *Torfaen BC v B&Q* ECLI:EU:C:1989:593.

[17] Case C-60/00 *Carpenter* ECLI:EU:C:2002:434.

[18] Dougan (n 5) 80–81.

MT v. Landespolizeidirektion Steiermark is the most significant recent judgment in the area of proportionality. In this case, the Court of Justice assessed in detail the proportionality of national criminal sanctions for infringing national restrictive legislation on provision of services. The Court first noted that such penalties are effective in ensuring compliance with that legislation and thus appropriate for attaining the objective pursued in that respect. The severity of the penalties imposed must, however, be commensurate with the seriousness of the infringements for which they are imposed.[19] The imposition of a minimum fine per unauthorised gaming machine does not appear to be disproportionate per se given the seriousness of the infringements at issue, since the illegal supply of gaming machines can have particularly serious harmful effects on society.[20] As regards the amount of that minimum fine, the national court must consider the relationship between the amount of the fine that may be imposed and the economic benefit that was derived from the infringement committed.[21] However, the imposition of a minimum fine, combined with an unlimited cumulative amount of fines in which the infringement concerns several unauthorised gaming machines, may lead to sizeable financial penalties being imposed and it must thus be ensured that the total amount of the fines imposed is not disproportionate in relation to that benefit. In relation to the imposition of a custodial sentence in lieu of a fine, the Court opined that such a penalty would not be disproportionate in light of the gravity of the infringements since it seeks to ensure that those infringements can be punished if it is not possible to recover the fine.[22] The Court nonetheless observed that since each gaming machine infringing the legislation is capable of providing grounds for the imposition of such a custodial sentence and the legislation does not provide for any limit on the total duration of such sentences, the accumulation of such penalties may lead to the imposition of a considerably lengthy custodial sentence in lieu of a fine, which might be disproportionate.[23]

In *MT v. Landespolizeidirektion Steiermark* many things were left to be decided by the national courts. Nonetheless, it is apparent that the Court of Justice had some serious doubts about the proportionality of the automatic replacement of unpaid fines with a custodial sentence and the absence of a cap to the total amount of the fine imposed. Having said that, it seems that the triggering of retrospective proportionality entails that the ECJ only considers itself capable of dictating fairly general criteria for the domestic court's scrutiny on the proportionality of

[19] Case C-679/18 *OPR-Finance*, ECLI:EU:C:2020:167, para 26; Case C-524/15 *Menci* ECLI:EU:C:2018:197, para 55.

[20] Case C-275/92 *Schindler*, ECLI:EU:C:1994:119, para 60; Joined cases C-338/04, C-359/04 and C-360/04 *Placanica and Others* ECLI:EU:C:2007:133, para 47; Case C-203/08 *Sporting Exchange* ECLI:EU:C:2010:307, para 27; Case C-347/09 *Dickinger and Ömer* ECLI:EU:C:2011:582, para 45.

[21] Case C-77/20 K.M. (Sanctions imposed on the master of vessel) ECLI:EU:C:2021:112, para 49.

[22] See: Joined Cases C-64/18, C-140/18, C-146/18 and C-148/18 *Maksimovic and Others* ECLI:EU:C:2019:723, para 45; *Lacatus v Switzerland* App No 14065/15 (ECtHR, 19 January 2021) para 110.

[23] Case C-482/18 *Google Ireland* ECLI:EU:C:2020:141, para 53.

the domestic sanctioning system. ECJ deference to national courts in the concrete proportionality assessment is thus the key principle in this line of case-law.

In summary, where national sanctions fall within the scope of EU law because the Member State is derogating from the Treaties, the ECJ's main aim is to temper the severity of national sanctions to the benefit of the individual defendant, since that best serves the objective of promoting free movement. This notion of proportionality thus clearly plays a central role in reviewing administrative and criminal penalties posing a burden on the enjoyment of internal market freedoms.[24]

III. Competence Proportionality and EU Sanctions

Competence proportionality in Article 5(4) TEU is about protecting too severe encroachments into state sovereignty. It is about with which intensity the EU – when it has competence – should legislate.[25] In general, the principle (also known as prospective proportionality) entails that all the measures taken must be proportionate to the objective to be achieved. This approach considers three essential prongs, namely: the suitability, necessity, and proportionality *sensu stricto* of the measures taken in relation to the objectives that it pursues. This is dependent on a variety of factors, such as the policy domain, the objectives pursued by the EU, the domestic legal context, the severity of sanctions established for other violations and the circumstances of an actual case.[26]

The key issue with regard to proportionality as a principle limiting the EU's power to determine sanctions is the question of the intensity of judicial review.

There is a strand of scholarship that argues that proportionality could be used effectively as a principle challenging the exercise of EU competences before the EU Courts. Davies and Kumm are proponents of such a view and, according to them, proportionality concerns the question of whether the loss of Member State autonomy and all disadvantages associated with it outweigh the benefits achieved by EU intervention or not.[27] Kumm takes the basis of this argument from the Court's existing jurisprudence on fundamental rights and submits that it is no more difficult to weigh policies against each other than it is to weigh policies against individual rights. The highly open-ended empirical and normative assessment of Member State acts in the Court's rights jurisprudence is not a qualitatively

[24] Dougan (n 5) 78–79.

[25] J Öberg, Limits to EU Powers: A Case Study of EU Regulatory Criminal Law (Oxford, Hart Publishing, 2017) ch 2.

[26] Asp (n 6); J Długosz, J 'The Principle of Proportionality in European Union Law as a Prerequisite for Penalization' (2017) *Przegląd Prawniczy Uniwersytetu Im. Adam Mickiewicza* 283, 289–290.

[27] See M Kumm, 'Constitutionalizing Subsidiarity in Integrated Markets: The Case of Tobacco Regulation in the European Union' (2006) 12 *European Law Journal* 503, 522; G Davies, 'Subsidiarity: the wrong idea, in the wrong place, at the wrong time' (2006) 43 *Common Market Law Review* 63, 81, 83.

different inquiry from jurisdictional proportionality analysis.[28] Davies argues that the Court's competence to engage in jurisdictional proportionality is demonstrated by the fact that the Court regularly assesses national measures in some detail to see if they are justified by the Member State's stated aim. Given this, and the fact that there is no other principle that can protect important areas of national autonomy from falling victim to less important Union action, the Court should apply jurisdictional proportionality intensively.[29]

However, there is a compelling case against putting trust in the principle of proportionality as being an effective shield against the imposition of EU sanctions in primary law instrument. First, the EU judiciary has, in the past, been very cautious in reviewing proportionality within the context of discretionary policy choices.[30] The guiding principle is, as stated in *British American Tobacco* case, that a low intensity review will be deemed appropriate whenever the EU legislature exercises a broad discretion involving political, economic, or social choices that require it to make complex assessments.[31] Since many Treaty articles will be of this nature, low intensity review will be the norm with a standard test of 'manifest disproportionality'. The core idea is that where the Treaties explicitly or implicitly accord a broad discretion to the legislative institutions, the courts should be wary of substituting their judgment for that of the primary decision-maker under the guise of proportionality.[32] There are numerous and complex factors to be balanced and weighed by the EU legislature in the context of broad policy schemes that involve discretionary economic, social, and political choice. Proportionality is also concerned with the balancing of policy choices and with the appropriateness of a certain policy. Whether a measure is 'suitable' for the implementation of a policy or what balance should be struck between different public and private interests are not questions the Court is well-equipped to adjudicate upon.[33]

Secondly, it seems that proportionality is conceptually not well-placed to be applied in competence disputes in respect of sanctions. The mere fact that a Member State believes that the legislation on which it was outvoted in the Council

[28] See Kumm (n 27) 521, 523–24, 528.

[29] See Davies, (n 27) 83.

[30] See J Öberg, 'The Rise of the Procedural Paradigm: Judicial Review of EU Legislation in Vertical Competence Disputes', (2017) 13 *European Constitutional Law Review* 248, 248–255.

[31] Case C-491/01 *R v Secretary of State for Health, ex p British American Tobacco (Investments) Ltd and Imperial Tobacco Ltd* ECLI:EU:C:2002:741, para 123; Case C-210/03 *R (on the application of Swedish Match AB and Swedish Match UK Ltd) v Secretary of State for Health* ECLI:EU:C:2004:802, para 48; Case C-58/08 *R (on the application of Vodafone Ltd and Others) v Secretary of State for Business, Enterprise and Regulatory Reform*, ECLI:EU:C:2010:321, paras 51–53.

[32] Case C-331/88 *R v Minister for Agriculture, Fisheries and Food, ex p Fedesa* ECLI:EU:C:1990:391, para 14; Case C-189/01 *Jippes v Minister van Landbouw, Natuurbeheer en Visserij* ECLI:EU:C:2001:420, 83–84.

[33] See Craig, *EU Administrative Law* (n 1) 592-593,600-604, 629-30, 639; Asp (n 6) 191; Joined cases C-27/00 and C-122/00 *Queen v Secretary of State for the Environment, Transport and the Regions* ECLI:EU:C:2002:161, para 63; Case C-176/09 *Luxemburg v Parliament and Council*, ECLI:EU:C:2011:290; J Öberg, 'Union Regulatory Criminal Law Competence after Lisbon Treaty' (2011) 19 *European of Crime, Criminal Law and Criminal Justice* 289.

involves too great an intrusion on its values does not mean that the measure infringes the proportionality principle. This is because a foundational feature of EU cooperation is premised on collective action in which Member States must make compromises and because the Treaties already balance Member State and EU interests. It is very difficult to imagine how a single Member State, or even a minority of Member States, could argue that a measure objectively entailed too great an intrusion on Member State values.[34] Moreover, if proportionality should work as a serious restraint on the exercise of Union competence to impose criminal sanctions, this presupposes that the national autonomy feature is integrated into the proportionality *stricto sensu* test. The Court only engages in this scrutiny when the applicant raises arguments that an incursion on Member State values is disproportionate *stricto sensu* in light of the EU objective before the Courts. This is not an easy task to discharge. The Union courts will already have decided that the contested measure withstands scrutiny under the suitability and necessity limbs of the test.[35]

However, the case-law on national sanctions implementing EU laws suggests a more intense scrutiny of the underlying EU measure at hand. This approach is influenced by the fact that such cases will commonly involve annulment either of a single administrative act or a particular article of a regulation, without calling into question the more general legislative schema.[36] In this case-law, the EU Courts normally consider the objectives of the relevant Treaty provisions or legislative scheme.[37] It is in particular the third limb of the Court's proportionality test, the *stricto sensu* enquiry of whether or not EU measures impose too disproportionate costs or inconveniences for individuals, which have proven significant in case-law.

In *Man (Sugar)*, the applicant was required to give a security deposit to the Board when seeking a licence to export sugar outside the Community but was four hours late in completing the paperwork. The Board, acting pursuant to an EU Regulation, forfeited the entire deposit of £1,670,370. The Court noted that where EU legislation makes a distinction between a primary obligation, compliance with which is necessary to attain the objective sought, and a secondary obligation essentially of an administrative nature, the EU legislator cannot penalise failure to comply with the secondary obligation as severely as failure to comply with the primary obligation. Although the Commission was entitled to impose a time limit for the submission of applications for export licences, the penalty imposed for failure to comply with that time-limit should have been significantly

[34] See P Craig 'Subsidiarity: A Political and Legal Analysis' (2012) 50 *Journal of Common Market Studies* 72, 83.

[35] Craig, *EU Administrative Law* (n 1) 601–604; A Alemanno, 'Regulatory Impact Assessment and European Courts: When Ex Ante Evaluation Meets Ex Post Judicial Control' (2011) 17 *European Public Law* 485, 498; Öberg, *Limits to EU Powers: A Case Study of EU Regulatory Criminal Law* (n 25).

[36] See Öberg, 'The Rise of the Procedural Paradigm' (n 30) 262–275.

[37] Craig, EU Administrative Law (n 1) 614.

less severe for the traders concerned than forfeiture of the entire security and it should have been more consonant with the practical effects of such a failure.[38]

The same reasoning underlies *Atalanta*,[39] where the ECJ held that provisions of an EU Regulation concerned with storage aid for pig meat – which required that the security would be forfeited if the obligations imposed by the storage contract were not fulfilled – were disproportionate. The Court noted that the underlying EU regulation drew a distinction between the principal obligations that are incumbent on the storer under the storage contract, the fulfilment of which is a condition of acquisition of the right to the aid and obligations intended to permit the supervision of the storage operations. Thus, although the storer cannot claim payment of the aid if they have not sent the particular documents relating to the storage operations to the agency, the mere fact that this was not done within the prescribed period cannot entail the loss of the right to aid when the principal obligations imposed in the contract have been fulfilled. The Court also noted that the absolute nature of a Commission implementing regulation was contrary to the principle of proportionality in that it did not permit the penalty to be made commensurate with the degree of failure to implement the contractual obligations.[40]

To summarise the discussion, there have been some successful actions for annulment in the field of individual administrative sanctions where the Court has declared some provisions on sanctions in an EU instrument as inapplicable or illegal. The Court's approach has been to declare such illegality without challenging the overall validity of the underlying EU legal act. Nonetheless, the Court's more general limited scrutiny of administrative sanctions in the area of proportionality and discretionary policy choices suggests that this principle is difficult to enforce when challenging the imposition of criminal sanctions in general EU instruments.

IV. Criminal Law Proportionality and the Charter

A. Conceptualising Proportionality in Criminal Law

Having discussed how proportionality could limit the imposition of criminal sanctions in the area of free movement and might constrain the exercise of EU

[38] Case 181/84 *R v Intervention Board, ex p ED & F Man (Sugar) Ltd*: ECLI:EU:C:1985:359, paras 20-31.

[39] Case 240/78 *Atalanta Amsterdam BV v Produktschap voor Vee en Vlees* ECLI:EU:C:1979:160; Case 122/78 *Buitoni SA v Fonds d'Orientation et de Régularisation des Marchés Agricoles* ECLI:EU:C:1979:43; Case 21/85 *Maas & Co NV v Bundesanstalt fur landwirtschaftliche Marktordnung* ECLI:EU:C:1986:449.

[40] Case 240/78 *Atalanta Amsterdam BV v Produktschap voor Vee en Vlees*, paras 10–12, 15.

legislative competencies prescribing sanctions, the following subsection analyses the implications of the criminal law notion of proportionality in the field of sanctions.

First, we should linger slightly on the central distinction between ordinal and cardinal proportionality in criminal law. In basic terms, the former is concerned with the proportionality of the sanction within the totality of the system whilst the latter is concerned with the relationship between a specific offence and the seriousness of the sanction.[41] This distinction is important for understanding how Article 49(3) of the Charter should be construed – the latter providing that 'the severity of penalties must not be disproportionate to the criminal offence'.

The argument here is that the Charter primarily relates to the concept of cardinal proportionality, which concerns the correlation between the gravity of the act committed and the statutory penalty scale for its commitment. In practice, this approach entails that national courts and the ECJ must determine whether or not the penalty laid down in the EU regulations is commensurate with the gravity of the offence. This means that the role of the EU legislature is to set criteria for determining what the maximum penalty must be for committing an offence of a particular type, so that the severity of that penalty is commensurate with the gravity of the act committed.[42]

With the retrospective notion of proportionality, the basis for the penalty is the fact that the act was committed by the perpetrator in the past. Historically it has been argued that this principle builds on the twofold notions of general prevention (deterrence) and the idea that punishment should involve censure and be distributed on grounds of desert. It is assumed that the cardinal proportionality function has two main components: the degree of fault of the perpetrator and the degree of social harm of the offences.[43]

At the EU level, ordinal proportionality plays a very confined role as it is nearly impossible to discuss ordinal proportionality in relation to the totality of the criminal law systems of the Member States. There is simply no common starting point for punishment in the Member States, whereas the general levels of repression differ considerably. This means that the EU cannot reasonably be expected to strive for ordinal proportionality in relation to the totality of the criminal law systems of the Member States. However, the concept of cardinal proportionality is useful as a flexible standard to assess sanctions that are part of the legal system.[44]

[41] Asp (n 6) 199–200.

[42] Długosz (n 26) 292–293; Asp (n 6) 188–193.

[43] Długosz (n 26) 289–290.

[44] Asp (n 6) is sceptical of the usefulness of retrospective proportionality arguing that the conclusion that a punishment is disproportionate will be drawn only under exceptional circumstances and that Article 49(3) of the Charter of Fundamental Rights thus does not set any clear borders for initiatives on the EU level.

B. Retrospective Proportionality as a Limit to the Imposition of EU Sanctions

The following analysis considers proportionality and EU sanctions in terms of the limits the former imposes on the nature and type of penalties that can be imposed within the context of in particular Article 49(3) of the Charter.

The now, more established case-law from the ECJ set forth some guidelines on the application of proportionality. First, the punitive measures permitted under national legislation must not go beyond what is necessary to attain the objectives legitimately pursued by that legislation. Furthermore, the severity of the sanctions must be commensurate with the seriousness of the breaches for which they are imposed but still ensure a genuinely dissuasive effect.[45] Another significant point in the Court's case-law is that it offers a wide margin of discretion for Member States to adopt an appropriate system of penalties for enforcing Union law, having regard to factors such as the objectives of prevention and deterrence, the difficulties of penalising infringements by alternative means and the importance of the public interest that the relevant EU legislation seeks to protect.[46]

The Court's review can sometimes assume a more intrusive character and can exert a direct influence on the relevant factors that the competent authorities should consider for the purposes of setting the actual punishment imposed to enforce EU obligations. *Louloudakis*, which was concerned with proceedings against an individual accused of evading the payment of the Greek vehicle tax by driving a vehicle registered in another Member State, provides a remarkable example of the Court's approach.[47] The ECJ noted here that in the absence of harmonisation of the EU legislation in the field of the penalties, the Member States are empowered to choose the penalties that seem appropriate to them. They must, however, exercise that power in line with the principle of proportionality, entailing that the penalties must not go beyond what is strictly necessary for the objectives pursued and must not be disproportionate to the gravity of the infringement.[48] Given that the objective of the directive at stake in *Louloudakis* was to encourage freedom of movement for EU residents and goods within the Union, the Court noted that the applicable penalties may prove to be disproportionate and could therefore constitute an obstacle to the said freedoms. This was because the penalties included flat-rate fixed penalties that were based solely on the vehicle's cubic capacity, without account being taken of the vehicle's age and increased duties, which may be as much as ten times the charges as issues imposed for the same breach. It was, however, for the *national court* to assess whether those penalties

[45] Case C-255/14 *Chmielewski* ECLI:EU:C: 2015:475, paras 21–23.

[46] Case C-326/88 *Hansen* ECLI:EU:C:1990:291; Case C-177/95 *Ebony Maritime* ECLI:EU:C:1997:89.

[47] Case C-375/95 *Commission* v *Greece* ECLI:EU:C:1997:505.

[48] C-36/94 *Siesse* ECLI:EU:C:1995:351, para 21; Case C-213/99 *De Andrade* ECLI:EU:C:2000:678 para 20.

appeared so disproportionate to the gravity of the infringement that they become an obstacle to the fundamental freedoms.[49]

In *Lindqvist* the Court also suggested that the Member States have a margin for discretion in implementing the EU Data Protection Directive. Initially, the Court observed that nothing suggested that its provisions were contrary to the fundamental rights protected by the EU legal order. This finding entails that it was at the stage of the implementation of the directive in national law in individual cases that a balance must be found between the rights and interests involved. In that context, fundamental rights have particular importance, as demonstrated by the case in the main proceedings, in which it was determined that Mrs Lindqvist's freedom to carry out activities contributing to religious life must be weighed against the protection of the private life of the individuals about whom Mrs Lindqvist had placed data on her internet site. Whilst the protection of private life requires the application of effective sanctions against people processing personal data inconsistently with the Data Protection Directive, such sanctions must always respect the principle of proportionality. This was so in light of the very wide scope of the directive and the far-reaching obligations for those processing personal data. It was thus for national courts to consider all the circumstances of the case before it, in particular the duration of the breach of the rules in implementing the directive and the importance for the persons concerned of the protection of the data disclosed.[50]

In its proportionality assessments, the ECJ regularly requires that penalties are distinguished in relation to the seriousness of the offence. In *Marton Urbán*, for instance, the Court considered a Bulgarian penalty addressing the breaches of a national regulation on road transport that required drivers to fill in information to demonstrate compliance with the legislation on road safety and drivers' working conditions. The Court noted that breaches likely to prevent the effective monitoring of drivers' working conditions and compliance with road safety cannot be ranked in the same category as minor infringements that do not hinder monitoring of compliance with the obligations laid down by EU legislation. It noted that the omission by a driver to enter the kilometre count on the record sheet at the end of the last journey has a minimal impact on road safety. That information is not vital to the successful completion of the check of compliance with the rules concerning driving times and rest periods. The imposition of flat-rate fines for all breaches of the rules on the use of record sheets without adjustment of the penalty in line with the seriousness of the breach thus appeared to be disproportionate in the light of the objectives pursued by the EU legislation.[51]

[49] Case C-262/99 *Louloudakis* ECLI:EU:C: 2001:407, paras 65–70; Case C-156/04 *Commission v Greece* ECLI:EU:C:2007:316.

[50] Case C-101/01 *Lindqvist* ECLI:EU:C: 2003:596, paras 84–88; Case C-262/99 *Louloudakis*. See also Case C-156/04 *Commission v Greece*, para 49.

[51] Case C-210/10 *Marton Urbán* ECLI:EU:C:2012:64.

Furthermore, the Court has regularly stressed that the acceptable choices for the means of coercive state enforcement might depend on factors specific to each individual territory.[52] *Commission v Greece* illustrates this approach. In this judgment, the Court noted firstly that the Greek legislation in question subjected to criminal penalties behaviours consisting of the evasion of national customs and tax provisions that concerned the movement of motor vehicles in which individuals who have their normal residence in Greece used vehicles registered in another Member State. Criminal punishment for that conduct is linked to the economic and social situation of the relevant Member State and the specific situation regarding the taxation of motor vehicles. It was common ground that registration fees in Greece were very high and that this could induce individuals to drive in that territory with cars registered in another Member State. The Court held that the requirements of enforcement and prevention may justify a Member State in setting penalties at a certain level of severity, but that those penalties must be proportionate. The Commission however, failed to adduce evidence that substantiated that the penalties imposed were disproportionate.[53]

A common notion in the case-law is that the ECJ is distinctively non-prescriptive when offering guidance on the proportionality principle, deferring markedly to national courts in applying the principle to the specific circumstances at hand. The recent *KM* judgment is a case in point for this approach. In this judgment, the ECJ considered whether or not the sanctions imposed on the defendant – the mandatory forfeiture of catches and prohibited or non-compliant fishing gear in addition to a fine – was proportionate to the attainment of the objective pursued by the legislation. The Court noted that it should be verified that for persons engaging in fishing activity there is a serious risk that infringements of the rules of the common fisheries policy will be detected and that offenders will have sufficiently severe sanctions imposed on them. The mandatory forfeiture of catches and non-compliant fishing gear was deemed sufficiently dissuasive to deter the persons concerned from infringing the prohibition relating to grading equipment, by depriving them of the unlawfully acquired profits that they could otherwise enjoy and the possibility of continuing to use such equipment. The Court also offered the national authorities at issue substantial leeway to ensure that the sanctions were dissuasive, observing that the sanctions at issue varied depending on the nature and gravity of the infringement and the offence in question. Thus, in the light of the seriousness of the infringement and the objective pursued, the mandatory forfeiture of catches and prohibited or non-compliant fishing gear were considered proportionate penalties.[54]

Enforcement in national legal orders constitutes one key aspect of the effectiveness of the proportionality principle in offering protection for individuals

[52] S Montaldo, 'Handle with care! The direct effect of the requirement of proportionality of sanctions and the remedy of disapplication: NE v. Bezirkshauptmannschaft Hartberg-Fürstenfeld' (2023) 60 *Common Market Law Review* 863, 879.

[53] Case C-156/04 *Commission v Greece*, paras 67–72.

[54] See Case C-77/20, *Criminal proceedings against K. M.* ECLI:EU:C:2021:112, paras 35–45.

from sanctions that are too severe. Acknowledging the direct effects of a provision of EU law creates two main implications: increased protection of individuals who are entitled to invoke the provision concerned against the Member States; and the strengthening of national courts' powers to set aside incompatible national rules.[55]

Link Logistics is a key judgment in this context. In this case, the Court of Justice ruled that the principle of proportionality in respect of national sanctions imposed within the context of Directive 1999/62 on the charging of heavy goods vehicles did not have a direct effect. The Court noted that for the principle of proportionality to be implemented, the Member States were required to adopt measures that were in line with their national law and they exercised a wide margin of discretion in that regard. The ECJ further observed that the directive did not contain precise rules regarding the establishment of those national penalties nor any express criterion for the assessment of their proportionality. The Court finally concluded that, since Article 9a of Directive 1999/62 necessitated the intervention of the Member States and left them a wide margin of discretion, it could not be regarded as sufficiently unconditional and precise to be granted direct effect.[56]

In a subsequent ruling – *NE v. Bezirkshauptmannschaft Hartberg-Fürstenfeld* – the Court made a significant departure from its previous case-law and declared the direct effect of the principle of proportionality.[57] In this ruling, the ECJ clarified that the proportionality requirement laid down in Article 20 of the amended Posting Workers Directive established an obligation framed in absolute terms – entailing a prohibition on adopting disproportionate sanctions – that was not conditional on any measure being taken by the Member State.[58] Such a requirement of proportionality had to be implemented by Member States under the directive and the fact that they enjoy a margin of discretion in that regard did not preclude judicial review from assessing whether or not the Member State had exceeded the limits of that discretion.[59] However, the Court held that legislation that provided for pecuniary penalties – the amount of which varies according to the number of workers affected by the failure to comply with certain obligations – was not in itself disproportionate.[60] On closer scrutiny, the ECJ nonetheless held that the national legislation provided disproportionate penalties due, in particular, to the accumulation of penalties without an upper limit of fines, which had to be higher than a predefined minimum amount.[61]

[55] See Montaldo (n 52).

[56] Case C-384/17 *Dooel Uvoz-Izvoz Skopje Link Logistic* ECLI:EU:C:2018:810, para 45–53.

[57] The case has been annotated by S Montaldo (n 52).

[58] Case C-205/20 *NE v. Bezirkshauptmannschaft Hartberg-Fürstenfeld* ECLI:EU:C: 2022:168, paras 22–32.

[59] Case C-72/95 *Kraaijeveld and Others* ECLI:EU:C: 1996:404, para 59; Case C-723/17 *Craeynest and Others* ECLI:EU:C:2019:533, para 45.

[60] Case C-645/18 *Bezirkshauptmannschaft Hartberg-Fürstenfeld* ECLI:EU:C: 2019:1108, para 32.

[61] Case C-205/20 *NE v. Bezirkshauptmannschaft Hartberg-Fürstenfeld*, paras 28–30, 40–41; Case C-645/18, *Bezirkshauptmannschaft Hartberg-Fürstenfeld*, paras 32–41.

NE v. Bezirkshauptmannschaft Hartberg-Fürstenfeld marks, as noted by Montaldo, a substantial reversal of the ECJ's approach in *Link Logistics*, which suggested that proportionality entails a positive obligation to design appropriate sanctioning regimes in the national legal orders. The former ECJ ruling proposes that the requirement at issue imposes a clear prohibition on adopting disproportionate penalties, relying on its previous case-law on direct effect.[62]

To summarise the discussion, it is clear that it is nearly impossible to identify in absolute terms what kind of measure, along with its severity, should be considered proportionate to an abstractly defined infringement of EU law. The nearly endless variability of legal and factual circumstances and the inherent complexities of the law of sanctions make it particularly difficult to identify clear guidelines about the measures that are considered to comply with the proportionality principle. Whilst there is an abundance case-law on the structure of the proportionality scrutiny, the application of criteria can lead to different outcomes depending on the specific features of a case, even to the same sanctioning regime.[63] This also entails that the ECJ has regularly opted for an approach of substantial deference to national courts in assessing concretely to what extent the national sanctions imposed on basis of EU law is in line with the principle of proportionality. However, as demonstrated by rulings such as *NE v. Bezirkshauptmannschaft Hartberg-Fürstenfeld*, *Louloudakis* and *Marton Urbán*, proportionality undoubtedly offers some protection for individual defendants by requiring the national courts to limit the Member State's obligation to penalise breaches of EU law and constrain their discretion to impose sanctions upon wrongdoing individuals.[64]

V. Conclusions and Reflections

This chapter aimed to explore how different notions of proportionality can constrain the imposition of criminal sanctions under EU law. The first section examined the implications of proportionality in the field of free movement and argued that the principle has a central role to play in this regard in situations Member State derogates from those freedoms and can invoke a legitimate justification for such a derogation.[65] The second section examined competence proportionality in Article 5(4) TEU.

There is, post-Lisbon, limited evidence in practice that the EU legislator adheres closely to the principle of proportionality when legislating in the area of criminal law.[66] A reasonable way of reading proportionality – as an expression of

[62] Case 28/67 *Firma Molkerei-Zentrale Westfalen/Lippe GmbH* ECLI:EU:C:1968:17; Montaldo (n 52) 871–873.

[63] Montaldo (n 52) 874–875, 885.

[64] Dougan (n 5) 78–79.

[65] See above Section I.

[66] See Öberg, *Limits to EU Powers* (n 25) ch 7; Öberg, 'Union Regulatory Criminal Law Competence' (n 33).

the principle of *ultima ratio* and paying due respect for national legal diversity[67] – is that the EU legislator should opt not to determine the type and the level of (criminal) penalties. This argument has been supported by the opinion of Advocate General (AG) Mazák in the *Ship Source Pollution* judgment in which the AG recommended that the EU's criminal competences should – due to concerns of coherence of national criminal justice systems – be limited to the principle of criminalisation and the definition of offences. On this point the AG mentioned that the Member States have quite different ideas as to the purpose of criminal law as an instrument of enforcement and that those ideas are reflected by differences in the national penal systems as regards the overall level of penalties and the balance between various forms of sentences. In line with this, the Member States are, as a rule, better placed to translate the concept of effective, proportionate, and dissuasive criminal penalties into their own legal systems and societal contexts.[68]

It nonetheless seems that new EU criminal law directives, as a rule, not only include provisions on criminal offences but also more precise specification of the penalties, going well beyond the *Greek Maize* formula of only prescribing effective, proportionate, and dissuasive sanctions. Montaldo has noted that EU legislation often provides for some measures to be made available in the sanctioning toolbox of the competent national authorities, ranging from compulsory implementation outcomes to optional choices from which the Member States may depart. Moreover, EU secondary law regularly establishes the specific penalties to be imposed mandatorily in response to a given type of violation of EU law and establishes the factors to be considered by the national authorities when determining the amount of a penalty.[69]

The EU legislator's more intrusive approach in sanctioning is particularly visible in terms of the use of quantitative thresholds of penalties, where EU legislation prescribes maximum and minimum level penalties to be imposed for the specific offences in the directive. This approach entails perforce that the least repressive Member States regularly need to adjust themselves to States that are more repressive. However, there is thin evidence to substantiate that there is a need for EU instruments that specify the scope and level of penalties to increase the effectiveness of criminal law. On the contrary, general research on deterrence suggests that the level and type of penalties has a limited impact on individual's choice to engage in wrongdoing and criminal activity.[70] Furthermore, real-life evidence

[67] See Art 67(3); Art 82(2) TFEU.

[68] Case C-440/05 *Commission v Council* ECLI:EU:C:2007:625, Opinion of AG Mazak, paras 96–106.

[69] Montaldo (n 52) 880–881.

[70] R Paternoster, 'How Much Do We Really Know about Criminal Deterrence?' (2010) 100 *Journal of Criminal Law and Criminology* 765; G Becker, 'Crime and Punishment: An Economic Approach' (1968) 76 *Journal of Political Economy* 169; JC Coffee Jr, 'No Soul To Damn – No Body To Kick – An Unscandalized Inquiry Into the Problem of Corporate Punishment' (1981) 79 *Michigan Law Review* 386.

also challenges the thesis that stricter criminal penalties have any demonstrable effect on criminal activity. Taking the example of the criminal justice systems in the Nordic countries, which in comparison to the rest of European countries have been marked by more lenient sanctions, we should, following the repressive deterrence argument, assume that they should be a paradise for criminals. However, there is limited evidence from the Nordic countries that organised crime has been a serious concern for those countries in the past.[71]

On a final note, the most significant developments in terms of sanctioning and proportionality have been those within the context of retrospective proportionality and Article 49(3) of the Charter. This chapter argues that the key function of proportionality for individuals is the retrospective aspect of the principle, which limits the imposition of sanctions that are too draconian in specific cases. The Court of Justice's progressive case-law, its reversal of its case-law to accept the direct effect of the principle of proportionality and its insistence on taking a more meticulous look at national sanctioning regimes, show that the principle is clearly actionable for individuals in this area. One of the key weaknesses of the ECJ case-law lies in its tendency to leave much of the assessment of the sanctioning regimes' compatibility with the principle of proportionality to the national courts. This approach is nonetheless defensible. Only national courts would sit with sufficient information on the national context, sanctioning regime, and the individual circumstances of the case to determine if the penalty is proportionate to the offence at issue and the objectives of the underlying EU legislation.[72]

[71] S Melander, 'Ultima Ratio in European Criminal Law' (2013) 3 *European Criminal Law Review* 45, 56–57. Asp (n 6) 188-206; Öberg, 'Limits to EU Powers' (n 25) ch 7; L Korsell and P Larsson, 'Crime and Justice in Scandinavia' (2011) 40 *Crime and Justice* 519. There is nonetheless tentative evidence that this trend is changing and that organised crime, at least politically, is becoming a concern in some Nordic countries: see Government of Sweden, 'Regeringens första 100 dagar: Kriminalitet', published 26 January 2023: www.regeringen.se/artiklar/2023/01/regeringens-forsta-100-dagar-kriminalitet/.

[72] See above Section III; Montaldo (n 52).

3

The Trinity of Proportionality

Different Dimensions of Proportionality as an EU Criminalisation Principle

GNIEWOMIR WYCICHOWSKI-KUCHTA

I. Introduction

Proportionality, especially when it comes to punishing individuals, is undoubtedly a central component of justice.[1] Its role in the Member States' legal orders is well known and described as limiting the state's power on the one hand and legitimising it on the other – thus providing just punishments, in particular when it comes to sentencing.[2] However, its physiognomy and function become more multifaced in the context of the Area of Freedom, Security and Justice (AFSJ) and, more specifically, within the harmonisation of domestic substantive criminal law. In the exercise of the Union's legislative competence, proportionality goes beyond its traditional role, usually associated with national criminal law. As the EU's competence within the harmonisation of national criminal law does not cover domestic enforcement or sentencing rules, proportionality remains mainly a legislative instrument. It thus becomes less individual-oriented, focused on justifying the EU's harmonisation of criminal offences and penalties rather than on weighing the desert, guilt and potential penalty, thereby shaping adequate coverage of the scope of the criminal prohibition and providing an argument for the choice of penalties and their severity. In this perspective, proportionality plays a more constitutional role.[3] To answer this peculiar nature of proportionality, three basic

[1] In this context, see J Raz, *Practical Reasons and Norms* (Oxford, Oxford University Press, 1999) 95 and MJ Fish, 'An Eye for an Eye: Proportionality as a Moral Principle of Punishment' (2008) 28 *Oxford Journal of Legal Studies* 57.

[2] The most notable works on the principle of proportionality in criminal law refer mainly to sentencing, e.g., A von Hirsch, 'Proportionality in the Philosophy of Punishment' (1992) 16 *Crime and Justice* 55; A von Hirsch and A Ashworth, *Proportionate Sentencing: Exploring the Principles* (Oxford, Oxford University Press, 2005) 75 et seq.

[3] See E Herlin-Karnell, *The Constitutional Dimension of European Criminal Law* (Oxford, Hart Publishing, 2012) 62 et seq and M Kaiafa-Gbandi, 'The 'constitutional' ruling on the Enforcement

notions of it are usually separately considered: general, prospective, and retrospective proportionality.

Prospective and retrospective proportionality emerge from the ECJ case-law[4] and have been broadly discussed in the literature.[5] However, the role of general proportionality in the context of EU harmonisation of criminal law competence and its interplay with other proportionality notions seems to get less traction. This does not mean it is clear and unproblematic. There is a need for an inquiry into what proportionality means in the context of introducing harmonised offences and penalties at the EU level since, exercising its competence in substantive criminal law falls under Article 5(4) TEU. Thus, the Union harmonisation shall not exceed what is necessary to achieve the objectives of the Treaties.

It is commonly agreed that general proportionality is particularly relevant in the AFSJ.[6] As mentioned before, the question of general proportionality is a matter of the scope of possible Union action. To understand this principle properly in the criminal context, it must therefore be confronted with Article 83(1) and (2) TFEU, Article 49(3) of the Charter, and Article 52(1) of the Charter, which provide limitations to the exercise of EU competence *vis-à-vis* the rights enshrined in it. This relation does not seem evident at first glance. In addition, the requirements that arise from this intersection of EU law provisions should structure the legislator's reasoning and should guide how the justification for the use of 'punitive' powers by the EU should be presented. The question is how the EU legislator should argue that the threshold justifying recourse to the harmonisation of national criminal law is met. I think that the trinity of proportionality – general, prospective and retrospective – that are derived from the constitutional sources of EU law can provide an answer to this pressing question.

In this chapter, I advance a conceptualisation of proportionality in the context of the EU's competence in substantive criminal law. Firstly, I am going to investigate how Articles 83(1) and (2) TFEU, 49(3) and 52(1) of the Charter influence the general proportionality principle derived from Article 5(4) TEU as a trinity. This set of legal principles establishes a higher threshold (or, as usually referred to in literature, a "strict proportionality test")[7] for the Union's legislation in

of Community Law (Case C-176/03) and its impact on EU law' in V Mitsilegas, A di Martino and L Mancano (eds), *The Court of Justice and European Criminal Law* (Oxford, Hart Publishing, 2021) 144 et seq.

[4] The ECJ does not use those terms but refers to those particular aspects of the proportionality principle; see Case 265/88 *Messner* ECLI:EU:C:1989:632, paras 9 and 14; Case 122/78 *Buitoni v. Fonds d' orientation et de régularisation des marchés agricoles (FORMA)* ECLI:EU:C:1979:43, para 16 et seq.

[5] See, e.g. V Mitsilegas and E Billis, 'Article 49 – Principles of Legality and Proportionality of Criminal Offences and Penalties' in S Peers, T Hervey, J Kenner and A Ward (eds.) *The EU Charter of Fundamental Rights – A Commentary* (Oxford, Hart Publishing, 2021) 1475 et seq.

[6] T Tridimas 'The Principle of Proportionality' in R Schütze and T Tridimas (eds), *Oxford Principles Of European Union Law: The European Union Legal Order: Volume I* (Oxford, Oxford University Press, 2018) 259–6, and I Wieczorek, *The Legitimacy of EU Criminal Law* (Oxford, Hart Publishing, 2020) 67–69.

[7] J Öberg 'Union Regulatory Criminal Law Competence after the Lisbon Treaty' (2011) 19 *European Journal of Crime, Criminal Law and Criminal Justice* 289, 289–290.

substantive criminal law. Secondly, I argue that general proportionality should be understood not only as a matter of competence, but also, together with other dimensions of proportionality, as a normative principle of criminalisation. This means that, for the EU action to be legitimate, it is important to provide grounds for criminalisation on the basis of the requirements of Article 5 TEU and Article 83 TFEU. Proportionality concerns the substantive content that the EU legislator has to provide, which refers to concurrent values or rights that come into play in the process of criminalisation (e.g. property and health or freedom and well-being of others).

II. Different Roles of Proportionality and its Sources

For the purposes of the analysis, it is necessary to first identify the different notions of proportionality in the context of the EU's criminal law framework, as well as their normative basis and then to trace the relationships between these notions. As mentioned, three concepts of proportionality can be encountered when the EU exercises its competence within criminal law: general, prospective, and retrospective proportionality.[8] Retrospective proportionality is based on the assumption that the severity of the penalty must be commensurate with the seriousness of the offence. This approach to proportionality is inherently connected with criminal law. Prospective proportionality, on the other hand, has evolved from administrative law. It defines the relationship between the measures taken and the objectives pursued and is usually divided into three elements: appropriateness, necessity and proportionality (*sensu stricto*).[9] The roles of those proportionality aspects were accurately described by RA Duff: 'The obvious example is that of present punishment to a past crime. (…) Retrospective proportionality figures in several ways in criminal law – not only in sentencing. (…) Prospective proportionality, by contrast, is of means to ends, of present action to the goal that it is intended to serve. (…) This species of proportionality is central to discussions of proportionality as a constitutional principle'.[10] General proportionality is perceived in the

[8] Sometimes general proportionality is fused with the notion of prospective proportionality, see, for instance, P Asp, *The Substantive Criminal Law Competence of the EU*' (Stockholm, Stiftelsen Skrifter utgivna av Juridiska fakulteten vid Stockholms Universitet, 2012) 188–90 and N Jareborg, 'Criminalization as Last Resort (Ultima Ratio)' (2004) 2 *Ohio State Journal of Criminal Law* 529, 532.

[9] 'The requirement of proportionality specifically requires verification that measures such as those at issue in the main proceedings, first, are appropriate for attaining the objective of general interest pursued, (…), second, are limited to what is strictly necessary, in the sense that that objective could not reasonably be achieved in an equally effective manner by other means less prejudicial to the rights and freedoms guaranteed to the persons concerned, and, third, are not disproportionate to that objective, which implies, in particular, a balancing of the importance of the objective and the seriousness of the interference with those rights and freedoms' (Case C-128/22 *Nordic Info* ECLI:EU:C:2023:951, para 77.

[10] RA Duff, 'Proportionality and the Criminal Law: Proportionality of What to What?' in E Billis, N Knust and J Petter Rui (eds), *Proportionality in Crime Control and Criminal Justice* (Oxford, Hart Publishing, 2021) 29–30.

ECJ's case-law as a 'general principle of the Union'.[11] It relies on the assumption that the EU, as a creator of legally binding rules, cannot introduce legal provisions if they are not necessary to achieve its aims, as the role of Article 5(4) TEU is to 'protect private rights against excessive public interference'[12] and to respect the autonomy of legal orders of the Member States.[13] Buisman rightly states that general proportionality influences how the EU should act.[14] This general principle in the realm of criminal law takes the form of an *ultima ratio* rule, which requires the legislative power to treat criminal law instruments as an exception – the last resort. The *ultima ratio* principle, which can be seen as an element of general proportionality,[15] should be treated as a first step in the criminalisation process, since it obliges the legislator to provide arguments that there are no other means to address the issue at stake, and the threshold for argumentation is structured by the requirements of Article 83 TFEU. The Commission, in its communication 'Towards an EU Criminal Policy: Ensuring the effective implementation of EU policies through criminal law', stated explicitly that general proportionality causes the legislator 'to analyse whether measures other than criminal law measures, e.g. sanction regimes of administrative or civil nature, could not sufficiently ensure the policy implementation and whether criminal law could address the problems more effectively'.[16]

As one can see, the three notions of proportionality share similar core themes and may even overlap to some extent within legislative processes. However, they are derived from various normative sources and serve different aims. General proportionality amounts to a general principle of EU law. It was initially developed in ECJ case-law,[17] although it is right now codified in Article 5(4) TEU, which states that the content and form of Union action shall not exceed what is necessary to achieve the objectives of the Treaties. It is refined in Protocol No 2 on the application of the principles of subsidiarity and proportionality,

[11] Case C-491/01 *British American Tobacco* ECLI:EU:C:2002:741, para 122.

[12] R Schütze, 'Subsidiarity after Lisbon' (2009) 68 *The Cambridge Law Journal* 533. See in this context the role of general proportionality in the assessment of EU institutions' decisions directly affecting individuals: Case T-446/05 *Amann & Söhne and Cousin Filterie v Commission* ECLI:EU:T:2010:165, para 171.

[13] See the discussion on this aspect P Craig, 'Subsidiarity: A Political and Legal Analysis' (2012) 50 *Journal of Common Market Studies* 72, 82 and G Davies, 'Subsidiarity: The Wrong Idea, in the Wrong Place at the Wrong Time' (2006) 43 *CML Rev* 43, 63.

[14] SS Buisman, 'The Future of EU Substantive Criminal Law. Towards a Uniform Set of Criminalisation Principles at the EU level' (2022) 30 *European Journal of Crime, Criminal Law and Criminal Justice* 172.

[15] Both the general principle of proportionality and the principle of *ultima ratio* share a common feature: they treat criminal law as an exception. The necessity of its application should therefore be proven beyond doubt. As the principle of *ultima ratio* does not have an explicit articulation in the Union's primary law and is undoubtedly an element of the common constitutional tradition of the Member States, Article 5(4) TEU should be seen as its normative basis.

[16] Commission Communication 'Towards an EU Criminal Policy: Ensuring the Effective Implementation of EU Policies Through Criminal Law', COM(2011) 573 final, 7.

[17] Case C-8/55, Fédération Charbonnière de Belgique v High Authority of the European Coal and Steel Community ECLI:EU:C:1956:7; Case C-19/61, Mannesmann AG v High Authority of the European Coal and Steel Community ECLI: EU:C:1962:31.

which specifies that all draft legislative acts shall take account of the need for any burden – whether financial or administrative, falling upon the Union, national governments, regional or local authorities, economic operators and citizens – to be minimised and to be commensurate to be achieved.[18] What is often overlooked, both in the literature and in legislative practice, is that Article 83(1) and (2) TFEU[19] contains elements that influence the proportionality assessment in its general and prospective aspects. In fact, the two provisions indicate the conditions for the Union to harmonise substantive criminal law of the Member States. Given this fact, they can be seen as direct indications of how the Union can act in substantive criminal law and are thus necessary requirements for fulfilling general proportionality demands. They show what exactly is mandatory for the EU to consider taking action in substantive criminal law (e.g. serious crimes of cross-border dimension or effectiveness of the EU's policies) and how the Union can act (harmonisation of definitions and minimum, maximum penalties).

Article 83(1) and (2) TFEU provides the *conditio sine qua non* for the EU's action, but it is not a sufficient condition: it requires taking into account other notions of proportionality. The prospective proportionality gains additional normative content from Article 52(1) of the Charter, which states that any limitation on the exercise of the rights and freedoms recognised by the Charter must, among other things, respect the essence of those rights and freedoms and can only be made if they are necessary and genuinely meet the objectives of general

[18] Art 5: 'Draft legislative acts shall be justified with regard to the principles of subsidiarity and proportionality. Any draft legislative act should contain a detailed statement making it possible to appraise compliance with the principles of subsidiarity and proportionality. This statement should contain some assessment of the proposal's financial impact and, in the case of a directive, of its implications for the rules to be put in place by Member States, including, where necessary, the regional legislation. The reasons for concluding that a Union objective can be better achieved at Union level shall be substantiated by qualitative and, wherever possible, quantitative indicators. Draft legislative acts shall take account of the need for any burden, whether financial or administrative, falling upon the Union, national governments, regional or local authorities, economic operators and citizens, to be minimised and commensurate with the objective to be achieved'.

[19] '1. The European Parliament and the Council may, by means of directives adopted in accordance with the ordinary legislative procedure, establish minimum rules concerning the definition of criminal offences and sanctions in the areas of particularly serious crime with a cross-border dimension resulting from the nature or impact of such offences or from a special need to combat them on a common basis.

These areas of crime are the following: terrorism, trafficking in human beings and sexual exploitation of women and children, illicit drug trafficking, illicit arms trafficking, money laundering, corruption, counterfeiting of means of payment, computer crime and organised crime.

On the basis of developments in crime, the Council may adopt a decision identifying other areas of crime that meet the criteria specified in this paragraph. It shall act unanimously after obtaining the consent of the European Parliament.

2. If the approximation of criminal laws and regulations of the Member States proves essential to ensure the effective implementation of a Union policy in an area which has been subject to harmonisation measures, directives may establish minimum rules with regard to the definition of criminal offences and sanctions in the area concerned. Such directives shall be adopted by the same ordinary or special legislative procedure as was followed for the adoption of the harmonisation measures in question, without prejudice to Article 76'.

interest recognised by the Union or the need to protect the rights and freedoms of others. It is an embodiment of the long-lasting ECJ approach, according to which: 'An intervention is deemed disproportionate and unacceptable when it detracts from the substance of the preserved rights'.[20] When it comes to criminalising a particular conduct, regardless of the scope of criminalisation, there is always at least one value, good or right being limited by the Union's action: the right to liberty, guaranteed by Article 6 of the Charter. Of course, other rights usually come into play (e.g., the right to property, the right to conduct business, or the right to freedom of expression). The conflict of competing values and interests in criminalisation thus seems inevitable because while some behaviour is prohibited, at least one Charter-protected liberty is always interfered with. As Möller accurately describes: 'there are at least two senses of balancing. The first we might call "interest balancing". It operates according to a cost-benefit analysis: the respective rights or interests are "measured," placed on a set of scales, and their weight is compared. The second kind of balancing we might call "balancing as reasoning" [i.e.] (…) making a moral argument as to which of the competing interests takes priority in the case at hand, and this moral argument may or may not proceed by way of interest balancing (interest balancing is one kind of moral reasoning but not the only one)'.[21] The conflict of values can only be solved by moral reasoning. So, while assessing the scope of the EU's harmonisation, the legislator is forced to rely not only on general proportionality, but also on prospective proportionality under Article 52(1) of the Charter. To that aim, the legislator shall identify the relevant conflict, verifies if the aim of the action can be seen as an objective of general interest recognised by the Union or is to protect the rights or freedom of others, and if the particular criminal conduct respects the essence of the limited right. The 'general interest recognised by the Union' should be interpreted broadly, not only as values indicated in Article 2 of the TEU but as all legal interests protected by the primary and secondary law of the EU.[22] Finally, one can find a direct embodiment of retrospective proportionality in Article 49(3) of the Charter, which explicitly states that the severity of penalties must not be disproportionate to the criminal offence. In this aspect it is essential that, to assess the severity of a given penalty, one has to take into account not only the degree of the potential penalty but also other circumstances that heavily influence the situation of the punished individual. The specific circumstances of the case need to be taken into account in determining the penalty,[23] in particular, the requirement of guilt, i.e. participation

[20] Case C-62/90 *Commission v. Germany* ECLI:EU:C:1992:169, para 23.

[21] K Möller, 'Proportionality: Challenging the Critics' (2012) 10 *International Journal of Constitutional Law* 715.

[22] JW Ouwerkerk, 'Herijking van Uniestrafrecht. Over de grondslagen voor strafrechtelijke regelgeving in de Europese Unie (Den Haag, Boom Juridisch, 2017) 13; Buisman (n 14), 163.

[23] Case C-384/17 *Dooel Uvoz-Izvoz Skopje Link Logistic N&N* ECLI:EU:C:2018:810, para 45, and Case C-210/10 *Márton Urbán* ECLI:EU:C:2012:64, para 54.

in one or all of the events which, in the context of the legal situation, make that person criminally responsible for the acts constituting the offence,[24] especially in the context of strict liability,[25] which sometimes may be qualified as criminal in the light of so called *Engel* criteria.[26]

III. Proportionality – Towards a Normative Criminalisation Principle

From this perspective, it is clear that there are several different constraints that limit the EU's actions in the substantive criminal law domain. Given that those constraints are entangled, pondering how they impact and give structure to the decision-making process is crucial. Proportionality, in its different iterations, raises very precise and practical questions from the perspective of the legislative process and guides the criminalisation process at the EU level. It thus becomes (together with the subsidiarity principle, which is beyond the scope of this chapter) what Duff calls the 'master criminalisation principle' – the foundational principle of criminalisation. It specifies the most fundamental reasons and criteria for criminalisation as a particular kind of EU activity – it is exclusive and exhaustive because it determines all the fundamental criteria for criminalisation.[27] That is why general proportionality should be understood not merely as a matter of competence but should be perceived, together with other dimensions of proportionality, as a normative criminalisation principle that shows not when (or not only when) the Unions' action is justified but how exactly the Union can act as a legislator when it comes to harmonisation of substantive criminal law.

Proportionality is always a matter of balance. It is so because it deals with principles that require optimisation, but they differ when it comes to subjects to be balanced. As Alexy aptly noticed: 'balancing is one part of what is required by a more comprehensive principle. This more comprehensive principle is the

[24] Case C-58/22 *NR* ECLI:EU:C:2024:70, paras 56–58. It also can potentially be referred to the situation such as force majeure ECJ has provided some argumentation for that notion, however it was not in the case of sanction which was clearly criminal and it is rather a standalone case, see case C- 210/00 *Käserei Champignon Hofmeister* ECLI:EU:C:2002:440, para 67.

[25] '(…) the imposition of a system of strict liability is not disproportionate in relation to the objectives pursued if that system is such as to encourage the persons concerned to comply with the provisions of a regulation and where the objective pursued is a matter of public interest which may justify the introduction of such a system' (Joined Cases C-497/15 and C-498/15 *Euro-Team and Spirál-Gép* ECLI:EU:C:2017:229, paras 53–54 and Case C-210/10, *Marton Urbán* ECLI:EU:C:2012:64, paras 47 and 48.

[26] See Case C-489/10 *Bonda* ECLI:EU:C:2012:319, paras 37–45. The discussion on the criminal nature of strict liability EU's sanction is echoed in Case C-683/21 *Nacionalinis visuomenės sveikatos centras prie Sveikatos apsaugos ministerijos* ECLI:EU:C:2023:376, Opinion of AG Emiliou, paras 74–77.

[27] RA Duff, *The Realm of Criminal Law* (Oxford, Oxford University Press, 2018), 234.

principle of proportionality (Verhältnismäßigkeitsgrundsatz). The principle of proportionality consists of three sub-principles: the principles of suitability, of necessity, and of proportionality in the narrow sense. All three principles express the idea of optimisation'.[28] The trinity of proportionality comes down to balancing different aspects and thus provides different justifications at different stages of the decision-making process – as de Búrca observed, proportionality always requires a set of conflicting interests that need to be 'balanced' and its role is to act as an intermediary.[29] Balancing means that one aspect is less satisfied than the other, but the core idea of balance, and therefore of proportionality in all its iterations, is that the greater the degree of non-satisfaction to one aspect, the greater the importance of satisfying the other.

General proportionality requires an analysis of the balance between interests, goods or rights from the perspective of whether or not criminalisation is necessary to achieve the pursued goal. Prospective proportionally, which derives from both Article 52(1) of the Charter as well as Article 5(4) TEU, urges the legislator to specify 'means and ends analysis' in the context of a particular criminal offence and to establish whether or not the essence of the limited rights is respected. It is thus necessary to answer if the scope of the criminal prohibition is appropriate, that is, if it is too narrow or too broad, and whether or not it can be effective, being mindful of cost-benefit analysis.[30] Finally, retrospective proportionality requires providing arguments that a penalty corresponds with the gravity of the crime. In this regard, it is especially required to take into account the minimum maximum penalties already harmonised at the EU level and the scale of penalties of the Member States. In fact, the EU does not have its own separate criminal justice system that might provide a point of reference and, as Jareborg notices, 'we are dealing with a retrospectively directed type of proportionality that is internal to the penal system'.[31] This aspect is also a reflection of proportionality, as the gravity of criminal offences and the severity of sanctions imposed for committing them may be seen as element of proportionality, since, as Scaccia notices, proportionality is a 'measure of the correct exercise of the Union's jurisdiction, together with subsidiarity, insofar as it conditions the choice between multiple manners of intervention, expressing a preference for those that grant a higher degree of respect for the Member States' identities'.[32] All those elements of proportionality are summarised in the table and conclusions presented below.

[28] R Alexy, 'Constitutional Rights, Balancing, and Rationality' (2003) 16 *Ratio Juris* 135. See also in similar vein M Kumm, 'Political Liberalism and the Structure of Rights', in G Pavlakos (ed), *Law, Rights and Discourse: The Legal Philosophy of Robert Alexy* (Oxford, Hart Publishing, 2007) 131, 137; Möller (n 21), 709 and 711.

[29] G de Búrca, 'The Principle of Proportionality and its Application in EC Law' (1998) 13 *Yearbook of European Law* 105, 106.

[30] IEMM Haenen, *Force & Marriage* (Cambridge, Intersentia, 2014), 135.

[31] Jareborg (n 8), 529.

[32] G Scaccia, 'Proportionality and the Balancing of Rights in the Case-law of European Courts' (2019) 4 *Federalismi* 1.

Table Differences between the three aspects of proportionality

	General proportionality	**Prospective proportionality**	**Retrospective proportionality**
Source	Article 5 (4) TEU General principle *Ultima ratio* reasoning Article 83 (1) and (2) TFEU: Threshold for criminal competence (seriousness of crimes with cross -border dimension/necessity for enforcing policy)	Article 5(4) TEU General principle Means/ends balance (three-fold test) Article 52 (1) Charter: Respect of the essence of values/goods/ rights limited by criminalistion Balance between general interest of criminalisation and the relevant legal good/value/interest	Article 49 (3) of the Charter: Severity of penalties
Subject of balance	Means and ends (*in abstracto)*	Means and ends (*stricto sensu*)	Severity of a penalty and seriousness of a crime
Stage of decision-making process	Admissibility of criminal law harmonisation	Shaping the scope of the prohibition	Shaping the penalty
What questions it answers?	Is it possible to use criminal law at all? Why other means do not work? What legal goods, rights and values are at stake? Are threshold requirements met? How?	Is the definition of the offence correct? Is it too broad or too narrow? How far can the concurrent legal good, right or value be limited? How harmonisation of the definition of the crime provides added value.	Is the criminal penalty shaped the right way? Does it reflect the seriousness of the crime? Should there be other means of responding to the crimes? Does it leave room for the court to take into the consideration individual circumstances of the case?

(continued)

Table ***(Continued)***

	General proportionality	**Prospective proportionality**	**Retrospective proportionality**
Requirements for the legislator	The legislator should identify the goods in conflict and should verify if the aim can be classified as general interest. They should provide reasons that non-criminal options are inefficient and requirements for the use of criminal law are met.	The legislator should provide reasons that particular criminal prohibition will allow the goal to be achieved and should show data that supports this policy option.	The legislator should show that sanction is proportionate, especially by comparing it to other euro-crimes or/and legal systems of Member States.

Given the above, it is worth mentioning that the ECJ case-law currently implies a rather loose standard of judicial review when it comes to assessing the proportionality of the EU's legal act. It implies that the choice to impose criminal sanctions is a political decision taken by the political institutions that are equipped with broad discretion.[33] Although the ECJ did not have the opportunity to exercise a proportionality assessment of substantive criminal law directives and framework decisions, existing case-law suggests that judicial review would be limited to extreme cases as it provides the Commission with broad political discretion when it comes to the choice of having recourse to the harmonisation of substantive criminal law.[34] Nevertheless, it is worth mentioning that the ECJ has referred to its case-law on the judicial review of EU own sanctions as setting the appropriate standard for judging the proportionality of Member State penalties and has cited its rulings concerning judicial review of domestic penalties for the enforcement of EU law as relevant for assessing the proportionality of Union own sanctions.[35] It therefore seems that the ECJ treats proportionality as a single standard, whether it is assessing EU or national legislation. The Union's competence to harmonise substantive criminal provisions is subject to the strict proportionality test, even though the ECJ provided the EU with a broader margin of appreciation in other branches of law.[36] This difference between the approach to criminal law and other

[33] J Öberg, 'Limits to EU Powers. A Case Study of EU Regulatory Criminal Law' (Oxford, Hart Publishing, 2019) 32–36.

[34] Case 265/87 *Hermann Schräder HS Kraftfutter* ECLI:EU:C:1989:303, para. 22 and case C- 45/05, Maatschap Schonewille- Prins, ECLI:EU:C:2007:296, para. 46.

[35] Case C-2/93 Exportslacterijen van Oordegem v. Belgische Dienst voor Bedrijfsleven en Landbouw and Generale Bank ECLI: ECLI:EU:C:1994:223, paras 19–20 and Case C-210/00 Käserei Champignon Hofmeister ECLI:EU:C:2002:440, para 59.

[36] A Suominen, 'Effectiveness and Functionality of Substantive Criminal Law' (2014) 3 *New Jorunal of European Criminal Law* 397.

areas of the Union can be explained by the specific nature of criminal law, with particular emphasis on its severity and its cultural context. In fact, as underlined by the German Federal Constitutional Court in the Lisbon judgment, criminal law is an area particularly close to the identity of the Member States.[37]

Given the unsettled approach of the Court, it is submitted here that proper justification of criminalisation and thorough assessment of the requirements mentioned above that stem from the trinity of proportionality should be provided in the legislative process. In fact, the way that judicial reviews function in relation to proportionality should have implications for the law-making process, as outlined above, should have implications for the law-making process, as law-making and judicial review are, after all, two sides of the same coin. The analysis of the proportionality trinity should thus be reflected in the law-making practices of the Union. The proportionality analysis should start with an assessment of the cost of non-action at the EU level and then on the benefits of action at the EU level. As van Ballegooij notes, the benefits of action at the EU level can 'be financial (cost savings due to efficiency gains), legal (more legal certainty, coherence), social (reduction in inequality), or political (enhanced mutual trust, effectiveness in achieving the policy aims of the Union in the area concerned)'.[38] The quantitative data shows how tools developed to measure the added value of EU legislative intervention may fall short of considering all the relevant factors influencing the need to introduce a penalty. As Asp notices, 'one cannot require full empirical support, but at the same time, it seems clear that the function of the essentiality requirement is to make sure that the EU legislature is not given full discretion as regards whether criminal law should be used'.[39] The issue of criminalisation thus remains a political decision; however, it should never be considered arbitrary –the legislator is obliged to provide good reasons that fulfil every step of the trinity proportionality requirement.

IV. Final Remarks

Given the above analysis, rather than viewing three different notions of proportionality, one should see them as a trinity – one normative criminalisation principle that influences criminal decision-making on three levels: choice of criminal instrument, the scope of the prohibition, and shaping the sanction. As Elohlm aptly describes: 'The distinction between retrospective and prospective concepts is important in order to illustrate two different ways of operating with proportionality in rule-of-law states. However, the distinction should not be exaggerated: the two approaches derive from the same principle and are closely related, using partly the same tools to measure proportionality, for example, the

[37] BVerfG, Judgment of the Second Senate of 30 June 2009–2 BvE 2/08, para 253.

[38] W van Ballegooij, 'Measuring the Added Value of EU Criminal Law', (2016) 2 *eucrim* 90, 91–2.

[39] Asp (n 8), 131.

notions of de minimis and appropriateness'[40]. The fact that different notions of proportionality are derived from different sources and used at different stages of the legislative process should not overshadow the fact that they ultimately derive from a common core – a particular conception of justice that limits the arbitrariness of those in power.

This concept of proportionality as a trinity has a deeply practical impact on the EU's legislative approach because it puts a normative burden on them to demonstrate the reasons to criminalise particular conduct in the proposed manner in the light of conditions derived from the Treaties and the Charter. Nevertheless, assessing proportionality in the criminal context is extremely challenging as it differs from other EU competences, especially the 'core' ones, such as a harmonising single market. Proportionality should not be limited to quantitative statistics but should also present the moral reasoning behind the values that coincide. It has to include the qualitative aspect and legal reasoning of prospective proportionality, especially the concurrent values that come into play when considering the criminalisation of particular conduct and the different factors that influence the mitigation of the penalty. It should also structure the law-making justifications by putting the burden on the legislators to justify their action.

[40] T Elholm, 'The Emotional Component of Proportionality' in E Billis, N Knust and J Petter Rui (eds), *Proportionality in Crime Control and Criminal Justice* (n 10) 80.

4

Proportionality of Sanctions under EU Law: Insights from Penal Theory

ADRIANO MARTUFI

I. Introduction

The principle of proportionality has played a major role in the case-law of the ECJ for decades. Long before the Lisbon Treaty entered into force,[1] references to proportionality abounded in rulings delivered by the Luxembourg judges in matters as diverse as free movement law, public procurement, and data protection.[2] In different shapes and forms, this principle is enshrined in multiple provisions of EU primary law,[3] so much so that proportionality has become almost 'forced passage' for both EU judicial reasoning and for policymaking. The wide resort to proportionality under EU law reflects a broader trend of contemporary constitutionalism.[4] In this perspective, proportionality is often regarded as having acquired a 'supra-constitutional status' (*Überverfassungsrang*),[5] being invoked in disputes involving conflicts between fundamental rights.[6] At the same time, proportionality arguments have historically been refined in the context of national administrative law,[7] most notably with a view to finding a balance between individual rights or interests and public policy goals.

[1] TJ Harbo 'The Function of the Proportionality Principle in EU Law' (2010) 16 *European Law Review* 158–185.

[2] E Bjorge and J Zglinski, 'The principle of proportionality in EU law and its domestic application: ni tout à fait le même, ni tout à fait un autre' in KS Ziegler, P Neuvonen, V Moreno-Lax (eds) *Research Handbook on General Principles in EU Law* (Cheltenham, Elgar, 2022) 191–208. See also Case C-120/94 *Commission v Greece* ECLI:EU:C:1995:109, Opinion of AG Jacobs, para 70: 'there are few areas of Community law, if any at all, where [proportionality] is not relevant'.

[3] For explicit references to proportionality see, for instance, Article 5(4) TEU, Article 296 TFEU, Article 49(3) and Article 52(1) of the Charter.

[4] A Stone Sweet and J Matthews, 'Proportionality Balancing and Global Constitutionalism' (2008) 47 *Columbia Journal of Transnational Law* 68–149.

[5] J Saurer, 'Die Globalisierung der Verhältnismäßigkeitsgrundsatzes' (2012) 51 *Der Staat*, 3–33.

[6] See for a categorisation of the proportionality principle as a meta-principle to settle conflicts between fundamental rights (such as, for instance, free speech and privacy) R Alexy, *A Theory of Constitutional Rights* (Oxford, Oxford University Press, 2010) 66 ff.

[7] The current shape of the 'proportionality assessment' under EU and ECHR law owes much to the theorisation of the *Verhältnismäßigkeitsgrundsatz* within the context of 19th century German

Similarly, proportionality has a long and disputed history within criminal justice theory: its origins are routinely linked back to primordial forms of justice in criminal matters (the infamous *lex talionis*),[8] that evoke the suggestive image of a 'balance' between rights and wrongs.[9] In modern times, proportionality can be found within several conceptualisations of state punishment. Crucially, references to proportionality of punishment appear in both desert-based and consequentialist accounts of sentencing. Desert-based theories regard punishment as retribution (literally 'paying back'), and build on deontological foundations in that they commonly see the 'hard treatment' involved by sanctions as a good-in-itself.[10] Consequentialists, in turn, deny that moral and legal justifications for punishment can be self-referred. From this standpoint, one must look forward to prospective consequences (e.g. in terms of crime reduction) to provide a solid foundation for the exercise of punitive powers.[11] By framing punishment as an outcome-oriented exercise, consequentialist theories link the moral question of 'why' a state should inflict hard treatment with the potential benefits thereof.

Theories on proportionality of punishment have developed accordingly, being articulated in retrospective terms (proportionality in light of *past* wrongdoing) by retributionists, while framed as forward-looking (proportionality in light of a *future* outcome) by consequentialists.

This chapter argues that, in accordance with most recent trends within penal theory, one must consider the role proportionality-as-a-right can play in bridging the gap between retributive and utilitarian views on punishment (and their seemingly opposite takes on what 'proportionate punishment' means).[12] This chapter also argues that proportionality can help to find a workable synthesis between opposed penal orientations if we endorse a 'thin' notion of proportionate punishment. In other words, we should not expect proportionality to provide us with a robust justification for punitive practices; instead, we should welcome a

'police law' and its subsequent development in the jurisprudence of German apex courts for the much part of the 20th century, see TJ Harbo, *The function of proportionality analysis in European law* (Brill, Leiden, 2015) 5 ff.; see also N Courakis and V Polyzoidou 'The Principle of Proportionality: Tracing its Historical Evolution' in E Billis, N Knust and JP Rui (eds), *Proportionality in Crime Control and Criminal Justice* (Oxford, Hart Publishing, 2021) 101–122.

[8] One of the best-known examples of this paradigm is to be found in the Bible in the Book of Exodus ('Eye for eye, tooth for tooth, hand for hand, foot for foot, burn for burn, wound for wound, stripe for stripe', Exodus 21: 23–25). The *lex talionis*, it is often claimed, reflects the long-lasting endurance of 'retributive emotions' within human societies, see JC Murphy, *Punishment and the Moral Emotions: Essays in Law, Morality, and Religion* (Oxford, Oxford University Press, 2012) 22.

[9] M Atwood, *Payback: Debt and the Shadow Side of Wealth*, (London, Bloomsbury, 2008) 23 ff.

[10] See below the literature cited in footnotes 32 and 33. Though Immanuel Kant and Georg WF Hegel are routinely presented as staunch retributionists, more recent scholarship has nuanced the judgement thereupon; see in this respect: S Byrd, 'Kant's Theory of Punishment: Deterrence in its Threat, Retribution in its Retribution' (1989) 8 *Law and Philosophy* 151–200; S Moccia, *Le teorie penali pure nel pensiero tedesco* (Naples, ESI, 2023) 37 ff.

[11] For a neat summary of consequentialist theories of punishment, see R Canton, *Why Punish?: An Introduction to the Philosophy of Punishment* (Palgrave, London, 2017) 83 ff.

[12] See, in the context of a recent revival of the mixed theories of punishment, MC Altman, *A Theory of Legal Punishment. Deterrence, Retribution, and the Aims of the State* (Routledge, London, 2021) 84.

more modest concept of proportionality as a 'side-constraint' (or 'negative proportionality'): a conception of proportionality that may be relied on to set upper limits for both penalties incurred *in abstracto* and sentences handed down by courts. Such a conclusion will be supported by claims that, under the Charter, proportionality must be construed first and foremost as a prerogative of the individual vis-à-vis the state's power to punish.

Significantly, the Charter lays down the requirement that penalties must not be disproportionate to criminal offences. The inclusion of a provision of this kind within a human rights catalogue is highly innovative when compared with prior international law instruments,[13] though the content of such a provision is formally declared to correspond to the constitutional *acquis* of the Member States.[14] Whether or not this is actually true,[15] it is telling that when 'codifying' the ideal of proportionality of penalties, drafters framed it as a *prohibition* (of disproportionate punishment) rather than as a *prescription*. This linguistic option must be seen as placing constitutional constraints on both EU and national penal policies when laying down penalties. The idea of a constitutional prohibition, in this case, reflects a deep-seated commitment to 'negative liberty' from state interference into one's legal sphere,[16] 'freedom' being one of the 'indivisible' values upon which the EU must be built pursuant to the preamble of the Charter.[17]

What is particularly notable about Article 49(3) of the Charter is that this provision the old-fashioned principle of 'retrospective proportionality' has gained the status of a fundamental right. What could once be regarded *only* as a penological tenet (or, more pertinently, in the case of EU case-law, as an interpretive criterion) has now turned into a full-fledged right of the individual under EU constitutional law. Though the ECJ's case-law regarding Article 49(3) is still scarce, this chapter argues that such a provision harbours an untapped potential that might strengthen the role of the individual within EU criminal justice. It is thus at least curious that the Luxembourg Court continues to refer to proportionality under Article 49(3) of the Charter as a two-faced principle, looking both at past wrongdoing and at future expected outcomes in terms of crime prevention. Most notably, it is submitted that the Court has watered down the uniqueness of what ought to be seen as a

[13] V Mitsilegas, E Billis, 'Article 49' in S Peers, T Hervey, J Kenners (eds) *The EU Charter of Fundamental Rights: A Commentary* (Oxford, Hart Publishing, 2021) 1473–1507, 1476.

[14] See the Explanatory Note on Article 49 of the Charter of Fundamental Rights of the European Union, OJ C 303/17, 14.12.2007: 'Paragraph 3 states the general principle of proportionality between penalties and criminal offences which is enshrined in the common constitutional traditions of the Member States and in the case-law of the Court of Justice of the Communities'.

[15] An analysis of constitutional case-law in Germany, for example, gives some reasons to harbour serious doubts about that: see RS Frase, C Momsen, T O'Malley, SL Washington, 'Proportionality of Punishment in Common Law Jurisdictions and in Germany' in *Core Concepts in Criminal Law and Criminal Justice: Volume 1, Anglo-German Dialogues* (Oxford University Press, Oxford, 2019) 213–260.

[16] See, for the all-important dichotomy between 'negative' and 'positive' liberty, I Berlin, 'Two Concepts of Liberty' in *Four Essays On Liberty* (Oxford, Oxford University Press, 1969) 118–172.

[17] 'Conscious of its spiritual and moral heritage, the Union is founded on the indivisible, universal values of *human dignity, freedom, equality* and *solidarity*', (emphasis added).

fundamental rights safeguard by referring to Article 49(3) within the *Greek Maize* test on domestic penalties.[18]

Against this background, I will proceed to set the scene by discussing proportionality in the context of traditional and modern theories of punishment. I will do so by highlighting the traces of both retributivist and utilitarian thinking within the case-law of the ECJ (II). In the following section, I devote my attention to the key dichotomy between 'cardinal' and 'ordinal' proportionality (III), arguing that while the former effectively provides the penological 'blueprint' for the prohibition of disproportionate penalties under Article 49(3),[19] the latter has sometimes surfaced in the case-law of the Court. Finally, I turn to the issue of whether a right not to be subject to disproportionate punishment may effectively be posited under the Charter (IV), by proposing a comparison with the adjudication by the US Supreme Court (USSC) on matters involving the eighth amendment. I conclude by suggesting a re-consideration of a right against excessive penalties or sentences as part of a human-rights based notion of punishment under EU law.

II. Proportionality and Penal Theories

The preliminary dilemma I address in this section is whether proportionality of punishment – in general terms – must be seen as a backward-looking or a forward-looking concept. I will argue that one must be very clear as to what is meant by 'proportionate punishment' if we are to consider this as a fundamental right of the individual under EU law. The risks of misunderstandings when speaking of proportionality of penalties is tangible when one considers the ECJ's case-law. It may be argued that it is in the Court's DNA to handle proportionality as a principle of administrative or public law: especially when dealing with restrictions to free movement being posed by national provisions that lay down criminal sanctions; the Luxembourg's judges would apply a proportionality test that bears resemblance to the tripartite structure of this test in other areas of EU law. Such a test entails that measures chosen are 'suitable', 'necessary' and that they do not impose 'excessive' burden on the interested person.[20]

[18] On the structure of the *Greek Maize* test see below. As for its implications for domestic criminalisation and sanctioning, see the contribution of S Montaldo to this volume.

[19] P Asp, 'Two Notions of Proportionality' in K Nuotio (ed) *Festschrift in Honour of Raimo Lahti* (Helsinki, University of Helsinki, 2007) 207–219; C Sotis, 'I principi di necessità e proporzionalità della pena nel diritto dell'Unione europea dopo Lisbona' (2012) 2 *Diritto penale contemporaneo. Rivista trimestrale*, 111–122, 118.

[20] TJ Harbo, *The Function of Proportionality Analysis in European Law* (Brill, Leiden, 2015) 23 ff. See, particularly, Case 8/74 *Dassonville* ECLI:EU:C:1974:82 and Case 120/78 *Cassis de Dijon* ECLI: ECLI:EU:C:1979:42; for a reading of these seminal rulings as a springboard for proportionality assessment in the context of EU free movement law, G Scaccia,'Proportionality and the Balancing of Rights in the Case-law of European Courts' (2019) 10 *Federalismi*, 2–34, 10.

The suitability requirement identifies the pursuit of a legitimate goal, which may lead the ECJ to rule out *in limine* the need for penalties under national law.[21] More relevant, in practice, is the necessity test, as it entails a purpose-oriented scrutiny of domestic sanctions. In the case-law regarding the free movement of goods and the legitimacy of restrictions on imports, the Court made it clear that both administrative and penal sanctions shall not go beyond 'what is strictly *necessary* for the purposes of enabling the importing Member State to obtain reasonably complete and accurate information on the movement of goods',[22] lest being defined as a measure that has an 'equivalent effect' to a restriction on imports. Both requirements look at the proportionality of sanctions from the perspective of their compatibility with the goal of securing the smooth functioning of internal market provisions and tend to frame penalties/sentences as one among many forms of interferences with the Treaty's market freedoms.[23]

Case-law on free movement of persons – referred to in this volume particularly by Öberg and Grossio – takes a visibly different stance as it places more emphasis on the third step of the test: that is, the question of whether the goals pursued by sanctions outweigh the 'damage' to the EU values or interests at stake.[24] This manner of understanding 'proportionate punishment' has often been regarded as being quintessentially retrospective, in that it seems to gauge proportionality only in relation to the seriousness of prior wrongdoing.[25] Admittedly, the Court of Justice has held, several times, that infringements of formal rules that relate to the exercise of a person's right to free movement must not be disproportionate to the 'gravity of the offence'.[26] On closer inspection, however, it seems that

[21] Case 88/77 *Schonenberg* ECLI:EU:C:1978:30; Case 179/78 *Rivoira* ECLI:EU:C:1979:73; Case C-13/01 *Safalero* ECLI:EU:C:2003:447; Case C-167/01 *Inspire Art* ECLI:EU:C:2003:512; Case C-12/02 *Grilli* ECLI:EU:C:2003:288; Joined Cases C-338/04, C-359/04 and C-360/04 *Placanica* ECLI:EU:C:2007:133.

[22] Case 41/76, *Donckerwolcke* ECLI:EU:C:1976:182, para 38; Case 52/77, *Cayrol* ECLI:EU:C:1977:196, para 39. Both rulings include the key finding pursuant to which an administrative or penal sanction would have to be regarded as a quantitative restriction to imports in so far as the omission or inaccuracy of declaration regarding the origins of imported goods 'were to attract penalties disproportionate to the nature of a contravention of a purely administrative character'.

[23] See, for instance, Case 122/78, *Buitoni*, ECLI:EU:C:1979:43, para 20, in which the ECJ combines a reference to an '*essentially* proportionate penalty' in relation to the infringements of an obligation to import or export (as provided for under Article 18(4) of Commission Regulation (EEC) No 193/75 of 17 January 1975) with the statement that such penalty shall not prove 'excessively severe in relation to the *objectives* of administrative efficiency in the context of the system of import and export licences', emphasis added.

[24] See particularly on the third step of the proportionality test, regarded as a balancing exercise, G de Búrca, 'The Principle of Proportionality and Its Application in EC Law' (1994) 1 *Yearbook of European Law* 1993, 105–50, 113.

[25] E Baker, 'The Emerging Role of the EU as a Penal Actor' in T Daems, D van Zyl Smit, S Snacken (eds), *European Penology?* (Oxford, Hart Publishing, 2017) 77–111, 84 and 100 with respect to the ECJ's ruling in Case C-193/94 *Skanavi* ECLI:EU:C:1996:70. See, however, for a more critical gaze on this case-law P Asp, *The Substantive Criminal Law Competence of the EU* (Stockholm, Jure, 2012) 192 ff.

[26] Case 8/77 *Sagulo* ECLI:EU:C:1977:131, paras. 12 and 13; Case C-265/88 *Messner* ECLI:EU:C:1989:632, para 14; Case C-378/97 *Wijsenbeek* ECLI:EU:C:1999:439, para 44; Case C-193/94 *Skanavi and Chryssanthakopoulos*, ECLI:EU:C:1996:70, para 37.

such a requirement is still embedded within the triadic proportionality assessment referred to above, as it mostly serves the purpose of allowing for a balancing exercise between EU liberties and national penal strategies to be undertaken when implementing EU law.

In *Pieck*, the question arose as to whether an EU national failing to comply with formalities required as proof of the right of residence in the host country could be punished by measures including fines, imprisonment and deportation.[27] Deportation was labelled as being *per se* in contrast with free movement, on the grounds that it would deny the very essence of rights conferred by the Treaty.[28] For fines and imprisonment, in turn, a case-by-case appraisal would be required. To be sure, imprisonment might turn into a penalty so disproportionate to the gravity of the offence that 'it becomes an obstacle to the free movement of persons'.[29] Only a nuanced reference is made to the inherent gravity of wrongdoing, while the Court's reasoning seems to revolve around the impact on free movement rights. A kindred argument[30] can be found within several subsequent rulings[31] and reveals the difficulty of the ECJ to disentangle retrospective proportionality from functionalist concerns, thereby laying the ground for a mixed (retrospective/prospective) assessment.

A. Proportionality and Desert-Based Theories

In light of the above, I will sketch out the traits of what proportionality could mean from the standpoint of penal theory. The main goal, as noted in the introduction, is to give some 'bite' to the prohibition laid down under Article 49(3) of the Charter. If one believes that such provision is to be read in no uncertain terms as a retrospective 'rule' governing the equilibrium between crime and punishment, there is no alternative than tapping into retributive theories for a response about its normative content. The relationship between proportionality and retributivism is far from straightforward, but it might be roughly summed up as follows: punishment is believed to rest on deontological foundations (state authority has a 'duty' to mete it out, and perpetrators might even be seen as having a 'right'

[27] Case 157/79, *Pieck*, ECLI:EU:C:1980:179, para 15 ff.

[28] What strikes, in this respect, is the lack of any reference to the prior ruling of the Court in Case 30/77 *Boucherau* ECLI:EU:C:1977:172, para 35, accepting derogations to free movement on grounds of 'public policy'.

[29] Case 157/79 *Regina v Pleck*, para 19. Interestingly, in the case at hand, the ECJ left no margin to the referring court and outlined a strict prohibition of resorting to a sentencing framework which might include imprisonment and deportation for trivial offences falling within the resort of EU free movement rights.

[30] Proportionality-based arguments are often coupled with references to the principle of non-discrimination, see Case C-35/20 *Criminal proceedings against A* ECLI:EU:C:2021:813, para 58.

[31] Case C-193/94 *Skanavi and Chryssanthakopoulos* ECLI:EU:C:1996:70, para 37; Case C-156/04 *Commission v Greece* ECLI:EU:C:2007:316.

to be punished);[32] in Kantian terms, the guilty, and only the guilty, must be visited with hard treatment;[33] while its infliction amounts to a 'categorical imperative', punishment 'should fit the crime'[34] and, thus, an offender's guilt.

The somewhat abstract idea that state-inflicted pain might fit the crime – while not being devoid of criticisms – reflects a deep-seated commitment to punish only if guilt is proven and to an extent that would be commensurate to the blameworthiness inherent to a person's wrongdoing. This latter term of reference (the 'seriousness' or 'gravity' of the crime), however, is all but easy to pinpoint. On this crucial aspect, scholarship has been torn for centuries. Yet, one might try to summarise the main lines of retributive thinking by ordering them along the dichotomy between moral and legal retribution.[35] While the former posits that punishing wrongdoers is a moral obligation, the latter purports to justify punishment as a counter-balancing factor, one offsetting the 'harm' to the legal order caused by the offence. Both approaches consider retribution – and the underlying tenet of distributive justice this conveys – as the essential 'function' of punishment. Proportionality, instead, contributes to linking punishment with its foundation. But how can one think of proportionality as a factor in justifying the infliction of punishment?

An answer can come only if we take the view that 'hard treatment' is visited on individuals who are thought to be morally responsible.[36] Punishment would thus be legitimate only to the extent that it is proportionate to the guilt of an offender (which, in turn, is believed to reflect the entire blameworthiness of her demeanour). This is what German scholars refer to as *Strafbegründungsschuld*[37] or guilt as a foundation for punishment. This view has been refined and renewed by modern-day advocates of 'just desert' as a founding principle of criminal justice. Andrew von Hirsch, in particular, has picked up on such a concept by framing punishment

[32] GWF Hegel, *Grundlinien der Philosophie des Rechts*, (Berlin, Nicolai, 1820 and Berlin, Hoffenberg, 2017) 81 ff.; see for an analysis of the 'right-to-punishment' doctrine, within both retributivist and utilitarian penal theory, M Dubber 'The Right to Be Punished: Autonomy and Its Demise in Modern Penal Thought' (1996) 16 *Law and History Review* 113–146.

[33] I Kant, *Grundlegung zur Metaphysik der Sitten* (Riga, 1785, Hartknoch and Berlin, Hoffenberg, 2016) 71 ff. See on Kant's theory of punishment M Dan-Cohen, 'Dignity, Crime, and Punishment: A Kantian Perspective' in M Dubber (ed) *Foundational Texts in Modern Criminal Law* (Oxford, Oxford University Press, 2014) 101–118, 116.

[34] The ideal that punishment must fit the crime is seen by many advocates of retribution of as the quintessential legacy of desert-based theories of punishment, see for instance Justice A Scalia's Opinion in USSC, *Ewing v. California*, 538 U.S. 11 (2003): 'the notion that the punishment should fit the crime is inherently a concept tied to the penological goal of retribution'.

[35] See for such dichotomy in the context of early-modern penal theory MA Cattaneo, *La filosofia della pena nei secoli 17. e 18. Corso di filosofia del diritto* (Ferrara, Editrice Universitaria, 1974) 54 ff.

[36] This premise seems to be well illustrated by John Rawls' view on retributivism: 'It is morally fitting that a person who does wrong should suffer in proportion to his wrongdoing. That a criminal should be punished follows from his guilt, and the severity of the appropriate punishment depends on the depravity of his act', J Rawls, 'Two Concepts of Rules' in (1955) 64 *The Philosophical Review*, 3–32, 4.

[37] See, among many, HH Jescheck, *Lehrbuch des Strafrechts. Allgemeiner Teil* (Berlin, Duncker & Hublot, 1996), 429 ff. A well-known provision of the German Criminal Code (§ 46(1) StGB) lays down that 'the guilt of the criminal ought to be the basis of punishment'.

as censure or disapprobation, in that it treats its recipient 'as someone capable of choice'.[38] Hard treatment merely conveys censure and seems to be based on a rather loose conception of 'normative guilt' (one is blamed for breaking the law, and not for its lack of morality).[39] According to this view, perpetrators must be visited with a degree of hard treatment that is commensurate with the blame their actions attract.

While there is much to commend in von Hirsch's attempt to provide insights into what public censure means for the offender, this gaze on punishment seems at odds with the principled view of EU law and, particularly, the Charter's take on proportionality. Instead, Article 49(3)'s prohibition of disproportionate punishment would seem to fit within a 'proportionality-as-parsimony' view of desert, such as that heralded by Micheal Tonry.[40] Penal parsimony reflects the ultimate goal of minimising suffering imposed on rule-breakers.[41] Within the penal theory, however, parsimony is often pitted against coherence and equality of sentencing.[42] To solve such a conundrum, some scholars have gone so far as to theorise proportionality as entailing the choice of the least restrictive or least punitive sanction while setting outer bounds to ensure that sentencing decisions are, at best, not undeserved.[43] Clearly, the principle of parsimony would seem to work well within the proportionality framework developed by the ECJ in the context of its case-law on free movement rights.[44] Still, one has to consider that the latter incorporates a balancing exercise. This poses the question of the policy objectives, against which the effort of minimising suffering must be weighed.

B. Proportionality and Consequentialist Theories

The notion of proportionality as a principle that entails a cost-benefit assessment takes us neatly into the consequentialist characterisation of punishment. For one, the need to engage in a balancing exercise seems to echo the utilitarian belief that hard treatment could never find a justification as a good-in-itself. Building on the very concrete need to reform criminal justice systems and to overturn the

[38] A von Hirsch, *Censure and Sanctions* (Oxford, Oxford University Press, 1993) 6 ff. and 19.

[39] A von Hirsch, 'Proportionality in the Philosophy of Punishment' (1992) 16 *Crime and Justice* 55–98.

[40] M Tonry, 'Fairness, Equality, Proportionality and Parsimony' in A du Bois-Pedain and AE Bottoms (eds), *Penal Censure: Engagements Within and Beyond Desert Theory* (Oxford, Hart Publishing, 2019) 277–295.

[41] As Tonry himself observes, parsimony is 'better understood, however, as deriving not from punishment principles but from the equality and human dignity principles with which punishment practices must be reconciled' (*Ibidem*, 294).

[42] See for a neat summary R Frase, 'Sentencing Principles in Theory and Practice' (1997) 22 *Crime and Justice*, 363–434.

[43] N Morris, 'Towards Principled Sentencing' (1977) 37 *Maryland Law Review*, 1161–1180; see, for a recent revamp of Morris' theory of 'penal parsimony', R Lippke, 'Retributive Parsimony', (2009) 15 *Res Publica*, 377–395, 394: '[retributive theory] is consistent with recognition of the ways in which [courts] must make difficult choices about how to balance the pursuit of retributive justice against the attainment of other goods to which individuals are arguably entitled'.

[44] This seems to be the view of Baker (n 25) 84.

penal practices of the *ancien régime*, early consequentialists (such as Montesquieu, Beccaria, and Bentham) seemed mostly concerned with measuring the potential effects of sentencing rather than its adequateness vis-à-vis the crime committed.[45] This turn on the effectiveness of penal strategies had arisen *inter alia* from the obvious concern to secularise the justification of punishment, moving away from transcendent ideals of 'distributive justice' that informed early penal codifications (such as the *Constitutio Carolina*), vaguely reminiscent of Thomistic conceptions of retribution as a means to re-establish a good 'order of justice'.[46]

Instead, consequentialism looks at the future with a view to prevent and reduce re-offending. With consequentialism, the justification for inflicting hard treatment can only lie in the reasonable expectation that such treatment will broadcast to society the negative impact of breaking the law and will thereby contribute to the common good. Importantly, among the early proponents of utilitarian theories of punishment, deterrence (or negative general prevention) was seen as its most compelling justification. A standard objection against strict consequentialists is that, for the sake of crime prevention, they might go a long way to justify punishment of the innocent.[47] It is argued that outcome-oriented sentencing could forego entirely any need to make punishment fit the crime.[48] And yet, it is telling that proportionality did not disappear altogether from the legal and political discourse of consequentialist thinkers.[49] Quite to the contrary, important appeals to proportionality can be found through the pages of both Beccaria and Bentham.[50] But what exactly is a proportionate punishment from a utilitarian standpoint?

Consequentialist proportionality corresponds to the two cumulative tenets of 'ends-benefits' and 'alternative-means':[51] (1) the costs and burdens of the sentence (or the added costs and burdens) may outweigh the likely benefits (or added benefits) generated by the sentence, and (2) the sentence may be disproportionate (that is, unnecessary, and therefore excessive) when compared with other, less costly or burdensome, means of achieving the same goals.

[45] See Courakis and Polyzoidou (n 7) 103.

[46] J Finnis, 'Aquinas, Punishment, and the Common Good' (2021) 21 *Cornell Legal Studies Research Paper*, 1 ff.

[47] A comprehensive literature review of arguments criticising utilitarianism on grounds of the framing-the-innocent's argument is neatly summarised in Altman (n 12) 124.

[48] While old-fashioned responses would point to the pain imposed on the innocent as lacking the real character of traditional 'punishment', most credited utilitarian responses to this emphasise that a legislation or a judicial ruling deliberately convicting the innocent would cast discredit and distrust on the legislature and the judiciary (thereby failing to uphold the ultimate goal of reducing re-offending and induce law-abiding behaviour); see for instance, Rawls (n 36) 10 ff. On the uneasy relationship between deterrence and proportionality see, among many, A von Hirsch, 'Proportionality in the Philosophy of Punishment' (1992) 16 *Crime and Justice* 55–98.

[49] See in particular N Lacey, 'The Metaphor of Proportionality' (2016) 43 (1) *Journal of Law and Society*, 27–44, 35: among Enlightenment thinkers' «appeals to the metaphor of proportionality in the law derive a good part of their power from the way in which they connect the exercise of legal power with doctrines and ideas of reason, fairness, fittingness, and order circulating within broader political and indeed cultural discourse».

[50] Lacey (n 49) 31.

[51] I explicitly borrow "the 'ends-benefits' vs. 'alternative-means' dichotomy" from Frase et al (n 15) 221 ff.

Both tenets resonate with the proportionality test employed by the ECJ, as they overlap with the second and the third steps of the general assessment developed by the Court in its interpretation of EU economic freedoms. Most notably, the 'ends-benefits' parameter coincides with the main rationale behind the case-law on sanctions and free movement rights, thereby requiring that penalties should not impose a burden (that is, a restriction of EU rights)[52] so great that it outweighs the expected benefits of the state reaction to an infringement. Similarly, several of the Court's rulings explicitly incorporate an 'alternative-means' reasoning, as they overtly require that national law provide for more lenient penalties.[53] As outlined above, it is hard to infer from these judgements any real element that would point to a sensible use of retrospective proportionality, to the extent that in such cases the intrinsic seriousness of the offence is almost entirely disregarded.

More worryingly, the ECJ's case-law interpreting the *Greek Maize* requirements seems to enhance the link between proportionality and prevention in such a way as to overemphasise deterrence. In some recent judgements that involved the interpretation of the 'holy triad' of requirements (effectiveness, proportionality, dissuasiveness of penalties)[54] guiding national discretion in the implementation of EU law, the Luxembourg judges have repeatedly highlighted that 'the severity of penalties must be commensurate with the seriousness of the infringements […], in particular by ensuring a genuinely dissuasive effect'.[55] In doing so, the Court's reasoning can be safely located within the consequentialist tradition of proportionality in that it seems to imply that: (1) an offence has been committed that reveals a certain degree of seriousness, (2) punishment must convey a level of censure that would provide reasons to abide by the law and induce norm-compliance and (3) such level of censure is enough to give the perpetrator and third parties a good reason to abide by the rules in the future.[56]

[52] Case 118-75 *Watson and Belmann* ECLI:EU:C:1976:106, para 21.

[53] Interestingly, the alternative-means principle is visible when the Court opines that a lesser penalty (e.g. a fine *in lieu* of a custodial sentence) is sufficient to achieve the goal of an effective implementation of EU law: see in addition to some of the rulings cited above Joined Cases C-64/18, C-140/18, C-146/18 and C-148/18, *Maksimovic*, ECLI:EU:C:2019:723, para 47: 'effective implementation […] could be achieved through less restrictive measures, such as a lower fine or the introduction of an upper limit on such fines, and without necessarily imposing a custodial sentence as an alternative penalty'. See also Case C-645/18, *Bezirkshauptmannschaft* ECLI:EU:C:2019:1108, para 40.

[54] F Giuffrida, 'Effectiveness, Dissuasiveness, Proportionality of Sanctions and Assimilation Principle: The Long-Lasting Legacy of the Greek Maize Case' in V Mitsilegas, A Di Martino and L Mancano (eds), *The Court of Justice and European Criminal Law. Leading Cases in a Contextual Analysis* (Oxford, Hart Publishing, 2019) 108.

[55] Case C-452/20 *Agenzia delle dogane e dei monopoli* ECLI:EU:C:2022:111, para 39; Case C-565/12 LCL *Le Crédit Lyonnais* ECLI:EU:C:2014:190, para 45; Case C-255/14 *Chmielewski* ECLI: ECLI:EU:C:2015:475, para 23. See also for a similar reasoning though with respect to free movement rights Case C-231/20, *MT v Landespolizeidirektion Steiermark* ECLI:EU:C:2021:845, para 45.

[56] Interestingly, there is some level of overlap between this approach to penal rationality and Von Hirsch's justification for inflicting hard treatment to convey censure: while censure is backward-looking, hard treatment responds mainly to preventative concerns ('a prudential reason for obedience to those insufficiently motivated by the penal censure's moral appeal'), see A von Hirsch,

C. The 'Modern' Trend Towards Proportionality as a Side-Constraint

It is submitted that the higher emphasis on deterrence in the 'Greek Maize' case-law must be understood as a consequence of the drive towards effectiveness that characterises this area of the ECJ's adjudication. As has been widely shown, the Union's penological gaze on national sanctions implementing secondary law must be understood in light of EU law's overarching principle of effectiveness.[57] While effectiveness remains implicit within the Court's jurisprudence on free movement rights, when asked about what makes for an *effective* enforcement of EU law, the ECJ tends to use the 'iron fist'.[58] As Advocate General Kokott once made clear, 'rules laying down penalties are *effective* where they are framed in such a way that they do not make it practically impossible or excessively difficult to impose the penalty provided for (and, therefore, to attain the objectives pursued by Community law)'.[59]

AG Kokott held the view that 'effectiveness' and 'dissuasiveness' of sanctions are roughly overlapping concepts. Arguing in such a way, the Attorney General made explicit reference to the ideal of the 'certainty of punishment' – a principle commonly associated with general deterrence since the times of early utilitarian philosophers[60] (see, in particular, the work of Cesare Beccaria).[61] In Kokott's view, there are three elements that allow sanctions to be thought as effective: i) the 'nature of the penalty'; ii) its 'severity'; iii) but also the 'likelihood of its being imposed'. This latter aspect is explained in the following terms: '[a]nyone who commits an infringement must fear that the penalty will in fact be imposed on him'.[62] This staunch utilitarian approach would call for a right to proportionality

'Proportionate Sentences: A Desert Perspective' in A von Hirsch, A Ashworth (eds) *Principled Sentencing. Readings on Theory and Policy* (Oxford, Hart Publishing, 2000) 168–179.

[57] E Herlin-Karnell, 'Effectiveness and Constitutional Limits in European Criminal Law' (2014) 5 *New Journal of European Criminal Law* 267–273. See also S Melander, 'Effectiveness in EU Criminal Law and Its Effects on the General Part of Criminal Law' (2014) 5 *New Journal of European Criminal Law* 274–300.

[58] M Dougan, 'From the Velvet Glove to the Iron Fist: Criminal Sanctions for the Enforcement of Union Law' in M Cremona (ed), *Compliance and the Enforcement of EU Law* (Oxford, Oxford University Press, 2012), 74–131.

[59] See Opinion of AG Kokott, ECLI:EU:C:2004:624, paras 87–89.

[60] As Bentham famously argued: 'pain and pleasure are the great springs of human action' J Bentham, *Rationale of Punishment* (London, Heward, 1830); J T McHugh ed (Amherst, Prometheus, 2009) 61. See, more broadly on penal utilitarianism, G Di Cristina, M Gottschalk, R Mayzer, 'Four currents of criminological thought' in B Arrigo and HY Bersot (eds), *The Routledge Handbook of International Crime and Justice Studies* (London, Routledge, 2013) 9–32.

[61] See C Beccaria, *Dei delitti e delle pene* (Leghorn, Coltellini, 1764) G Francioni, L Firpo ed (Milano, Mediobanca, 1984). See for an early English translation, C Beccaria, *An Essay on Crimes and Punishments*, H Philip ed (Philadelphia, Nicklin, 1819) 54: '[t]he certainty of a small punishment will make a stronger impression than the fear of one more severe, if attended with the hopes of escaping'.

[62] Joined Cases C-387/02, C-391/02 and C-403/02 *Silvio Berlusconi and Others* ECLI:EU:C:2004:624, Opinion of AG Kokott, paras 89–90.

to act as an 'equaliser', offsetting the risk that sentences are constantly driven upwards by consequentialist concerns. If read properly, Article 49(3) of the Charter would indeed suggest that we understand proportionality as an external constraint, allowing only dissuasive penalties that are not disproportionate.

Before looking more closely into the Court's case-law to explore the way in which the ECJ and national judges could gauge the severity of penalties (and compare this with an infringement's seriousness), one could probably conclude that a sound way to interpret proportionality under the Charter is to embrace some form of 'negative retributivism'.[63] It is safe to say that the justification for hard treatment under EU law cannot lie, as retributivists would suggest, in the inherent blameworthiness of an act. As things stand, a rationale for hard treatment could only be cast in utilitarian terms. Incidentally, however, the ECJ has long made clear that punitive sanctions are, in essence, different from merely preventative measures:[64] the former are, by definition, 'reactive' to a prior violation and may serve in the event of a serious and repeated lack of compliance. The Court insisted that the implementation of EU law can only be made through punitive measures, while some preventive measures (such as a civil forfeiture) would not be sufficient to guarantee the expected outcome in terms of enforcement.[65]

If the essence of any punitive sanction lies in its being a reaction to past wrongdoing, it may be possible to build on the seriousness of such demeanour to, at least, set upper limits to the severity of penalties and constrain sentencing *in concreto* to minimise suffering. This view of proportionality is reminiscent of what Robert Nozick referred to as 'side-constraint'.[66] The idea of proportionality as a 'constraint' as opposed to a 'goal',[67] is eloquent about the role this principle can play. Not only is proportionality understood as a 'thin concept'[68] (thus unable to provide a robust justification for punishment), but it must be framed as an individual guarantee

[63] The concept of negative retributivism is often understood as a nod to the absence of any foundational link between the gravity of an offence and the justification of punishment. Negative retributivism, instead, is the 'position of choice for theorists who insist that the fundamental justifying aim of legal punishment is the reduction of crime but who acknowledge the drawbacks to such an exclusively forward-looking justification', R Lippke, 'Some Surprising Implications of Negative Retributivism' (2014) 31 *Journal of Applied Philosophy* 49–62.

[64] Case C-265/95 *Commission v French Republic* ECLI:EU:C:1997:595, para 19 ff.

[65] Case C-265/95 *Commission v French Republic* ECLI:EU:C:1997:595, para 20. The Court found that French domestic legislation had not been adequate nor proportionate for the purpose of deterring vandals from disrupting the importation and transit in France of fruit and vegetables originating in other Member States, in a way that ended up disrupting the free movement of goods. In particular, the failure to prosecute and indict violent acts committed by private individuals and by protest movements of French farmers against agricultural products from other Member States resulted in a violation of both the freedom of movement of goods under the Treaty and the related duty of sincere cooperation.

[66] R Nozick, *Anarchy, State, and Utopia* (New York, Basic Books, 1974) 29.

[67] Y Lee, 'The Constitutional Right against Excessive Punishment' (2005) 91 *Virginia Law Review* 677–746; A Ristroph, 'Proportionality as Principle of Limited Government (2005) 55 *Duke Law Journal* 263–332.

[68] F Viganò, *La proporzionalità della pena. Profili di diritto penale e costituzionale* (Torino, Giappichelli, 2021) 213 ff.

(proportionality *ex parte civium*) and not as an attribute of the sovereign power to punish (proportionality *ex parte principis*). This notion speaks to a form of 'weak' or 'negative' retributivism, which fits well into mixed theories of punishment.[69] This composite strand of penal theories holds that one may well posit punishment on preventive grounds (deterrence, positive prevention, rehabilitation) at the statutory level; however, at the stage of sentencing, an individual assessment should prevail.[70]

III. Proportionality between Justice and Equality

If proportionality is to be understood as a 'side-constraint', its main role would be to lead to a reduction of sentences determined only on preventive grounds. In particular, when meting out punishment, one should not only consider the extent to which a sentence is conducive to deterring but also must set upper limits to its severity. If a sentence is to be calculated only based on preventative concerns, the chances are high that this could lead to an excess of punishment *in concreto*. Linking the measure of sentences to the blameworthiness of the individual, in turn, may reduce the severity of the sentence handed down *if* such sentence turns out to be excessive or exaggerated.[71] By contrast, nothing would prevent a court from determining the entity of a sentence in such a way that it dips below the lower limits set out by the law. This would be the case if, by reasoning on grounds of general and individual deterrence (and/or rehabilitation), the judge is satisfied that punishment may be reduced or even dispensed with.[72]

A. Cardinal Proportionality

While we might be able to endorse a thin version of proportionality, the question of which term of reference should be relied on to gauge whether or not a penalty or sentence is 'excessive' remains unsolved. According to a traditional mixed theory of punishment – popular among German,[73] Spanish[74] and Italian[75]

[69] See M Altman, 'In Defense of a Mixed Theory of Punishment' in M Altman (ed) *The Palgrave Handbook on the Philosophy of Punishment* (Cham, Palgrave Mc Millan, 2023) 195–241.

[70] Lippke (n 63) 51 ff.

[71] Lee (n 67) 742.

[72] See for this argument, with specific reference to a multifactorial theory of sentencing, C Roxin, 'Sinn und Grenzen staatlicher Strafe' in C Roxin, *Strafrechtliche Grundlagenprobleme* (Berlin, De Gruyter, 1974) 1–31.

[73] C Roxin and L Greco, Strafrecht, Allgemeiner Teil. Volume I: Grundlagen. Der Aufbau der Verbrechenslehre (Munich, Beck, 2020) 156.

[74] GJ Basso, Determinacion judicial de la pena y proporcionalidad con el hecho (Madrid, Marcial Pons, 2019) 177 ff.

[75] E Dolcini, La commisurazione della pena (Padova, Cedam, 1979) 176 ff. See also Viganò (n 68) 152 ff.

scholars – side-constraint proportionality is, at closer inspection, a by-product of the principle of culpability. It is often argued that, because of the very essence of punishment (understood as a reaction to a prior and culpable wrongdoing), sentences must be commensurate to an offender's guilt. The idea of penal parsimony, within this theoretical framework, can be derived from the notion that perpetrators can be blamed for something and shall not be visited with a harder treatment than what such blame requires. In this view, it would fall beyond the inherent logic of punishment to impose a sentence that exceeds what an offender has proven to deserve, through its culpability, in terms of blame/reprobation.

Anchoring proportionality to a perpetrator's guilt lays down the frame of reference for cardinal proportionality, or proportionality in relation to the seriousness of a single offence. In this perspective, if punishment is excessive in relation to one's guilt it would come across as unjust, thereby proving unable to meet any further preventive and correctional goal.[76] Yet, placing guilt at the very centre of a theory of sentencing may be problematic on at least three accounts: (1) regulatory criminal law is notoriously riddled with strict liability offences, (2) it is still doubtful if *mens rea* requirements apply in their full stringency within the context of administrative violations, even though sanctions are substantively 'criminal' as per the *Engel* criteria,[77] and (3) to the extent that criminal/administrative sanctions can be imposed on legal persons, it would be uneasy to build proportionality around a unitary notion of guilt.[78] This might go some way to explain why traditional scholarship in the English-speaking tradition anchors cardinal proportionality to the dual requirement of (a) harm and (b) culpability.[79]

In the Luxembourg Court's case-law, one can find some traces of cardinal proportionality based on harm. In *K.M.*, when explicitly applying Article 49(3) of the Charter, the ECJ ruled that 'in order to assess the proportionality of the sanction, account should also be taken of the relationship between the amount of the fine that may be imposed and the economic benefit derived from the infringement committed, in order to deter offenders from committing such

[76] Italian scholars have often emphasised the conceptual link between the principle of guilt and the correctional goal of social rehabilitation (the latter being the most consistent interpretation of the principle that 'punishments shall tend towards the convict's re-education' laid down by Article 27(3) of the Italian Constitution), see T Padovani, 'Teoria della colpevolezza e scopi della pena' in (1987) 30 Rivista italiana di diritto e procedura penale, 798–835.

[77] The ECtHR (having to accommodate different constitutional traditions of the Member States) does not explicitly recognise the principle of culpability as such. It does, however, acknowledge certain aspects of mens rea, while not outlawing strict liability offenses. See Salabiaku v France App No 10519/83 (ECtHR, 7 October 1988), para 27 and 28; GIEM v Italy App No 1828/06 34163/07 19029/11 (ECtHR, 28 June 2018), para 243.

[78] See for the notion of organisational fault liability, breaking out from derivative models based on individual liability, WS Laufer 'Corporate bodies and Guilty Minds' (1994) 43 *Emory Law Journal* 647–730; JL Coffee, 'No Soul to Damn: No Body to Kick: An Unscandalized Inquiry into the Problem of Corporate Punishment' (1981) 79 *Michigan Law Review* 386–459.

[79] See, among many, RA Duff, *Punishment, Communication and Community* (Oxford, Oxford University Press, 2001) 135.

an infringement'.[80] What is striking here is that, although the Court seems to refer to the seriousness of the offence, it employs a one-sided yardstick to measure it: that is, the economic return of crime. This choice is motivated by (1) the omnipresent need to put proportionality at the service of deterrence and (2) the difficulty of measuring the seriousness of criminal behaviour objectively. The ruling's findings, in addition, are only of limited utility because they apply exclusively to financial penalties or fines.

Clearly, it would seem unlikely, if not impossible, to extend the same reasoning when the content of a sanction and the proceeds of crime are of a different nature (e.g. a financial benefit *vis-à-vis* a custodial sentence).

The complexity of carrying out a one-sided assessment of cardinal proportionality explains why, in some rulings, the ECJ has used a triadic model of assessment to appraise the proportionality of punishment. The triadic model involves a *tertium comparationis*, that is a sentencing scale provided for a different category of crimes other than the statutory provision under scrutiny. This triadic test is typical of an appraisal of proportionality based on considerations of equality, such as to avoid unevenness and incoherence while sanctioning comparable forms of wrongdoing. In a number of cases regarding free movement rights, the Court has thus linked proportionality of punishment and non-discrimination clauses provided for under EU primary law. In *Drexl*, for instance, it was found that the penalty provided for the failure to pay VAT on imported goods (a term of imprisonment and the confiscation of goods) was manifestly disproportionate (not in itself, but) when compared to penalties applicable to non-payment of value-added taxes on domestic transactions.[81]

It is notable that, while the Court acknowledged the different nature of the two categories of offences it compared,[82] it still found that the sentencing scale provided for non-compliance of tax duties on imported goods amounted to disproportionate punishment. Though the two sets of violations shall not be punished equally, provisions on domestic transactions provide a benchmark with which to measure the proportionality of sentences applicable to EU law-relevant cases.

B. Ordinal Proportionality

The most plausible way to understand retributivism as a side-constraint is through embedding both ordinal and cardinal limits within the proportionality

[80] Case C-77/20 K. M. (Sanctions infligées au capitaine de navire) ECLI:EU:C:2021:112, para 49.

[81] Case 299/86 Criminal proceedings against Rainer Drexl ECLI:EU:C:1988:103, para 23.

[82] Ibidem, para 22: 'it must be stated in that regard that the two categories of offences in question are distinguished by different circumstances concerning both the constituent elements of the offence and the greater or lesser extent of the difficulty of discovering it. Value-added tax on importation is charged simply when the goods actually enter the territory of the member state concerned, rather than on a transaction'.

test.[83] Ordinal proportionality implies a holistic gaze on the system of sanctions as it requires penalties and sentences to be comparatively just, such that more serious offences are punished more harshly than less serious offences. Though cases exist in which a penalty is manifestly disproportionate,[84] any assessment on cardinal grounds presupposes a scale that ranks violations based on their severity.[85] Sentencing theorists have long shown that for an assessment of cardinal proportionality to be well-founded, one has to rely on some ordinal classification of the seriousness of crimes, from high to low.[86] Only then can one anchor the severity of penalties to a pre-existing and viable benchmark.

This might go some way to show why the ECJ has often opted for a triadic assessment while gauging the proportionality of domestic sanctions. Similarly, the Court has sometimes built on the very ranking of EU law violations, as outlined under EU secondary law, to conclude that some flat-rate fines would, by default, result in a disproportionate punishment when applied to all sorts of violations of the same set of EU rules, irrespective of their gravity. In *Urbán*, the Luxembourg Court has built on a scale of seriousness among different types of infringements, sketched out by relevant provisions in the dispute at hand, to argue that violations of duties on the use of record sheets for lorry-drivers and their employers – set out by Regulation No 3821/85 of the Council – would not warrant a sanction-by-default regardless of their gravity.[87] Instead, national legislation should consider the different degree of seriousness of the infringement of each EU law prescription,[88] taking particular account of their impact on the goal of ensuring road safety.[89]

I would agree that, in other instances, developing a proportionality test that builds on ordinal concerns would prove somewhat uneasy.[90] This might be the case, especially when EU legislation in the field concerned is rather sketchy or

[83] Lippke (n 63) 53.

[84] As is well known, the ECtHR has vented the possibility to expand on the concept of 'grossly disproportionate punishments' in its case-law on Article 3 ECHR, but has rarely applied this prohibition in practice; see N Mavronicola 'Crime, Punishment and Article 3 ECHR: Puzzles and Prospects of Applying an Absolute Right in a Penal Context' (2015) 15 *Human Rights Law Review* 721–743.

[85] See on the existential nexus between cardinal and ordinal proportionality, von Hirsch (n 38) 18 ff.

[86] M Matravers, 'Is twenty-first century punishment post-desert?' in M Tonry (ed) *Retributivism has a past: Has it a future?* (Oxford, Oxford University Press, 2011) 30–45.

[87] Case C-210/10 *Urbán* ECLI:EU:C:2012:64, paras 33 ff.

[88] Annex III to Directive 2006/22, though not applicable to the case at issue, had drawn a distinction between groups of infringements of Regulation No 3821/85, stating for each type of obligations, their legal basis, the type of infringements and their level of seriousness. The latter are classified in three levels, namely 'very serious infringement', 'serious infringement' and 'minor infringement'.

[89] See, accordingly, the Court in *Urbán*, para 33: 'breaches likely to prevent the effective monitoring of drivers' working conditions and compliance with road safety cannot be ranked in the same category as minor infringements which, although indeed constituting breaches of the provisions of the regulations in question, do not, however, hinder monitoring of compliance with the obligations laid down by European Union legislation'.

[90] See the contribution by Öberg in this volume.

poorly harmonised.[91] However, it would seem fair to say that when a domestic judge employs a triadic test, involving – as a term of comparison – some equivalent national provision, the ranking of offences on ordinal grounds might be restored. Unfortunately, this ranking would not reflect an appraisal entirely made by EU law but rather a combination of penal priorities followed under national and EU law, respectively, so much so that it might be asked if we would end up comparing apples and oranges. Ordinal rationality, in turn, might be weighed against the need to safeguard some margin of manoeuvre for domestic authorities (thereby including both the legislator and the system of courts/administrative bodies in charge of meting out sanctions).

That is clearly the case if we look at criminal law *stricto sensu* and in its harmonisation under Article 83 TFEU. Thus far, the approximation of criminal penalties has always been built on minimum-maximum thresholds. Accordingly, the Council in both 2002[92] and 2009[93] relied on a set of guidelines that rank offences according to four different levels, thus establishing corresponding echelons of criminal penalties for each group of offences. The level of harmonised penalties however, corresponds to the minimum of the maximum sanction incurred. Though this system has been rightly criticised for its limited operational impact,[94] and accurate proposals have been laid down to replace it,[95] it also lays bare the difficulty of finding the 'anchoring points of a penalty scale'[96] even when (or especially because) the EU is committed to harmonising criminal sanctions at the domestic level.

IV. Proportionality as a Fundamental Right

Based on this overview, we are left with the question of whether Article 49(3) of the Charter gives individuals a right not to be subject to a disproportionate punishment. While the prevailing view that retributivism can only work as a

[91] That was clearly not the case with respect to the record-keeping duties of lorry drivers as per Regulation No 3821/85. Though the choice of sanctions was left to national law (in accordance with the 'holy triad' of effectiveness, proportionality, and dissuasiveness), conduct norms had been subject to approximation under EU secondary law, thereby allowing for a ranking of the violations on grounds of their varying degree of severity.

[92] Council Conclusions on the approach to apply regarding approximation of penalties, doc. 9141/02, 27 May 2002, 3 ff.

[93] Council conclusions on guidelines for future criminal law in EU legislation, doc. 14162/09, 9 October 2009, 5.

[94] P Asp, 'Harmonisation of Penalties and Sentencing within the EU' (2013) 1 *Bergen Journal of Criminal Law and Criminal Justice*, 53–62.

[95] H Satzger, 'The Harmonisation of Criminal Sanctions in the European Union' (2019) 14 *Eucrim* 115–120. See also F. Zimmermann, 'Strafrechtliche Sanktionen und das Recht der Europäischen Union: eine Bestandsaufnahme' in H. Satzger (ed), *Harmonisation of Criminal Sanctions in the European Union* (Baden-Baden, Nomos, 2020) 577–614.

[96] A Von Hirsch, 'Proportionality in the Philosophy of Punishment: From 'Why Punish?' to 'How Much?'' (1990) 1 *Criminal Law Forum* 259–290.

side-constraint would seem to lean towards answering in the affirmative, one must grapple with the distinctive orientation of EU law in favour of negative general prevention. Building a sound theoretical interpretation of the Charter as a set of provisions that addresses *both* public bodies (at the national and EU level) *and* individuals, some remarks are in order. First, it seems erroneous to hold that proportionality of criminal penalties 'follow[s] both from Article 52(1) of the Charter and from the principle of proportionality of penalties in Article 49(3) of the Charter'.[97] Arguing for such a connection would obscure the uniqueness of proportionality as an individual guarantee and constraint to legislative and judicial penal excesses.

Second, though Article 52(1) speaks to a different form of goal-oriented and forward-looking proportionality (one that Article 49(3) is meant to offset), the right to avoid disproportionate penalties should maintain its distinctiveness and should not be conflated with the third step of the tripartite assessment. The latter is thought of as a balancing exercise between the burden imposed on the norm-recipient and public goals pursued by EU law. By contrast, the prohibition against disproportionate punishments is meant to protect individual rights no matter what. If we are not to water down the unique meaning of this essential provision, we have to disentangle it from any possible balancing test so as to interpret it as placing an upper limit to maximum penalties. This understanding of proportionality requires efforts (on the part of both the ECJ and domestic courts) to ground the prohibition laid down by the Charter on both cardinal and ordinal considerations.

Third, the individual right not to suffer an excessive punishment must be understood as involving an entirely retrospective assessment ('what was one punished for?'), placing a limit on the state's power to punish. To give this prohibition some bite, the ECJ could engage in a rather unprecedented exercise of cross-fertilisation and build on the lesson offered by its American counterparts.

For more than a century, the US Supreme Court (USSC) has developed a rather sophisticated – albeit at times contradictory – case-law regarding the Eighth Amendment's prohibition of 'cruel and unusual punishments'. In such a context, the USSC fleshed out the general principle pursuant to which 'punishments' that are grossly disproportionate in comparison with the seriousness of the offence are to be deemed unconstitutional.[98] Though such reasoning originally applied to death penalties[99] (and, more recently, to life sentence without parole[100]), the gist of this prohibition has also been extended to cover financial

[97] Joined Cases C-64/18, C-140/18, C-146/18 and C-148/18 *Maksimovic* ECLI:EU:C:2019:723, para 97. See for a similar take Case C-384/17 *Link Logistik N&N* ECLI:EU:C:2018:810, para 42.

[98] See for an evolutionary reading of the Eighth Amendment originalist meaning, thus laying the groundwork for contemporary case-law on 'grossly disproportionate punishment' *Weems v United States* 217 US 349 (1910).

[99] See, for instance, *Atkins v Virginia*, 536 US 304 (2002).

[100] See, among many, *Solem v Helm*, 463 US 277 (1983).

penalties, including fines and confiscation measures.[101] As the analysis of the ECJ's case-law suggests, nothing would prevent the Luxembourg Judges from taking a similar stance and finding some penalties (such as fixed or flat-rate fines or even custodial sanctions)[102] disproportionate and to do this regardless of whichever goals the legislator or the sentencing court are purportedly trying to attain (as no balancing exercise would be admitted). In the most recent case law of the ECJ, Article 49(3) of the Charter is recognised to have direct effect and is conducive to disapplication of national provisions contrary to such right[103]. After all, the doctrine of direct effect is traditionally regarded as the source of rights which individuals may invoke against the state within the sphere of application of EU law. The judges in Luxembourg, however, have been ambiguous as to whether the right at hand can be seen as an absolute limit to the state's *ius puniendi*. It is submitted that, instead of framing proportionality as a unified concept – bringing together utilitarian concerns and rights-protection under the aegis of articles 52 and 49 of the Charter – Article 49(3) must be read as a standalone prohibition against disproportionate penalties, one that leaves no room for weighing in opposing interests. This would mean interpreting the right to proportionate punishment as an absolute prohibition. The absolute character of such prohibition can be derived by the underlying connection between punishment and dignity (Article 1 of the Charter).

Though the Charter recognises an explicit prohibition of inhuman and degrading treatment or punishment (Articles 4 of the Charter), nothing prevents the Court to adopt a systemic interpretation of punishment-related provisions within the Charter itself. It makes little sense to rule out a combined interpretation of Articles 1, 4 and 49(3) of the Charter, thereby setting out a ban on (at least) grossly disproportionate penalties. It seems rather meaningful, instead, to construe such provisions as a systemic whole, arguing that individuals can obtain a direct application of their right not to suffer disproportionate penalties whenever a sufficient threshold is met. In light of the above, the individual right in question trumps any utilitarian concerns and cannot be the subject of a balancing exercise as the Court's case law on free movement rights routinely suggested.

[101] See for the 'excessive fine clause' as developed by the USSC on the basis of Eight Amendment, with regard to civil forfeiture: *Bajakajian v United States*, 524 US 321 (1998); *Timbs v Indiana*, 586 US 146 (2019) for an application of the *Bajakajian*'s doctrine to state criminal law.

[102] See Case C-655/21 *G. ST. T.* ECLI:EU:C:2023:791, para 81: while a national provision threatening a custodial sentence for a violation of EU trade mark rules 'is not necessarily disproportionate in certain instances of trade mark infringements, it must nevertheless be stated that a provision such as Article 172b(2) of the [Bulgarian] Criminal Code, which links an especially broad description of an offence to a custodial sentence of a minimum of five years, does not guarantee that the competent authorities are able to ensure in each individual case, in accordance with the obligation under Article 49(3) of the Charter [...] that the severity of the penalties imposed does not exceed the seriousness of the offence identified'.

[103] Case C-205/20, *Bezirkshauptmannschaft Hartberg-Fürstenfeld*, ECLI:EU:C:2022:168, para. 32.

V. Conclusion

This chapter has sought to illustrate why insights from penal theory suggest a partial rethinking of proportionality under Article 49(3) of the Charter is in order. The core of my argument is that we should reconsider what this principle/right is designed for. Building on arguments of 'negative retributivism' and 'penal parsimony', I concluded that this peculiar form of proportionality is meant to place the individual centre stage (proportionality *ex parte civium*), thereby antagonising the authority's 'right to punish'. A question for future research is whether, once we have managed to disentangle a fundamental right to proportionality from utilitarian concerns, we might further this humanitarian virtuous circle by grounding proportionality on a broader human-rights-oriented understanding of punishment under EU law. If one rules out 'grossly disproportionate' penalties as being contrary to the Charter, it will be possible to enhance this claim by positing that – at least in some instances – an axiological connection exists between Article 49 and Article 4 of the Charter, which prohibits any inhuman or degrading treatment or *punishment*.

5

The Proportionality and Harm Principles in the European Perspective

A Comparative and Complementary Reading

VITTORIO CAMA

I. Introduction

Although inherently elusive, the proportionality and harm principles are at the heart of the European criminal law debate.[1] The elusiveness of proportionality can be attributed to its multifaceted nature, which is evidenced by its various recognitions within EU primary and secondary law, supported by the jurisprudence of the European Court of Justice (ECJ), and comprehensively discussed in the academic

[1] The issue of normative justifications of European criminal law is the object of an increasingly advanced and lively debate. Inter alia, see, in alphabetical order, P Asp et al, 'The Manifesto on European Criminal Policy in 2011' (2011) 1 *European Criminal Law Review* 86; M Böse, 'The Principle of Proportionality and the Protection of Legal Interests (Verhältnismäßigkeit und Rechtsgüterschutz)' (2011) 1 *European Criminal Law Review* 35; SS Buisman, 'The Future of EU Substantive Criminal Law: Towards a Uniform Set of Criminalisation Principles at the EU Level' (2022) 30 *European Journal of Crime, Criminal Law and Criminal Justice* 161; P Caeiro, 'Constitution and Development of the European Union's Penal Jurisdiction: Responsibility, Self-Reference and Attribution' (2022) 27 *European Law Journal* 441; S Coutts, 'Supranational Public Wrongs: The Limitations and Possibilities of European Criminal Law and a European Community' (2017) 54 *Common Market Law Review* 771; E Herlin-Karnell, 'What Principles Drive (or Should Drive) European Criminal Law?' (2010) 11 *German Law Review* 1115; M Kaiafa-Gbandi, 'The Importance of Core Principles of Substantive Criminal Law for a European Criminal Policy Respecting Fundamental Rights and the Rule of Law' (2011) 1 *European Criminal Law Review* 7; M Kaiafa-Gbandi, 'Approximation of Substantive Criminal Law Provisions in the EU and Fundamental Principles of Criminal Law' in A Weyembergh, F Galli (eds), *Approximation of Substantive Criminal Law in the EU: The Way Forward* (Brussels, Edition de l'Université de Bruxelles, 2013); A Klip, *European Criminal Law: An Integrative Approach*, 3rd edn (Cambridge, Intersentia, 2016); V Mitsilegas, *EU Criminal Law*, 2nd edn (Oxford, Hart Publishing, 2021); J Öberg, *Limits to EU Powers: A Case Study of EU Regulatory Criminal Law* (Oxford, Hart Publishing, 2017); JW Ouwerkerk, 'Old Wine in a New Bottle: Shaping the foundations of EU Criminal Law through the Concept of Legal Interests (Rechtsgüter)' (2022) 27 *European Law Journal* 426; N Peršak, 'EU Criminal Law and Its Legitimation: In Search for a Substantive Principle of Criminalisation' (2018) 26 *European Journal of Crime, Criminal Law and Criminal Justice* 20; H Satzger, *International and European Criminal Law*, 2nd edn (Munich, CH Beck-Hart-Nomos, 2018); I Wieczorek, *The Legitimacy of EU Criminal Law* (Oxford, Hart Publishing, 2020).

theorisation on the subject. In contrast, the harm principle's puzzling nature is rooted in the absence of a universally accepted definition, both academically and positively throughout Europe, as evidenced by the differences between 'harm-oriented doctrines'.[2]

Despite possessing different theoretical bases, both the principle of proportionality and the harm principle share a common feature: their silence on the content of the objects they evaluate. In this sense, proportionality requires balancing means and ends, while the harm principle needs a specific target of harm, yet both lack clarity on the value-based criteria for selecting these elements. This ambiguity plays a crucial role in the scope and legitimacy of European criminal law, as the selection of reference objects not only affects national legislation, but also deeply influences the extent of authority over individual freedoms. These choices – which should reflect deeper values – require a meticulous balancing of rights that are recognised and protected at the European 'constitutional' level. Consequently, this issue ties into the wider debate on legally protectable interests in Europe, echoing the fundamental notions of the German *Rechtsgut* theory. The necessity for the incorporation of additional axiological parameters to assess the legitimacy of European criminal policy choices therefore paves the way for integrating these concepts, along with the inherently related principle of harm, into European criminal law.

In this perspective, this chapter aims to explore a comparative and complementary reading of the principles of proportionality and harm at the European level, focusing on their influence on the proportionality of criminal penalties. Although a detailed analysis of other EU principles, such as subsidiarity[3] and effectiveness,[4] or criminal law principles, such as *ultima ratio*,[5] is beyond the scope

[2] This definition is taken from W Hassemer, 'The Harm Principle and the Protection of "Legal Goods" (Rechtsgüterschutz): a German Perspective in Criminalisation Theory' in AP Simester, A du Bois-Pedain, U Neumann (eds), *Liberal Criminal Theory* (Oxford, Hart Publishing, 2014) 187 ff.

[3] P De Hert, I Wieczorek, 'Testing the Principle of Subsidiarity in EU Criminal Policy: The Omitted Exercise in the Recent EU Documents on Principles for Substantive European Criminal Law' (2012) 3 *New Journal of European Criminal Law* 394; E Herlin-Karnell, 'Subsidiarity in the Area of Justice and Home Affairs Law – A Lost Cause?', (2009) 15 *European Law Journal* 351; I Wieczorek, 'The Principle of Subsidiarity in EU Criminal Law' in C Brière, A Weyembergh (eds), *The Needed Balances in EU Criminal Law: Past, Present and Future* (Oxford, Hart Publishing, 2017).

[4] N Peršak, 'Principles of EU Criminalisation and their Varied Normative Strength: Harm and Effectiveness' (2022) 27 *European Law Journal* 463–476.

[5] Proportionality and *ultima ratio* are 'negative formal principles', as opposed to harm-oriented doctrines that provide positive material justifications to criminalise. In this respect, N Peršak, *Criminalising Harmful Conduct. The Harm Principle, its Limits and Continental Counterpart* (New York, Springer, 2007) 22 and Wieczorek (n 1) 66. On the *ultima ratio* principle in European Criminal Law J Bengoetxea, H Jung, K Nuotio, 'Ultima Ratio, a Principle at Risk: European Perspectives' (2013) 3 *Oñati Socio-legal Series* 1–5; S Melander, 'Ultima ratio in European Criminal Law' (2013) 3(1) *Oñati Socio-legal Series* 42–61; JW Ouwerkerk, 'Criminalisation as a Last Resort: A National Principle under the Pressure of Europeanisation?' (2012) 3 *New Journal of European Criminal Law* 228; On the principle and its relationship with proportionality, E Herlin-Karnell *The Constitutional Dimension of EU Criminal Law* (Oxford, Hart Publishing, 2012) 124–128 and R Wendt, 'The Principle of "Ultima Ratio" and/or the Principle of Proportionality' (2013) 3 *Oñati Socio-legal Series* 81; ME Florio, 'Struggle in Favour of a Criminal Law as an 'ultima ratio'' (2023) 2 *European Criminal Law Review* 135.

of this contribution, their interaction with the principles of proportionality and harm is nevertheless relevant as they form the broader context of the research and inform its key passages.

The chapter will begin with an overview of the principle of proportionality in European criminal law, highlighting its pivotal role and multifaceted nature. It will then explore the essential features of harm-oriented doctrines, comparing how these are articulated within continental European and common law systems. However, in light of the perceived crisis of these doctrines, it will also examine, albeit briefly, their critical aspects and potential alternative theories. Following this analysis, the chapter will establish the relevance of identifying a European dimension for the principle of *nullum crimen sine iniuria*, and will evaluate its potential foundations and identify the most significant obstacles to its recognition. With these foundations laid, the focus will shift to the core of the chapter: a complementary reading of the proportionality and harm principles in European criminal law through the lens of Article 52(1) of the Charter of Fundamental Rights of the European Union (hereinafter 'the Charter'). Finally, the chapter will conclude by assessing the implications of this interpretation also in the light of the 'implicit' direct effect entrusted to the principle of proportionality of penalties enshrined in Article 49(3) of the Charter.

II. The Polyhedral Principle of Proportionality as a Normative Foundation of EU Criminal Law

The principle of proportionality in EU law, notably elusive,[6] manifests in various aspects within the European 'constitutional' framework.

It can first be noted that Article 5(4) Treaty on European Union (TEU) highlights proportionality, alongside subsidiarity, as a guiding principle for the exercise of EU competences.[7] Furthermore, an examination of the Charter reveals that proportionality encompasses an additional dimension. In this respect, Article 52(1) states that 'any *limitation* on the exercise of the rights and freedoms recognised by this Charter must be provided for by law and *respect the essence* of those rights and freedoms. Subject to the principle of *proportionality*, limitations

On the *ultima ratio* principle in general, N Jareborg 'Criminalisation as a Last Resort (Ultima Ratio)' (2005) 2 *Ohio State Journal of Criminal Law* 53; D Husak, 'The Criminal Law as a Last Resort' (2004) 24 *Oxford Journal of Legal Studies* 207; P Mikkinen, '"If Taken in Earnest": Criminal Law Doctrine and the Last Resort' (2006) 45 *Howard Journal* 521.

[6] S Montaldo, 'EU Sanctioning Power and the Principle of Proportionality' in S Montaldo, F Costamagna, A Miglio (eds), *EU Law Enforcement: The Evolution of Sanctioning Powers* (London, Routledge, 2022) 114.

[7] P Asp, *The Substantive Criminal Law Competence of the EU* (Stockholm, Stiftelsen Skrifter utgivna av Juridiska fakulteten vid Stockholms universitet, 2012) 188 ff; See also Herlin-Karnell (n 5) 127 ff; T Tridimas, *The General Principles of EU Law*, 2nd edn (Oxford, OUP, 2006) 139 and more generally chs 3–5.

may be made only if they are *necessary* and *genuinely* meet *objectives of general interest recognised by the Union* or the *need* to *protect* the *rights and freedoms of others*' (emphasis added). Thus, a 'human-rights based' perspective on proportionality, focusing on individual rights protection,[8] has been incorporated into the European constitutional framework.[9]

Altogether, the notions of proportionality arising from the synergy between Article 5(4) and Article 52(1) of the Charter evoke a prospective dimension.[10] In this sense, Article 5(4) TEU requires a balance between the aim pursued by a particular policy and the means used to achieve it. To verify compliance with the principle, the ECJ adopts a tripartite test based on the elements of suitability, necessity, and proportionality *stricto sensu*.[11] Structured in this way, the assessment of proportionality is ultimately based on relative considerations[12] and constitutes, in terms of criminal law, a principle that concerns the exercise of powers, rather than the legitimacy of the decision to exercise those powers. Indeed, the principle does not provide guidance on the values that should inform the selection of a certain purpose.[13] Thus, reasoning by extremes, if the objective was the purest form of authoritarian terrorism or symbolic repression,[14] then very severe penalties (or even the death penalty) might be considered proportionate.[15]

Against this background, the human-rights-based proportionality can be useful in 'giving voice' to the more general principle of proportionality. In this respect, Article 52(1) of the Charter identifies 'objectives of general interest' or 'the need to protect the rights and freedoms of others' as the only legitimate aims that any measure (not only criminal) imposing a limitation on individual rights and freedoms can pursue.

At this stage, it is appropriate to place Article 52(1) of the Charter in the context of criminal law. As sharply highlighted,[16] the criminalisation of conduct constitutes *per se* a limitation of rights and freedoms. Firstly, the more general

[8] For an analysis of the intersection of the EU principle of proportionality of penalties with the European Convention on Human Rights (ECHR) system, see the contribution of L Grossio to this book.

[9] V Mitsilegas, *EU Criminal Law after Lisbon* (Oxford, Hart Publishing, 2016) 133–134. More generally on the interaction between human rights and criminal law, M Delmas-Marty, *Le flou du droit* (Paris, Presses Universitaires de France, 1986), 171 ff. On human rights in criminal law as 'sword' and 'shield', Y Cartuyvels et al (eds), *Les droits de l'homme, bouclier ou épée du droit pénal?* (Bruxelles, FUSL, 2007).

[10] Mitsilegas (n 9).

[11] Asp (n 7) 188–189.

[12] Wieczorek describes prospective proportionality as a 'neutral' principle. Wieczorek (n 1) 65 ff.

[13] This explains why the Manifesto on European Criminal Policy, proposed as a prerequisite the identification of a legitimate purpose. On this subject, Ouwerkerk (n 1) 429.

[14] cf T Elholm, R Colson, 'The Symbolic Purpose of EU Criminal Law' in R Colson, S Field (eds), *EU Criminal Justice and the Challenges of Diversity: Legal Cultures in the Area of Freedom, Security and Justice* (Cambridge, Cambridge University Press 2016).

[15] cf V Masarone, 'Il "diritto penale europeo" al vaglio dell'offensività: fondamento ed esiti' (2019) 1 *Archivio penale* 10 ff. The article is fundamental also in addressing various issues connected to the legitimacy of European criminal policies.

[16] Wieczorek (n 1) 65 ff.

autonomy of the individual – and therefore, the freedom to act and self-determine – is restricted.[17] This first limitation is connected to further restrictions related to the specific type of criminalised conduct (i.e. the criminalisation of hate speech limits the general freedom of expression, associative crimes limit freedom of association, etc.). Such restrictions become effective when a conviction (or even a precautionary measure) is actually enforced. The individual thus sees their personal freedom, freedom of movement, full disposal of their property, etc, restricted.

Criminalisation can also lead to less obvious restrictions of rights. For instance, the criminal labelling or stigma that the individual who (allegedly) engages in criminalised conduct suffers, even before conviction, has an impact on rights such as psychological and physical integrity, reputation and privacy and carries social and economic consequences (before, after and independently from actual conviction):[18] the criminal process itself becomes a 'pre-conviction sanction'.[19] Furthermore, a hidden outcome is the potential chilling effect that criminalisation can have on the expressions of individual rights.[20] For instance, the criminalisation of humanitarian assistance, insofar as it discourages assistance to migrants, entails a restriction of rights such as life, physical integrity, respect for private and family life, asylum, etc.[21]

A second dimension of the principle of proportionality that stems from the Charter is, instead, more properly related to the field of criminal law. In particular, Article 49(3) of the Charter, which enshrines the principle of proportionality of penalties, presents a predominantly retrospective dimension in the implementation of criminal sanctions.[22] However, the principle stipulated in Article 49(3) is silent as well. This provision merely requires that the 'severity of penalties' must not be disproportionate to the 'criminal offence' without clarifying the meaning of these elements. The jurisprudence of the ECJ does not provide much clarity on the issue, relying instead on the notion of the 'seriousness' of the infringement or

[17] cf, inter alia, T Hörnle, *Grob anstößiges Verhalten. Strafrechtlicher Schutz von Moral, Gefühlen und Tabus* (Frankfurt a. M., Klostermann, 2005) 18 ff and 65–71.

[18] K Hadjimatheou, 'Criminal Labelling, Publicity, and Punishment' (2016) 35 *Law and Philosophy* 567 and E Rasmusen, 'Stigma and Self-Fulfilling Expectations of Criminality' (1996) 39 *The Journal of Law & Economics* 519.

[19] cf V Manes, *Il principio di offensività nel diritto penale* (Torino, Giappichelli, 2005) 140 ff. On trials by media, cf S Moccia, *La perenne emergenza* (Napoli, ESI, 1997) 161 ff.

[20] cf T Baumbach, 'Chilling Effect as a European Court of Human Rights' Concept in Media Law Cases' (2018) 6 *Bergen Journal of Criminal Law & Criminal Justice* 92.

[21] S Zirulia, 'Non c'è smuggling senza ingiusto profitto' (2020) 3 *Diritto penale contemporaneo* 167 ff. More generally on the chilling effect and on the principle of prospective proportionality in the Italian legal system, N Recchia, *Il principio di proporzionalità nel diritto penale* (Torino, Giappichelli, 2020) 251 ff.

[22] For an analysis on retrospective proportionality, see the contribution of J Öberg to this book. For the difference between 'proportionality to the purpose of punishment' and 'proportionality to the offence committed', see F Viganò, *La proporzionalità della pena. Profili di diritto penale e costituzionale* (Torino, Giappichelli, 2021) 116 ff.

of the offence, without explaining the factors to be considered when assessing this parameter.[23]

III. *Nullum Crimen Sine Iniuria*: Harm-Oriented Doctrines in a Comparative Context

Similar to proportionality, the harm principle is polyhedral. However, its complexity arises not as much from multiple positive references in European legislation, as it does with proportionality, but rather from the variety of interpretations across different legal traditions. A shared notion underpins these variations: legislators may – or must, according to the *ultima ratio* principle – criminalise only behaviours that cause significant harm to specific interests. This concept finds resonance in the common law harm principle, the German *Rechtsgüterschutz*, and the principles of *offensività*, *ofensividad*, and *ofensividade* in the Italian, Spanish, Portuguese, and Latin-American legal systems.[24]

In the common law tradition, the harm principle, as originated by John Stuart Mill and elucidated by Joel Feinberg, functions as a preliminary filter. It restricts criminalisation to behaviours that are both wrongfully and seriously harmful to others. The principle is further defined by, among others, Simester and von Hirsch who identify crime as a violation of a person's normative claim over their resources.[25]

When discussing harm-oriented theories from a 'continental' perspective, the *Rechtsgüterschutz* theory often takes centre stage. This theory posits that criminalisation is justified primarily to protect 'legal goods' (*Rechtsgüter*). While this premise is broadly accepted, divergences arise over defining the concept of legal good. Roxin and Greco, for instance, advocate an individualistic or personalistic approach,[26] identifying legal goods as 'conditions or purposes necessary for the

[23] Masarone (n 15); cf V Mitsilegas, E Billis, 'Article 49 – Principles of Legality and Proportionality of Criminal Offences and Penalties' in S Peers et al (eds), *The EU Charter of Fundamental Rights – A Commentary*, 2nd edn (Oxford, Hart Publishing, 2021) 1489.

[24] For references on these principles, L Micheletto, 'Towards an Integrated (and Possibly Pan-European?) *Prima Facie* Legitimacy Test: Merging the *Rechtsgut* Theory, the *Offensività* Principle, and the Harm Principle' (2021) 29 *European Journal of Crime, Criminal Law and Criminal Justice* 241–263.

[25] For an overview of the content and functions of the harm principle, Peršak (n 5) 35–94. Ch V also draws a comparison between the harm principle and the *Rechtsgüterlehre*. For further comparison, A Eser, 'The Principle of "Harm" in the Concept of Crime: A Comparative Analysis of the Criminally Protected Legal Interests' (1965) 4 *Duquesne Law Review* 345.

[26] For a personal conception of the legal good, W Hassemer, 'Grundlinien einer personalen Rechtsgutslehre' in L Philipps and H Scholler (eds), *Jenseits des Funktionalismus. Arthur Kaufmann zum 65. Geburtstag* (Heidelberg, Decker & Müller, 1989) 90–91; See also F Palazzo, 'I confini della tutela penale: selezione dei beni e criteri di criminalizzazione' (1992) *Rivista italiana di diritto e procedura penale* 453; S Moccia, Il diritto penale tra essere e valore (Napoli, ESI, 1992) 175; G Fornasari,

free development of the individual, the realisation of their fundamental rights and the functioning of a human-rights-based state system'.[27]

It is generally recognised that the *Rechtsgut* concept serves two primary functions. The first, often termed as methodological, positivistic, descriptive, formal, intra-systemic or heuristic suggests that legal goods derive from and are defined by the norms of positive law, embodying the underlying *ratio* of criminalisation.[28] This function, however, lacks in justifying and legitimising decisions on criminalisation and is mainly useful for the classification or interpretation of offences. The second function, referred to as critical, normative, material and system-transcendent, positions legal goods as pre-existing and independent entities, that serve as constraints and as benchmarks for the legitimacy of criminal law choices.[29]

The principles of *offensività*, *ofensividad*, and *ofensividade* in civil law countries, influenced by the Italian academic discourse, primarily originate from a critical perspective of the *Rechtsgut*.[30] From a constitutional law viewpoint,[31] *offensività* is underpinned by the Italian Constitution's emphasis on personal liberty (Article 13), suggesting that the most severe restriction of individual freedom, i.e. the criminal sanction, is justifiable only in cases of harm (or danger of harm) to a 'constitutionally relevant' legal good that is at least equal in value compared to the personal interests sacrificed.[32] Importantly, this principle is not merely a theoretical guide for lawmakers but also a binding norm for judges,

Il concetto di economia pubblica nel diritto penale. Spunti esegetici e prospettive di riforma (Milano, Giuffré, 1994) 131 ff; A Cavaliere, 'Riflessioni sul ruolo dell'offensività nella teoria del reato costituzionalmente orientata' in G Giostra and G Insolera (eds) *Costituzione, diritto e processo penale* (Milano, Giuffré, 1998) 152; cf O Lagodny, *Strafrecht vor den Schranken der Prinzipien* (Tübingen, Mohr, 1996); O Lagodny, 'Basic Rights and Substantive criminal Law: The Incest Case' (2011) 61 *The University of Toronto Law Journal* 761.

[27] C Roxin, L Greco, *Strafrecht Allgemeiner Teil Bd. 1: Grundlagen. Der Aufbau der Verbrechenslehre*, 5th edn (München, CH Beck, 2020) 26.

[28] T Hörnle, 'Theories of Criminalization' in T Hörnle and M Dubber (eds), *The Oxford Handbook of Criminal Law* (Oxford, Oxford University Press, 2014) 686 ff. For a never-dated analysis, F Angioni, *Contenuto e funzioni del concetto di bene giuridico* (Milano, Giuffré, 1983).

[29] C Roxin, 'The Legislation Critical Concept of Goods-in-law under Scrutiny' (2013) 1 *European Criminal Law Review* 1 ff.

[30] G Fornasari, 'Offensività e postmodernità: un binomio inconciliabile?' (2018) 3 *Rivista Italiana di diritto e procedura penale* 1514–1539.

[31] On the incorporations of criminal-law principles in Constitutional Law, also in common law traditions, A du Bois-Pedain, 'The Place of Criminal Law Theory in the Constitutional State' in Simester, du Bois-Pedain, Neumann (n 2) 305 ff.

[32] F Bricola, 'Teoria Generale del Reato' (1973) *XIX Novissimo Digesto Italiano*, 15 ff. For a constitutional approach to the *Rechtsgut* and *offensività*, W Sax, 'Grundsätze der Strafrechtsplege' in KA Bettermann, HC Nipperday, U Scheuner (eds), *Die Grundrechte*, Bd 3, 2 Halbband (Berlin, Duncker & Humboldt, 1959) 909; HJ Rudolphi, 'Die verschiedenen Aspekte des Rechtsgutsbegriffs' in *Festschrift für Richard M. Honig* (Göttingen, Schwartz, 1970) 158 ff; C Roxin, *Strafrechtliche Grundlagenprobleme* (Berlin, De Gruyter, 1973) 1 ff; cf A Engländer, 'Revitalisierung der materiellen Rechtsgutslehre durch das Verfassungsrecht?' (2015) 127 *Zeitschrift für die gesamte Strafrechtswissenschaft* 620–621.

prohibiting convictions unless there is actual harm or a concrete danger to legal goods.[33]

Despite these variances, it is crucial to underscore the existence of a general principle – and eventually a common constitutional tradition as per Article 6(3) TEU –[34] epitomised by the formula *nullum crimen sine iniuria* which asserts that, given that criminalisation limits individual freedom and rights, only actions that cause harm, even indirectly, to valuable legal interests should be criminalised.

IV. Crisis of Harm-Oriented Doctrines and their Alternatives

A common thread among the three briefly outlined theories is a widespread belief in their limited effectiveness as binding parameters for legislative choices. In this perspective, a prevailing sense of a crisis has emerged: legislators, regardless of country or tradition, continue to criminalise harmless conducts, and supreme and constitutional courts, tasked with enforcement, make little use of these theories or explicitly deny their applicability.[35]

Given these premises, there is a quest for alternative theories.[36] Among these, a predominant role is awarded to the revival of Feuerbach's *Rechtsverletzung* theory.[37] The foundational idea behind this theory – criticisms of which catalysed the birth of the *Rechtsgüterlehre* –[38] is that crime should be understood as a 'violation of a right'. Despite this shared core, the conceptualisations of the theory diverge significantly in their trajectories.

For instance, Hörnle adopts an approach that is constitutionally oriented. Accordingly, criminal norms, which limit general freedom, can only be justified

[33] L Pasculli, 'Harm, Offence and *Offesa* in the English and the Italian Criminal Law. For a Constitutionalisation of a Unitary Principle of Harm in the English Legal System, also as Criterion of Judicial Interpretation' (2016) 2 *Diritto penale XXI Secolo* 349.

[34] On the issue, S Moccia, 'Funzione della pena ed implicazioni sistematiche: tra fonti europee e Costituzione italiana' (2012) 8 *Diritto e procedura penale* 929 and Masarone (n 15) 13 ff.

[35] For an account of these criticisms in the Italian debate, see Fornasari (n 30) 1518 ff; for the *Rechtsgüterlehre*, see C-F Stuckenberg, 'The Constitutional Deficiencies of the German Rechtsgutslehre' (2013) 3 *Oñati Socio-legal Series* 31; for the harm principle, see Pasculli (n 33); MC De Maglie, 'Il declino dell'harm principle' in A Cavaliere et al (eds), *Politica criminale e cultura giuspenalistica. Scritti in onore di Sergio Moccia* (Napoli, ESI, 2017); BE Harcourt, 'The Collapse of the Harm Principle' (1999) 90(1) *Journal of Criminal Law and Criminology* 109.

For a discussion of why court decisions should not be relied upon to derive a criminal principle, see Hörnle (n 28) 680–684.

[36] For instance, as concerns the harm principle, RA Duff, 'Towards a Modest Legal Moralism' (2012) 8(1) *Criminal Law and Philosophy* 217 and A Ripstein, 'Beyond the Harm Principle' (2006) 34 *Philosophy & Public Affairs* 215. On the *Rechtsgüterschutz*, S Swoboda, 'Die Lehre vom Rechtsgut und ihre Alternativen' (2010) 122 *Zeitschrift für die gesamte Strafrechtswissenschaft* 24.

[37] L Greco, *Lebendiges Und Totes in Feuerbachs Straftheorie* (Berlin, Duncker & Humboldt, 2009).

[38] Inter alia, P Sina, *Die Dogmengeschichte des Strafrechtlichen Begriffs 'Rechtsgut'* (Basel, Verlag Helbing und Lichtenhahn, 1962).

if they are deemed necessary to protect others' fundamental rights as defined by Article 2(1) of the *Grundgesetz*. These rights are not limited to those recognised by positive law but also include human interests worthy of protection based on values that transcend positive law.[39] Thus, a crime fundamentally constitutes a violation of the subjective 'rights of others'.[40] Conversely, Haas and Renzikowski focus on the tripartite legal relationship between a legal object or interest, its holder, and the obligated subject.[41] The latter's unlawful conduct violates not so much an 'objective' legal good as the legal power of another individual over that good.[42] Furthermore, according to PA Hirsch, a crime should be understood as a violation of rights, which, in the case of infringement of individual rights, occurs normatively on two levels: a violation of an interpersonal duty of conduct, which constitutes a subjective violation of rights, and a violation of a norm of conduct, which is seen as an objective violation of law.[43] While these theories are argumentatively valid and share liberal objectives, they also face challenges arising from the 'manipulability' of the concept of human rights.[44] Notwithstanding, their focus on the relational aspect of crime, highlighting the interplay between the legal status of the victim and the perpetrator – and eventually the horizontal dimension of human rights (*Drittwirkung*) – may positively reflect proportionality's balancing exercise.[45]

It is also important to emphasise that the boundaries between 'alternative' and 'mainstream' theories often blur, with mutual incorporations between the harm principle, the 'rights of others'[46] and the *Rechtsgut* theories,[47] and suggestions to align the *Rechtsgüterlehre* with fundamental human rights, endorsing

[39] Inter alia, Hörnle (n 17) 18 ff.

[40] T Hörnle, '"Rights of Others" in Criminalisation Theories' in Simester, du Bois-Pedain, Neumann (n 2) 169–186.

[41] For instance, V Haas, *Kausalität und Rechtsverletzung* (Berlin, Duncker & Humboldt, 2002) 81 ff and J Renzikowski, 'Pflichten und Rechte. Rechtsverhältnis und Zurechnung' (2007) 154 *Goltdammer's Archiv für Strafrecht* 561 ff.

[42] For an analysis and critique, see Roxin, Greco (n 27) 102 ff.

[43] PA Hirsch, *Das Verbrechen als Rechtsverletzung Subjektive Rechte im Strafrecht* (Berlin, Duncker & Humboldt, 2021), 48 ff and 70 ff.

[44] A Cavaliere, '"Diritti" anziché "beni" e "principi" in diritto penale?' (2023) 10 *Sistema penale* 63, 67 ff. Thus, for example, it is noted that the affirmation of a right to security served to justify the use of a criminal law 'of the enemy'; cf K Amelung, 'Der Begriff des Rechtsguts in der Lehre vom strafrechtlichen Rechtsgüterschutz' in R Hefendehl, A von Hirsch and W Wohlers (eds), *Die Rechtsgutstheorie. Legitimationsbasis des Strafrechts oder dogmatisches Glasperlenspiel?* (Baden-Baden, Nomos, 2003) 172–173; cf F Viganò, 'Diritto penale e diritti della persona' in G Mannozzi et al (eds), *Studi in onore di Carlo Enrico Paliero* (Milano, Giuffrè, 2022) 845–875.

[45] On balancing human rights, S Besson, 'Human Rights in Relation: A Critical Reading of the ECtHR's Approach to Conflicts of Rights' in S Smet, E Brems (eds), *When Human Rights Clash at the European Court of Human Rights: Conflict or Harmony?* (Oxford, Oxford University Press, 2017).

[46] cf von Hirsch (n 43) 71 ff.

[47] cf K Ambos, 'The Overall Function of International Criminal Law: Striking the Right Balance Between the Rechtsgut and the Harm Principles' (2015) 9 *Criminal Law and Philosophy* 301.

minimum criminal law[48] and the instrumental role of collective goods for individual rights.[49]

V. The Harm Principle in European Criminal Law: Limited Normative References and Complementary Perspectives

The harm principle, unlike proportionality, lacks strong normative status in European criminal law, exists mainly in soft-law documents that recommend it for EU criminal policy without binding force on European co-legislators. Summarising the reflections of Peršak,[50] it can be said that EU policy documents on criminal law reflect varied considerations of harm. The Council's 2009 Conclusions highlight a form of the harm principle, that emphasise that criminal provisions should target conducts that cause actual harm or serious threats to protected rights, and avoid anticipated and premature criminalisation.[51] The European Commission's 2011 Communication focuses on the seriousness and character of legal breaches without explicitly mentioning harm but implying it through the gravity of the crime.[52] Similarly, the European Parliament in 2012 references harm as 'damage', stressing that criminal law should address conduct causing significant 'damage' to society or individuals.[53]

On the contrary, in the academic debate there have been various approaches leading to a complementary reading of the principles of harm and proportionality. A first attempt in this regard was made by the Manifesto on European Criminal Policy, in which the requirement of a legitimate purpose, further refined consonantly with harm-oriented doctrines, was derived from the principle of proportionality.[54] Similarly, in a 'filtering' construction, Peršak proposes an effective integration between the common law conception of harm and proportionality,

[48] For principles of minimum criminal law in the Italian debate, see A Baratta, 'Principi del diritto penale minimo. Per una teoria dei diritti umani come oggetti e limiti della legge penale' (1985) 3 *Dei delitti e delle pene* 443 ff; and all the more essential considering that it applies the concept of minimum criminal law to European criminal policy, A Baratta 'Il Corpus Juris e la cultura giuridico-penale europea' in S Moccia (ed), *Ambito e prospettive di uno spazio giuridico-penale europeo* (Napoli, ESI, 2004); cf L Ferrajoli, *Diritto e ragione. Teoria del garantismo penale* (Roma-Bari, Laterza, 1989). Outside of the Italian context, A Ashworth, J Horder, *Principles of Criminal Law*, 7th edn (Oxford, Oxford University Press, 2013).

[49] Above n 26.

[50] Peršak (n 1) 29–31.

[51] Council of the European Union, 'Conclusions on model provisions, guiding the Council's criminal law deliberations', Brussels, 30 November 2009.

[52] European Commission, 'Towards an EU Criminal Policy: Ensuring the effective implementation of EU policies through criminal law', 20.9.2011, COM(2011) 573 final.

[53] European Parliament, 'Resolution of 22 May 2012 on an EU approach to criminal law', 2010/2310(INI).

[54] Asp et al (n 1) 87 ff.

assigning logical priority to the former.[55] On similar theoretical premises, an interesting test has been proposed to integrate the harm principle, *offensività*, and *Rechtsgüterschutz*.[56] Furthermore, Buisman suggests placing the harm principle and the concept of *Rechtsgut* as thresholds for the legitimisation of criminalisation, and prospective proportionality as a moderating principle for the justification of criminalisation.[57] Finally, it has been argued that the principle of *offensività* is already part of the proportionality test[58] and properly pertains to the suitability of the means to the end.[59]

Notwithstanding, the significance of critiques that argue that European criminal law fails to meet the standards of *nullum crimen sine iniuria*, primarily due to the lack of a defined catalogue of legal goods protectable at the European level, cannot be overlooked.[60] The question thus intersects with theoretical attempts to identify the foundations around which a theory of European legal goods could revolve.[61]

The 'debate' seems to be settling on the existence of two different categories of 'European' legal goods. Firstly, there are inherently European legal goods, i.e., they are intrinsically linked to the institutional structure of the European Union and are only meaningful in the context of that structure.[62] Accordingly, these legal goods are mostly supranational and collective in nature. Secondly, there are legal goods that are non-inherently European, which are interests that are nationally recognised for criminal protection and fundamental values, such as the right to life. According to Coutts, these would be interests 'shared' by the EU and all Member States[63] or, following Öberg, 'transnational interests'.[64] In particular, for

[55] Peršak (n 1) 29–31 and Peršak (n 4) 463–476. However, it bears noting that the possibility to derive the principle from grounds of exercise of competences such as Art. 83(1) TFEU appears to be founded on a methodological perspective.

[56] Micheletto (n 24) 241–263.

[57] Buisman (n 1) 164–175.

[58] cf G Stea, 'L'offensività europea come criterio di proporzione dell'opzione penale' (2013) 3 *Archivio penale* 1. See also A De Lia, '"Ossi di Seppia"? Appunti sul principio di offensività' (2019) 2 *Archvio penale* 31. The author posits that the harm principle is understood in a 'weak', rather than 'strong', sense at the European Level. On this topic, see also A Bonomi, 'Il principio di offensività del reato nella giurisprudenza costituzionale' (2021) 1 *Diritto pubblico* 197.

[59] A Molinarolli, 'Una possibile dimensione europea del principio di offensività' (2016) 2 *Diritto penale contemporaneo* 19.

[60] Masarone (n 15); cf M Donini, 'Il principio di offensività. Dalla penalistica italiana ai programmi europei' (2013) 4 *Diritto penale contemporaneo* 4.

[61] According to Ouwerkerk, the *Rechtsgüterlehre* is more suitable for European criminal law than the harm principle. Ouwerkerk (n 1) 433-436; cf CPM Cleiren, JM ten Voorde, 'Harmonising Legal Interests: Legal Interests under Criminal Law in a Multilevel Legal Order' in JW Ouwerkerk et al (eds), *The Future of EU Criminal Justice Policy and Practice: Legal and Criminological Perspectives* (Leiden, Brill/Nijhoff, 2019) 121–142.

[62] Caeiro draws a distinction between 'institutional' and 'functional' legal interests, Caeiro (n 1) 452 ff; cf G Grasso, *Comunità Europee e diritto penale* (Milano, Giuffré, 1989) 12.

[63] Coutts (n 1) 771–804.

[64] J Öberg, 'Normative justifications of EU criminal law: European public goods and transnational interests' (2023) 27 *European Law Journal* 408.

the second category, European protection is primarily based on the simultaneous occurrence of harmful conducts in several Member States and on the inadequacy of decentralised decision-making by States due to various types of cross-border challenges. However, it should be noted that the latter category poses significant challenges in justifying the 'attraction' – and therefore the extension – of the competence to protect these goods at the European level and hence the risk of over-criminalisation.[65]

VI. For a Complementary Reading between Harm and Proportionality in European Criminal Law

A complementary reading of the *nullum crimen sine iniuria* and proportionality principles requires applying successive filters and – to become legislatively binding and judicially enforceable – verifying whether or not each filter enjoys a constitutional anchorage in EU law.

As discussed, both harm and proportionality are silent principles, incapable of serving *per se* as guiding forces.[66] Using a metaphorical image, navigating European criminal policies based on both principles is like sailing a boat without wind. In this perspective, the proportionality relationship between means and ends alone is insufficient to ensure a rights-respecting criminal law, considering that the ends could be as nefarious as pure repressive terrorism. Similarly, establishing that only conduct which harms 'something' can be criminalised dangerously implies that the target of harm could be identified in society as a whole or even in concepts like individual morality, public morals, and the infamous 'healthy sentiment of the people'.[67] This approach would therefore deprive the principles of their critical function and would risk justifying repressive, authoritarian, and symbolic usage of criminal law.

To transform these principles into clear guiding lines, it is necessary to 'inflate their sails' with a value-based and axiological approach. This role can be well played by the notion of 'legal interest', as mediated by the *Rechtsgüterlehre*, acting as a *trait d'union* between various theories of *nullum crimen sine iniuria*. Clearly, for the theoretical construction to effectively guide the choices of the European legislator, the 'object' of protection must perform a critical function and not just a 'methodological' one which still remains useful to offer interpretative and classificatory

[65] Ouwerkerk (n 1) 436 ff.

[66] However, being quintessentially linked to a critical function of the legal good, the Italian *offensività* cannot be considered 'silent'. In this sense, it can be argued that the Italian legal system incorporates a 'strong' dimension of the principle of harm, unlike other legal systems and, allegedly, European criminal law. In this respect, see De Lia (n 58).

[67] K Loewenstein, 'Law in the Third Reich' (1936) 45 *The Yale Law Journal* 779. On the issue see Masarone (n 15) 10.

guidance.[68] The subsequent challenge then becomes how to select legal goods to be protected at the European level, given that even the 'omnivorous' concept of legal goods can be prone to manipulation.

As previously discussed, Article 52(1) of the Charter provides a formidable lock-pick through which such axiological parameters of the legitimacy of criminalisation choices can be introduced into European criminal law.

A. Identifying the First Term of Reference: Freedoms and Rights as 'Sacrificed' Interests

The initial element that must be met in order for Article 52(1) of the Charter to be applied to criminal law policies is the provision of a limitation of a fundamental right or freedom. In this regard, as previously and in greater detail noted, it is crucial to emphasise that criminalisation *per se* constitutes a limitation of fundamental rights and freedoms protected at the EU 'constitutional' level.

The identification of the fundamental freedoms and rights that may be 'sacrificed' through criminalisation should not be limited to the Charter but should also extend to all primary EU law. In this perspective, Article 2 TEU is of paramount importance in establishing that the 'Union is founded on the values of respect for human dignity, freedom, democracy, equality, the rule of law and respect for human rights, including the rights of persons belonging to minorities.'[69] The reference to freedom substantiates that limitations of liberty implied by criminalisation must respond to an enhanced justification insofar as they affect the free development of an individual's personality and self-determination.[70] Therefore, under Article 2 TEU, freedom is afforded an elevated status, similar to that of individual liberty in Article 13 of the Italian Constitution, as elucitated by Bricola's theory,[71] and to that of free development of personality in Article 2(1) *Grundgesetz*, as per Hörnle's 'rights of others' theory.[72]

Moreover, the concept of human dignity is inextricably connected with this perspective.[73] Accordingly, the criminalisation of conducts that do not meet the canons of harm and proportionality in the offered reading, implies, as axiologically

[68] According to Manes, the eclipse of a 'rigid' paradigm of *offensività* linked to the critical theory of the legal good, would entail a 'transliteration' of the principle of harm into the principle of proportionality. The fundamental question thus shifts from 'whether' (*an*) to 'how' (*quomodo*) to criminalise. Manes (n 19) 136–138, 150–158.

[69] cf Wieczorek (n 1) 40 ff.

[70] cf Hörnle (n 17) 18 ff.

[71] See Bricola (n 32) 15–16.

[72] cf Hörnle (n 40) 180 ff.

[73] On the notion of human dignity generally and as a possible legal interest, see T Hörnle, 'Criminalising Behaviour to Protect Human Dignity' (2012) 6 *Criminal Law and Philosophy* 307 and T Hörnle and M Kremnitzer, 'Human Dignity as a Protected Interest in Criminal Law' (2009) 44 *Israel Law Review* 145.

empty and manipulable, an instrumentalisation of the individual by virtue of whatever *ratio* the legislator decides to follow and, therefore, a violation of human dignity. Similar parallels could be proposed with reference to 'democracy' and 'equality' and, above all, to 'rule of law' in its 'material' dimension.[74]

Furthermore, since criminalisation restricts not just the general freedom of the individual, but also rights linked to the expression of that freedom, the broader requirement of 'respect for human rights' enshrined in Article 2 TEU and expanded by Articles 6(1) and (3) TEU to encompass the rights and freedoms guaranteed by the ECHR – as mediated by Article 52(3) of the Charter – and common constitutional traditions, is crucial.

In conclusion, it can be observed that the fundamental rights and freedoms that are 'sacrificed' by the criminalisation of certain behaviours enjoy a particularly enhanced status in European 'constitutional' law, being recognised and protected in both the Charter and the Treaties.

B. Identifying the Second Term of Reference: Selecting Legitimate Legal Goods as Protected Interests

Once the first term of comparison has been identified, it is necessary to identify the second object of balancing under Article 52(1) of the Charter. In this respect, criminalisation, as limitation of liberty and rights, is legitimate only if it responds to the 'need to protect the rights and freedoms of others' or 'objectives of general interest'.

While 'rights and freedoms of others' echoes both the notion of individual legal goods and that of 'rights of others' and thus appears consonant with harm-oriented doctrines, more challenging questions arise on the notion of 'objectives of general interest'. Speaking of 'objectives', the norm seems to recall a methodological understanding of the legal good, where this concept is viewed as the mere purpose or *ratio*, and, therefore, 'objective' of criminalisation choices. In this perspective, it should be noted that, according to the currently prevailing interpretation, the notion of 'objectives of general interest' is considered particularly broad, to the extent of including objectives arising from secondary sources. Consequently, this broad interpretation also limits the 'prescriptive' scope of Article 52(1) of the Charter.[75]

Nevertheless, there are good reasons – not least because of the principle of *ultima ratio* – for the most pervasive limitation of fundamental rights, such as criminalisation, to be guided by a reinforced and an enhanced legitimacy.

[74] cf M Kettunen, *Legitimizing European Criminal Law. Jusitifications and Restrictions* (Cham, Springer, 2020) 75–110 and ch IV.

[75] See S Peers, S Prechal, 'Art 52 – Scope and Interpretation of Rights and Principles' in Peers et al (n 23) 1624 ff.

In this sense, the proportionality test under Article 52(1) should require that the second term of reference of the test, i.e. 'rights and freedoms of others' and 'objectives of general interest', enjoys at least equal status in 'constitutional' or primary sources of law, as the fundamental rights and freedoms restricted and 'sacrificed' by criminalisation. In this respect, two further arguments can be advanced.

Firstly, legitimate objectives must be of '*general* interest' (emphasis added). This expression seems to refer not just to simply 'public' interests – as such, properly 'belonging' to the State – but to 'general' interests as shared by the EU community of citizens or, in other words, collective legal goods, interests, or rights that are merely 'recognised [and not just established by Act] by the Union'.[76] This requirement appears to guide the selection of protectable interests towards a constitutional or primary legal basis. Indeed, believing that such recognition could stem from secondary law or other legal sources would mean methodologically inverting the logical relationship between sources of law (*Inversionsmethode*), because it would allow a subordinate act, such as a Regulation, a Directive, or a soft-law document, to influence the content of a provision with a broadly constitutional scope, such as Article 52(1).

Secondly, it is important to note that Article 52(1) of the Charter requires any limitation to respect the 'essence of the limited freedoms and rights'. Thus, instead of strictly adhering to a single theory when selecting protectable interests, a new filter bridging *Rechtsgüterschutz* and *Rechtsverletzung* theories can be suggested. This may involve selecting legal goods that directly or, if collective, instrumentally promote subjective rights. For instance, this filter implies constructing the internal market as instrumental for European citizens' economic freedoms.[77] In this sense, the parameter of respect for the essence of rights bolsters the selection filter among protectable legal goods and supports a markedly critical conception thereof.

Consequently, justifying limitations on rights for macroscopic public interests, such as security, is challenging as these rarely align with the 'essence' of the rights being limited. True respect for the essence of these rights is only maintained if the criminalised behaviour actually harms, or poses a threat to, other rights or freedoms that are of equivalent value and dimension, in line with the principle of proportionality. It follows that if the conduct in question does not harm, or even potentially promotes rights, it should not be legitimately criminalised.

A careful selection of protectable interests also follows from the principle of *ultima ratio* and minimum criminal law, according to which only those interests for which all other forms of protection through not only civil and administrative,

[76] cf Baratta (n 48).

[77] Above n 26; cf P Asp et al, 'A Manifesto on European Criminal Policy' (2009)12 *Zeitschrift für Internationale Strafrechtsdogmatiek*, 707, and Asp et al (n 1) 86–103.

but also social, economic and cultural measures – and thus 'a complex of normative responses' addressing the root causes of crime –[78] have failed can legitimately be protected by criminal law.[79]

The subsequent challenge becomes to determine if certain legal goods should be protected at the European level. This requires an assessment of whether the goods – regardless of their inherently European nature – fall under European competence and whether there is a 'constitutional' or primary basis for the involvement of the European legislator, guided by subsidiarity, proportionality, and effectiveness (in a restrictive, not expansive, sense). This implies that it must be proven that a certain legal good cannot be adequately protected by the Member States, that criminalisation at European level is proportionate for its protection, and that its protection can only be effectively pursued through the exercise of European competences. It is important to note that the implication of this approach does not suggest that all provisions of the Charter or of the Treaties may serve as a legal basis for criminalisation. Rather, it implies that the exercise of powers derived from recognised legal bases should be assessed through the proposed axiological filters, thus entrusting Article 52(1) with a more prescriptive status.[80]

C. Protecting Interests from Harm as the 'Aim' in the Proportionality Test

The previous filter 'voices' the principle of harm by clarifying the object to which the harm should be directed. In this perspective, within criminal law, the protection of certain rights or collective legal goods, requested by Article 52(1) of the Charter in the sense delineated above, is logically justifiable only if they are actually harmed or endangered by the behaviours intended to be criminalised. In fact, respecting the 'essence' of limited rights necessitates that these are not sacrificed for general purposes that are disconnected from individual interests or for the protection of goods that do not suffer significant harm. It would otherwise be very difficult to prove that criminalisation 'responds effectively' to their protection, since the criminalisation of harmless conducts would rarely be effective in protecting rights that are not remotely affected by it. As for the previous step, a supporting argument may also derive from the *ultima ratio* principle and the 'necessity' parameter, insofar as they require that criminalisation should be limited

[78] A Cavaliere, 'Il diritto penale minimo in Alessandro Baratta: per un'alternativa alla "cultura del penale"' (2018) 3 *Archivio Penale* 15.

[79] In this respect 'the law's most coercive and censuring technique (criminalisation) should be reserved for the most serious invasions of interests', A Ashworth, 'Is the Criminal Law a Lost Cause?' (2000) 116 *Law Quaterly Review* 225 and Ashworth and Horder (n 48) 33.

[80] cf JW Ouwerkerk, 'Criminalisation Powers of the European Union and the Risks of Cherry-Picking between Various Legal Bases: The Case for a Single Legal Framework for EU-Level Criminalisation' (2016) 23 *Columbia Journal of European Law* 503.

to harmful conduct to such an extent that no other instrument would be effective in counteracting it.[81]

In its turn, the principle of *nullum crimen sine iniuria*, when considered in light of the protection for legitimate interests, substantiates and 'voices' the principle of proportionality. In this perspective, according to Article 5(4) TEU and Article 52(1) of the Charter, criminalisation under Article 83 Treaty on the Functioning of the European Union, as a means, is legitimate only insofar as it is proportionate to achieve the end of protecting interests from harm. The 'usual' test of proportionality (suitability, necessity, and proportionality *stricto sensu*) can also be finalised to this end.

It follows that, since proportionality presupposes and refines the principle of *nullum crimen sine iniuria*, the latter finds also 'implicit' or 'logical' coverage: in this sense, criminalising a non-harmful conduct is always to be deemed disproportionate. It bears noting that the implicit nature or coverage of a principle should not be considered a strong argument for detracting from its value. Indeed, even the principle of proportionality, which now enjoys extensive positivistic coverage, was theorised as an implicit principle in the early years of 'EU' law.[82]

Furthermore, under Article 52(1) of the Charter, a complementary reading of proportionality and harm translates into a requisite of proportionate balance – including, therefore, the respective degree of compression – between the limited interests and those being protected, thereby permitting the protection of interests with at least equivalent value to those being 'sacrificed' and that enjoy, as previously mentioned, equal 'constitutional' or primary anchorage. In this perspective, the 'necessity' requirement, aligning with *ultima ratio*, calls for selecting the least rights-intrusive alternative.

Finally, 'genuinely meets' and 'effectively responds' call the legislator to an evidence-based approach. Without such an approach, principles risk remaining theoretical, as demonstrated by the 'self-certification' or 'self-exculpatory' clauses with which the European legislator sanctions the conformity of criminal law instruments to fundamental rights.[83] Indeed, respect for fundamental rights cannot simply result from their proclamation but should be inherent in the discipline itself.[84] In this respect, an important testing field for the principle of *nullum*

[81] cf V Mitsilegas, 'From Overcriminalisation to Decriminalisation: The Many Faces of Effectiveness in European Criminal Law' (2014) 5 *New Journal of European Criminal Law* 416.

[82] G Scaccia, 'Proportionality and the Balancing of Rights in the Case-law of European Courts' (2019) 4 *Federalismi* 8.

[83] For some criticisms, P de Hert, 'EU Criminal Law and Fundamental Rights' in V Mitsilegas, M Bergstrom, T Konstantidines (eds), *Research Handbook on EU Criminal Law* (Cheltenham, Edward Elgar, 2016) 105.

[84] On the issue, A Cavaliere, 'L'influenza sull'ordinamento italiano del diritto penale europeo delle organizzazioni criminali' in S Mir Puig, M Corcoy Bidasolo and V Gòmez Martìn (eds), *Garantìas constitucionales y Derecho penal europeo*, (Madrid, Marcial pons, 2012) and M Kaiafa-Gbandi, 'Terrorismusbekämpfung in der Europäischen Union und das vor-präventive Strafrecht' in F Herzog and U Neumann (eds), *Festschrift für Winfried Hassemer* (Heidelberg, Müller, 2010) 1164.

crimen sine iniuria at the European level may be the legitimacy of criminalising the mere instigation of conducts that only remotely harm (individual) legal goods.[85]

Altogether, establishing a constitutional foundation for the discussed principles is essential, as it empowers the ECJ's review alongside national parliaments' oversight during implementation. However, whether or not criminal instruments will be deemed illegitimate based on the Charter will largely depend on the political courage of the ECJ to prioritise principles and human rights protection over efficiency and securitisation.[86]

D. Implications for the Principle of Proportionality of Penalties in EU Law in Abstracto and in Concreto

A complementary reading of the principles of harm and proportionality is also essential to ensure the proportionality of penalties, as stipulated in its retrospective dimension in Article 49(3) of the Charter. As generally recognised, this principle prevents the legislator – both the European one in setting minimum penalties and the national one in implementing them – from setting penalties that are disproportionate to the offence. However, as previously noted, the latter element is not further specified either at the positive level or in the case law of the ECJ, which merely requires a proportion between the penalty and the 'seriousness' of the offence. In this regard, a complementary approach plays a crucial role both *in abstracto* and *in concreto*.

In abstracto, it clarifies that the 'seriousness' of the offence is to be determined by taking into account the degree of harm suffered by the interests protected by criminal law. The terms of the proportionality balancing must therefore be understood as the severity of the (minimum) penalty, on the one hand, and the degree of harm caused to the protected interests, on the other. It follows that, logically, a penalty established for a non-harmful act can never be considered proportionate. The criminalisation of non-harmful conduct would thus be violating not only Article 52(1) of the Charter and therefore the principles of harm and proportionality, but also the principle of proportionality of penalties under Article 49(3) of the Charter.

Furthermore, regarding the gradation of the minimum penalty, it is important to consider not just the extent of the harm to legal goods but also the varying value these goods may hold.[87] For instance, an attempt, being less harmful, should

[85] cf A Cavaliere and V Masarone (eds), *L'incidenza di decisioni quadro, direttive e convenzioni europee sul diritto penale italiano* (Napoli, ESI, 2018) *passim*.

[86] The reflections presented seem to resonate with a request for a preliminary ruling (Case C-460/23 *Kinshasa*) brought before the ECJ on the 21 July 2023 (a few months after the Conference) with reference to the assessment of proportionality under Article 52(1) of the criminalisation of humanitarian assistance by the Facilitators Package and the Italian Act implementing it.

[87] The role played by the importance of the interests affected is highlighted by J Feinberg, *Harm to Others: The Moral Limits of the Criminal Law* (Oxford, Oxford University Press, 1984) 36.

incur a less severe penalty than a completed offence. Similarly, an act that damages a merely instrumental good should be penalised less severely than one directly harming a fundamental good, such as life.

In concreto, a complementary reading of the principles of harm and proportionality may serve as a judicial criterion for 'measuring' punishment.[88] Hence, when applying criminal laws domestically, the judge must consider the harm caused by the perpetrator's actions to protected interests, including those belonging to the victim 'in the flesh'. This perspective therefore also reflects the 'relational' dimension of crime proposed by some of the 'violation of rights' theories, while not ruling out other factors, such as the perpetrator's guilt, in determining the penalty.[89]

VII. Concluding Remarks

This chapter provided an opportunity to review and reaffirm the importance of the principle of *nullum crimen sine iniuria* in European criminal law. While defining a common understanding of this principle presents substantial challenges, the necessity for new dimensions of this principle becomes particularly significant in times of crisis. Indeed, it would appear that the much-vaunted crisis of harm-oriented doctrines is more properly attributable to the inability or unwillingness of the national and European legislators to be guided by them than to the intrinsic validity of the doctrines themselves. In light of these considerations, the exploration of additional axiological parameters for the legitimacy of both European and national criminal policies – in conjunction with alternative theoretical perspectives – is indeed of critical importance to the advancement of a European criminal law that prioritises the protection of fundamental rights and adheres to the guarantees of the rule of law.

In conclusion, two additional and final questions emerge, open up prospects for future research. The first question is whether the suggested reading implies that the harm principle can influence the judicial application of penalty, thereby preventing judges from convicting individuals for actions that are, *in concreto*, harmless. The second question pertains to the 'direct effect' implicitly recognised by the ECJ to Article 49(3) of the Charter and whether,[90] according to

[88] Montaldo (n 6) 114.

[89] Wieczorek (n 1) 68–69 and A Ashworth, L Zedner, 'Prevention and Criminalisation: Justification and Limits' (2012) 15(4) *New Criminal Law Review* 542, 544.

[90] In fact, in the recent *NE* case, the Grand Chamber held that the requirement of proportionality of penalties laid down in the *Greek Maize* formula and, in the present case, in Directive 2014/67/EU, which itself 'recalled' the general principle of Article 49(3) of the Charter, has direct effect (Case C-205/*20 NE v Bezirkshauptmannschaft Hartberg-Fürstenfeld* ECLI:EU:C:2022:168). For a comment on the judgment, F Viganò, 'La proporzionalità della pena tra diritto costituzionale italiano e diritto dell'Unione europea: sull'effetto diretto dell'Art. 49, paragrafo 3, della Carta alla luce di una recentissima sentenza della Corte di Giustizia' (2022) *Sistema penale* 1.

a complementary reading, *nullum crimen sine iniuria* and proportionality as per Article 52(1) of the Charter are afforded the same status as prior logical conditions. Affirmatively answering the question has interesting – albeit not devoid of criticalities – implications, as it would mean acknowledging that domestic judges are empowered to disapply European-derived criminal laws that fail to adhere to these principles. Whether this is a desirable outcome, in light of the principles of legality, legal certainty and equality before the law,[91] remains a matter for further discussion.

[91] On these doubts, see Opinion of Advocate General Bobek (23 September 2021) in the same case, paras 92–111. For a 'reply' arguing that judicial review of the proportionality of penalties should be entrusted – at least in the Italian context – to the 'centralised' control of the Constitutional Court, rather than to the delocalised control of ordinary judges, see ibidem.

6

Proportionality of Criminal Penalties between EU Law and the ECHR

An Unattainable Convergence of Standards?

LORENZO GROSSIO

I. Introduction

The first part of the book has advanced a conceptual appraisal of proportionality of criminal penalties in EU law. The topic of this chapter may therefore appear awkward. The law of the EU is profoundly different from the European Convention on Human Rights (ECHR): the former postulates a complex legal order derived from progressive integration between the Member States, while the latter constitutes a fundamental rights instrument governed by international law. In what ways could a combined assessment of proportionality of penalties between the two systems be beneficial for its theoretical understanding?

Against this premise, two main reasons support the approach taken in this chapter. Firstly, Member States' criminal systems are systematically confronted with overlapping obligations that derive from both EU law and the ECHR. In this context, proportionality plays a crucial role, as it shapes the clash between domestic (criminal) measures and the protection of rights and freedoms secured by the law of the EU and the ECHR. However, proportionality of penalties may be differently construed and applied under the two systems. A combined analysis would therefore contribute to disclosing the complex array of proportionality limits to the domestic *ius puniendi* stemming from EU law and the ECHR.

Secondly, with the prospect of the Union's accession to the ECHR, the interplay between EU law and the Convention becomes crucial for framing the limits of the EU legislative action in substantive criminal law. Following the ECJ striking down the draft accession agreement in 2014,[1] new negotiations are as of 2024 at the final stage.[2] Should a new agreement be concluded, any inconsistency of

[1] *Adhésion de l'Union à la CEDH* Avis 2/13, ECLI:EU:C:2014:2454.

[2] On 17 March 2023, the "46+1" negotiation group announced that the Parties have agreed on a new draft accession agreement, which is still to be adopted. For an in-depth analysis, see N Bergamaschi,

the EU approach to the harmonisation of penalties with the ECHR fundamental rights standards may trigger the Union's responsibility under the Convention. A combined assessment of the EU and ECHR's understanding of proportionality of penalties would thus shed light on proportionality constraints on the definition of harmonised penalties.

Following a systematisation of the place of proportionality of penalties under the law of the EU and ECHR (II), this chapter explores whether the two legal systems feature some elements of convergence on the theorisation and application of the principle. To that aim, the chapter assesses firstly the role of the European Court of Human Rights (ECtHR) proportionality standards for the EU harmonisation of criminal penalties (III) and, secondly, the respective approaches of the ECJ and the ECtHR in the review of domestic criminal sanctions (IV). The last paragraph (V) outlines the answer to the research question, together with some concluding remarks.

II. Setting the Scene: The Multiple Places and Understandings of Proportionality of Criminal Penalties between EU Law and the ECHR

As previous chapters have shown, Article 49(3) of the Charter codifies the retrospective understanding of proportionality of criminal penalties.[3] However, the scope of this principle in the EU legal order is broader, as it enjoys at least four dimensions. Firstly, domestic penalties may amount to an interference with fundamental rights secured by the Charter as the proportionality requirement stems not only from Article 49(3) but also Article 52(1) therein. Secondly, proportionality limits the exercise of Member States' *ius puniendi* even where criminal sanctions clash with the enjoyment of internal market freedoms.[4] Thirdly, proportionality constitutes a key obligation under the *Greek Maize* paradigm: domestic penalties established to secure the effectiveness of EU law shall be not only effective and adequately dissuasive but also proportionate in that respect. Finally, proportionality amounts to a limit to the exercise of supranational legislative powers in

'Prime considerazioni sul nuovo tentativo di adesione dell'Unione alla CEDU e sui suoi principali ostacoli' (2024) 1 *Quaderni AISDUE* 1; E Di Franco, M Correia de Carvalho, 'Mutual Trust and EU Accession to the ECHR: Are We Over the Opinion 2/13 Hurdle?' (2023) 8 *European Papers* 1221.

[3] See, in particular, the contributions of J Öberg and A Martufi to this book.

[4] On this topic, among many, see D Doukas, 'Morality, Free Movement and Judicial Restraint at the European Court of Justice' in P Koutrakos, NN Shuibhne, P Syrpis (eds), *Exceptions from EU Free Movement Law* (Oxford, Hart Publishing, 2016) 162. For a broader account of proportionality as a criterion for the legitimacy of domestic measures impairing the exercise of internal market freedoms, among many, see T Tridimas, *The General Principles of EU Law* (Oxford, Oxford University Press, 2007) 193–241; J Snell, 'General Principles in Free Movement Law: Applicability and Application', in KS Ziegler, PJ Neuvonen, and V Moreno-Lax (eds), *Research Handbook on General Principles in EU Law* (Cheltenham, Elgar, 2022) 388–389.

the harmonisation of criminal penalties. In this regard, the general principle of proportionality as enshrined in Article 5(4) TEU does not constitute the only limitation to the Union legislative action. In fact, the approximation of penalty scales is also subject to proportionality constraints flowing from Articles 52(1) and 49(3) of the Charter.

The scope of proportionality of criminal penalties is narrower under the ECHR than under EU law, as it only regards its fundamental rights dimension. Indeed, the proportionality of penalties has a twofold role under the ECHR. On the one hand, the principle constitutes a key factor in the review of domestic sanctions posing a burden on the enjoyment of fundamental rights under the ECHR. That is the case, in particular, of conditional rights, such as the protection of private and family life (Article 8 ECHR), freedom of thought, conscience and religion (Article 9 ECHR), freedom of expression (Article 10 ECHR), freedom of assembly (Article 11 ECHR), the right to property (Article 1 of Protocol No 1 to the ECHR), and freedom of movement (Article 2(3)–(4) of the Protocol No 4 to the ECHR). Disproportionate penalties amount to an interference with those rights, which is not 'necessary in a democratic society'.[5] Moreover, manifestly disproportionate criminal penalties may also be illegitimate *vis-à-vis* the prohibition of torture and inhuman or degrading treatments and penalties under Article 3 ECHR. On the other hand, Contracting Parties shall adhere to proportionality even when positive obligations deriving from the ECHR require them to resort to criminal penalties.

The principle's multiple places under the law of the EU and the ECHR entail a plurality of theoretical understandings. Firstly, proportionality may be construed in prospective terms, which entails a forward-looking relationship between the penalty and the attainment of an aim. The latter may be a legitimate policy objective – such as for the general principle of proportionality under Article 52(1) of the Charter – or a penological non-retributive goal, with particular emphasis on general prevention.[6] Secondly, proportionality of criminal penalties may be construed in a retrospective fashion, intended as a backward-looking relationship of commensurability between the penalty and the seriousness of the wrongdoing.[7]

The different theoretical schemes of the principle coexist under the law of the EU and the ECHR. In both legal systems, proportionality of criminal penalties is inextricably linked to the traditional understanding of the principle of proportionality, materialised in the threefold suitability, necessity and proportionality *stricto sensu* test. The latter applies to criminal measures as well: however, in this

[5] Among many, see SJ Summers, *Sentencing and Human Rights* (Oxford, Oxford University Press, 2022) 155.

[6] See, in particular, the contribution of Adriano Martufi in this book.

[7] On the dichotomy between prospective and retrospective proportionality in EU criminal law, among many, see: E Herlin-Karnell, 'General Principles and EU Criminal Law' in KS Ziegler, PJ Neuvonen, and V Moreno-Lax (eds), *Research Handbook on General Principles in EU Law* (n 3) 527; RA Duff, 'Proportionality and the Criminal Law: Proportionality of What to What?' in E Billis, N Knust and JP Rui (eds), *Proportionality in Crime Control and Criminal Justice* (Oxford, Hart Publishing, 2021) 30–39.

context proportionality assumes a distinct theoretical trait. As the practice will show, prospective standards – that consider whether the penalty constitutes an unnecessary deterrent against a given conduct – and retrospective standards – that consider whether the penalty is disproportionate to the seriousness of the wrongdoing – are crucial for assessing whether a given sanction is necessary and proportionate *stricto sensu* to the attainment of a legitimate policy aim.

III. Proportionality in the Harmonisation of Domestic Criminal Penalties: Do ECHR Standards Influence the EU Legislator?

Article 83 TFEU empowers the Union to adopt harmonising provisions on criminal offences and penalties in some 'areas of particularly serious crime with a cross-border dimension', as well as 'to ensure the effective implementation of a Union policy in an area which has been subject to harmonisation'.[8] By relying on this legal basis, the EU legislature has adopted several legislative instruments providing for minimum standards on the type of sanction to be imposed with respect to given wrongdoings, as well as the maximum term of penalty scales.[9]

It is worth noting that no proportionality objection against harmonising provisions of criminal penalties has so far been adjudicated by the ECJ. Hence, there is no judicial practice in this regard.[10] At the same time, legislative practice

[8] As outlined by Mitsilegas, the two prongs composing the EU competence under Article 83 TFEU reflect the double rationale driving the approximation of substantive criminal law. On the one hand, the harmonisation of offences and penalties may be warranted to tackle global security threats by means of criminal law, thus giving rise to 'securitised criminalisation'. On the other hand, approximation of Member States' criminal law provisions may serve a functional purpose, by ensuring the effective implementation of Union policies (V Mitsilegas, *EU Criminal Law after Lisbon. Rights, Trust and the Transformation of Justice in Europe* (Oxford, Hart Publishing, 2016) 54; V Mitsilegas, *EU Criminal Law* 2nd ed. (Oxford, Hart Publishing, 2022) 114–119). Against this background, Monar has suggested that the recent EU legislative practice on Article 83 TFEU discloses the emergence of a third rationale for the approximation of substantive criminal law, consisting of the promotion of common values. Monar frames this rationale as the 'constitutional dimension' of EU criminal law (J Monar, 'Reflections on the Place of Criminal Law in the European Construction' (2021) 27 *European Law Journal* 356, 360–364). The concept of 'constitutional' is not totally new in EU substantive criminal law. While Wieczorek has clarified that harmonisation constitutes in itself a value-based operation (I Wieczorek, *The Legitimacy of EU Criminal Law* (Oxford, Hart Publishing, 2020) 85), Herlin-Karnell has traced back a constitutional dimension even to functional criminalisation (E Herlin-Karnell, *The Constitutional Dimension of European Criminal Law* (Oxford, Hart Publishing, 2012) 64–65).

[9] For an analysis of the reasons underlying the absence of harmonising provisions on minimum penalties, see the contribution of C Brière to this book.

[10] It is worth noting that a similar contestation has been recently lodged with the ECJ in Case C-460/23 *Kinsa*, currently pending. The case consists of a preliminary ruling that originates from an Italian criminal court that seeks to ascertain whether EU provisions on facilitating illegal immigration, with particular emphasis on Framework Decision 2002/946/JHA, are compatible with fundamental rights under the Charter insofar as they do not provide that the purpose of humanitarian assistance can justify the exclusion of criminal liability.

is particularly indicative of how the EU institutions weigh conflicting interests against the angle of proportionality of penalties and of the influence of ECHR standards. In the *travaux préparatoires* of relevant Directives and Framework Decisions,[11] the issue of the proportionality of harmonised penalties mostly arises while assessing the compatibility of the legislative proposal with fundamental rights pursuant to Article 52(1) of the Charter. The 2017 Proposal for a Directive on Combating Fraud and Counterfeiting of Non-Cash Means of Payment is explicative of this approach: to qualify as legitimate interferences with fundamental rights under Article 52(1) of the Charter, the proposed legislation shall comply with 'the principle that criminal offences and penalties must be set out in law and be proportionate'.[12] Conversely, the retrospective proportionality requirement enshrined in Article 49(3) of the Charter seems to play a minor role in shaping the EU legislative approach. This provision is merely recalled among the fundamental rights that EU substantive criminal law instruments shall abide by.[13]

From a theoretical viewpoint, this reticent approach towards Article 49(3) of the Charter may appear quite surprising. At the same time, the limited role attributed to this provision appears coherent with the EU's own understanding of proportionality of penalties which, under Article 52(1) of the Charter, enshrines not only retrospective but also prospective features. From a prospective viewpoint, harmonised standards shall entail 'the lowest realistic penalty which still exerts a deterring effect'.[14] From a complementary retrospective side, minimum maximum penalty thresholds shall not be disproportionate to criminal offences they seek to penalise.[15]

Notwithstanding the emphasis on the fundamental rights aspect of proportionality of criminal penalties, references to the Strasbourg Court's jurisprudence are extremely scarce in the *travaux préparatoires* of EU substantive criminal law instruments. Moreover, these rare references do not unveil any influence on the EU legislature's proportionality assessment. On the one hand, ECHR standards are

[11] This analysis is based upon a complete assessment of the Explanatory Memoranda and Impact Assessment Reports accompanying legislative proposals of Directives and Framework Decisions currently in force or pending before the Parliament and the Council, as well as Parliament Legislative Resolutions and Council Positions and General Approaches thereof.

[12] Proposal for a Directive on Combating Fraud and Counterfeiting of Non-Cash Means of Payment, COM(2017) 489 final, 15.

[13] The Proposal for a Directive of the European Parliament and of the Council on Combating Terrorism, COM(2015) 625 final, 02.12.2015, 14, as well as the Proposal for a Directive of the European Parliament and of the Council on the Fight Against Fraud to the Union's Financial Interests by Means of Criminal Law, COM(2012) 363 final, 8 and the Proposal for a Directive of the European Parliament and of the Council on the Protection of the Euro and Other Currencies against Counterfeiting by Criminal Law, COM(2013) 042 final, 8 are prominent examples of this legislative approach.

[14] Commission Staff Working Paper – Impact Assessment Accompanying the Proposal for a Directive of the European Parliament and of the Council on the Fight Against Fraud to the Union's Financial Interests by Means of Criminal Law (Part I), SWD (2012) 195 final, 35.

[15] Proposal for a Directive of the European Parliament and of the Council on the Protection of the Euro and Other Currencies against Counterfeiting by Criminal Law, and Replacing Council Framework Decision 2000/383/JHA, COM (2013) 042 final, 7.

sometimes called upon to better substantiate the meaning of Charter rights upon which harmonised penalties are parameterised. That is the case, for instance, of the 2010 Proposal for a Directive on Sexual Abuse, Sexual Exploitation of Children and Child Pornography, according to which the proposed standards on penalties have been analysed not only with respect to Article 7 of the Charter, but also Article 8 ECHR.[16] On the other hand, ECHR rights are sometimes invoked to justify the purported approximation on grounds of positive obligations stemming from the Convention itself. That is the approach featured in the 2022 Proposal for a Directive on Gender-Based Violence, which emphasised the obligations 'to prevent, investigate and punish this kind of violence'[17] as ensuing from the Convention.

It follows that the legislative proportionality scrutiny of harmonising standards on penalties is exclusively based upon EU-own paradigms – most notably, Article 52(1) of the Charter – without any meaningful influence from ECHR ones.

IV. Proportionality in the Review of Domestic Criminal Penalties: A Comparison between the ECJ and ECtHR Approaches

Criminal punishment may either ensure the effective implementation of obligations that stem from the law of the EU and ECHR or pose a burden on the enjoyment of rights and liberties secured therein. Proportionality of criminal penalties emerges as an issue in both domains, which deserve separate consideration.

A. Domestic Criminal Penalties Securing the Effectiveness of the Law of the EU and ECHR: Between Upper and Lower Limits to States' *Ius Puniendi*

Further to harmonisation under Article 83 TFEU, positive obligations in EU substantive criminal law emanate, respectively, from the principle of assimilation and the *Greek Maize* paradigm. As defined by the ECJ in the well-known *Greek Maize* judgment,[18] the principle of assimilation requires that 'infringements of Community law are penalised under conditions, both procedural and substantive, which are analogous to those applicable to infringements of national law of a

[16] Proposal for a Directive on Sexual Abuse, Sexual Exploitation of Children and Child Pornography, COM (2010) 94 final, 4.

[17] Commission Staff Working Document – Impact Assessment Report accompanying the Proposal for a Directive of the European Parliament and of the Council on Combating Violence Against Women and Domestic Violence, SWD (2022) 62 final, 46.

[18] Case 68/88 *Commission v Greece* ECLI:EU:C:1989:339.

similar nature and importance'.[19] Assimilation does not require an accommodation between conflicting interests, which constitutes the hallmark of any proportionality assessment. Rather, it entails an equation between two distinct – although equally reprehensible – wrongdoings.[20] The analysis of proportionality of penalties under EU positive obligations shall therefore focus on the *Greek Maize* paradigm, which requires Member States to sanction violations of EU law through effective, dissuasive and proportionate penalties.[21]

Several ECHR rights require Contracting Parties to resort to criminal penalties, and their proportionality represents a key aspect of their compatibility with the Convention. However, proportionality of criminal penalties under the *Greek Maize* paradigm and ECHR positive obligations materialises two opposite limits to the domestic *ius puniendi*. On the one hand, proportionality represents an upper limit to the severity of criminal penalties against violations of EU law (i). On the other hand, the same principle entails a lower limit for those penalties required for the effective protection of ECHR rights, thereby ensuring that these sanctions adequately reflect the seriousness of the wrongdoing (ii).

i) Proportionality of Criminal Penalties under the Greek Maize *Paradigm: An Upper Limit to the Domestic* Ius Puniendi

The *Greek Maize* paradigm postulates a compound obligation upon the Member States. On the one hand, violations of EU law shall be subject to effective and dissuasive penalties. The concepts of 'effectiveness' and 'dissuasiveness' are distinct, although intertwined. In particular, the former postulates in general terms the capacity of a given legal arrangement to attain its purpose.[22] 'Dissuasiveness', on its part, is a specific criminal law concept, inherently linked to the general prevention function of the punishment. More specifically, it postulates the capability of the sanction to deter the public from committing a given action or omission.[23] 'Effectiveness' and 'dissuasiveness' both foster domestic criminalisation under the *Greek Maize* paradigm, as they require a minimum level of severity from the Member States' criminal law response against violations of EU law. On the other hand, proportionality constitutes an upper limit to the severity

[19] *Ivi*, para 24.

[20] As underlined by Mitsilegas, assimilation derives not only from the principle of effectiveness, but also of equivalence (Mitsilegas, *EU Criminal Law after Lisbon* (n 8), 75). In literature, see also F Giuffrida, 'Effectiveness, Dissuasiveness, Proportionality of Sanctions and Assimilation Principle: The Long-Lasting Legacy of the Greek Maize Case' in V Mitsilegas, A Di Martino and L Mancano (eds), *The Court of Justice and European criminal law. Leading cases in a contextual analysis* (Oxford, Hart Publishing, 2019) 108.

[21] On the key features and implications of the *Greek Maize* paradigm for domestic criminalisation and sanctioning, see the contribution of S Montaldo to this book.

[22] Among many, see: M Accetto and S Zleptnig, 'The Principle of Effectiveness: Rethinking Its Role in Community Law' (2009) 11 *European Public Law* 375, 378–379.

[23] On the uneasy relationship between deterrence and proportionality, among many, see A von Hirsch, 'Proportionality in the Philosophy of Punishment' (1992) 16 *Crime and Justice* 55, 58.

of domestic penalties:[24] they shall be effective and dissuasive to the extent that they are not disproportionate in that respect.

When EU law provides for the adoption of effective and dissuasive penalties, the ECJ may be called upon to review their proportionality through the preliminary reference procedure. The ECJ case-law has provided crucial insights into the meaning of 'proportionate'. Proportionality in this context entails a finalistic assessment, as the severity of sanctions must be commensurate to the aim pursued. More specifically, the sanctions 'must not go beyond what is necessary to attain the objectives legitimately pursued by that legislation'.[25] The aim of criminal penalties depends upon the specific goals attained by each piece of secondary law providing for the establishment of 'effective, proportionate and dissuasive' penalties. However, all of these objectives can be resumed with an all-encompassing general purpose: the effectiveness of EU law. In fact, the *Greek Maize* paradigm seeks effective penalisation at the domestic level for violations of EU law.[26]

The ECJ proportionality test is based on the necessity requirement: to qualify as proportionate, the type and amount of the penalty shall not overstep the minimum level of severity required for ensuring the effective implementation of EU law. This standard of review is quite elusive in itself. However, the Luxembourg Court has sought to better clarify its meaning by relying on prospective and retrospective proportionality. The two schemes complement the ECJ assessment: 'the severity of penalties must be commensurate with the seriousness of the infringements [...], in particular by ensuring a genuinely dissuasive effect, while respecting the general principle of proportionality'. This affirmation, which has become a refrain in the ECJ case-law,[27] envisages a complementary role for prospective and retrospective proportionality in the Court's review of criminal penalties under the *Greek Maize* paradigm. The ECJ may rely on both schemes to assess whether the severity of domestic penalties goes beyond what is necessary to ensure the effective implementation of EU law. On the one hand, the severity of the penalties under scrutiny shall not be disproportionate to the seriousness of the wrongdoing; on the other hand, the penalty shall not result in a level of deterrence contrary to the principle of proportionality, thus overstepping what is necessary to ensure a genuinely dissuasive effect'. It follows that the ECJ proportionality review of

[24] M Dougan, 'From the Velvet Glove to the Iron Fist: Criminal Sanctions for the Enforcement of Union Law' in M Cremona (ed), *Compliance and the Enforcement of EU Law* (Oxford, Oxford University Press, 2012), 82.

[25] Among many, see: Case C-77/20 *K. M. (Sanctions infligées au capitaine de navire)* ECLI:EU:C:2021:112, para 37; Case C-255/14 *Chmielewski* ECLI:EU:C:2015:475, para 22; Case C-210/10 *Urbán* ECLI:EU:C:2012:64, paras 24 and 53; Case C-210/91 *Commission v Greece* ECLI:EU:C:1992:525, para 20.

[26] S Montaldo, 'EU Sanctioning Power and the Principle of Proportionality' in S Montaldo, F Costamagna and A Miglio (eds), *EU Law Enforcement. The Evolution of Sanctioning Powers* (Torino, Giappichelli – Routledge, 2021), 121–122.

[27] For some (although not exhaustive) references, see: Case C-452/20 *Agenzia delle dogane e dei monopoli and Ministero dell'Economia e delle Finanze* ECLI:EU:C:2022:111, para 39; Case C-565/12 *LCL Le Crédit Lyonnais* ECLI:EU:C:2014:190, para 45; Case C-255/14 *Chmielewski* ECLI:EU:C:2015:475, para 23.

domestic penalties shall be construed as a compound assessment, enshrining both the prospective and retrospective schemes.

Against this premise, the ECJ case-law discloses that the prospective scheme takes prominence over the retrospective one, as it influences decisively the Court's standard of review. When providing national courts with guidance in the context of the preliminary reference procedure, the Court emphasises the need to ensure that the severity of domestic penalties adequately deters offenders from violating EU law. This is apparent, for instance, from the ECJ ruling in *K. M. (Sanctions infligées au capitaine de navire)*. While confronted with financial criminal penalties against violations of EU provisions on fishery, the Court underlined that 'in order to assess the proportionality of the sanction, account should also be taken of the relationship between the amount of the fine that may be imposed and the economic benefit derived from the infringement committed, *in order to deter offenders from committing such an infringement* (emphasis added)'.[28]

Having identified the minimum level of severity required to deter potential offenders, prospective proportionality envisages a necessity review of the penalty. Following this approach, the ECJ in *Schenker* underlined that financial sanctions whose amount is equivalent to the value of the wrongdoing's object are disproportionate.[29] In the same line of reasoning, the Court's order in *Bezirkshauptmannschaft Hartberg-Fürstenfeld* concluded the proportionality test on Austrian penalties against violations of provision on posted workers by acknowledging that 'effective implementation [...] could be achieved through less restrictive measures, such as a lower fine or the introduction of an upper limit on such fines, and without necessarily imposing a custodial sentence as an alternative penalty'.[30]

Retrospective proportionality exercises a narrower influence on the ECJ scrutiny under the *Greek Maize* paradigm, as the relevant case-law discloses a self-restraint approach. The Court relies on the retrospective scheme only for providing general guidance to the referring court. Firstly, the ECJ usually verifies whether national criminal systems allow for graduating the penalty considering the seriousness of the wrongdoing for which it is imposed. To that aim, substantive criminal law provisions leave a margin of discretion to trial courts for determining the type and amount of the penalty within a given scale, depending upon the circumstances of each case.[31] Consequently, subject to verification by domestic courts, fixed penalties may be disproportionate from a retrospective viewpoint.[32] Domestic sanctioning schemes that make high minimum penalties applicable to

[28] Case C-77/20 *K. M. (Sanctions infligées au capitaine de navire)* ECLI:EU:C:2021:112, para 49.

[29] Case C-655/18 *Schenker* ECLI:EU:C:2020:157, para 44.

[30] Case C-645/18 *Bezirkshauptmannschaft Hartberg-Fürstenfeld* ECLI:EU:C:2019:1108, para 40.

[31] Case C-384/17 *Link Logistik N&N* ECLI:EU:C:2018:810, para 45.

[32] Case 8/77 *Sagulo and Others* ECLI:EU:C:1977:131, para12. It is interesting to notice that the ECJ in Agenția Națională de Integritate has applied a similar retrospective assessment even with respect to a non-criminal sanction, consisting in the prohibition on holding elective public offices following a conviction for corruption (Case C-40/21 *Agenția Națională de Integritate* ECLI:EU:C:2023:367, para 67).

a wide range of conducts may be contrary to the proportionality requirement as well. That abstract minimum penalty threshold could appear excessive for the seriousness of the concrete wrongdoing.[33] These affirmations in the case-law only amount to broad criteria directed to the referring courts. Except in cases of evidently disproportionate penalties,[34] the ECJ does not assess the absolute or relative worthiness of a given domestic criminal penalty from a retrospective viewpoint. Conversely, this verification is usually reserved for domestic courts, which follow the ECJ general guidance when assessing retrospective proportionality considering all the circumstances of the case.

The ECJ's approach of self restraint is not surprising for two reasons. Firstly, the reduced role of retrospective proportionality reflects the Court's peculiar position *vis-à-vis* domestic courts. In the preliminary reference procedure, ECJ rulings are intended to provide domestic courts with abstract guidance on how to apply proportionality of penalties at the domestic level, without supplementing the determination of penalties by domestic trial courts. The Luxembourg Court is therefore prevented from exercising an in-depth review of the retrospective appropriateness of a given penalty. This assessment requires a specific focus on the factual circumstances of the given case which, in the context of proceedings pending before national judicial authorities, shall be reserved to the referring courts. It follows that retrospective proportionality allows the ECJ only to provide national courts with broad criteria or stigmatise manifestly disproportionate sanctioning schemes.

Secondly, the ECJ's emphasis on evaluating the penalties' level of deterrence under prospective proportionality may also be explained by the ultimate function of criminal penalties under the *Greek Maize* paradigm: securing the effectiveness of EU law. In the Luxembourg Court's view, the sanction's capability to attain this goal is measured in terms of dissuasiveness against the violation of the relevant EU provisions. It therefore appears logical for the Court to take into due consideration the level of deterrence of criminal penalties in the proportionality assessment. This approach ultimately allows the ECJ to accommodate the need to ensure the effectiveness of EU law *vis-à-vis* the protection of individuals against the excessive exercise of *ius puniendi*.

ii) Proportionality of Criminal Penalties under ECHR Positive Obligations: A Lower Threshold for the Severity of Criminal Penalties

To ensure effective protection of fundamental rights, the Convention may require Contracting Parties to resort to criminal penalties. The Strasbourg Court has framed similar positive obligations from several ECHR provisions, including the

[33] Case C-655/21 *G. ST. T. (Proportionnalité de la peine en cas de contrefaçon)* ECLI:EU:C:2023:791, para 81.

[34] Such as, for instance, the establishment of a financial penalty in abstracto without a predefined maximum amount and the provision of a fixed additional penalty in case of dismissal of the defendant's appeal, even if qualified as a contribution to the costs of the procedure (Joined Cases C-64/18, C-140/18, C-146/18 and C-148/18 *Maksimovic* ECLI:EU:C:2019:723, para 50).

right to life (Article 2 ECHR), the prohibition of torture and inhuman or degrading treatments and punishments (Article 3 ECHR), the prohibition of slavery and forced labour (Article 4 ECHR), and the right to respect for private and family life (Article 8 ECHR).[35]

Proportionality of penalties is the tool used by the ECtHR to review the Contracting Parties' criminal law response to wrongdoings that impair the enjoyment of fundamental rights. However, in this context the principle of proportionality has a radically different function compared with the *Greek Maize* paradigm. Under positive obligations to criminalise, proportionality does not establish upper limits for the exercise of *ius puniendi*. Rather, the principle is intended to set a lower threshold for the severity of criminal penalties. More specifically, proportionality in this context is intended as a 'by default' requirement: it entails assessing whether the penalty imposed adequately reflects the seriousness of the wrongdoing, thereby sufficiently deterring its commission.[36] Thus construed, proportionality of penalties is a guarantee for the victims of violations of ECHR rights resulting from the committed crime, rather than for the offender against excessively harsh punishments. This aspect follows the inherently different features of the *Greek Maize* paradigm and ECHR positive obligations. In fact, the former enshrines compound obligations on the Member States, as it drives and limits the domestic *ius puniendi*: criminal penalties shall be dissuasive and ensure the effective implementation of EU law, but also be proportionate. Conversely, the Convention entails a distinction between positive and negative obligations in fundamental rights protection, whereby only the latter concern issues of excessive penalisation.

The opposite functions pursued by the principle of proportionality of criminal penalties trace a clear dividing line between the *Greek Maize* paradigm and the ECHR's positive obligations. But this is not the only difference between the Luxembourg and Strasbourg Court's understandings of proportionality of criminal sanctions securing the effectiveness of EU law and ECHR obligations. Different to the ECJ approach analysed in the previous section, the ECtHR case-law manifests an inherently retrospective proportionality assessment. Following a well-established trend, the Strasbourg Court's scrutiny consists of verifying whether the penalty is manifestly disproportionate to the seriousness of the wrongdoing.[37] The choice to limit the ECtHR's standard of review to manifestly disproportionate penalties is a consequence of the margin of discretion enjoyed by Contracting Parties in selecting the most appropriate measure for giving

[35] For an assessment of the relevant case-law, see among many: A Ashworth, *Positive Obligations in Criminal Law* (Oxford, Hart Publishing, 2013) 196–211; L Lavrysen, 'Positive Obligations and the Criminal Law: A Bird's-Eye View on the Case Law of the European Court of Human Rights' in L Lavrysen and N Mavronicola (eds), *Coercive Human Rights: Positive Duties to Mobilise the Criminal Law under the ECHR* (Oxford, Hart Publishing, 2020).

[36] F Viganò, 'Les obligations de protection pénale des droits fondamentaux' in G Giudicelli-Delage, S Manacorda and J Tricot (eds), *Devoir de punir? – Le système pénal face à la protection internationale du droit à la vie* (Paris, Société de législation comparée, 2013) 68.

[37] *Myumyun v Bulgaria* App No 67258/13 (ECtHR, 3 November 2015), para 67.

effect to Convention rights. Resorting to criminal penalties and determining their amount is the primary responsibility of domestic authorities, to which the Strasbourg Court shall pay a certain degree of deference.[38]

At the same time, the same Court 'must still exercise a certain power of review and intervene in cases of *manifest disproportion between the gravity of the act and the punishment imposed* (emphasis added)'.[39] The level of gravity of the wrongdoing follows from the importance attached to the right whose enjoyment is impaired by the offence. For instance, the ECtHR in *Myumyun v Bulgaria* and *Gafgen v Germany* qualified the crimes at issue as particularly serious since they amounted to 'a breach of one of the core rights of the Convention',[40] namely, the prohibition of inhuman and degrading treatments.[41] Building upon the retrospective assessment just outlined, the Strasbourg Court has clarified that financial penalties are in principle manifestly disproportionate by default with respect to the seriousness of acts amounting to inhuman or degrading treatments.[42] By way of exception, financial criminal sanctions may suffice where mitigating circumstances apply, but their amount could not in any case be derisory or result in a token penalty.[43] In this context, the retrospective assessment absorbs prospective proportionality. Should the Court conclude that the penalty at stake is manifestly disproportionate to the seriousness of the conduct, the same penalty 'could not be regarded as having the necessary dissuasive effect'.[44]

It follows that the ECJ's and the ECtHR's understandings of proportionality of criminal penalties implementing EU and ECHR obligations differ widely for two main reasons. On the one hand, proportionality under the *Greek Maize* paradigm entails an upper limit to the severity of penalties, while ECHR positive obligations establish a lower threshold. On the other hand, the ECJ proportionality assessment is mainly grounded on prospective proportionality, whereas the ECtHR approach is based on a retrospective assessment.

B. Domestic Criminal Penalties Clashing with EU Law and ECHR Rights: A Different Interaction between Prospective and Retrospective Proportionality

Whenever domestic sanctions clash with the enjoyment of rights and liberties secured by the law of the EU and the ECHR, proportionality is meant to set an

[38] Among many, see: *Barovov v Russia* App No 9183/09 (ECtHR, 15 June 2021), para 38; *Külah and Koyuncu v Turkey* App No 24827/05 (ECtHR, 23 April 2013), para 41; *Kasap and Others v Turkey* App No 8656/10 (ECtHR, 14 January 2014), para 59.

[39] *Nikolova and Velichkova v Bulgaria* App No 7888/03 (ECtHR, 20 December 2007), para 62.

[40] *Gäfgen v Germany* App No 22978/05 (ECtHR, 1 June 2010), para 124.

[41] Article 3 ECHR.

[42] *Darraj v France* App No 34588/07 (ECtHR, 4 November 2010), para 49; *Austrianu v Romania* App No 16117/02 (ECtHR, 12 February 2013), paras 73–74.

[43] *Gäfgen v Germany* App No 22978/05 (ECtHR, 1 June 2010), para 124.

[44] *Myumyun v Bulgaria* App No 67258/13 (ECtHR, 3 November 2015), para75; *Gäfgen v Germany* App No 22978/05 (ECtHR, 1 June 2010), para 124.

upper limit to the severity of criminal penalties, thereby protecting individuals from excessive penalisation. The proportionality limits to the domestic *ius puniendi* are framed by the Luxembourg (i) and Strasbourg (ii) Courts by relying on prospective and retrospective paradigms but, once again, to a different extent.

i) The Uneasy Relationship between Prospective and Retrospective Proportionality in the ECJ Scrutiny of Domestic Penalties

Depending on the nature of the rights and liberties impeded by domestic sanctions, a plurality of sources under EU law provides for a proportionality assessment. Should penalties amount to an interference with internal market freedoms, their review can be envisaged under the various Treaty provisions on limitations to their enjoyment.[45] In case of criminal penalties posing a burden on fundamental rights under the Charter, their proportionality may be assessed under Article 52(1) therein.

The Charter gives distinct significance to retrospective proportionality of penalties in Article 49(3), a provision that was, for a long time, scarcely considered in the ECJ jurisprudence. However, a recent trend in case-law suggests the emergence of a renewed approach in this regard. In fact, the Court has recently established a legal connection between Article 49(3) and other proportionality paradigms, such as Article 52(1) of the Charter and Treaty provisions on limitations to internal market freedoms. In particular, the ECJ now recognises that proportionality of criminal penalties 'follow[s] both from Article 52(1) of the Charter and from the principle of proportionality of penalties in Article 49(3) of the Charter'.[46] In the same line of thought, other rulings have construed Article 49(3) of the Charter and Treaty provisions on limitations to internal market freedoms as providing for overlapping requirements. That is the approach manifested in *Landespolizeidirektion Steiermark and Others (Machines à sous)*, where the Court reviewed financial criminal sanctions on illegal gaming activities *vis-à-vis* the free provision of services. In that case, the preliminary question warranted a review based on both Articles 49(3) of the Charter and 56 TFEU. The Court, on its part, grounded its assessment on the latter provision, while

[45] See, in particular, Articles 36, 45(3), 52(1) and 65(1)-(3) TFEU. In fact, the ECJ well-established case-law has regularly interpreted these provisions as entailing a proportionality assessment (in literature, among many, see K Lenaerts, 'Proportionality as a Matrix Principle Promoting the Effectiveness of EU law and the Legitimacy of EU Action' in Continuity and Change – How the Challenges of Today Prepare the Ground for Tomorrow. ECB Legal Conference 2021 (Frankfurt, European Central Bank, 2022), 28).

[46] Joined Cases C-64/18, C-140/18, C-146/18 and C-148/18 *Maksimovic* ECLI:EU:C:2019:723, para 97; Case C-384/17 *Link Logistik N&N* ECLI:EU:C:2018:810, para 42. Even before this development in case-law, legal scholarship has envisaged a strict bond between Articles 52(1) and 49(3). In particular, Fichera framed Article 52(1) of the Charter as a broader declination of the proportionality requirement enshrined in Article 49(3) therein (M Fichera, 'EU Fundamental Rights and the European Arrest Warrant', in S Douglas-Scott and N Hatzis (eds), Research Handbook on EU Law and Human Rights (Cheltenham, Elgar, 2019) 428).

recalling Article 49(3) of the Charter as an ancillary provision.[47] It thus appears that Article 49(3) of the Charter and Treaty provisions on limitations to internal market freedoms also entails interchangeable proportionality paradigms.

These findings elicit a syllogism: since Article 52(1) of the Charter is equivalent to proportionality of penalties under Article 49(3), and the latter paradigm is interchangeable with the one enshrined in Treaty provisions on limitations to internal market freedoms, the latter paradigms are also equivalent to Article 52(1) of the Charter. Article 49(3) of the Charter thus emerges as a unifying paradigm for proportionality of penalties which, as evocatively suggested by the ECJ in the *NE* ruling, all other relevant proportionality requirements 'merely reiterate'.[48]

Notwithstanding the Court's renewed emphasis on Article 49(3) of the Charter, the ECJ's understanding of proportionality is not limited to its retrospective declination. Similarly to the *Greek Maize* paradigm, the Luxembourg Court construes proportionality of penalties as a broader assessment that combines prospective and retrospective considerations. As clearly illustrated by the Court's reasoning in *ECOTEX Bulgaria*, 'the administrative or punitive measures permitted under national legislation must not go beyond what is necessary to attain the objectives legitimately pursued by that legislation'.[49] To assess whether domestic criminal sanctions comply with that standard, prospective and retrospective proportionality come once again into question. Especially 'the severity of the penalties imposed *must also be commensurate with the seriousness of the infringements* for which they are imposed, particularly *by ensuring a genuinely deterrent effect, while not going beyond what is necessary to attain that objective*' (emphasis added).[50]

At first sight, it appears that the ECJ approach in this context does not differ in principle from the one that features the proportionality review under the *Greek Maize* paradigm. In fact, the Luxembourg Court assesses retrospective proportionality cautiously, as its position *vis-à-vis* domestic courts in preliminary reference procedures only allows for the dictation of general guidance. Building upon the need to ensure a relationship of commensurability between the severity of sanctions and the seriousness of the wrongdoing, the ECJ case-law demands that domestic penalty scales leave enough room for trial courts to determine sanctions to be imposed in the concrete case. During this assessment, domestic courts are required to take into consideration not only the nature of the conduct but also the offender's personal characteristics.[51] Moreover, while the absence of an upper

[47] Case C-231/20 *Landespolizeidirektion Steiermark and Others (Machines à sous)* ECLI:EU:C:2021:845, para 45.

[48] Case C-205/20 *Bezirkshauptmannschaft Hartberg-Fürstenfeld (Effet direct)* ECLI:EU:C:2022:168, para 31.

[49] Case C-544/19 *ECOTEX Bulgaria* ECLI:EU:C:2021:803, para 99. On the same point, see Case C-430/05 *Ntionik and Pikoulas* ECLI:EU:C:2007:410, para 54.

[50] Case C-231/20 *Landespolizeidirektion Steiermark and Others (Machines à sous)* ECLI:EU:C:2021:845, para 45. On the same point, see also: Case C-679/18 *OPR-Finance* ECLI:EU:C:2020:167, para 26; Case C-42/15 *Home Credit Slovakia* ECLI:EU:C:2016:842, para 63; Case C-565/12 *LCL Le Crédit Lyonnais* ECLI:EU:C:2014:190, para 45; Case C-418/11 *Texdata Software* ECLI:EU:C:2013:588, para 51.

[51] Case C-544/19 *ECOTEX Bulgaria* ECLI:EU:C:2021:803, para 105.

limit to penalty scales may lead to the imposition of disproportionate penalties,[52] high minimum penalties may be justified from a retrospective viewpoint by the inherent seriousness of the relevant conduct.[53]

Still, there is a noteworthy difference with the *Greek Maize* case-law. Compared to the latter, the ECJ proportionality assessment on penalties interfering with the enjoyment of EU rights and liberties attaches less emphasis on the need to ensure an adequate level of deterrence under the prospective scheme. Penalties in this domain are not intended to secure EU-derived interests like in the *Greek Maize* context; there is therefore no need for the ECJ to warn domestic courts to pay due regard to their deterrent nature when exercising a proportionality assessment. Following this approach, prospective proportionality exercises a twofold influence on the Court's review. In some cases, this scheme has been employed to supplement the general criteria derived from retrospective proportionality. That is the case, for instance, of *ECOTEX Bulgaria* and *Zheng*, where the Court ruled that fines corresponding to the total amount of the benefit that the offender derived from the crime would exceed what is necessary to ensure compliance.[54] In other cases, prospective proportionality takes precedence over the retrospective scheme, as it constitutes the crucial assessment to hold a given sanctioning system as disproportionate. This is the approach featured in *Maksimovic*: after assessing the capability of domestic criminal law provisions to ensure that penalties imposed are not disproportionate to the seriousness of the wrongdoing, the Court concluded that less onerous sanctions would be sufficient for ensuring compliance.[55]

To sum up, the ECJ case-law on penalties clashing with EU-derived rights and liberties unveils an uneasy relationship between prospective and retrospective assessments. On the one hand, the Luxembourg Court appears eager to rely on both proportionality techniques; on the other hand, when domestic sanctioning systems do not appear manifestly disproportionate from a retrospective viewpoint, only a prospective review allows the Court to hold them contrary to the principle of proportionality.

ii) The Key Role of Retrospective Proportionality in the ECtHR Case-law

Unlike the ECJ case-law, retrospective proportionality amounts to the crucial aspect of the Strasbourg Court's review of criminal penalties. When sanctions clash with the enjoyment of conditional rights under the ECHR, the proportionality

[52] Joined Cases C-64/18, C-140/18, C-146/18 and C-148/18 *Maksimovic* ECLI:EU:C:2019:723, para 42.

[53] Case C-231/20 *Landespolizeidirektion Steiermark and Others (Machines à sous)* ECLI:EU:C:2021:845, para 46.

[54] Case C-544/19 *ECOTEX Bulgaria* ECLI:EU:C:2021:803, para 110; Case C-190/17 *Zheng* ECLI:EU:C:2018:357, para 45.

[55] Joined Cases C-64/18, C-140/18, C-146/18 and C-148/18 *Maksimovic* ECLI:EU:C:2019:723, para 47.

standard of review tends to be more lenient compared with the ECJ scrutiny. Contracting Parties enjoy a margin of appreciation in the sentencing domain.[56] Therefore, and differently from the ECJ approach, the necessity assessment does not constitute the key step of the ECtHR proportionality test, as the latter is mainly grounded on balancing under proportionality *stricto sensu*.

The Court's emphasis on proportionality *stricto sensu* leaves much more room for evaluating the severity of penalties *vis-à-vis* the seriousness of the wrongdoing. The ECtHR consistently relies on this possibility, thereby recalling that 'in assessing the proportionality of the interference, *the nature and severity of the penalties imposed* are also factors to be taken into account (emphasis added)'.[57] Following this approach, the Strasbourg Court regularly verifies whether the criminal sanction under review is commensurate to the seriousness of the wrongdoing. Should the outcome of this evaluation be negative, the same penalty cannot be regarded as posing a legitimate and proportionate interference with the fundamental right invoked.[58] By relying on this retrospective assessment, the Strasbourg Court has provided insights into the proportionality limits posed by the Convention to the severity of criminal penalties. Notably, in cases involving political speech,[59] defamation,[60] and media offences,[61] the ECtHR has highlighted that only a serious prejudice for other fundamental rights resulting from the wrongdoing may justify the imposition of custodial penalties. Concerning the amount of the penalty, reviewing its proportionality *vis-à-vis* the seriousness of the offender's conduct warrants an in-depth assessment of the relevant factual circumstances of the conduct. To that aim, the ordinal proportionality technique – which involves a comparison between sanctions against differently harmful conducts[62] – may supplement the ECtHR's retrospective assessment. Following this approach, for instance, in *Raichinov v Bulgaria* the Strasbourg Court underlined that those insults made in public are more serious than those made in the presence of a limited number of people.[63]

[56] The scope of Contracting Parties' discretion varies depending upon the nature of interference with the right posed by the given wrongdoing. In particular, should the criminal measure affect one of the most intimate facets of the individual's identity, the margin of appreciation is reduced. Conversely, Contracting Parties are afforded broader discretion in cases where the imposition of penalties touches upon moral or ethical issues (among many, see: *Stübing v Germany* App No 43547/08 (ECtHR, 12 April 2012), para 60).

[57] Among many, see: *Tammer v Estonia* ECHR 2001–I, para 69; *Skałka v Poland* App No 43425/ 98 (ECtHR, 27 May 2003), para38; *Kincses v Hungary* App No 66232/10 (ECtHR, 27 January 2015), para42; *Krasulya v Russia* App No 12365/03 (ECtHR, 22 February 2007), para 44.

[58] Summers (n 5), 94.

[59] *Otegi Mondragon v Spain* App No 2034/07 (ECtHR, 15 March 2011), para 59.

[60] Among many, see: *Mariapori v Finland* App No 37751/07 (ECtHR, 6 July 2011), para 67; *Balaskas v Greece* App No 73087/17 (ECtHR, 5 November 2020), para 61; *Matalas v Greece* App No 1864/18 (ECtHR, 25 March 2021), para 59.

[61] Among many, see: *Sallusti v Italy* App No 22350/13 (ECtHR, 7 March 2019), para 59; *Cumpănă and Mazăre v Romania* ECHR 2004–XI, para 115.

[62] A von Hirsch (n 23), 79.

[63] *Raichinov v Bulgaria* App No 47579/99 (ECtHR, 20 April 2006), para 48.

Prospective proportionality, conversely, has a narrower influence on the ECtHR review. In some cases, the ECtHR proportionality assessment entails verifying not only retrospective proportionality but also whether penalties are so harsh as to have a 'chilling effect' on the exercise of the rights invoked.[64] In particular, criminal sanctions entail chilling effects whenever they amount to an excessive deterrent, thereby dissuading the public from exercising fundamental rights secured by the Convention.[65] The 'chilling effect' doctrine is a powerful tool for assessing if the severity of domestic sanctions under review strikes a fair balance between the defendant's rights and the public interests secured by criminal penalties.[66] However, the scope of this prospective assessment in the ECtHR case-law is limited. In fact, the level of deterrence created by criminal penalties only emerges from the Strasbourg Court's case-law on freedom of expression[67] and, to an even more limited extent, freedom of assembly.[68] Retrospective proportionality therefore amounts to the key assessment of criminal penalties under conditional rights.

The same paradigm plays an even more important role under Article 3 of the Convention. This finding may appear as surprising as the provision enshrines an absolute right: no limitation to its enjoyment may be admitted on proportionality grounds.[69] However, according to the well-established case-law of the ECtHR, domestic measures need to attain a minimum level of severity to fall under the prohibition of torture and inhuman or degrading treatments or punishments.[70] In the context of criminal penalties, retrospective proportionality has emerged as the tool for assessing whether Contracting Parties' sanctions are so severe as to reach this threshold. More specifically, 'while, in principle, matters of appropriate sentencing largely fall outside the scope of Convention [...], a *grossly disproportionate sentence could amount to ill-treatment contrary to Article 3* (emphasis added)'.[71] The ECtHR case-law provides few insights on how the 'grossly disproportionate' concept shall be construed, but this threshold appears as particularly demanding.

[64] T Baumbach, 'Chilling Effect as a European Court of Human Rights' Concept in Media Law Cases' (2018) 6 *Bergen Journal of Criminal Law and Criminal Justice* 92.

[65] Among many, see RÓ Fathaigh, 'Article 10 and the Chilling Effect Principle' (2013) 3 *European Human Rights Law Review* 304, 305.

[66] In case-law, see *Barfod v Denmark* (1989) Series A no 149, para 29, according to which '[w]hen striking a fair balance between these interests, the Court cannot overlook, as the applicant and the Commission rightly pointed out, the great importance of not discouraging members of the public, for fear of criminal or other sanctions, from voicing their opinions on issues of public concern (emphasis added)'.

[67] Among many, see *Cumpănă and Mazăre v Romania* ECHR 2004–XI, para114; *Marchenko v Ukraine* App No 4063/04 (ECtHR, 19 February 2009), para 52; *Mariapori v Finland* App No 37751/07 (ECtHR, 6 July 2010), para 68.

[68] *Yaroslav Belousov v Russia* App Nos 2653/13 and 60980/14 (ECtHR, 4 October 2016), para 181.

[69] On this premise, the Strasbourg Court has usually affirmed that 'the nature of any offence allegedly committed by the applicant is [...] irrelevant for the purposes of Article 3' (in particular, see: *Al-Saadoon and Mufdhi v The United Kingdom* App No 61498/08 (ECtHR, 2 March 2010), para 122).

[70] *Tyrer v The United Kingdom* (1978) Series A no 26, para 29; *Saadi v Italy* App no 37201/06 (ECtHR, 28 February 2008), para 135.

[71] *Vinter and Others v The United Kingdom* App Nos 66069/09, 130/10 and 3896/10 (ECtHR, 9 July 2013), para 103.

It may be reached in extreme situations in which criminal penalties lack any relationship of commensurability to the wrongdoing they seek to penalise. This may be the case, for instance, of life sentences imposed while there was no real culpability on the defendant.[72] The cautious approach by the Strasbourg Court can be explained by the lack of a coherent sentencing practice among Contracting Parties. Since 'in principle, matters of appropriate sentencing largely fall outside the scope of Convention',[73] only penalties that are absolutely and evidently disproportionate to the seriousness of the wrongdoing may fall under the scope of the prohibition of inhuman or degrading treatments or punishments.

In conclusion, it appears that the reason for the diverging approaches of the Luxembourg and Strasbourg courts lies not only in the ECtHR's emphasis on proportionality *stricto sensu*, rather than the necessity test employed by the ECJ but also – once again – in the two courts' different position *vis-à-vis* domestic authorities. The Strasbourg Court usually reviews the proportionality of penalties imposed in concrete cases after all domestic remedies have been exhausted. From a similar standpoint – and differently from the ECJ – the ECtHR can rely upon a wide range of factual circumstances whose consideration allows the Court to firmly ground its retrospective proportionality assessment on the penalty.

V. Concluding Remarks: A (Tendentially) Unattainable Convergence of Standards between EU Law and the ECHR

Is there a convergence of standards between EU law and the ECHR on proportionality of criminal penalties? The current practice and case-law suggest a negative answer.

Firstly, the EU legislative practice on the harmonisation of criminal penalties features no connection with ECHR standards. As the relevant *travaux préparatoires* have disclosed, findings deriving from the Strasbourg Court's case-law play almost no influence on the Commission, Parliament and Council's proportionality scrutiny of harmonised standards on criminal penalties.

Secondly, while both legal systems envisage prospective and retrospective tests for reviewing the severity of domestic criminal sanctions, there are profound differences between the law of the EU and the ECHR on the principle of proportionality's understanding and application. Concerning domestic criminal penalties

[72] *Ivi*, para 139. The need to consider the offender's culpability fits the retributive theory underlying retrospective proportionality. In this perspective, offenders shall always be regarded as moral agents, thereby imposing criminal penalties that are commensurate to their culpability (N Mavronicola, 'Crime, Punishment and Article 3 ECHR: Puzzles and Prospects of Applying an Absolute Right in a Penal Context' (2015) 15 *Human Rights Law Review* 721, 733).

[73] *Harkins and Edwards v The United Kingdom* App Nos 9146/07 and 32650/07 (ECtHR, 17 January 2012), para 133.

aimed at securing the effectiveness of the law of the EU and the ECHR, the principle of proportionality features two radically different theoretical understandings between the two legal systems. In particular, the principle under the *Greek Maize* paradigm entails an upper limit to the exercise of *ius puniendi*; conversely, the ECtHR construes positive obligations flowing from the Convention as setting lower proportionality thresholds for the severity of those sanctions.

Concerning domestic criminal penalties interfering with the enjoyment of rights and liberties secured by EU law and the ECHR, the principle of proportionality follows here a coherent understanding: it postulates upper limits to the severity of domestic sanctioning schemes. However, the ECJ and ECtHR rely on the prospective and retrospective techniques to a different extent. While prospective proportionality generally amounts to the decisive test in the ECJ review, the ECtHR assessment is mainly based on retrospective proportionality.

Following these considerations, it appears that there is no convergence of standards between EU law and the ECHR on proportionality of criminal penalties. However, is such a convergence unattainable, meaning that there is no room to develop a holistic approach between the two legal systems? This final question elicits a nuanced conclusion. On the one hand, should the EU accede to the ECHR, the EU legislature may be incentivised to comply with the ECHR standards when drafting harmonising provisions on criminal penalties. As previously underlined, any inconsistency with ECHR proportionality requirements may trigger the EU's responsibility for violating the Convention. On the other hand, no further convergence of standards between the two systems might be envisaged. Indeed, this analysis revealed that the different approaches between the ECJ and the ECtHR towards proportionality review of domestic criminal penalties derive from the profound institutional differences between the EU legal order and the ECHR system, which a potential EU membership to the Convention would not obliterate. More specifically, conceptualising proportionality of criminal penalties as an upper or lower limit to the exercise of *ius puniendi* depends on the different nature of obligations flowing from the *Greek Maize* paradigm and ECHR positive obligations. In the same line of thought, key reliance on either the prospective or retrospective technique depends on the ECJ and the ECtHR's respective positions *vis-à-vis* domestic courts.

In conclusion, not only do the law of the EU and the ECHR not disclose a holistic approach towards proportionality of criminal penalties, a similar convergence of standards is also tendentially unattainable in the future.

PART B

The Role of Proportionality of Penalties in EU Criminal Law

7

Proportionality of Penalties in EU Substantive Criminal Law Legislative Instruments

CHLOÉ BRIÈRE

I. Introduction

Penalties are usually defined as a legal punishment for an offence, and consist of measures pronounced against a person, natural or legal, after the conclusion of proceedings that determine their responsibility in the commission of such an offence. National laws provide for different types (criminal or administrative) and levels of penalties, which consist of various measures that range from the death penalty, or life imprisonment for the most severe, to prison sentences of various lengths, fines, etc. The modalities of their execution – such as a suspended sentence, allowing for an early release, etc. – may also vary from one country to another. Well-known at the national level and the case-law of the European Court of Human Rights (ECtHR), the requirement of proportionality of penalties also applies in EU law and in that context encompasses various meanings and dimensions: it must be respected whenever the European Union is directly exercising sanctioning powers to remedy the incorrect implementation or violations of EU law.[1] It also applies whenever Member States exercise at the domestic level their sanctioning power within the scope of EU law and complement the requirements stemming from the European Convention on Human Rights (ECHR). Lastly, it applies when the EU legislature is enacting legislative instruments in which it provides for the penalties to be applied.

This chapter will focus on the last dimension, namely the level of penalties in EU law instruments, and will further restrain its scope to the instruments adopted on the basis of Article 83 TFEU. Relying on a comparative analysis of 14 instruments

[1] S Montaldo, 'EU Sanctioning Power and the Principle of Proportionality' in S Montaldo, F Costamagna, A Miglio, *EU Law Enforcement, The Evolution of Sanctioning Powers* (London – Torino, Routledge – Giappichelli, 2021) 129.

(directives and proposals for directives) based on Article 83 TFEU that have been presented and/or adopted since 2009,[2] this chapter examines whether the EU legislature, when adopting EU instruments in the field of substantive criminal law, complies with the retrospective proportionality of penalties, understood as a requirement to ensure a balance between the severity of the penalty applied and the gravity of the crime committed,[3] and does so consistently.

Under such meaning, the principle of proportionality of penalties may influence the decision of the EU legislator to criminalise certain forms of behaviour and to select the type and level of sanctions to be applied, eventually following a scaled approach to reflect the severity of each offence.[4] This dimension of the principle is enshrined in Article 49 (3) of the Charter of Fundamental Rights,[5] which refers to the 'general principle of proportionality between penalties and criminal offences which is enshrined in the common constitutional traditions of the Member States and the case-law of the Court of Justice of the Communities.'[6] It is always binding on the EU institutions and must be taken into consideration when the Commission, the Council and the European Parliament propose, negotiate and adopt EU legislative instruments aiming to define minimum rules on penalties.

Such analysis is relevant as the exercise of this EU competence has always been and remains extremely sensitive. As reflected in the Commission's 2004 Green Paper, it implies that the EU interferes with the well-arranged sanctions system established in national criminal justice systems, resulting from 'historical, cultural and legal reasons (…), deeply rooted in (national) legal systems, which have evolved and are the expression of how Member States have faced and answered fundamental questions about criminal law.'[7] This results in diversity among the national systems of penalties and a certain reluctance to see EU standards disrupting carefully crafted national scales of penalties. Complying with the principle of proportionality of penalties can thus be considered as a way for the EU to claim additional legitimacy in its approximation efforts, and almost all of the instruments reviewed mention the importance of the Charter and the principles of the legality and proportionality of criminal offences and sanctions in their preambles, except for the proposal for a directive on violence against women and domestic violence.

[2] The full list is available at the end of the chapter.

[3] SS Buisman, 'The Future of EU Substantive Criminal Law, Towards a Uniform Set of Criminalisation Principles at the EU Level', (2022) 2 *European Journal of Crime, Criminal Law and Criminal Justice* 30, 184–185. See also I Wieczorek, *The Legitimacy of EU Criminal Law* (Oxford, Hart Publishing, 2020) 68–69.

[4] Wieczorek, ibid.

[5] ibid.

[6] M Steirt and N Coghlan (eds), *The Charter of Fundamental Rights of the European Union: the 'travaux préparatoires' and selected documents* (Florence, European University Institute, 2020) 194.

[7] Commission, Green paper on the approximation, mutual recognition and enforcement of criminal sanctions in the European Union, COM(2004) 334 final, 47.

The chapter begins by framing the limited scope of the EU's competences on penalties and the techniques developed to circumvent it (II). The analysis continues with an assessment of the content of EU instruments, focusing on those proposed in 2022 and 2023, as they denote a certain evolution in the approach followed (III). The chapter concludes with the finding that while the EU legislature formulates rules reflecting a concern for the proportionality of penalties, consistency is far from being ensured (IV).

II. The Limitations Faced by the EU's Legislature

The competence of the EU in criminal matters has always been perceived as particularly sensitive. This can be explained by the nature of criminal law itself. As H. Wechsler observed, it is the law 'on which men place their ultimate reliance for the protection against all the deepest injuries that human conduct can inflict on individuals and institutions'. However, it is also the law that 'governs the strongest force that we permit official agencies to bring to bear on individuals'.[8] The enactment of criminal norms, defining the constitutive elements of a criminal offence, or providing for the appropriate level of sanctions, is a delicate exercise, reflecting societal choices and values. This nature of criminal law explains why the conferral of competences in criminal matters to the EU has been a slow process, marked by the persistence of intergovernmental decision-making procedures, the limited competences granted to EU institutions other than to the Council of Ministers and the choice to maintain, until 2009, specific instruments different from classic Community law instruments. The legal regime foreseen in the Maastricht treaty tailored an *ad hoc* legal regime for the adoption of measures supporting police and judicial cooperation in criminal matters, and such specificities remained through the revisions introduced by the Amsterdam and Nice treaties, and partially subsisted after the Lisbon Treaty. The purpose of this part is not to retrace extensively the historical evolution of the EU's competence in adopting norms approximating criminal penalties, or the policy documents adopted to define guidelines and model provisions on the matter, as these issues have already been analysed elsewhere.[9] It aims first and foremost at examining why the EU legislature faces some limitations that prevent it from developing a complete scale

[8] H Wechsler, 'The Challenges of a Model Penal Code' (1952) 65 *Harvard Law Review* 1097, 1098.

[9] K Zompoulakis, 'Approximation of Sanctions in the European Union: A Wild Goose Chase?' (2022) 13 *New Journal of European Criminal Law* 3, 333–345; A Giannakoula, 'Approximation of Criminal Penalties in the EU: Comparative Review of the Methods Used and the Provisions Adopted: Future Perspectives and Proposals' (2015) 5 *European Criminal Law Review* 2, 133–160; or JAE Vervaele, 'Harmonised Union Policies and the Harmonization of Substantive Criminal Law' in F Galli, A Weyembergh (eds), *Approximation of Substantive Criminal Law in the EU: The Way Forward* (Bruxelles, Editions de l'Université de Bruxelles, 2013) 58.

of penalties at the EU level, and the impact they have on the content of EU legislative instruments.

Originally, the Treaty on the European Union was particularly vague on the competence of the EU to approximate national criminal legislation. The Treaty provisions (Articles K1, K2 and K3) simply referred to its competence to legislate in areas of common interest, in compliance with the European Convention on Human Rights. The instruments adopted on the basis of these provisions, also known as 'first-generation instruments', were specific to the EU competence in criminal matters (joint actions, conventions, etc.), and their provisions relating to the approximation of penalties were particularly vague. As an example, the Joint Action adopted in 1997 to combat trafficking in human beings and sexual exploitation of children[10] merely required that Member States re-examined their legislation and their practices to ensure that the offence of trafficking and secondary behaviour can be subject to 'effective, proportionate and dissuasive criminal penalties'.[11] The Treaty of Amsterdam was considered a leap forward in relation to the EU's competence in criminal matters as it allowed for the adoption of common standards. Article 31(e) TEU provided for the EU's competence to progressively adopt measures establishing minimum rules relating to the constituent elements of criminal acts and penalties in the fields of organised crime, terrorism and illicit drug trafficking. The conferral of an expanded competence to the EU to legislate in criminal matters was nonetheless strictly framed. The European Council pinpointed in its Tampere Conclusions the "limited number of sectors of particular relevance" for which the efforts to agree on common definitions, incriminations and sanctions should focus.[12] The consecration of an explicit legal basis raised questions as to the way the EU would enact legislation containing provisions on sanctions and penalties to be applied, and a strong concern was expressed by the Member States against the resort to the adoption of minimum sanctions. Their concern resulted in the adoption of a Declaration,[13] which specifically excluded minimum sanctions as a potential technique for the approximation of penalties in EU law. Their reluctance can be understood as not all EU countries include minimum sanctions in their national system of penalties,[14] and these types of sanctions can be perceived as restraining the capacity of judges and courts to adapt the level of penalties to the specific circumstances of a case, thus potentially undermining their proportionality.[15]

[10] Joint Action 97/154/JHA of 24 February 1997 concerning action to combat trafficking in human beings and sexual exploitation of children [1997] OJ L63/2.

[11] Title II, A, b) of the Joint Action.

[12] Tampere European Council of 15 and 16 October 1999, Presidency Conclusions, para 48.

[13] Declaration on Article K.3 (e) of the Treaty on European Union.

[14] W de Bondt, S Miettinen, 'Minimum Criminal Penalties in the European Union: In Search of a Credible Justification' (2015) 21 *European Law Journal* 6, 723. For an overview, see European Commission, Study on minimum sanctions in the EU Member States, 2015, 155.

[15] H Satzger, 'The Harmonisation of Criminal Sanctions in the European Union, A New Approach' (2019) *EUCRIM* 2, 116.

In a similar vein, the possibility to approximate standards via the adoption of maximum sanctions, i.e. defining the highest penalty to be imposed, was not an available option, due to – once more – the diversity of the national criminal justice systems. As an example, the possibility to provide for and/or pronounce life imprisonment is excluded in some Member States, while in others such sentences are foreseen and regularly pronounced, and such diversity is not undermined by the careful case-law of the ECtHR on that matter.[16]

These limitations led the Member States and the Council, the sole legislator at the time, to define in Council conclusions adopted in 2002[17] a dual approach,[18] distinguishing between situations in which it may be sufficient to simply provide that the offences concerned are punished by effective, proportionate and dissuasive criminal penalties, and those for which it may be necessary to go further and thus include in the text indications about the desired level of penalty agreed upon. The Council developed a specific system based on the adoption of common norms establishing 'minimum requirements for the maximum level of penalties to be provided in national law',[19] also referred to as the 'minimum-maximum system' and defined four different levels providing for increasingly severe penalties. With such an approach, the Council can be considered as establishing the premises of an EU-scale of penalties, close to the ones existing in some Member States, such as France,[20] establishing a link between the degrees of severity inherent to the behaviours criminalised and the penalties suggested to the national legislators. These 2002 Conclusions represent the peak of the efforts of the Member States for a greater systematisation of the sanctioning requirements.[21] They are also particularly interesting as they produced concrete results in favour of the proportionality of penalties in EU second-generation legislative instruments, supporting the choice of the most appropriate level of sanction for each offence. The Council went as far as to adopt model provisions in 2009 and repeated the assessment to be conducted when deciding whether to include elements regarding the approximation of penalties.[22] As demonstrated by Athina Giannakoula, their application led to a lowering of the level of minimum-maximum penalties provided for in Framework Decisions, and the negotiations within the Council addressed specifically the need to differentiate between different levels of penalties according to the gravity of the offences.[23]

[16] ECtHR, Press Unit, Factsheet on Life imprisonment, May 2023.

[17] Council conclusions on the approach to apply regarding approximation of penalties, 27 May 2002, doc. 9141/02.

[18] Vervaele (n 9) 58.

[19] Ibid, 59.

[20] M-L Rassat, *Droit pénal général*, ch. 2 Les différentes sanctions pénales, Ellipses, 2017, para 498.

[21] Satzger (n 15) 117.

[22] Council Conclusions on model provisions, guiding the Council's criminal law deliberations, 30 November 2009, doc. 16542/2/09 REV 2.

[23] Giannakoula (n 9) 141. See in particular the quote of Council, Proposal for a Council Framework Decision on combating the sexual exploitation of children and child pornography, doc. 6623/02, 2–3.

The Treaty of Lisbon further amended the provisions relating to the competence of the EU in criminal matters, now defined in Article 83 TFEU. This provision grants the EU legislature the competence to adopt Directives that establish minimum rules concerning the definition of criminal offences and sanctions in specific areas of crime and whenever such approximation proves necessary to ensure the effective implementation of a Union policy in an area which has been the subject of harmonisation measures. Under Article 83(1) TFEU, the EU competence is justified as necessary to combat specific areas of crime, that have been elevated as global security threats by the international community and the EU.[24] On the other hand, Article 83(2) TFEU confirms a functional view of criminal law, used as a tool to achieve the effectiveness of other Union policies. As phrased by the Working Group on the Area of Freedom, Security and Justice (AFSJ), approximation of criminal law should be part of the toolbox of measures for the pursuit of a common policy of the Union, whenever a crime is directed against a shared European interest (protection of the EU's financial interests, counterfeiting the euro, etc.) and non-criminal rules do not suffice. More generally, Article 83 TFEU and the competence it grants to the EU to adopt 'minimum rules' on penalties has given rise to discussions regarding its distinction from minimum sanctions; the extent to which the EU legislature shall not encroach upon the discretion of national legislators in defining penalty levels for specific offences,[25] and the need to take into account the complex national sanctioning systems, not limited to prison penalties.[26] These elements were notably echoed in the Commission's position expressed in 2011, signalling that the EU's competence should be mobilised to reduce the degree of variation between the national systems, leading to an inconsistent application of EU rules.[27] In practice, the EU legislature remains bound by the limited competence it receives in the Treaties, and the need to rely on the 'minimum-maximum system' whenever it wishes to enact provisions approximating the level of penalties. The prevalence of such a system can be illustrated by the fact that, in 2013, when the Commission put forward a proposal for a directive foreseeing the adoption of minimum sanctions, presented as contributing 'to a consistent EU wide system for the protection of the euro',[28] the Member States promptly discarded the idea.[29]

[24] V Mitsilegas, EU Criminal Law after Lisbon: Rights, Trust and the Transformation of Justice in Europe (Oxford, Hart Publishing, 2016) 58.

[25] Zoumpoulakis (n 9) 338 and the literature referred to in footnotes 32 and 33.

[26] W Bogensberger, 'Article 83', in M Kellerbauer, M Klamert, J Tomkin, *Commentary on the EU Treaties and the Charter of Fundamental Rights* (Oxford, Oxford University Press, 2019) 899.

[27] Commission, Communication 'Towards an EU Criminal Policy: Ensuring the effective implementation of EU policies through criminal law', COM(2011) 573 final, 9–10.

[28] Commission, Proposal for a Directive on the protection of the euro and other currencies against counterfeiting by criminal law, COM(2013) 42, Art 5(4).

[29] Council, Proposal for a Directive on the protection of the euro and other currencies against counterfeiting by criminal law – General Approach, doc. 14761/13, 13.

The Commission's capacity to influence the level of penalties applied is thus quite restrained, as already stressed in 2004.[30] First, the national legislators may reflect and decide upon what they consider to be the appropriate level of penalties within their national criminal justice system, leading to possible divergences in the rules applied across the Member States. Second, the concrete evaluation of what constitutes a proportionate penalty remains in the hands of the national criminal courts, which retain broad discretion in defining the most appropriate sentence. The consecration of the Charter of Fundamental Rights as part of EU primary law seems to impact the assessment of the proportionality of penalties envisaged at the national level in such concrete cases, i.e. relating to the execution of European arrest warrants, rather than the legislative work of the EU institutions.[31] Yet, the exercise of the EU's legislative competence has been marked by a new impetus in the last two years, with new proposals being put forward, revising and updating previous instruments, or expanding the scope of the EU's competence in criminal matters to new crimes.[32] Their examination may thus allow us to verify if the principle of proportionality of penalties has benefitted from a proper consideration and whether the EU legislature pushed the boundaries of its competence to integrate new elements interfering with the appreciation *in concreto* of the appropriate penalty.

III. Proportionality of Penalties in the Exercise of the EU's Competence

The examination of the EU criminal law instruments adopted since the entry into force of the Lisbon Treaty and the level of penalties prescribed therein is not a complete novelty. As a way of example, Athina Giannakoula[33] reviewed the level of penalties prescribed in the Directives adopted between 2009 and 2014. The mobilisation of the EU's competence in approximating penalties has thus partially already been assessed. The standardisation of the provisions included, notably through the wording used, has been pinpointed, demonstrating that the Model Provisions adopted by the Council in 2009 remain a strong basis for the EU legislature.[34] Yet, the work it previously undertook to develop an EU-scale of penalties had been mentioned in the first two Directives adopted in 2011 but

[30] Commission, Green Paper on the approximation, mutual recognition and enforcement of criminal sanctions in the European Union, COM(2004) 334 final, 22 and 48.

[31] T Locke, 'Article 49 of the Charter', in M Kellerbauer, M Klamert, J Tomkin, *Commentary on the EU Treaties and the Charter of Fundamental Rights* (n 26) 2235.

[32] Council Decision (EU) 2022/2332 on identifying the violation of Union restrictive measures as an area of crime that meets the criteria specified in Article 83(1) TFEU [2022] OJ L308/18. For an analysis, see the contribution of L Bernardini and F Finelli to this book.

[33] Giannakoula (n 9).

[34] Zoumpoulakis (n 9) 340–341.

was progressively left aside,[35] and the references to Article 49 (3) of the Charter and/or the question of proportionality of penalties are addressed in rather vague and abstract ways.[36]

One may thus wonder whether a new analysis is warranted, and the argument to sustain such analysis can be found in the recent dynamism of the EU legislature, which is – as of January 2024 – negotiating no less than five directives based on Article 83 TFEU and quickly progressing towards their adoption before the suspension of the European Parliament's activities ahead of the European elections in June 2024. Among the instruments under negotiation, three of them are the object of a provisional agreement between the European Parliament and the Council and are thus close to adoption, namely the revised versions of the Environmental Crime Directive[37] and the Trafficking in Human Beings Directive,[38] and the adoption of the Directive on the violation of the EU restrictive measures.[39] One proposal, the draft Directive on combating violence against women and domestic violence, has already been the object of three trilogues, but the negotiations are partially blocked due to divergent positions on the definition of rape. Lastly, the latest draft instrument is the proposal for a Directive on the facilitation of unauthorised entry, transit and stay in the Union, presented in November 2023, and preparing the long-awaited revision of the Facilitators' Package.[40]

The purpose of this part of the chapter will thus be to delve into these instruments to identify possible patterns of evolution in the way that penalties and their proportionality are being dealt with by the EU legislature, and to what extent it strengthens or diminishes the consideration given to the principle of proportionality of penalties. For clarity, the analysis will be divided between the sanctions envisaged for offences committed by legal persons on the one hand, and by natural persons on the other. For each category, different elements were reviewed, including but not limited to the nature of the penalties prescribed, the severity of the sanctions envisaged, the definition of aggravating and/or mitigating circumstances, or the non-application of penalties in restrictive cases.

A. Proportionate Penalties Applicable to Legal Persons?

The penalties applicable to legal persons are probably the trickiest to address from the perspective of the EU legislature. Contrary to the provisions relating to the

[35] Directive 2011/36/EU, Preamble, para 12, and Directive 2011/93/EU, Preamble, para 11.

[36] L Grossio, The Principle of Proportionality of Criminal Offences and Penalties between EU Law and the ECHR, defended on 16 February 2024, 155. The Article is regularly mentioned in the proposals for new Directives presented by the Commission when examining their compliance with fundamental rights, but it is only referred to expressly in the preamble of the Directive on Market Abuse that lists it among the Charter's provisions it complies with (Directive 2014/57/EU, Preamble, para 27).

[37] Provisional agreement reached on 16 November 2023.

[38] Provisional agreement reached on 23 January 2024.

[39] Provisional agreement reached on 12 December 2023.

[40] Proposal for a Directive of the European Parliament and of the Council laying down minimum rules to prevent and counter the facilitation of unauthorised entry, transit and stay in the Union,

penalties applicable to natural persons, the possibility to foresee criminal liability and the application of criminal sanctions to legal persons are far from being unanimously shared across EU Member States. Several Member States do not provide for the criminal liability of legal persons, despite long-standing debates and proposals to harmonise that aspect. As a consequence, the Model provisions adopted by the Council remain on purpose vaguely drafted, referring to 'criminal and non-criminal fines', and listing a few possible penalties to be selected and implemented by the Member States.[41] The first instruments adopted on the basis of Article 83 TFEU, being either instruments linked to the fight against a specific crime or criminal activity, or instruments mobilising criminal law to better enforce EU law, retained this formula. The relevant provisions on sanctions concerning legal persons are drafted in very close if not identical terms in the Directives on trafficking in human beings, child pornography, money laundering, terrorism, non-cash fraud payment, etc.

Yet a clear evolution may be noticed in the more recently presented and negotiated texts. The proposal for the revision of the Directive on trafficking in human beings is probably the most explicit on the rationale presiding such reform. In the explanatory memorandum, the Commission stresses how the penalty regime previously in place failed to meet the objectives of the Directive, notably due to its optional nature and the extent to which it is transposed and applied in the Member States.[42] Another argument linked to the diversity of the penalties applicable is made within the proposal for a Directive on the violation of Union restrictive measures, as the Commission stressed the diversity not only in the criminal or administrative nature of the penalties applied but also in the level of the penalties imposed (maximum fine ranging from 133,000 euros to 37·5 million euros).[43] The change proposed in these draft instruments constitutes a shift in favour of minimum rules on the liability of legal persons with mandatory penalties to be made available in the national legal systems.[44] Even though the nature of the penalties likely to be incurred is not harmonised, and the Member States retain the capacity to choose between criminal or administrative measures, the provisions are far more prescriptive requiring the Member States to implement when appropriate the penalties envisaged. Interestingly, the compromise text on the Directive for the protection of the environment through criminal law, or the proposal for a Directive on migrant smuggling does not include such innovation and relies on the traditional formulation and penalty regime.[45] Such a difference may be explained by

and replacing Council Directive 2002/90/EC and Council Framework Decision 2002/946 JHA, COM/2023/755 final.

[41] Model provisions (n 22) 5.

[42] Commission, Proposal for a Directive revising Directive 2011/36/EU, 2.

[43] Commission, Proposal for a Directive on the definition of criminal offences and penalties for the violation of Union restrictive measures.

[44] See the difference between Article of the Directive 2011/36/EU and the proposal for its revision and the shift from 'sanctions (….) that may include other sanctions' to 'ensure that a legal person is liable […] if appropriate of the following sanctions'.

[45] The proposal for a Directive on violence against women does not, at least in the Commission's version, contain provisions of the liability of legal persons and the penalties to be applied to them.

the legal bases used, respectively Article 83(1) or (2) TFEU, that reflect the rationales behind the mobilisation of the EU's competence in criminal matters and the distinction between functional objectives and security objectives.

This specificity is further emphasised when examining the additional elements provided for in the proposals based on Article 83(2) TFEU concerning the fines to be imposed on legal persons. Both texts include additional rules determining the level of the fines, whose maximum level shall be inferior to 3%, 5% or 6% of the total worldwide turnover of the legal person concerned.[46] This fining technique – borrowed from other fields of EU law, especially competition law,[47] and/or from some domestic penalty systems[48] – calls for the following remarks. Firstly, the proportionality of the fines is a clear concern and motivation of the EU legislator, which stresses that the amount of the fines 'shall be proportionate to the seriousness of the conduct and to the individual, financial and other circumstances of the legal person concerned'. This fining technique is most likely chosen to reinforce the dissuasiveness of the fines to be imposed, as stressed in the preambles of both texts.[49] Moreover, the concern for proportionality of penalties also translates in the percentages being put forward, the highest one applying to the offences considered more serious, committed with aggravating circumstances. The regime is far from homogeneous, however, and the draft smuggling Directive may be subject to changes during the negotiations. Indeed, the compromise text of the Directive on environmental crimes offers flexibility to the Member States to choose between this fining method and absolute amounts, depending on their national systems, while the draft smuggling Directive only refers to percentages of the turnover. In that regard, the proposal for a directive on the violation of Union restrictive measures stands out as the odd one out: while the text is based on Article 83(1) TFEU, it does also include a provision foreseeing the application of this fining regime. This may reflect the particularity of this text and its objectives: while it pursues a functional logic of ensuring the proper enforcement of the Union's restrictive measures, it cannot be based on Article 83(2) TFEU, as the Common Foreign and Security Policy remains in a particular position within the EU's legal order and cannot be considered as 'a Union policy in an area which has been subject to harmonisation measures'.

This analysis reveals how the EU provisions defining the penalties to be applied to legal persons are evolving towards a more prescriptive regime. The EU legislature still respects the legal traditions of the Member States and accommodates their diversity in the liability incurred by legal persons, or in the way fines may

[46] Compromise text for Directive on environmental crime, Art 7(3)(a) and Proposal for a Directive on smuggling, Art 8.

[47] See the contribution by P Caeiro to this volume.

[48] See eg in Finland, or Sweden, where the amount of the fine is a function of the net income of the offender. European Transport Safety Council, Traffic Law Enforcement in the EU. 2011, 6.

[49] Compromise text for Directive on environmental crime, para 15 and Proposal for a Directive on smuggling, para 13.

be calculated. Nevertheless, the wording is more prescriptive and the concern for the effective dissuasiveness of the penalties envisaged pushed for the inclusion in EU criminal law instruments for additional details on the way to calculate fines, considering the wealth and resources of the legal persons sanctioned.

B. Proportionate Penalties Applicable to Natural Persons?

For natural persons, and the adoption of minimum rules on the penalties that Member States may then provide in their national legal systems, the analysis of the proportionality of penalties is trickier. First, the EU legislature only provides for minimum rules regarding the minimum–maximum level of prison sentences, and this has not evolved in all the instruments adopted and/or negotiated since the entry into force of the Lisbon Treaty.[50] Nevertheless, there are some hints or indications that the EU legislature has been increasingly aware of the need to ensure the proportionality of penalties. While stressing the importance of the discretion of national judges when deciding upon the sentence to be pronounced,[51] EU criminal law instruments are including more and more provisions guiding such assessment, thus potentially interfering with the appreciation of what would constitute a proportionate penalty in specific circumstances.

The first example lies in the definition of minimum rules regarding which behaviour(s) shall be criminalised and considered by national judges as aggravating circumstances, hence justifying a higher penalty. The definition of aggravating instruments in EU criminal law instruments is far from being a new trend, and the instruments adopted under the Lisbon Treaty under the legal basis of Article 83(1) include such provisions.[52] Their inclusion is not automatic, and some texts do not refer to such circumstances.[53] Among those that include details on aggravating circumstances, two approaches can be distinguished. In some texts, the level of penalties and the possible aggravating circumstances are described in the same provision, with a higher level of penalties prescribed for offences committed with aggravating circumstances, reflecting a concern for proportionality (a higher minimum-maximum penalty for a more severe crime).[54] In others, aggravating circumstances are listed in a separate provision and their impact on the possible level of penalties applicable is not expressly addressed in the core of

[50] With a nuance maybe with the proposal for a Directive on migrant smuggling that mentions that third country nationals who commit the offences defined in this Directive should be subject to return and may be prohibited to re-enter the EU's territory (preamble, para 11).

[51] Directive (EU) 2019/713, para 17; Directive 2017/541, para 19 or Compromise text for Directive on environmental crime, para 14a.

[52] Directive 2011/36/EU, Art 4 (2) and (3), or Directive (EU) 2018/1673, Art 6.

[53] Directive (EU) 2017/541 on terrorism is silent about them.

[54] Directive 2011/36/EU, Art 4 (2), or proposal for a Directive on violence against women and domestic violence, Art 12.

the Directives.[55] Nevertheless, the preambles of these instruments include a paragraph on aggravating circumstances, insisting that Member States should provide for their application within their national legal system, ensuring that they are available for judges to consider when sentencing offenders, either to take into account specific factual circumstances or the cumulation of several offences.[56] Most surprisingly, the proposal for a Directive on migrant smuggling follows a new and third approach: it contains a provision dedicated to aggravated criminal offences (Article 4), which are to be subject to higher-level penalties (Article 6 (3) and (4)). The concern for the proportionality of the penalties to the severity of the crime is clearly expressed in the proposal, with the preamble insisting on the need to distinguish the aggravated criminal offences that 'create higher harm to individuals and to society', and more severe criminal penalties that reflect the 'higher social concern regarding more serious and harmful conducts'.[57] The text also foresees a more severe penalty for smuggling attempts that caused the death of third-country nationals (Article 6(4)), addressing here for instance the situations in which attempts to reach the EU by boat result in the death of passengers.

In contrast with the provisions defining minimum rules on aggravating circumstances, recent instruments (adopted or negotiated) include provisions on mitigating circumstances. Such a provision was first included in the Framework Decision on terrorism[58] and maintained when it became a Directive in 2017. It invites Member States to provide for a possible reduction of the penalties envisaged should the person renounce terrorist activity or provide specific information to the competent national authorities.[59] The latter element reflects a specific concern of the Member States, best demonstrated by the adoption back in 1996 of a Council Resolution on individuals who cooperate with the judicial process in the fight against international organised crime.[60] Two recent proposals put forward by the Commission include such a provision on mitigating circumstances: the revised Directive on environmental crime and the proposal for a Directive on smuggling. The compromise text on the former still includes it, and its adoption is thus forthcoming. It provides for the possibility to make available for judges the consideration of situations in which the offender restored nature to its previous condition or took action to minimise the impact of the offence; and in case of collaboration with competent authorities.[61] The proposal for a Directive on smuggling refers also

[55] Directive 2011/93/EU, art 9; Directive (EU) 2018/1673, Art 6; Proposal for a Directive on the violation of Union restrictive measures, Art 8, or Compromise text for the Environmental Crime Directive, Art 8.

[56] eg Directive 2011/93/EU, para 21; or Compromise text for the Environmental Crime Directive, para 16.

[57] Proposal for a Directive on migrant smuggling, para 9.

[58] Council Framework Decision of 13 June 2002 on combating terrorism [2002] OJ L164/3, Art 6.

[59] Directive (EU) 2017/541, Art 16, which corresponds to the unchanged text of Art 6 the Framework Decision 2002/475/JHA.

[60] Council Resolution of 20 December 1996 on individuals who cooperate with the judicial process in the fight against international organised crime [1997] OJ C10/1.

[61] Compromise text for the Environmental Crime Directive, para 16a, and Art 9.

to such cooperation with competent national authorities as a mitigating circumstance (Article 10), and in its explanatory memorandum, the Commission spells out how such a set of aggravating and mitigating circumstances serves to 'ensure the proportionality of the criminal penalties, in line with the principle of criminal penalties enshrined in Article 49(3) of the Charter.'[62]

Finally, the concern of the EU legislature for the proportionality of penalties can be found through provisions and/or considerations excluding criminalisation and/or the application of penalties to certain situations. The first example can be found in the Directive on combating human trafficking, which includes a provision on the 'non-prosecution or non-application of penalties to the victim', which shall apply to victims compelled to commit offences as a direct consequence of being subject to trafficking.[63] Such an exemption, justified in the preamble on the ground of the necessary protection of the victims' rights, has been largely commented on by authors who stress its objective to incite victims to report to the competent authorities[64] and its relatively weak formulation.[65] Its implementation also proved particularly sensitive, and while the revision proposed by the Commission left the text untouched, the European Parliament adopted amendments to strengthen it. The amended version notably foresees the annulment of any related penalties and the expunction of their police and criminal records and makes explicit that such provision should not be conditional to the victims' cooperation with criminal proceedings.[66] A similar provision addresses the situation of child victims of sexual abuse and sexual exploitation compelled to commit criminal activities as a direct consequence of their abuse.[67] But similar provisions have never been adopted or proposed since, and instead, the Commission chose alternative approaches to exclude from criminalisation certain behaviours. As a way of example, the proposal for a Directive on the violation of restrictive measures excludes from criminalisation the provision of goods and services of daily use fulfilling basic needs of the natural persons subject to EU restrictive measures, and their dependent family members, as well as the provision of humanitarian assistance to persons in need.[68] It does so by listing those behaviours at the end of the provision that define the minimum rules on the definition of criminal offences. However, this provision has been substantially reduced by the Council, which only refers in its general approach to the exemptions or derogations that may be granted

[62] Proposal for a Directive on migrant smuggling, 8.

[63] Directive 2011/36/EU, para 14 and Art 8.

[64] E Symeonidou-Kastanidou, 'Directive 2011/36/EU on Combating Trafficking in Human Beings, Fundamental Choices and Problems of Implementation' (2016) 7 *New Journal of European Criminal Law* 4, 475.

[65] T Obokata and B Payne, 'Implementing Action Against Trafficking of Human Beings under the TFEU: A Preliminary Analysis' (2012) 3 *New Journal of European Criminal Law* 298, 310.

[66] European Parliament, Report on the proposal for a directive of the European Parliament and of the Council amending Directive 2011/36/EU on preventing and combating trafficking in human beings and protecting its victims, 10.10.2023, A9-0285/2023.

[67] Directive 2011/93/EU, Art. 14.

[68] Proposal for a Directive on the violation of EU restrictive measures, Art 6(3).

in the EU restrictive measures.[69] This contrasts with the approach followed in the proposal for a draft Directive on migrant smuggling. The proposal is subject to strict scrutiny on the criminalisation or non-criminalisation of humanitarian assistance to migrants. Many commentators stressed the limits of the Facilitators' Package concerning this issue,[70] and the risks of prosecution and conviction faced by those who would assist migrants to enter, transit or reside in Europe, best illustrated with repeated proceedings monitored by NGOs and human rights bodies. The Commission adopted guidelines on the matter in 2019,[71] but the proposal for a revised legal framework constitutes an excellent opportunity to clarify and harmonise the rules applicable in that regard, clearly excluding from criminalisation such humanitarian assistance. The proposal does partially answer to such demands as it introduces in the definition of 'smuggling' the requirement of material or financial gain, in line with the definition provided in the UN Protocol on the smuggling of migrants. Yet the text does not include a provision that expressly provides for the non-criminalisation of – or to a lesser extent the non-prosecution or the non-application of penalties to – those assisting migrants with a humanitarian objective. The text only refers, in its preamble, to the fact that the constitutive elements of the offence 'will usually not be fulfilled when it comes to assistance among family members or the provision of humanitarian assistance or the support of basic human needs', and that the purpose of the text is not to criminalise assistance provided to family members or humanitarian assistance.[72] It is, however, uncertain whether this formulation will prevent the prosecution and conviction of those assisting migrants, as the weaknesses of the previous legal framework, not corrected with such formulation, have led to such prosecutions and convictions, including in States providing for the non-prosecution of humanitarian assistance. It nevertheless illustrates the concern raised by the risk of applying unjustified and disproportionate penalties to persons who did not act with criminal intent.

IV. Conclusion

The approximation of penalties reached through the adoption of EU criminal law instruments is far less intense than in other fields of EU law. As previously mentioned, the provisions reviewed in this chapter only contain minimum rules and leave ample discretion to the national legislatures to adapt the level of penalties

[69] Council, Proposal for a Directive on the violation of EU restrictive measures – General approach, doc. 10366/23, para 4a.

[70] See, eg A Marletta, 'Le droit pénal européen à l'épreuve de la solidarité : L'incrimination de l'aide humanitaire aux migrants', (2021) 57 *Cahiers de droit européen* 3, or S Carrera *et al*, 'Countering Migrant Smuggling: The EU's Policy Approach' in *Policing Humanitarianism: EU Policies Against Human Smuggling and their Impact on Civil Society* (Oxford, Hart Publishing 2019) 18.

[71] European Commission, *Guidance on the implementation of EU rules on definition and prevention of the facilitation of unauthorised entry, transit and residence* (Communication C(2020)6470 final).

[72] Proposal for a Directive on migrant smuggling, para 7.

to the national systems in place and to the national interpretation of proportionality. Assessing the proportionality of penalties provided for in EU instruments would therefore require an exploration going beyond the mere content of EU legislative instruments to dissect the transpositions at the national level and the sentencing practices of national judges. Such an exercise is far beyond the scope of this chapter. Our analysis nevertheless reveals some interesting insights. The limits of the EU's competence in criminal matters did not prevent the EU legislature from considering the principle of proportionality of penalties. This is evidenced by the documents adopted by the Council in 2002 and 2009, but also from the substance of the instruments adopted before and after the entry into force of the Lisbon Treaty that reflects an imperfect scale of penalties at the EU level, by grading the penalties incurred depending on the severity of the offences. The instruments proposed and negotiated since 2022 reinforce such a trend as they include more provisions that guide the determination of the appropriate penalties, specifying possible aggravating, or mitigating circumstances, and /or excluding from criminalisation or penalties certain situations. Such a trend can translate to the willingness of the EU legislature to reduce the diversity and heterogeneity of sentencing practices across Member States. This is particularly important to address criminal cases often presenting a cross-border dimension and requiring the determination of the most appropriate jurisdiction. A better approximation of the level of penalties and guidance on sentencing may prevent the risk of forum shopping, i.e. the attempt to bring the case to trial in the Member State in which the penalties are stricter or more lenient. It is also important to ensure a stronger enforcement of common EU rules, since discrepancies may reduce the existence of a common playing field and result in the unequal enforcement of common standards across the EU. Such concerns are also reflected by the insertion in the latest draft instruments of provisions that contain minimum rules on limitation periods for the investigation, prosecution and trial of offences, and/or for the enforcement of penalties.[73]

However, despite these hints, the principle of proportionality of criminal penalties is not taken into consideration consistently by the EU legislature. Some discrepancies may be explained by the evolution in time of the political agreement of the Member States to insert new types of provisions in EU legislative instruments, and the differences between instruments adopted ten years apart are understandable. A distinction between those adopted under Article 83(1) TFEU and Article 83(2) TFEU also seems to emerge, notably regarding the fining regime applicable to legal persons, and may be explained by the different logics presiding to the adoption of minimum rules on penalties under each legal basis. Yet it is not completely coherent, as demonstrated by the proposal for a Directive on the violation of EU restrictive measures. Similarly, the provisions excluding criminalisation

[73] Proposal for a Directive on migrant smuggling, Art 11, or Compromise text for the Environmental Crime Directive, Art 11.

and/or the application of penalties are particularly diverse, reflecting their potential political sensitivity and the lack of consensus among Member States on their inclusion in legally binding instruments. Such a panorama is further accompanied by the disappearance of policy documents that reflect on the EU's policy and/or priorities in criminal matters. The possibility of solving inconsistencies through the adoption of new and updated model provisions seems a very unlikely solution, and the preparation of legislative proposals by different Directorates within the Commission, and their negotiation involving potentially different parliamentary committees or working groups, may further undermine consistency.

List of instruments analysed (as of February, 2024 1st)

1. Directive 2011/36/EU of the European Parliament and of the Council of 5 April 2011 on preventing and combating trafficking in human beings and protecting its victims, and replacing Council Framework Decision 2002/629/JHA, *OJ L 101, 15.4.2011, p. 1–11.*
2. Directive 2011/93/EU of the European Parliament and of the Council of 13 December 2011 on combating the sexual abuse and sexual exploitation of children and child pornography, and replacing Council Framework Decision 2004/68/JHA, *OJ L 335, 17.12.2011, p. 1–14.*
3. Directive 2013/40/EU of the European Parliament and of the Council of 12 August 2013 on attacks against information systems and replacing Council Framework Decision 2005/222/JHA, *OJ L 218, 14.8.2013, p. 8–14.*
4. Directive 2014/57/EU of the European Parliament and of the Council of 16 April 2014 on criminal sanctions for market abuse (market abuse directive), *OJ L 173, 12.6.2014, p. 179–189.*
5. Directive 2014/62/EU of the European Parliament and of the Council of 15 May 2014 on the protection of the euro and other currencies against counterfeiting by criminal law, and replacing Council Framework Decision 2000/383/JHA, *OJ L 151, 21.5.2014, p. 1–8.*
6. Directive (EU) 2017/541 of the European Parliament and of the Council of 15 March 2017 on combating terrorism and replacing Council Framework Decision 2002/475/JHA and amending Council Decision 2005/671/JHA, *OJ L 88, 31.3.2017, p. 6–21.*
7. Directive (EU) 2017/1371 of the European Parliament and of the Council of 5 July 2017 on the fight against fraud to the Union's financial interests by means of criminal law, *OJ L 198, 28.7.2017, p. 29–41.*
8. Directive (EU) 2018/1673 of the European Parliament and of the Council of 23 October 2018 on combating money laundering by criminal law, *OJ L 284, 12.11.2018, p. 22–30.*
9. Directive (EU) 2019/713 of the European Parliament and of the Council of 17 April 2019 on combating fraud and counterfeiting of non-cash means of payment and replacing Council Framework Decision 2001/413/JHA, *OJ L 123, 10.5.2019, p. 18–29.*

10. Proposal for a Directive of the European Parliament and of the Council on the protection of the environment through criminal law and replacing Directive 2008/99/EC, COM/2021/851 final.
11. Proposal for a Directive of the European Parliament and of the Council on combating violence against women and domestic violence, COM/2022/105 final.
12. Proposal for a Directive of the European Parliament and of the Council on the definition of criminal offences and penalties for the violation of Union restrictive measures, COM/2022/684 final.
13. Proposal for a Directive of the European Parliament and of the Council amending Directive 2011/36/EU on preventing and combating trafficking in human beings and protecting its victims, COM/2022/732 final.
14. Proposal for a Directive of the European Parliament and of the Council laying down minimum rules to prevent and counter the facilitation of unauthorised entry, transit and stay in the Union, and replacing Council Directive 2002/90/EC and Council Framework Decision 2002/946 JHA, COM/2023/755 final.

8

Violations of EU Sanctions and Criminal Penalties: Proportionality at Peril?*

LORENZO BERNARDINI AND FRANCESCA FINELLI

I. Introduction

Restrictive measures, also known as sanctions, are a prominent tool of Common Foreign and Security Policy (CFSP). Their effectiveness depends to a large extent on the implementation and enforcement mechanisms that are employed at the national level. Accordingly, the Union has called upon Member States to take all appropriate measures to ensure that sanctions are adhered to within their respective jurisdictions.[1] Traditionally, Member States have been entrusted with the task of designing 'effective, proportionate and dissuasive' penalties, whether administrative or criminal, applicable to infringements of restrictive measures.[2] The Union has never provided further guidance.

However, the war in Ukraine and the unprecedented need to address the phenomenon of evasion of sanctions has resulted in a paradigm shift. For the first time, the general obligation to provide for 'effective, proportionate and dissuasive' penalties has been perceived as insufficient, and the need for (harmonised) *criminal* penalties has emerged.[3]

* The authors have jointly developed the ideas that form the basis of this essay. The introduction and conclusions were written jointly. Lorenzo Bernardini wrote Section III (and its subsections); Francesca Finelli wrote Section II (and its subsections).

[1] Pursuant to the principle of sincere cooperation, as set out in Art 4(3) TEU, as well as Art 24(3) TFEU.

[2] According to the 'Greek Maize' formula, see Case C-68/88 Commission v Greece ECLI:EU:C:1989:339, para 24. See also General Secretariat of the Council, Guidelines on implementation and evaluation of restrictive measures (sanctions) in the framework of the EU Common Foreign and Security Policy (2018) doc. 5664/18.

[3] In the context of the 6th package of sanctions adopted in early June 2022, Regulations 833/2014 and 269/2014 departed, for the first time, from the standard wording, and explicitly invited Member States to lay down 'appropriate criminal penalties' applicable to infringement of those Regulations.

In this context, the Commission has put forward unprecedented proposals to redesign the national enforcement of EU restrictive measures.[4] On 25 May 2022, the Commission tabled down (i) a Council Decision for the introduction of a new 'Euro-crime', more precisely, for the addition of the violation of sanctions to the areas of crime laid down in Article 83(1) TFEU;[5] (ii) a Communication explaining the content of a successive Directive for the harmonisation of national criminal penalties in the field;[6] (iii) a Directive to reinforce rules on asset recovery and confiscation.[7]

While the proposed Directives (ii and iii) are still under negotiation, the Council Decision (i) has been adopted and we have recently witnessed the birth of a new 'Euro-crime' under Article 83(1) TFEU. In fact, on 28 November 2022, following the consent of the European Parliament,[8] the Council unanimously added the violation of restrictive measures to the list of Euro-crimes.[9] This step represents the main prerequisite for the Commission to present a final proposal for a Directive 'on the definition of criminal offences and penalties for the violation of Union restrictive measures', which it indeed did a few days later, on 2 December 2022.[10]

The introduction of a new Euro-crime and the legislative developments that have accompanied it represent the most important paradigm shift for a closer integration since the beginning of the Russia/Ukraine war. These recent developments will soon reform the enforcement of EU restrictive measures at the national level. In addition, it is worth noticing that the Union has successfully completed, for the first time, the procedure set forth in Article 83(1) TFEU, thereby supplementing the list of Euro-crimes initially provided by the Lisbon Treaty[11] and expanding its competences to address a new area of particularly serious crime with a cross-border dimension. Since then, CFSP and Area of Freedom, Security and Justice (AFSJ) are meant to become two intertwined areas of EU law – whereby the effective enforcement of CFSP Decisions relies on the effective application of AFSJ provisions.

[4] Press release of 25 May 2022, 'Ukraine: The Commission proposes rules on freezing and confiscating assets of oligarchs violating restrictive measures and of criminals'. On the Commission's role of 'leading promoter of closer European integration' see A Bradford, The Brussels Effect: How the European Union Rules the World, 1st edn (Oxford, Oxford University Press, 2020) 15.

[5] COM(2022) 247 final, Proposal for a Council Decision.

[6] COM(2022) 249 final, 'Towards a Directive on criminal penalties for the violation of Union restrictive measures'.

[7] COM(2022) 245 final, Proposal for a Directive of the European Parliament and of the Council.

[8] On 7 July 2022, the European Parliament gave its consent to the draft Council Decision on identifying the violation of EU sanctions as a new area of EU crime. See document P9_TA(2022)0295.

[9] See Council Decision (EU) 2022/2332 identifying the violation of Union restrictive measures as an area of crime that meets the criteria set out in Article 83(1) of the Treaty on the Functioning of the European Union [2022] OJ L308/18.

[10] COM(2022) 684 final. This draft Directive will be discussed and adopted by the Council and the European Parliament in accordance with ordinary legislative procedure.

[11] The areas of crime explicitly listed in the second paragraph of Art 83(1) TFEU are: terrorism, trafficking in human beings, sexual exploitation of children, drug trafficking, arms trafficking, corruption, money laundering, counterfeiting of means of payment, computer-related crime and organised crime.

The recourse to Article 83(1) TFEU and the consequent harmonisation of criminal offences and penalties for the violation of EU restrictive measures raises several (new) questions, including numerous concerns in relation to the principle of proportionality. This contribution intends to analyse two different declinations of the proportionality principle: one *prospective* (II) and one *retrospective* (III). The first concerns the relationship between means and ends: proportionality is deemed to be breached if the (criminal) means are excessively burdensome, intrusive or otherwise costly for achieving the objectives (i.e., countering the violations of restrictive measures). The latter concerns the relation between the criminalised conduct and the severity of the penalty. Here, proportionality is deemed to be breached if the penalty (for the violations of restrictive measures) is too severe or lenient.[12]

II. Prospective Proportionality under Article 83(1) TFEU

European institutions have moved rapidly towards the creation of a new Euro-crime under Article 83(1) TFEU. In little more than 6 months, the Commission proposal became Council Decision (EU) 2022/2332.

In the words of the Commission, 'the decision to add the violation of Union restrictive measures to the list of EU crimes in Article 83(1) TFEU would be proportionate in view of the fact that the criteria specified under Article 83(1) TFEU are met'.[13] It suggests that recourse to Article 83(1) TFEU is not subject to any specific proportionality test. In fact, proportionality between *means* (e.g., resorting to EU criminal law under Article 83(1) TFEU) and *ends* (e.g., combating Euro-crimes) is presumed without conducting any assessment. If the European Parliament and the Council agree on the need to add the violations of restrictive measures as a new area 'of particularly serious crime with a cross-border dimension',[14] the Commission argues that there is no reason (and no need) to evaluate the *prospective* proportionality of the EU intervention. However, this chapter will challenge such an approach, arguing that proportionality cannot be presumed but must always be demonstrated when recourse is made to EU criminal law.

For the purposes of this chapter, we propose to follow the 'ideal criminalisation' process proposed by Nina Peršak, according to which the legislative activity of the Union in the field of criminal law should resemble a funnel with three filters

[12] On the principles of *prospective* and *retrospective* proportionality see N Jareborg, 'Criminalization as Last Resort (Ultima Ratio)' (2005) 2 *Ohio State Journal of Criminal Law* 521, as well as the contributions of J Oberg, G Wycichowski-Kuchta, A Martufi and L Grossio to this book.

[13] COM(2022) 247 final, p. 11. See also COM(2022) 684 final, 9: the proposed Directive 'does not go beyond what is necessary to achieve its objective. The approximation of definitions of criminal offences and the types and levels of criminal penalties is limited to what is needed to effectively address the violation of Union restrictive measures in Member States'.

[14] Art 83(1) TFEU.

into which a legislative proposal is fed.[15] The first filter requires the EU legislator to identify a fundamental legal interest to be protected by criminal law; the second filter calls for the legislator to assess the use of criminal law in the light of the principle of *ultima ratio*; and the third filter asks the EU legislator to weigh the practical costs of criminalisation. If the proposed criminalisation passes through all three filters successfully, it can be deemed compliant with the principle of *prospective* proportionality.

A. Prospective Proportionality and the Identification of Fundamental Legal Interests

At the level of the first filter, the legislator should determine whether the criminalisation in question satisfies the harm principle, namely whether it is intended to counter wrongful and harmful conduct that infringes a fundamental legal interest, legal good or *Rechtsgut*. The harm principle requires that criminalisation powers should only be used to protect *fundamental* interests. In other words, criminal law should protect a limited number of interests, i.e. limited *Rechtsgüter*. If the harm principle is not satisfied (as the legislator does not identify fundamental interests to protect), recourse to criminal law will be completely disproportionate.

According to the Commission, the violation of EU restrictive measures constitutes:

> a particularly serious area of crime, which presents, in gravity, a similar seriousness to the areas of crime already listed in Article 83(1) TFEU, since it may perpetuate threats to international peace and security, undermine the consolidation and support for democracy, the rule of law and human rights and result in significant economic, social/societal and environmental damage.[16]

The identified *Rechtsgüter* are international peace and security, democracy, the rule of law and human rights. These legal interests are undoubtedly fundamental ones in the EU legal order, as enshrined in the Treaties,[17] but it is the first time that the legislator has identified the *Rechtsgüter* in such a broad manner. Safeguarding international peace and security and upholding the EU's values in its relations with the wider world have traditionally been objectives to be pursued under the framework of the CFSP,[18] rather than the AFSJ.[19] However, the proposed criminalisation of the violation of sanctions seems to intertwine the two areas of EU law and their objectives.

[15] N Peršak, 'Principles of EU Criminalisation and Their Varied Normative Strength: Harm and Effectiveness' (2022) 4 *European Law Journal* 463. See also N Peršak, *Criminalising Harmful Conduct* (New York, Springer, 2007).

[16] COM(2022) 247 final, p. 7.

[17] See Arts 2 and 3 TEU.

[18] Art 3(5) TEU. See also Art 21 TEU.

[19] The maintenance (and restoration) of international peace and security is usually addressed by the 'highly political' European Council or by Member States in the framework of other international fora, such as the United Nations. In addition, prosecuting 'the most serious crimes of concern to the international community' is the main competence of international (*ad hoc*) tribunals, as well as the International Criminal Court (see Art 5 of the Rome Statute).

The Union's intervention in extending the list of 'Euro-crimes' (pursuant to Article 83(1) TFEU) has so far responded to wrongful and harmful conduct that is considered to have an impact on individual victims and their communities on the one hand, and on (European) society as a whole on the other. Nonetheless, the identified *Rechtsgüter* in the criminalisation of the violation of sanctions appear to be directed only at the wider community, with no specific reference to the potential individual victims (as illustrated in Table 1 below). It is not clear therefore who exactly are the victims to be protected from the violation of sanctions that perpetuate threats to international peace and security.

Table 1 New Euro-crimes and the identification of fundamental legal interests

Proposed EU legislation (Legal basis: Art. 83(1) TFEU)	**Identified *Rechtsgüter***	**Individual victims**	**Society at large**
Proposal for a Directive on the definition of criminal offences and penalties for the violation of Union restrictive measures[20]	International peace and security, as well as the consolidation and support for democracy, the rule of law and human rights (beyond EU borders)	N/A	✓ The EU (and international) society
Proposal for a Council Decision on adding hate speech and hate crime to the areas of crime laid down in Art. 83(1) TFEU[21]	Human dignity, freedom, democracy, equality, rule of law and respect for human rights, including the rights of persons belonging to minorities, pluralism, non-discrimination, tolerance, justice, solidarity and equality between women and men	✓	✓
European Parliament resolution on adding gender-based violence to the areas of crime laid down in Art. 83(1) TFEU[22]	Equality between women and men, the right to equal treatment and non-discrimination, human dignity, the right to life, the right to physical and mental integrity, the prohibition of torture and inhuman or degrading treatment or punishment, the prohibition of slavery and forced labour, the right to liberty and security and the right to respect for private and family life	✓	✓

[20] COM(2022) 684 final.

[21] COM(2021) 777 final. Hate speech and hate crime affect both 'the individual victims and their communities, causing them sufferance and limiting their fundamental rights and freedoms, [and] society at large'.

[22] European Parliament Resolution of 16 September 2021 with recommendations to the Commission on identifying gender-based violence as a new area of crime listed in Art 83(1) TFEU, P9_TA(2021)0388.

Thus, in deciding to criminalise the violation of restrictive measures, the EU legislator has significantly broadened the interpretation of the harm principle, looking at the impact that the violation of sanctions has on the wider international (rather than EU) society, and ultimately identifying the need to protect Rechtsgüter beyond the territorial borders of the EU. This approach has stretched the interpretation of both the harm principle and the prospective proportionality of EU criminal law. In fact, the broader the interpretation of harm (and Rechtsgüter), the broader the possibility for recourse to be made to EU criminal law – without defining clear limits and proportionality tests.

B. Prospective Proportionality and Ultima Ratio

Moving on to the second filter of the 'ideal criminalisation' process, the legislator should consider whether other possible means, less coercive and intrusive than criminal means, could counter the wrongful and harmful conduct in question. In this second step, the legislator should assess the *prospective* proportionality of EU criminal law in light of the *ultima ratio* principle.[23]

The legislator should first assess 'the decision on whether to adopt criminal law measures *at all*' (emphasis added)[24] and evaluate whether non-criminal means are sufficient. In other words, the least burdensome, intrusive, or otherwise costly means should be used to achieve the given ends (i.e., countering the violations of restrictive measures) before resorting to EU criminal law. Only when non-criminal means have proven to be insufficient (or have been exhausted) can the legislator resort to criminal law. This principle ensures that criminalisation 'always remain[s] a measure of last resort'.[25]

When it appears necessary to adopt new criminal law provisions, the EU legislator should take into account 'the expected added value or effectiveness of criminal provisions *compared to other measures*' (emphasis added).[26] Nevertheless, in deciding to add the violation of restrictive measures to the list of Euro-crimes, the Commission regrettably does not explain why criminal law is the proportionate choice compared to other means of enforcement. On the

The Parliament recognizes that 'gender-based violence affects' not only individual victims, but 'all areas of society'.

[23] Jareborg (n 12). See also S Melander, 'Ultima Ratio in European Criminal Law' (2013) 1 *European Criminal Law Review* 45.

[24] Commission, Communication on 'Towards an EU Criminal Policy: Ensuring the Effective Implementation of EU Policies Through Criminal Law', COM(2011) 573 final, 7.

[25] ibid, 6. See also Council Conclusions on Model Provisions, Guiding the Council's Criminal Law Deliberations, 30 November 2009, 2; The Stockholm Programme – An Open and Secure Europe Serving and Protecting Citizens [2010] OJ C115/01, para 3.3.1; and European Parliament Resolution of 22 May 2012 on an EU Approach to Criminal Law (2010/2310(INI)), letter I.

[26] Conclusions on Model Provisions, Guiding the Council's Criminal Law Deliberations, 30 November 2009, 2.

contrary, the Commission invokes the exceptional need to resort to criminal law under a 'fast-track' procedure, as follows:

> Given the exceptional urgency, *no* impact assessment could be conducted, and the relevant obligation was lifted. The proposal to add the violation of restrictive measures to the areas of crime laid down in Article 83(1) TFEU does not have, in itself, any impact on national governments, regional or local authorities, economic operators or citizens.[27]

Impact assessments are probably the most important *ex ante* guarantee for the creation of evidence-based legislation[28] and evidence-based criminalisation. Both the Commission and the European Parliament have endorsed the need for 'clear factual' evidence to prove the 'necessity' of new criminal law provisions.[29] However, this fundamental requirement has been bypassed in view of the exceptional circumstances of the war in Ukraine, and the need (or presumed need) to resort to repressive criminal means to (most effectively) counter the violation of sanctions.

In the absence of an impact assessment, how can the EU legislator have an adequate understanding of the problem to be addressed (including its existence, size, scale, causes and consequences)? How can it determine whether criminalising the violation of sanctions satisfies the *ultima ratio* principle and *prospective* proportionality? The Commission highlighted (only) one main piece of evidence, pointing to the fact 'that insufficient priority is given to investigating and prosecuting the violation of the Union's restrictive measures in many Member States'.[30] In other words, EU intervention is deemed necessary and proportionate because of the inconsistent enforcement of restrictive measures at the national level.[31]

> [...] the different definitions of, and heterogeneous sanctions for, the violation of Union restrictive measures under Member States' administrative and/or criminal law represent an obstacle to the consistent application of the Union policy on restrictive measures. They may even lead to forum shopping by offenders and ultimately their impunity because they could choose to conduct their activities in the Member States that provide for less severe responses to the violation of Union restrictive measures. Harmonisation would also increase the deterrent effect of sanctions for the violation of Union restrictive measures.[32]

[27] COM(2022) 247 final, p 12.

[28] J Ouwerkerk, 'Evidence-Based Criminalisation in EU Law: Evidence of What Exactly?' in J Ouwerkerk, J Altena, J Öberg, S Miettinen (eds), *The Future of EU Criminal Justice Policy and Practice* (Leiden, Brill | Nijhoff, 2019). See also COM(2015) 215 final, 'Better Regulation for Better Results – An EU Agenda'.

[29] COM(2011) 573 final, 8; and European Parliament Resolution (2010/2310(INI)), para 3.

[30] COM(2022) 247 final, 3. See also the study conducted by Genocide Network Secretariat, 'Prosecution of Sanctions (Restrictive Measures) Violations in National Jurisdictions: A Comparative Analysis' (2021), www.eurojust.europa.eu/publication/expert-report-prosecution-sanctions-restrictive-measures-violations-national-jurisdictions.

[31] Inconsistent enforcement undermines the effectiveness of restrictive measures and, ultimately, the EU's ability to speak with one (credible) voice, see COM(2021) 32 final, 16.

[32] COM(2022) 247 final, 8. See also COM(2022) 684 final, 8.

Although supranational harmonisation is clearly a solution to address the inconsistent enforcement of EU restrictive measures at the national level, the Commission does not address the main question, that is, 'why EU criminal law?'

Prior to the unprecedented proposals presented, respectively, on 25 May 2022 and 2 December 2022, the majority of Member States had *not* opted for exclusive criminal enforcement to tackle the violation of sanctions in their domestic jurisdiction. Indeed, in 13 Member States, the violation of restrictive measures would amount to either an administrative or criminal offence,[33] while in two Member States[34] it would only result in administrative penalties. These 15 states chose not to rely solely on criminal enforcement, perhaps because they had taken the *ultima ratio* principle into account.

The EU intervention thus raises several concerns in terms of prospective proportionality. First, '[…] we do not have *any* evidence that a failure to criminalise the violation of sanctions in some Member States, or the existence of dual administrative and criminal regimes in others, is the reason for low levels of detection, prosecution and conviction for the offence'.[35] More generally, we lack clear data concerning investigations and punishment of the violation of sanctions. The expansion of EU criminal harmonisation in this area therefore appears difficult to reconcile with the *ultima ratio* principle, which requires the legislator to resort to criminal law only when alternative measures have *proved* insufficient to achieve the desired objectives.

Second, one may ask whether Article 83(1) TFEU requires a pre-existing consensus on the need to use criminal means of enforcement in all 27 Member States. In other words, we may ask whether Article 83(1) TFEU should only be invoked to endorse national criminal law. It has been argued that some crimes 'would simply not exist without the EU' (e.g., fraud against the EU budget, misappropriation of EU funds, corruption of EU officials) and that the Union therefore has a responsibility to protect the interests underlying such crimes.[36] In those scenarios, a lack of consensus among Member States does (and should) not prevent the EU from regulating a certain issue through criminal law means. However, the protection of international peace and security is not inherently European, and their violations do not constitute 'European core crimes'.[37] These legal goods exist even without the EU.

If the introduction of a new Euro-crime is not intended to uphold and confirm 'shared conceptions of wrongs amongst the Member States',[38] then Article 83(1)

[33] Belgium, Bulgaria, Czech Republic, Germany, Estonia, Ireland, Greece, Italy, Lithuania, Austria, Poland, Romania, Slovenia.

[34] Spain, Slovakia.

[35] See Report of the European Parliament on the proposed Directive (A9-0235/2023), Minority position (Ms. Clare Daly on behalf of The Left).

[36] P Caeiro, 'Beyond Competence Issues: Why and How Should the EU Legislate on Criminal Sanctions?' in R Kert, A Lehner (eds), *Vielfalt des Strafrechts im internationalen Kontext. Festschrift für Frank Höpfel zum 65. Geburtstag* (Wien, Neuer Wissenschaftlicher Verlag, 2018) 652.

[37] ibid.

[38] Except in cases where purely European legal goods are at stake.

TFEU would lose its 'ancillary' (or complementary) function.[39] This leads to the third and final question: to what extent can the Union intervene to pursue its own criminal law agenda, detached from national choices? Does Article 83(1) TFEU require a bottom-up approach (i.e., from Member States to the Union)[40] to the *ultima ratio* principle or does it allow for a top-down approach (i.e., from the Union to Member States) for combating serious crimes *'à l'européenne'*?[41]

In a 'fast-track' criminalisation, these questions (unfortunately) remain open. In the context of the war in Ukraine, it seems that exceptional geopolitical circumstances can lift any obligation to produce evidence-based criminal legislation, which risks leading to over-criminalisation (or 'precautionary criminalisation'),[42] contrary to the *ultima ratio* principle, as well as the prospective proportionality of EU criminal law.[43]

C. Prospective Proportionality and the Costs of Criminalisation

At the level of the third and final filter, the legislator should consider more pragmatic issues, inter alia the cost, time, utility, efficiency, and overall effectiveness,[44] of criminalisation. If and only if the benefits of criminalisation outweigh its costs, recourse to EU criminal law pursuant to Article 83(1) TFEU would be considered to be in line with the principle of *prospective* proportionality.

The criminalisation in question is intended to put an end to impunity for violations of restrictive measures, but the Commission does not provide clear factual evidence as to whether criminal means are more cost-effective if compared to other-than-criminal means. Regrettably, it remains unclear how (and why) EU criminal law will better combat impunity.

[39] S Coutts, 'Supranational Public Wrongs: The Limitations and Possibilities of a European Community', *Citizenship, Crime and Community in the European Union* (Oxford, Hart Publighing, 2021) 204.

[40] On 'translating' national legal interests into EU ones, see JW Ouwerkerk, 'Old Wine in a New Bottle: Shaping the Foundations of EU Criminal Law through the Concept of Legal Interests (Rechtsgüter)' (2021) 27 *European Law Journal* 426.

[41] F Meyer, D. Tsilikis, 'Criminal Law Enforcement of EU Law and the Impact of Europeanization' in M Scholten (ed), *Research Handbook on the Enforcement of EU Law* (Cheltenham, Edward Elgar Publishing 2023) 59.

[42] E Herlin-Karnell, 'The Development of EU Precautionary Criminalisation' (2011) 1 *European Criminal Law Review* 149. See also D Husak, *Overcriminalization: The Limits of the Criminal Law*, 1st edn (New York, Oxford University Press, 2007).

[43] 'The stronger the pull of external factors, the stronger the necessity to have proper safeguards in place and, in particular, the stronger the need to follow a tailor-made, evidence-based approach. […] New initiatives should [not] be purely symbolic […].' See N. Franssen and A. Weyembergh, 'From Facts and Political Objectives to Legal Bases and Legal Provisions: Incremental European Integration in the Criminal Law Field' (2021) 27 *European Law Journal* 368, 376.

[44] 'Effectiveness can appear different depending on the actor or part of the criminal justice system we look at.' See A Suominen, 'Effectiveness and Functionality of Substantive EU Criminal Law' (2014) 5 *New Journal of European Criminal Law* 388, 395.

On a general note, criminal enforcement entails strong procedural and substantive guarantees, including the rights to interpretation and translation, to information, to access to a lawyer, to legal aid and to the presumption of innocence. It may not therefore automatically guarantee a higher chance of detection, prosecution and punishment of (new) crimes, especially in relation to conduct that is difficult to prove, such as facilitating sanction evasion or failing to exercise due diligence in the processing of financial transactions. Accordingly, competent national authorities (e.g., supervisory bodies in the financial sector) may be able to react more swiftly (and more cost-efficiently) to sanction evasion by non-criminal means. Indeed, the burden of proof for the imposition of administrative sanctions would be lower and procedural safeguards for 'suspects' less demanding, making the investigative and sanctioning processes less burdensome and less costly.

D. 'Securitised' or 'Functionalised' Criminalisation under Article 83(1) TFEU?

Traditionally, it has been argued that Article 83 TFEU 'puts forward a dual model of criminalisation':[45] on the one hand, Article 83(1) TFEU reflects the securitised approach to criminalisation by defining the EU's competence to combat certain areas of crime, i.e., areas of particularly serious crime with a cross-border dimension; on the other hand, Article 83(2) TFEU regulates the functional criminalisation approach, which grants the Union with the competence to harmonise national criminal laws if such approximation 'proves essential to ensure the effective implementation of a Union policy in an area which has been subject to harmonisation measures'. On the basis of the essentiality requirement put forward in Article 83(2) TFEU, the academic discussion has dealt extensively with the limits of recourse to functional criminalisation.[46] This is also because the EU legislator has never succeeded in using Article 83(1) to introduce a new area of crime before 2022. However, the purpose of Section II was to show that Article 83(1) TFEU also deserves special attention to ensure compliance with the prospective proportionality principle and to avoid any attempt to instrumentalise EU criminal law.

Furthermore, Section II was intended to demonstrate that the recent introduction of a new Euro-crime for countering sanction violations – pursuant Article 83(1) TFEU – has blurred the traditional distinction between securitised and functionalised criminalisation. The resort to EU criminal law is deemed

[45] V Mitsilegas, 'Substantive Criminal Law: From Securitised to Functional Criminalisation', *EU Criminal Law* (Oxford, Hart Publishing, 2022).

[46] For instance, J Öberg, 'Do We Really Need Criminal Sanctions for the Enforcement of EU Law?' (2014) 5 *New Journal of European Criminal Law* 370; V Franssen, 'EU Criminal Law and Effet Utile: A Critical Examination of the Union's Use of Criminal Law to Achieve Effective Enforcement' in JB Banach-Gutierrez and C Harding (eds) *EU Criminal Law and Policy: Values, Principles, and Methods* (Oxon, Routledge, 2016).

functional 'to [first] ensure the effective implementation of the Union's policy on restrictive measures'.[47] We may therefore wonder whether the fast-track criminalisation of sanction violations is in fact perceived as a means to an end (the end being the effective implementation of EU sanctions), rather than reflecting a securitised approach to criminalisation.

III. Retrospective Proportionality and Criminal Penalties for Breaches of EU Restrictive Measures

Among the principles governing the application of criminal law, one of considerable importance is that of proportionality of criminal penalties, enshrined in Article 49(3) of the Charter of Fundamental Rights of the European Union ('the Charter'), which succinctly states: 'the severity of penalties must not be disproportionate to the criminal offence'. This principle, dubbed as *retrospective* proportionality, holds a central position in EU criminal law, particularly at (but not limited to)[48] the legislative level 'when prescriptive norms are designed and sanctions for their breach must be selected'.[49] It serves as the yardstick for our analysis in this section, the main focus of which will be an evaluation of whether the proposed criminal penalties contained in the Commission Proposal for a Directive (hereinafter: 'the Proposal')[50] for the violation of EU sanctions are in keeping with the aforementioned fundamental principle.

A. Retrospective and Retributivist Paradigm of Proportionality of Penalties

Article 49(3) of the Charter serves as the normative benchmark for the principle of proportionality of criminal penalties in EU criminal law, stipulating that the severity of penalties must not be disproportionate to the committed criminal offences.[51] Grounded in the common constitutional traditions of Member States,[52] this principle mandates a balance between the severity of penalties and the gravity

[47] COM(2022) 247 final, p. 7. See also the preamble of the proposed Directive on the definition of criminal offences and penalties for the violation of restrictive measures, COM(2022) 684 final.

[48] The principle of retrospective proportionality plays also a key-role in sentencing, that is, at the adjudication level. See, in this regard, E Herlin-Karnell, 'What Principles Drive (or Should Drive) European Criminal Law?' (2010) 10 *German Law Journal* 1126.

[49] I Wieczorek, *The Legitimacy of EU Criminal Law* (Oxford, Hart Publishing 2022) 65.

[50] COM(2022) 684 final. The Proposal also encompasses penalties against both natural and legal persons. However, this Chapter focuses on criminal penalties against *natural persons*.

[51] R Sicurella, M Panzavolta, 'Articolo 49' in S Allegrezza, R Mastroianni, F Pappalardo, O Pollicino, O Razzolini (eds), *Carta dei diritti fondamentali dell'Unione europea* (Milano, Giuffrè, 2017).

[52] Explanations relating to the Charter of Fundamental Rights [2007] OJ C 303/17.

of the offence.[53] The EU and domestic authorities are thus tasked with identifying the most appropriate penalty in alignment with the criminal conduct at stake.[54]

The CJEU has repeatedly underscored the importance of aligning penalty severity with the seriousness of infringements, emphasising the need for a genuinely deterrent effect without surpassing what is necessary to achieve this objective.[55] As highlighted by the Luxembourg Court, the principle of proportionality requires consideration of individual circumstances in determining penalties.[56] This perspective reveals two inherent features of the principle, which are entrenched in 'proportionalism' theories.[57]

Firstly, Article 49(3) embraces a *retrospective* conception of proportionality, seeking to administer justice for 'a crime already committed'.[58] The severity of the current State's response should mirror the degree of culpability of past criminal behaviour, with the penalty calibrated according to the measure of the offence.[59] This relative notion of proportionality is discernible in connection with the offender's behaviour.

Secondly, Article 49(3) aligns with *retributivist* theories, asserting that individuals should receive punishment commensurate with their 'just' or 'commensurate' deserts.[60] This approach emphasises proportionality as a form of "fittingness", where the offence should be 'reflected' in the penalty.[61] This implies that, while identical crimes deserve identical punishments, different crimes warrant distinct punishments based on varying degrees of culpability.[62]

In this context, concerns may arise about a possible violation of Article 49(3) of the Charter if the penalties are too severe or too lenient in relation to the gravity of the offence. This concern is particularly pronounced in cases of overtly disproportionate penalties.[63] However, the absence of a clear method for determining the appropriate magnitude of punishment reflects the traditional challenge in depicting an absolute degree of 'commensurability' between penalties and offences. To fix this issue, legal scholars have traditionally relied on the notions of 'ordinal' and

[53] T Lock, 'Article 49 CFR' in M Kellerbauer, M Klamert and J Tomkin (eds), *The EU Treaties and the Charter of Fundamental Rights: A Commentary* (Oxford, Oxford University Press, 2019) 2234.

[54] V Mitsilegas, E. Billis, 'Article 49', in S Peers, T Hervey, J Kenner, A Ward (eds), *The EU Charter of Fundamental Rights – A Commentary*, 2nd ed. (Oxford, Hart Publishing, 2021).

[55] See, to that effect, Case C-231/20 *MT v Landespolizeidirektion Steiermark* ECLI:EU:C:2021:845, para 45 and further case law cited therein, and Case C-77/20 *KM* ECLI:EU:C:2021:112, paras 37–38.

[56] See, among others, Case C-384/17 *Link Logistik N&N* ECLI:EU:C:2018:810, para 45.

[57] G Duus-Otterström, 'Do Offenders Deserve Proportionate Punishments?', (2021) 3 *Criminal Law and Philosophy* 463.

[58] C New, 'Time and Punishment' (2005) 1 *Ohio State Law Journal* 283.

[59] Jareborg (n 12).

[60] A von Hirsch, 'Proportionate Sentences: A Desert Perspective' in M Tonry (ed), *Why Punish? How Much? A Reader on Punishment* (Oxford, Oxford University Press, 2011), 210 ff., and Y Lee, 'Why Proportionality Matters' (2012) 6 *University of Pennsylvania Law Review* 1835.

[61] V Tadros, *The Ends of Harm: The Moral Foundations of Criminal Law* (Oxford, Oxford University Press 2011) 332–333.

[62] K Greenawalt, 'Punishment' (1983) 2 *The Journal of Criminal Law and Criminology* 347, 347–348.

[63] e.g., imposing the death penalty for acts of defamation.

'cardinal' retrospective proportionality. As famously clarified by von Hirsch, the former necessitates a relative perspective, stipulating that offences of comparable gravity should incur penalties of comparable severity; thus, more serious transgressions should result in more severe punishments than less severe transgressions. Conversely, the latter entails an absolute approach, requiring the establishment of a penalty hierarchy that categorises crimes based on their inherent seriousness. This would facilitate the State's evaluation of the manner in which the punishment, considered in a non-relative context, aligns with a specific offence (e.g., a nine-year sentence for theft is absolutely disproportionate, even if ordinal proportionality is maintained).[64]

It is therefore essential to distinguish between petty and serious offences and to justify such distinctions. In other words, it is important not only to tailor penalties to the specific (illegal) behaviour in question, but also to clarify *some criteria* for distinguishing between petty and serious offences.[65]

Against this background, the main concern over disproportionate penalties leading to over-punishment is significant from different standpoints. It is worth noting, inter alia, that they impose an unnecessary sacrifice of individual goods, i.e. personal freedom, private and family life, reputation, etc. What is more, disregarding the principle of proportionality in sentencing could also undermine the perceived fairness and equity of the entire criminal justice system.[66]

To sum up, in line with Article 49(3) of the Charter, both national and EU authorities are responsible for determining the most appropriate punishment for a given offence. The broad concept of this benchmark requires that the relationship between the severity of the penalty and the seriousness of the behaviour to be punished be established[67] As the EU's criminalisation policy is grounded in the assumption that offenders should be punished to the extent they deserve – requiring careful definition of behaviours to be penalised through criminal sanctions – it will be crucial, throughout the 'offence construction phase',[68] to identify the main features of the behaviour at stake, the corresponding criminal sanction, and strike a balance between these factors. Retrospective proportionality takes centre stage in this process.

[64] A von Hirsch, 'Proportionality in the Philosophy of Punishment: From "Why Punish?" to "How Much?"' (1990) 16 *Criminal Law Forum* 282–290.

[65] On the differences between the EU and national approaches to retrospective proportionality, see, inter alia, C Sotis, 'Les principes de nécessité et de proportionalité', in G Giudicelli-Delage, C Lazerges (eds), *Le droit pénal de l'Union Européenne au lendemain du Traité de Lisbonne* (Paris, Société de Législation Comparée, 2012) 71–74. Indeed, the EU can establish criminal offences and set proportionate penalties. However, it should also leave some room for manoeuvre to Member States to adapt said offences and penalties at the national level, according to *their* domestic idea of retrospective proportionality.

[66] A von Hirsch, 'Proportionality in the Philosophy of Punishment' (1992) 16 *Crime & Justice* 68.

[67] A Duff, 'Proportionality and the Criminal Law: Proportionality of What to What?' in E Billis, N Knust, J Petter Rui (eds), *Proportionality in Crime Control and Criminal Justice* (Oxford, Hart Publishing, 2021) 35.

[68] SS Buisman, 'The Future of EU Substantive Criminal Law. Towards a Uniform Set of Criminalisation Principles at the EU level' (2022) 2 *European Journal of Crime, Criminal Law and Criminal Justice* 161.

IV. Petty or Serious Offences? The 'Vertical' Distinction

The Proposal delineates two distinct categories of offences related to the breach of EU sanctions – 'minor' and 'serious' offences. This categorisation is grounded on the fact that, as will be explained, lighter penalties are designated for the former, while more severe penalties are prescribed for the latter category. The construction of criminal offences in adherence to the ordinal facet of the principle of proportionality raises the question of why certain offenses warrant more lenient treatment than others.[69] Obviously, if this reasoning is not clarified, there is a risk that penalties will be imposed that are not commensurate with the seriousness of the offence.

The Proposal primarily addresses violations of restrictive measures, encompassing both direct infringements and actions aimed at circumventing those measures.[70] The comprehensive nature of this catalogue reflects a commitment to criminalise all potential breaches of sanctions through criminal penalties. Given its accuracy in listing all these behaviours, it can contribute to clarity as to what is prohibited under EU law.

The various types of conduct referred to in Article 3 are subject to a maximum penalty involving imprisonment, with varying severity. Indeed, a 'vertical distinction' is established between two categories of criminal offences, each with its own set of punishments, reflecting the 'seriousness' of the illicit behaviour.[71]

The first group comprises acts of circumvention listed in Article 3(2), points (h)(iii), (iv) and (v) (characterised by 'failing' to comply with certain obligations under EU sanctions law), which are punishable by a minimum-maximum imprisonment penalty of at least one year, provided they involve funds or economic resources valued at least EUR 100,000. The second group includes various both breaches and circumvention of EU sanctions, punishable by a minimum-maximum penalty of at least five years of imprisonment if they involve funds or economic resources of a value of at least EUR 100,000. The following table provides an overview.

Table 2 The 'vertical' distinction

	Minor offences	**Serious offences**
Threshold	Art 3(2), points (h)(iii), (iv) and (v)	Art 3(2), points (a)–(g), (h)(i)–(ii) and (i)
< EUR 100,000	Imprisonment	
> EUR 100,000	Max > at least 1 year	Max > at least 5 years

[69] See, in this regard, D Pulitanò, 'Proporzione' in C Piergallini, G Mannozzi, C Sotis, C Perini, M Scoletta, F Consulich (eds), *Studi in onore di Carlo Enrico Paliero* (Milano, Giuffrè, 2022) 1757–1766 and, more broadly, F Viganò, *La proporzionalità della pena* (Torino, Giappichelli, 2021) 160 ff.

[70] See Art 3 of the Proposal (see n 3 above). On this blurred distinction, with a specific focus on circumventing conducts, see the comprehensive analysis provided by F Finelli, 'Countering circumvention of restrictive measures: The EU response' (2023) 60 *CML Rev* 733.

[71] Explanatory Memorandum to the Proposal (see n 3 above), 13.

The Explanatory Memorandum's failure to clarify the rationale behind the 'vertical' distinction raises an issue – the absence of precise explanations or supporting evidence, such as references to Member State provisions or best practices, or other EU instruments, diminishes the guidance provided in this regard.[72] In addition, the wide range of behaviours categorised under a single group of 'violations of restrictive measures' may highlight the need for more detailed grounds to justify said vertical distinction, which are not provided by a mere reference to the seriousness of the offences in question.

Moreover, the absence of an impact assessment in drafting the Proposal, driven by unprecedented geopolitical circumstances, raises concerns (in addition to those outlined in Section II.B above).[73] Achieving a balance between offences and their penalties, as required by Article 49(3) of the Charter, becomes difficult without an evidence-based rationale for distinguishing between minor and serious offences.[74] This may be illustrated by the fact that, for example, the failure to provide information to the competent national authorities on assets that have not been properly frozen is punished less severely than the failure to freeze assets belonging to or owned, held or controlled by a designated person without undue delay (or the concealment of such assets), even though the former conduct may result in the loss of traceability of the assets to be frozen.[75]

The proposed division may also be vulnerable on another front, as the same monetary threshold triggering imprisonment, i.e., the involvement of 'funds or economic resources of a value of at least EUR 100 000' – that is, in simple terms, the same 'damage' as in the material case – applies to both groups of offences. Nevertheless, two sets of imprisonment penalties have been laid down, i.e., either one or five years of imprisonment. It may therefore appear disproportionate, in retrospect, to establish different groups of offences (and consequently different penalties) without a valid justification for this choice.

Finally, an identical punishment is provided for certain circumvention offences and serious direct violation offences, which again raises the question of why both behaviours merit the same penalty.[76] This lack of distinction may warrant further consideration and clarification in the legislative process.

V. Meeting the Monetary threshold: The 'Horizontal' Distinction

The criminal offences and associated penalties outlined in the Proposal are not determined solely by the 'vertical' distinction between minor and serious conduct.

[72] ibid.

[73] See, in this vein, the Opinion of the European Economic and Social Committee (EESC) on the Proposal (Rapp. Moreno Dìaz), SOC/739, 15 March 2023, para 4.2.

[74] On the importance of impact assessment during the criminalization process, see Sotis (n 65) 66–71.

[75] Compare Art 3(2)(h)(iv) of the Proposal (see n 3 above) with Art 3(2)(b) and 3(2)(h)(i) thereof.

[76] Compare, eg, Art 3(2)(a) and (g) of the Proposal (see n 3 above).

Within each category, an additional factor should be taken into account, namely the monetary threshold of EUR 100 000.This threshold, which relates to the funds or economic resources involved in the criminal conduct, acts as a 'horizontal' distinction. If this threshold is reached, Member States are obliged to establish a minimum-maximum penalty of either one or five years of imprisonment, depending on the offence. In other words, the monetary threshold or EUR 100 000 acts as a factor that, *irrespective of the conducts at stake*, triggers Member States' obligations to establish minimum-maximum penalties. The table below illustrates the situation envisaged by the Proposal.

Table 3 The 'horizontal' distinction

Threshold	Minor offences	Serious offences
	Article 3(2), points (h)(iii), (iv) and (v)	Article 3(2), points (a)–(g), (h)(i)–(ii) and (i)
< EUR 100,000	Imprisonment	
> EUR 100,000	Max > at least 1 year	Max > at least 5 years

A crucial question thus arises: why has the EUR 100,000 threshold been considered appropriate to trigger Member States' obligations to establish specific minimum-maximum penalties? Understanding the rationale behind the Commission's approach is crucial in assessing whether the criminal sanctions align with the principle of retrospective proportionality. Regrettably, the Proposal provides no guidance in this regard. The Explanatory Memorandum's sole reference states that the EUR 100,000 threshold distinguishes more serious offences deserving a maximum imprisonment term of at least five years, which is what happens with 'serious' offences.[77] Not only is this statement unsupported, but it also overlooks the application of the same threshold to 'minor' offences.

Although the Proposal lacks a justification in this area,[78] it is noteworthy that the same threshold has already appeared in another EU criminal law instrument – the so-called 'PIF Directive'.[79] In dealing with criminal penalties against natural persons for breaches of EU restrictive measures, the Commission explicitly refers to Article 7 of the latter Directive, where this specific monetary benchmark is explicitly employed.[80] That reference may imply that the incorporation of such a benchmark in the Proposal is grounded in the pre-existing presence of the same in the PIF Directive. Since the monetary benchmark of EUR 100,00 is not a 'novelty'

[77] Explanatory Memorandum to the Proposal (see n 24 above), 13.

[78] One could therefore wonder whether, for instance, thresholds of EUR 50,000 or 150,000 might have been more appropriate. This is an issue linked to a cardinal proportionality assessment.

[79] Directive (EU) 2017/1371 of the European Parliament and of the Council on the fight against fraud to the Union's financial interests by means of criminal law [2017] O.J. L198/29 (hereinafter: 'PIF Directive').

[80] COM(2022) 249 final, 3, fn 9.

in EU criminal law, its utilisation could enhance consistency across various EU criminal law instruments.

Specifically, an analysis of Article 7 of the PIF Directive will confirm that it serves as a blueprint for the current Proposal as it imposes a minimum-maximum penalty of at least four years of imprisonment if the damage or advantage resulting from the criminal offence in question (e.g., fraud affecting the Union's financial interests) exceeds EUR 100,000.[81] Notably, throughout the drafting of the PIF Directive, the Commission maintained that the foreseen penalties were 'proportionate with the seriousness of the offences and [were] in line with the sanctions currently provided in the majority of Member States',[82] and, additionally, that the minimum sanction types and levels were 'in line with best practices in Member States [and] consistent with other EU instruments and the seriousness of each of the offences'.[83]

Two issues emerge from this context. Firstly, adopting the same monetary threshold as the PIF Directive may not be the most appropriate choice for addressing breaches of EU restrictive measures, which also encompass non-economic offences, such astravel ban violations.[84] Secondly, the threshold originated from a distinct EU legal instrument (i.e., the PIF Directive) and was justified within a different context, that is, combating fraud and protecting the EU's financial interests. Adopting such a monetary benchmark for the current Proposal without clear justification raises concerns as to whether the relevant minimum-maximum penalties remain commensurate with the severity of the respective criminal offences, provided they meet the same limit.

VI. Multiple Types of Conduct: The 'Cumulative Effect'

Another issue linked to the EUR 100,000 monetary threshold in the Proposal warrants further analysis. Specifically, 5(3) of the Proposal allows the threshold to be also met 'through a series of linked offences' committed by the same offender.[85] This pertains to situations in which multiple violations of EU restrictive measures are committed. For the threshold to be met, these related offences must fall into the same category: they are either all minor offences or they are all serious offences.[86] The 'cumulative effect' is triggered when the funds or economic resources involved in the multiple criminal behaviours amount to at least EUR 100,000, thus leading to the imposition, as already explained, of a minimum-maximum penalty of

[81] Article 7(3), first and second subparagraphs, PIF Directive.
[82] COM(2012) 363 final, Explanatory Memorandum, 10.
[83] SWD(2012) 195 final, 34, where a specific reference to the "minimum thresholds set in anti-money laundering legislation" can be found.
[84] See Art 3(2)(c).
[85] Art5(3) *in fine* and 5(4) *in fine* of the Proposal (see n 3 above).
[86] ibid.

one or five years of imprisonment, depending on the seriousness of the offence in question. However, this approach raises concerns regarding the principle of retrospective proportionality of penalties. In fact, the Proposal seemingly compels Member States to apply an identical minimum-maximum penalty across highly dissimilar scenarios.[87]

Consider, for example, two situations: first, ten bank transfers of EUR 10,000 made by the same individual, each intended to conceal a total of EUR 100,000 owned, held or controlled by a single designated person who should have been frozen;[88] and second, an individual who provides false information to the authorities in order to conceal that a designated person is the ultimate beneficiary of a certain amount of funds,[89] making funds available to another designated person[90] and executing a bank transfer in favour of a third designated individual,[91] totalling EUR 100,000 and involving three distinct blacklisted persons. In the former case, ten identical operations were undertaken for the benefit of a single blacklisted person, while in the latter case only three operations were carried out but involved three distinct designated individuals.

The Proposal envisages the same minimum-maximum penalty for both situations, emphasising the importance of the total amount of money involved and minimising the manifestation of different behaviours. This implies an equal degree of blameworthiness, according to the EU legislator's viewpoint, despite fundamentally different behaviours exhibited in the two scenarios. Advocating the application of the same sanction in both cases implies that the means, modalities or number of illegal acts are irrelevant. What is more, the number of blacklisted individuals involved in the illicit behaviour seems irrelevant in this context. This perspective, where the monetary threshold acts de facto as an absolute benchmark, potentially conflicts with retrospective proportionality, as the latter mandates a case-specific assessment of the conduct to determine the most appropriate penalty in the material case.

VII. Conclusions

The (rapid) criminalisation of sanction violations under Article 83(1) TFEU leaves us with more open questions than ever.[92] On the one hand, the EU Treaties proclaim that 'the Union's aim is to promote peace'.[93] On the other hand, it is

[87] Here, considerations of *ordinal* proportionality may arise.
[88] Art 3(2)(h)(i) of the Proposal (see n 3 above).
[89] Art 3(2)(h)(ii) of the Proposal (see n 3 above).
[90] Art 3(2)(a) of the Proposal (see n 3 above).
[91] Art 3(2)(h)(i) of the Proposal (see n 3 above).
[92] S Allegrezza, 'La rose des vents de la politique pénale européenne: Hommage à Mireille Delmas-Marty' (2023) *Archives de politique criminelle* 197, 207.
[93] Art 3(1) TFEU.

unclear whether EU criminal law should pursue the same goal and be used to counter threats to international peace and security. For instance, one might wonder whether international crimes, such as the crime of aggression, could also be added to the list of EU crimes in the future.[94]

Along with the need to ensure the effective implementation of restrictive measures throughout the Union, it is equally important to ensure that there are no legitimate grounds for questioning the lawfulness (and proportionality) of the proposed criminal penalties. The introduction of disproportionate penalties not only contravenes a fundamental principle of criminal law but could also undermine the legitimacy of the EU in regulating this sensitive area. Building on what Advocate General Maduro said in his 2008 Opinion in the landmark *Kadi* case, it is the Union's responsibility 'to ensure that the political necessities of today do not become the legal realities of tomorrow'.[95] Accordingly, it is the Union's responsibility to take into due consideration the principle of proportionality (both prospectively and retrospectively), notwithstanding the unprecedented geopolitical circumstances that undoubtedly require an effective response.

[94] See A Rosas, 'From Freezing to Confiscating Russian Assets?' (2023) 48 *European Law Review* 337, 345.

[95] Opinion of AG Poiares Maduro in Case C-402/05 P *Kadi v Council and Commission* ECLI:EU:C:2008:11, para 45.

9

Broadly Unknown, but Deservedly Unloved?

*Turnover-based Fines and their Transplant from Competition Law to EU Criminal Law**

PEDRO CAEIRO

'For most European criminal lawyers, special criminal law and punitive administrative law remain unknown and unloved.'

John A. E. Vervaele (Valedictory Lecture, 2023)

I. The Sanctions Applicable to Legal Persons under EU Criminal Law: On the Verge of Changing the Model?

The various framework decisions and directives enacted to approximate the criminal laws of Member States usually include provisions regarding the liability of legal entities for criminal offences and the corresponding penalties.[1] The first

* This paper is dedicated to Professor John A. E. Vervaele – scholar and friend – whom I was unable to honour on the appropriate occasion.

I consulted an unusually large number of colleagues – experts in various legal branches – for comments and suggestions on draft versions of this manuscript. Their feedback prevented me from making more and worse mistakes and helped me better shape my ideas. I am therefore thankful to Adán Nieto Martin, Carolina Cunha, Filipe Cassiano dos Santos, Miguel França, Patricia Faraldo Cabana, Pedro Maia and, especially, Stefano Montaldo. Any remaining mistakes or unclarities are my sole responsibility.

Part of the manuscript was crafted during a research stay at the IISL – International Institute for the Sociology of Law in late spring 2023. I wish to thank them, including their awesome staff, for hosting me and providing access to their resources, amidst the inspiring atmosphere of Oñati.

[1] For the theoretical foundations and legal-political meaning of the EU's competence to legislate on criminal *penalties*, see P Caeiro, 'Beyond Competence Issues: Why and How Should the EU Legislate on Criminal Sanctions?' in R Kert and A Lehner (Hrsg.), *Vielfalt des Strafrechts im internationalen Kontext. Festschrift für Frank Höpfel zum 65. Geburtstag* (Wien, Neuer Wissenschaftlicher Verlag, 2018) 645–665; and the collective work of the European Criminal Policy Initiative in H Satzger (Hrsg.),

instrument of secondary law that aimed at such a goal was Framework Decision of 29 May 2000 on counterfeiting in connection with the introduction of the euro,[2] enacted under the Amsterdam Treaty, which established 'minimum rules' concerning the sanctions applicable to legal persons 'held liable' for the criminal offences outlined therein.[3] Article 9 required Member States to ensure that legal entities faced 'effective, proportionate and dissuasive sanctions, which shall include criminal or non-criminal fines and may include other sanctions', exemplified in the same provision.[4]

This model, which leaves the method for determining fines broadly to the discretion of Member States, was adopted with slight variations by the framework decisions and directives on the approximation of criminal law that followed,[5] including the most recently enacted Directive.[6] The sole exception was Framework Decision 2005/667/JHA of 12 July 2005 on ship-source pollution:[7] on the one hand, Article 6(1)(a) provided for mandatory quantitative (minimum maximum) thresholds for the financial sanctions applicable to legal entities; on the other hand, Article 6(3) *allowed* Member States to:

> implement paragraph 1(a) by applying a system, whereby the fine is proportionate to the turnover of the legal person, to the financial advantage achieved or envisaged by the commission of the offence, or to any other value indicating the financial situation of the legal person, provided that such system allows for maximum fines, which are at least equivalent to the minimum for the maximum fines established in paragraph 1(a).

However, the Framework decision was annulled by the Court of Justice[8] and the Directive that replaced it – possibly drawing on the Court's considerations in that

Harmonisierung strafrechtlicher Sanktionen in der Europäischen Union, Harmonisation of Criminal Sanctions in the European Union (Baden-Baden, Nomos Vlg., 2020).

[2] Council Framework Decision 2000/383/JHA on increasing protection by criminal penalties and other sanctions against counterfeiting in connection with the introduction of the euro [2000] OJ L140/1.

[3] It is not entirely accurate to use the expression 'criminal sanctions applicable to legal persons', since the sanctions can have a 'non-criminal' nature, in order to accommodate domestic legal orders that do not provide for the criminal liability of legal entities: see P Faraldo Cabana, 'Acerca de la idoneidad de la sanción pecuniaria para personas jurídicas. Una reflexión de Derecho español con apuntes de Derecho italiano' in *Economía y Derecho penal en Europa: una comparación entre las experiencias italiana y española. Actas del Congreso hispano-italiano de Derecho penal económico (Università degli Studi di Milano, Milano, 29-30 de mayo de 2014)* (A Coruña, Universidade da Coruña, 2015) 253–254; see also n 70.

[4] eg, exclusion from entitlement to public benefits or aid, temporary or permanent disqualification from the practice of commercial activities, placement under judicial supervision, or judicial winding-up order.

[5] See A Klip, *European Criminal Law: An Integrative Approach* 4th edn (Cambridge, Intersentia, 2021) 426 et seq; and F Mazzacuva, *Le Pene Nascoste. Topografia delle Sanzione Punitive e Modulazione dello Statuto Garantistico* (Torino, Giapicchellli, 2017) 98, fn 77.

[6] cf Article 11 of Directive (EU) 2019/713 of the European Parliament and of the Council on combating fraud and counterfeiting of non-cash means of payment and replacing Council Framework Decision 2001/413/JHA [2019] OJ L 123/18.

[7] Council Framework Decision 2005/667/JHA to strengthen the criminal-law framework for the enforcement of the law against ship-source pollution [2005] OJ L 255/164.

[8] Case C-440/05 *Commission v Council* ECLI:EU:C:2007:625.

judgment[9] – restored the previous model and provided that legal persons should be punishable by 'effective, proportionate and dissuasive penalties'.[10]

In fact, turnover-based sanctions are well-known to EU and domestic *administrative* or *non-criminal* punitive law:[11] they were adopted for the first time in competition law,[12] from where they expanded to other fields.[13] But, so far, no EU instrument has *compelled* Member States to implement turnover-based *criminal* fines. Even the annulled Framework decision on ship pollution left the implementation of such a method (which was mentioned in vague terms, as a reference among others that may ensure proportionate punishment) to the discretion of the Member States. From then on, the EU legislator seemed keen to keep turnover-based sanctions outside criminal law, as the regime of market abuse exuberantly shows. While Article 30(2)(j) of the Market Abuse Regulation[14] provides for administrative turnover-based fines, Article 9 of the Market Abuse Directive[15] resorts to the traditional formula, by directing Member States to adopt a criminal law entailing 'effective, proportionate and dissuasive sanctions, which shall include criminal or non-criminal fines', which should apply, as per the legislator's explicit instruction, to the 'most serious' infringements.[16]

Nevertheless, the recent proposals of the European Commission for directives on the approximation of criminal law establish that the maximum limit of financial penalties applicable to legal entities for selected offences should not be less than a *certain percentage of the total worldwide turnover of the legal person in the*

[9] ibid, para 70: 'the determination of the type and level of the criminal penalties to be applied does not fall within the Community's sphere of competence'.

[10] Article 8c of Directive 2005/35/EC of the European Parliament and of the Council on ship-source pollution and on the introduction of penalties for infringements [2005] OJ L255/11, as amended by Directive 2009/123/EC of the European Parliament and of the Council amending Directive 2005/35/EC on ship-source pollution and on the introduction of penalties for infringements [2009] OJ L280/52.

[11] For the purposes of this paper, administrative sanctions are understood in a broad sense, encompassing all public law sanctions that do not formally fall under criminal law. This definition does not imply that every non-criminal law sanction should be labelled as 'administrative' by the EU legislator: cf M Kärner, 'Interplay between European Union criminal law and administrative sanctions: Constituent elements of transposing punitive administrative sanctions into national law', (2022) 13 *New Journal of European Criminal Law* 49, *passim*.

[12] cf Articles 65(5) and 66(6) of the Treaty establishing the European Coal and Steel Community (1952); see also below, Section II.

[13] cf, eg, Articles 66(2)(c) and 67(2)(e) of Directive 2013/36/EU of the European Parliament and of the Council on access to the activity of credit institutions and the prudential supervision of credit institutions and investment firms, amending Directive 2002/87/EC and repealing Directives 2006/48/EC and 2006/49/EC [2013] OJ L176/338; Article 83(4)(5)(6) of Regulation (EU) 2016/679 of the European Parliament and of the Council on the protection of natural persons with regard to the processing of personal data and on the free movement of such data, and repealing Directive 95/46/EC (General Data Protection Regulation) [2016] OJ L119/1; see also Kärner (n 11) 48.

[14] Regulation (EU) No 596/2014 of the European Parliament and of the Council of 16 April 2014 on market abuse (market abuse regulation) and repealing Directive 2003/6/EC of the European Parliament and of the Council and Commission Directives 2003/124/EC, 2003/125/EC and 2004/72/EC [2014] OJ L173/1.

[15] Directive 2014/57/EU of the European Parliament and of the Council on criminal sanctions for market abuse (market abuse directive) [2014] OJ L 173/179.

[16] For a critical assessment of the combination of administrative and criminal sanctions in the field of market abuse, see V Mitsilegas, *EU Criminal Law*, 2nd edn (Oxford, Hart Publishing, 2022) 120–121, and Kärner (n 11) 54–55.

business year preceding the fining decision.[17] This suggests that the EU – or, at least, the Commission – intends to introduce, as a pattern, a 'new' method for sanctioning legal entities in the realm of criminal law, which Mongillo calls 'the new frontier of financial sanctions applicable to legal entities'.[18]

This chapter assesses whether such an approach is sound and constitutes a viable blueprint for designing an innovative criminal sanctions system for legal entities. Section II briefly describes turnover-based sanctions in competition law, their justification, and their evolution over time. In Section III, turnover-based fines are scrutinised through the lenses of legality, proportionality, and adequacy to the pursued goals, as well as compatibility with the 'minimum rules' clause contained in Article 83 of the TFEU, or at least with the coherence principle. Section IV acknowledges the overall positive amendments recently introduced by the Council in both the *PDirEnv* and the *PDirVRM*, thereby linking the discussion to the issues raised in Section III and sketches out a model that might better reconcile the several conflicting interests. Finally, Section V gathers some concluding reflections.

II. The Origins of the 'New' Financial Sanctions: Competition Law and Its Evolution

A. Justification of Turnover-Based Sanctions

Turnover-based sanctions are notorious features of administrative EU competition law.[19] Prior to the entry into force of Article 15(1) of Directive ECN+,[20] their implementation in domestic law was not required by EU law,[21] but many Member States have voluntarily replicated it in their competition laws.

[17] See Article 7(4)(5) of the Proposal for a Directive of the European Parliament and of the Council on the protection of the environment through criminal law and replacing Directive 2008/99/EC, COM(2021) 851 final (*PDirEnv*); Article 7(2)(3)) of the Proposal for a Directive on the violation of EU restrictive measures, COM(2022) 684 final (*PDirVRM*; incidentally, there is a typo in all three paragraphs of Article 7: the mention to 'article 7' intends to refer to 'article 6'); Article 17(2)(a) of the Proposal for a Directive of the European Parliament and of the Council on combating corruption, replacing Council Framework Decision 2003/568/JHA and the Convention on the fight against corruption involving officials of the European Communities or officials of Member States of the European Union and amending Directive (EU) 2017/1371 of the European Parliament and of the Council, COM(2023) 234 final.

[18] V Mongillo, 'Il sistema delle sanzioni applicabili all'ente collettivo tra prevenzione e riparazione. Prospettive de iure condendo', (2022) 3 *Rivista trimestrale di diritto penale economico* 582.

[19] cf Article 23(1)(2) of Council Regulation (EC) No 1/2003 on the implementation of the rules on competition laid down in Articles 81 and 82 of the Treaty [2003] OJ L1/1, and Article 14(1)(2) of Council Regulation (EC) No 139/2004 on the control of concentrations between undertakings (the EC Merger Regulation) [2004] OJ L 24/1.

[20] Directive (EU) 2019/1 of the European Parliament and of the Council to empower the competition authorities of the Member States to be more effective enforcers and to ensure the proper functioning of the internal market [2019] OJ L11/3 [Directive ECN+].

[21] The provisions mentioned in n 19 are addressed exclusively to the European Commission, not to Member States or national authorities: see Ritter, 'VO 1/2003 Art. 5. Zuständigkeit der

The reason usually given for introducing this method into competition law is twofold. On the one hand, it is said to allow for accommodating sanctions with appropriate (individual and general) deterrent effect, given the wealth and economic power of some enterprises,[22] as well as enabling the confiscation of proceeds deriving from the infringements.[23] Traditional quantitative frameworks would fail to achieve these goals and 'crime' could 'pay'. On the other hand, it ensures that fines remain commensurate with enterprises' financial capacity, thereby averting their potential demise, which would run counter to the overarching goal of protecting competition.

B. The Evolution of Turnover-Based Sanctions in Competition Law

There might have always been a place for two distinct readings of the fining method in competition law, especially in what concerns the role played by the turnover percentage that limits the fines amount. However, it is submitted that there has been an actual 'evolution', a change of perspective in that respect, which was paradigmatically instantiated by a judgment of the German Supreme Court.[24] I will therefore refer to two *stages* of the fining method in competition law.

i) The First Stage: The Turnover Percentage as an 'External' Cap ('Kappungsgrenze')

According to Article 15(2) of Regulation No 17/62,[25] the Commission could decide to impose on undertakings or associations of undertakings 'fines of from 1000 to 1 000 000 units of account, or a sum in excess thereof but not exceeding 10% of the turnover in the preceding business year … In fixing the amount of the fine,

Wettbewerbsbehörden der Mitgliedstaaten' in U Immenga and J Mestmäcker (Hrsg.), *Wettbewerbsrecht. Band 1 (EU)*, 5th edn (München, C. H. Beck, 2012) mn. 7; Dannecker and Biermann, 'Vorbemerkung vor § 81' in U Immenga and J Mestmäcker (Hrsg.), *Wettbewerbsrecht. Band 2 (GWB)*, 5th edn (München, C. H. Beck, 2014) mn. 20–22; P Caeiro, 'Punível com coima de até 10% de um montante qualquer: a inconstitucionalidade das normas sancionatórias do Regime Jurídico da Concorrência, na parte em que (não) fixam um limite máximo para as coimas aplicáveis ao *Abuso de posição dominante*' in J Lobo Moutinho, H Salinas, E Vaz de Sequeira, P Garcia Marques (eds), *Homenagem ao Prof. Doutor Germano Marques da Silva*, vol. IV (Lisboa, Universidade Católica Editora, 2020) 2429–2439.

[22] See WPJ Wils, 'The European Commission's 2006 Guidelines on antitrust fines: a legal and economic analysis' (2007) 30 *World Competition* 200. For a critical analysis of deterrence in this field see IS Forrester, 'Due process in EC competition cases: A distinguished institution with flawed procedures', (2009) 34 *EL Rev* 823; and L Calzolari, 'Sanctions in EU Competition Law: Ensuring Deterrence within the Decentralised Enforcement System of Articles 101 and 102 TFEU' in S Montaldo, F Costamagna and A Miglio (eds), *EU Law Enforcement. The Evolution of Sanctioning Powers* (London-Torino, Routledge-Giappichelli, 2021) 241 et seq.

[23] cf European Commission, *XXIst Report on Competition Policy 1991*, Publications Office, 1992, 101, mn. 139.

[24] cf below, II. B. ii).

[25] Regulation No 17: First Regulation implementing Articles 85 and 86 of the Treaty [1962] OJ 13/204.

regard shall be had both to the gravity and to the duration of the infringement.' Paragraph (4) of the same provision clarified that '[d]ecisions taken pursuant to paragraphs 1 and 2 shall not be of a criminal law nature.'

Before 1998, the Commission imposed fines corresponding to a certain percentage of enterprises' 'turnover',[26] even if the concept of relevant turnover varied. Such construction equated to interpreting the 10% limit as a proper threshold for the sanctioning framework. This method was endorsed by Advocate General Warner in the *Miller* case in 1978,[27] and prompted Wils' criticism,[28] who also noted that the Court of Justice never suggested such an approach.[29]

In 1998, the Commission adopted guidelines to ensure 'the transparency and impartiality of the Commission's decisions' while applying fines under competition law.[30] According to the GL 1998, the Commission should start by setting a 'basic amount' related to 'the gravity and duration of the infringement, which are the only criteria referred to in Article 15(2) of Regulation No 17'. The gravity of the infringement depended on a series of circumstances ('its nature, its actual impact on the market, where this can be measured, and the size of the relevant geographic market'), which allowed infringements to be split into three categories under different general descriptions. The applicable 'likely fines' (sic) would range from: ECU 1 000 to ECU 1 million for minor infringements; ECU 1 million to ECU 20 million for serious infringements; and 'above ECU 20 million' for very serious infringements. Finally, the GL 1998 recalled: '[i]t goes without saying that the final amount calculated according to this method (basic amount increased or

[26] cf EL Camilli, 'Optimal fines in cartel cases and the actual EC fining policy' (2006) 29 *World Competition* 592.

[27] 'Thus the Commission's discretion as to the amount of a fine may be taken to lie *in the range between 0% and 10% of the turnover of the undertaking concerned.* (…) Accordingly, a fine of 10% of turnover may be taken to be appropriate to an intentional infringement of the gravest kind and of considerable duration. At the other end of the scale, a fine of less than 1% is appropriate for a merely negligent infringement, of the most trivial kind and continuing only for a short time, in a case where, nonetheless, the circumstances warrant the imposition of some fine' (Case 19/77 *Miller International Schallplatten GmbH v Commission of the European Communities* ECLI:EU:C:1978:1, Opinion of AG Warner; emphasis added).

[28] 'If there is no legal reason to calculate fines as a percentage of turnover, an economic justification is not easy to find either. To achieve effective deterrence, fines should optimally be equal to the harm caused by the infringement, or alternatively equal to the benefit gained by the violator plus some safety margin, divided by the probability of detection and punishment. (…) In the end, the method of calculation of fines as a percentage of the relevant turnover creates an illusion of scientific rigour, as there is no good reason for fines to be proportional to turnover nor any criterion to select the percentage figure to apply to the turnover' (WPJ Wils, 'The Commission's New Method for Calculating Fines in Antitrust Cases' (1998) 23 *EL Rev* 255, 255–256); see also D Geradin and D Henry, *The EC fining policy for violations of competition law: An empirical review of the Commission decisional practice and the Community courts' judgments*. The Global Competition Law Centre Working Papers Series. GCLC Working Paper 03/05, at https://www.coleurope.eu/sites/default/files/research-paper/gclc_wp_03-05_0.pdf.

[29] Quite the contrary: see below, n 35.

[30] Guidelines on the method of setting fines imposed pursuant to Article 15 (2) of Regulation No 17 and Article 65 (5) of the ECSC Treaty (98/C 9/03) [1998] OJ C9/3 (GL 1998).

reduced on a percentage basis) may not in any case exceed 10% of the worldwide turnover of the undertakings, as laid down by Article 15(2) of Regulation No 17'.

Most provisions of Regulation No 17/62 were repealed and replaced with Regulation (EC) No 1/2003,[31] which is currently in force. Article 23 of the new Regulation does not mention any quantitative thresholds, but it keeps the general criteria for setting the fines (gravity and duration of the infringement) and the 10% of the turnover cap. Article 23(5) also denies the 'criminal law nature' of the European Commission's 'decisions' to impose fines.

Eventually, with a view to implementing the rules brought by Regulation (EC) No 1/2003, the Commission adopted revised Guidelines on the method of setting fines for infringements of Articles 81 and 82 of the EC Treaty (currently, Articles 101 and 102 TFEU).[32] The basic amount shall be set as 'a proportion of the value of sales [usually 15%-30%], depending on the degree of gravity of the infringement, multiplied by the number of years of infringement' (point 19), which can then be increased or decreased according to the circumstances (points 25 and 27), and 'the final amount of the fine shall not, in any event, exceed 10% of the total turnover in the preceding business year of the undertaking or association of undertakings participating in the infringement, as laid down in Article 23(2) of Regulation No 1/2003' (point 32).

The analysis of all those instruments shows that there are references to several percentages and factors to be considered while determining the fine, and there is abundant case-law of the EU Courts in that respect, but the sole limit of a *legal* nature is the turnover percentage established in both Regulations.[33] This limit was consensually understood as being extraneous to the procedure of *calculating* fines: it rather worked as an *external* cap[34] intended to protect undertakings (and, ultimately, production as a whole) by taking into consideration their *capacity to pay*.[35] Hence the reference of the turnover to *the year preceding the fining decision*,

[31] Council Regulation (EC) No 1/2003 on the implementation of the rules on competition laid down in Articles 81 and 82 of the Treaty [2003] OJ L1/1.

[32] Guidelines on the method of setting fines imposed pursuant to Article 23(2)(a) of Regulation No 1/2003 [2006] OJ C210/2 (GL 2006). These Guidelines explicitly limit their scope to Articles 101 and 102 infringements (point 8: 'fines imposed pursuant to Article 23(2)(a) of Regulation No 1/2003') and apparently leave out the fines applicable to enterprises that contravene a decision ordering interim measures under Article 8 or fail to comply with a commitment made binding by a decision pursuant to Article 9 (Article 23(2)(b)(c) of the Regulation). Arguably, such a limitation was already implicit in the GL 1998, considering the calculation method they provided.

[33] See also Calzolari (n 22) 256.

[34] The word 'external' is aptly used by Camilli (n 26) 590–591: 'the major function of the provision is the determination of the limit above which the size of the fine is per se deemed to be dangerous for the existence of the undertaking, hence not proportional. However, this ceiling does not impose any binding provision on the utilization of the turnover as a proxy for the determination of the actual fine. This constraint on the Commission's fining power is due to the need to respect the "external" proportionality of the decision'. However, the author hesitatingly mixes, to a certain extent, 'internal' and 'external' proportionality: 'a fine above the limit would be considered not to be proportionate to the *infringement*, because it could endanger the *financial stability of the firm*' (ibid, emphasis added).

[35] See, eg, Case C-189/02 P *Dansk Rørindustri and Others v Commission* ECLI:EU:C:2005:408, paras 280–283: '280. As the Commission contended, that upper limit seeks to prevent fines being

because it is the most up-to-date picture of the enterprise's financial capacity, whereas the basic amount of the fine is determined in relation to the *value of sales related to the infringement*, and therefore refers to the years it was perpetrated.[36]

As a consequence, under this construction, fines are not determined within a previously given legal framework, with lower and upper limits, by reference to which the imposed fine might express the gravity of the infringement and the guilt/blameworthiness of the perpetrator. Instead, the quantum (the 'basic amount') of the fine is calculated as a proportion of the value of sales related to the infringement, totally unbound. It can be a fraction (eg, 30%), the whole value (100%)[37] or, potentially, a multiple of it (eg, 200%):[38] no *law* prevents such possibility. If the amount exceeds 10% of the turnover of the year preceding the fining decision, it is correspondingly reduced.[39]

ii) The Second Stage: The Turnover Percentage as the Upper Limit of the Sanctions Framework

In 2013, the German Supreme Court (BGH) issued a landmark judgment in the case *Grauzement-kartell*, where the defence challenged the conformity of § 81(4)(2) [currently, § 81c(2)] of the German Competition Law (*GWB*), which contained a provision similar to Article 23(2) of Regulation 1/2003, with the legality principle.[40] The Court rightly found that sanctions, including those

imposed which it is foreseeable that the undertakings, owing to their size, as determined, albeit approximately and imperfectly, by their total turnover, will not be able to pay (see, to that effect, Musique Diffusion française and Others v Commission, paragraphs 119 and 121). 281. That limit is therefore one which is uniformly applicable to all undertakings and arrived at according to the size of each of them and seeks to ensure that the fines are not excessive or disproportionate. 282. That upper limit thus has a distinct and autonomous objective by comparison with the criteria of gravity and duration of the infringement. 283. *The only possible consequence of the upper limit is that the amount of the fine calculated on the basis of those criteria will be reduced to the maximum permitted level.* Its application implies that the undertaking concerned *will not pay the fine which in principle would be payable if it were assessed on the basis of those criteria*' (emphasis added). See also: Commission Decision 1999/60/EC relating to a proceeding under Article 85 of the EC Treaty (Case No IV/35.691/E-4: – *Pre-Insulated Pipe Cartel*) [1999] OJ L24/1, para 179, where several enterprises received a significant reduction of the fines that *had been set* following the common calculation procedure, *exceeding* the 10% threshold. In the same direction, WPJ Wils, 'The European Commission's 2006 Guidelines on antitrust fines: a legal and economic analysis' (2007) 30 *World Competition* 197, 199: '*whenever the amount thus set exceeds the statutory maximum* of 10 percent of the total turnover in the preceding business year of the undertaking concerned, as laid down in Article 23(2) of Regulation No. 1/2003, it will be *capped* at that ceiling' (emphasis added); and H Gilliams, 'Proportionality of EU Competition Fines: Proposal for a Principled Discussion' (2014) 37 *World Competition* 449, 452.

[36] GL 2006, point 13.

[37] GL 2006, points 21, 25 and 28.

[38] GL 2006, point 37.

[39] cf I Bos and MP Schinkel, 'On the scope for the European Commission's 2006 fining guidelines under the legal maximum fine' (2006) 2 *Journal of Competition Law and Economics* 673, 675: 'Recent studies report only 10 out of more than 60 Article 81 and 82 EC infringement decisions resulting in a fine between 1998 and 2006 in which the total turnover cap *limited the fine the Commission intended to impose*' (emphasis added).

[40] BGH, *Grauzement-kartell*, 26.02.2013 – KRB 20/12. For a summary of the judgment and its consequences in Germany, see Biermann, '§81c' in J Immenga and U Mestmäcker (Hrsg.), *Wettbewerbsrecht. Band 2 (GWB)*, 7th edn (München, C. H. Beck, 2024) mn 39–46.

provided for by administrative punitive law (*Ordnungswidrigkeiten*), must have a maximum legal limit,[41] which is an indispensable ('*unverzichtbar*') requirement for complying with the legality principle.[42] However, the BGH did not join the predominant construction in German literature (at least after 2005), according to which the percentual limit of competition fines (similar to EU law) worked as a cap (*Kappungsgrenze*),[43] which ultimately left fines without an upper legal limit that might serve as a reference for their determination and thus violated the legality principle.[44] Instead, the BGH contradicted the explicit reasoning followed by the German legislator and ruled that the percentual threshold should be understood as the maximum legal limit of the sanction framework (*Bussgeldobergrenze*),[45] which, in the Court's view, would redeem the provision in the eyes of the Constitution.[46]

Whether or not the BGH's ruling can be reconciled with the 2002 judgment of the German Constitutional Court (BVerfG) concerning the 'wealth penalty' (*Vermögenstrafe*) provided for by former § 43a of the German Penal Code for individuals[47] is a controversial issue.[48] This penalty consisted of a payment order for an amount with no limit other than the actual value of the convict's property at the time of sentencing, to be determined by the court. By five votes to three, the majority of the Second Senate found that the provision violated the legality principle and hence the German Constitution.[49] At the time of writing, the

[41] BGH, *Grauzement-kartell*, para 51.

[42] ibid, para 56.

[43] H Achenbach, 'Die Kappungsgrenze und die Folgen – Zweifelsfragen des § 81 Abs. 4 GWB' (2009) 7 *Zeitschrift für Wettbewerbsrecht* 3; see also further references in BGH, *Grauzement-kartell*, para 52.

[44] See, eg, U Soltész, C Steinle and H Bielesz, 'Rekordgeldbußen versus Bestimmtheitsgebot – Die Kartellverordnung auf dem Prüfstein höherrangigen Gemeinschaftsrechts' (2003) 14 *Europäische Zeitschrift für Wirtschaftsrecht* 204, 204–210, esp. 207; H Achenbach, 'Die Bussgeldtatbestände des GWB' in H Achenbach, A Ransiek and T Rönnau (Hrsg.), *Handbuch Wirtschaftsstrafrecht*, 4th edn (Heidelberg, C. F. Müller, 2015) 1554, with extensive references; in the same direction, M Dreher and M Kulka, *Wettbewerbs- und Kartellrecht: Eine systematische Darstellung des deutschen und europäischen Rechts*, 10 edn (Heidelberg, C. F. Müller, 2018) 720, mn. 1777.

[45] When enacting the '6. GWB-Novelle' in 1998, the German legislature explicitly rejected the introduction of a turnover-based upper limit, citing concerns related to 'the rule of law' ('*rechtsstaatlichen Gründen*'): cf. Biermann (n 40) mn. 32.

[46] But see the criticism by H Achenbach, 'Die Bussgeldtatbestände des GWB', mn 53, who aptly argues that § 81(4)(2) (currently § 81c(2)) of the GWB violates the legality principle and is unconstitutional in either construction; cf also Biermann (n 40) mn 54: 'Insbesondere mangels Bezugs zum Unrecht bilden die in § 81c Abs. 2–4 enthaltenen Rahmen also nur eine absolute Obergrenze, können jedoch für sich genommen – *problematisch im Hinblick auf die Anforderungen des Bestimmtheitsgrundsatzes* – keinen Orientierungsrahmen im Sinne einer Schwereskala für die konkrete Festsetzung der Geldbuße zu liefern' (emphasis added). Biermann also outlines the several legislative amendments to the GWB that followed the *Grauzement-kartell* judgment, which he deems unsatisfactory; the author advocates for a comprehensive critical reassessment of German and EU cartel sanctions law, possibly resulting in a new statutory framework (ibid, mn. 59).

[47] BVerfG, *Judgment* 20.03.2002 – 2 BvR 794/95 (lexetius.com/2002,273), esp. para. 92–96.

[48] See Biermann (n 40), with further references.

[49] In the Court's assessment, the norm was unconstitutional for various reasons, including its establishment of a '«wandering» penalty framework' [*wandernden Strafrahmen*] and 'its delegation of determination to judicial interpretation'. As stated in the judgment, 'the judge is mandated to ascertain the upper limit defined by the value of the wealth as a reference point for the sanction' (para. 94). Hence, '[t]he upper limit of the wealth penalty is based solely on the amount of the actual property [...].

German Constitutional Court has not yet addressed on the merits the constitutional conformity of competition law sanctions.

The paradigm shift operated by the BGH in *Grauzement-kartell* – which, in the Court's view, saved the constitutional validity of German competition law sanctions – also took place, around the same time, in other jurisdictions,[50] as if it suddenly became generally apparent that competition sanctions could not dispense with a proper legal maximum limit.

By contrast, the EU bodies seem to have retained the original 'cap-construction' method.[51] It is therefore somewhat surprising that Directive ECN+ clearly sets the turnover percentage as the *upper limit* of fines applicable to infringements of articles 101 and 102 TFEU, rather than a cap designed to protect the capacity to pay. The connection between turnover percentage and deterrence enhancement results already from Recital 49 of the Directive, according to which,

> The deterrent effect of fines differs widely across the Union, and in some Member States the maximum amount of the fine that can be imposed is very low. To ensure NCAs can impose dissuasive fines, the maximum amount of the fine that is possible to be imposed for each infringement of Article 101 or 102 TFEU should be set at a level of not less than 10% of the total worldwide turnover of the undertaking concerned. This should not prevent Member States from maintaining or introducing a higher maximum fine that can be imposed.[52]

In the same vein, Recital 43 bluntly reads that '[f]ines should be determined *in proportion to the total worldwide turnover* of the undertakings and associations of undertakings concerned' (emphasis added) – not in proportion to the value of sales, as indicated in the GL 1998 and GL 2006.

This undermines, in a constitutionally unacceptable manner, the predictability of an anticipated wealth penalty, especially since the law has refrained from specifying particular criteria for its determination' (para 96; my translation, citations omitted).

[50] See, eg, the Decision of the Portuguese Competition Authority, Case No. 2011/1, 18.07.2013, para 590: 'the *abstract framework of the fine* corresponds to the range indicated in Article 43 of the [former] Portuguese Competition Law, as a percentage of the turnover, for each type of infringement' (emphasis added). As a matter of fact, Article 43(1) of the former Portuguese Competition Law (Law no. 18/2003, of 11.06.2003), which read '(…) a fine that cannot exceed, for each of the companies involved in the infringement, 10% of the turnover *in the last year*' (emphasis added), could be interpreted either way. See also, following the current construction of the Portuguese NCA, the recent Judgment of the Tribunal da Relação de Lisboa, case no. 322/17.1YUSTR.L1-PICRS, of 19.02.2024 (available at www.dgsi.pt).

[51] See, eg, European Commission, Directorate-General for Competition, Report on competition policy 2018 – Including Commission staff working document, Publications Office, 2019, https://data.europa.eu/doi/10.2763/296993, 42: 'ACW's fine was *capped* due to the application of the *10% ceiling*. The General Court found that this fine *reduction* for one party (ACW) breached the principle of equal treatment, and should have been attributed proportionately between the two other parties (…)' (emphasis added).

[52] This justification was already articulated in the Explanatory Memorandum of the Commission's proposal: 'To ensure NCAs can set deterrent fines on the basis of a common set of core parameters: first, there should be a common legal maximum of no less than 10% of the worldwide turnover and second, when setting the fine, NCAs should have regard to the core factors of gravity and duration of the infringement' (COM(2017) 142 final, 22.03.2017, Chapter V).

The new approach to the percentual limit is confirmed by Article 15 of the Directive ('Maximum amount of the fine'), whose para 1 provides that

> Member States shall ensure that the maximum amount of the fine that national competition authorities may impose on each undertaking or association of undertakings participating in an infringement of Article 101 or 102 TFEU is not less than 10 % of the total worldwide turnover of the undertaking or association of undertakings in the business year preceding the decision referred to in Article 13(1) (emphasis added).

As a consequence, Member States, unbound by EU law, can provide for *higher* upper limits if they deem it fit. Establishing a 'minimum-maximum' for the fines aims at setting sanction frameworks – much like the minimum-maximum penalties for individuals usually provided for in the directives on the approximation of criminal law –, not at protecting an enterprise's capacity to pay. Incidentally, it should be noted that such protection does not enjoy any consideration in the Directive, which is difficult to understand. Of course, if the turnover percentage were an actual *maximum* limit, there would be no need to keep the 10% cap, as the imposable fines could not go beyond such limit. But, as the percentage is now construed as a *minimum* upper threshold, there should be some kind of cap to ensure that the fines do not go beyond what the enterprise can pay.[53]

In turn, fines applicable to infringements other than violations of Articles 101 and 102 TFEU, regulated in Article 23(2)(b)(c) of Regulation (EC) No 1/2003, do not seem to be subject to any precise maximum limit in the Directive – in contrast, again, to the 10% turnover threshold set in the Regulation. Apparently, Member States are allowed to (continue to) establish, in those cases, whichever limits they deem appropriate, as long as the fines are 'effective, proportionate and dissuasive' (Article 13(3) of Directive ECN+).

The method introduced by Directive ECN+ for calculating the fines applicable to Articles 101 and 102 TFEU infringements arguably replaces the previous ones completely. The logic behind taking the value of sales in the year(s) of the infringement as a basis for the determination of the fine is completely different from assessing the gravity and the duration of the infringement on a scale of 1%-10% of the enterprise's turnover in the year preceding the decision. Furthermore, there is now a logical contradiction embedded in the method to be followed by national authorities. The *value of sales in the year of the infringement* taken by national guidelines as a framework for calculating the fine – replicating the model provided by EU guidelines – cannot be related to a maximum *limit* drawn from a completely different magnitude and nature, such as the *turnover of the year preceding the decision*. Those are heterogeneous values that cannot be integrated in a scale.

The consequences that might bring such disparities between *EU law* binding on the Commission (per Regulation (EC) No 1/2003) and on Member States (per Directive ECN+) are outside the remit of this chapter. However, it seems quite clear that the same infringement committed by the same enterprise will be fined

[53] See below, IV.B.

with completely different amounts depending on whether the procedure takes place before the Commission or a (any) national authority:[54] only by chance will a calculation based on the value of sales in the year of commission equate the sum calculated as a percentage of the annual global turnover of the year preceding the decision.

III. The Problematic Nature of Turnover-Based Fines

A. Are Competition Law Fines Subject to the Same Guarantees as Established for Criminal Penalties?

As mentioned, Article 15(4) of Regulation No 17/62 and Article 23(5) of Regulation (EC) No 1/2003 explicitly denied the criminal law nature of the European Commission's 'decisions' to impose fines – and, by extension, of the fines themselves – in the field of competition law. The same caveat can be found in other instruments that provide for sanctions in administrative punitive law (eg, merger control).[55] Denying the sanctions' 'criminal law nature' is arguably driven by two goals: in the first place, it purports to avoid any issues concerning the EU's *competence* to establish (and apply) sanctions in those fields;[56] in the second place, it points to setting aside the *guarantees* established for criminal sanctions by the ECHR and the Charter of Fundamental Rights.

The first issue is unproblematic, since it is clear that the boundaries set by the Treaties to the legislative competence of the EU in criminal matters do not concern sanctions that do not bear a criminal law nature *stricto sensu*.[57]

The second issue, however, raises more questions.

In *Volkswagen v Commission* (2003), the Court of Justice relied on Article 15(4) of Regulation No 17/62 to find that competition law fines 'are not of a criminal law nature'; otherwise, the Court added, 'the effectiveness of Community competition law would be seriously affected'.[58] As a consequence, the establishment of the intentional nature of the infringement did not require 'the identification of the persons who had acted improperly within the undertaking or who ought to have been held responsible for any defective organisation of the undertaking'.[59]

[54] This means that Directive ECN+ can worsen the problems arising from the unpredictability of the allocation of cases – which is already an issue vis-à-vis the legality principle: cf S Brammer, *Horizontal aspects of the decentralisation of EU competition law enforcement*, PhD Diss. KU Leuven, 2008, https://lirias.kuleuven.be/retrieve/68393, 155 et seq.

[55] Article 14(4) of Council Regulation (EC) No 139/2004 on the control of concentrations between undertakings (the EC Merger Regulation) [2004] OJ L24/1.

[56] cf Brammer (n 54) 264.

[57] See WPJ Wils, 'The Increased Level of EU Antitrust Fines, Judicial Review and the ECHR' (2010) 33 *World Competition* 12; J Öberg, 'The definition of Criminal Sanctions in the EU' (2014) 3 *European Criminal Law Review* 273.

[58] Case C-338/00 P *Volkswagen AG v Commission* ECLI:EU:C:2003:473, paras 95–98.

[59] ibid.

The same line of reasoning was adopted by the General Court in *Compagnie maritime belge SA v Commission* (2008). The Court explicitly relied on the *Volkswagen* judgment – including the need to preserve the 'effectiveness of Community competition law' – and denied its criminal law nature.[60] Consequently, the Court ruled that it was unnecessary to examine whether or not the law applicable to the infringements and the penalties had changed to the applicant's advantage between the first (partially annulled) and the second fining decisions because the latter was not bound to take such eventual changes into consideration. Thus, the Court dismissed the retroactive application of the more lenient law.[61]

Notwithstanding, in other rulings, the EU courts and the ECtHR have recognised the criminal law nature of competition law to the effect of protecting some individual rights in specific situations.[62]

The ambiguity of the stance taken by EU courts and the ECtHR in this respect[63] is mirrored by the approach pursued in the notorious *Jussila* judgment, where the ECtHR found that 'the criminal-head guarantees [of Article 6 ECHR] will not necessarily apply with their full stringency' when the sanctions do not pertain to the hard core of criminal law.[64] Arguably, this 'flexible approach' applies to other criminal law guarantees, such as those enshrined in Article 7 ECHR.

[60] Case T-276/04 *Compagnie maritime belge SA v Commission* ECLI:EU:T:2008:237, paras 65–67.

[61] ibid, para 67: '… even on the assumption that competition law had evolved in a manner favourable to the applicant, which the applicant has wholly failed to demonstrate, the parts of Decision 93/82 establishing the infringements and the applicant's participation in them could not be impugned without infringing the principle of legal certainty and the principle of res judicata'. Invoking the principle of legal certainty in punitive proceedings as a basis for setting aside the retroactive application of the *lex mitior* is, to say the least, rather unusual.

[62] See, eg, Human Rights Commission Report of 30 May 1991 in *Société Stenuit v France* (1992) 14 E.H.R.R. 509, 62–64: the proceedings initiated by the French authorities for an infringement against French competition law constituted a 'criminal charge' under Article 6 ECHR given, *inter alia*, the severity of the sanction (on this case, see the analysis by Brammer (n 54) 265 et seq, with further references); Case T-279/02 *Degussa v Commission* ECLI:EU:T:2006:103 and Case C-266/06 *Degussa v Commission* ECLI:EU:C:2008:295: the fines applicable to competition law infringements are subject to the principles of legality and proportionality of penalties; Case C-17/10 *Toshiba Corporation and Others v Úřad pro ochranu hospodářské soutěže* ECLI:EU:C:2012:72: the principle *ne bis in idem* applies to competition law infringements; *Menarini Diagnostics S.r.l. v. Italy* App No 43509/08A (ECtHR, 27 September 2011): the fine imposed for a competition law infringement was criminal in nature and therefore Article 6 of the ECHR applied.

[63] This ambiguity dates back from the time when Regulation 17/62 was still in force: see J Schwarze, 'Rechtsstaatliche Grenzen der gesetzlichen und richterlichen Qualifikation von Verwaltungssanktionen im europäischen Gemeinschaftsrecht' (2003) 9 *EuZW* 268 et seq; see also F Dethmers and H Engelen, 'Fines Under Article 102 of the Treaty on the Functioning of the European Union' (2011) 2 *European Competition Law Review* 95; JAE Vervaele, *European Criminal Justice in the Post-Lisbon Area of Freedom, Security and Justice* (Trento, Università degli Studi di Trento, 2014) 210.

[64] *Jussila v Finland* App No 73053/01 (ECtHR, 23 November 2006) para 43. For insights into the impact of this judgment on competition law, WPJ Wils, 'The Increased Level of EU Antitrust Fines, Judicial Review and the ECHR', (2010) 33 *World Competition* 14; and WPJ Wils, 'The Compatibility with Fundamental Rights of the EU Antitrust Enforcement System in Which the European Commission Acts Both as Investigator and as First-Instance Decision Maker' (2014) 37 *World Competition* 8. For a discussion on the 'autonomous notion' of criminal matters adopted by the ECtHR and the applicability of ECHR guarantees to laws, procedures, and sanctions not explicitly labelled as criminal by national law, see, among many, AMV Vugt, 'Administrative Sanctions in EU law' (2012) 5 *Review of European Administrative Law* 5; the collective volume F Galli and A Weyembergh (eds), *Do Labels Still Matter?*

Consequently, while the criminal law nature of competition procedures and fines raises little doubt in the light of the *Engel* (or should we say: *Engel+*) criteria,[65] especially given their severity and purpose, it might not be always clear to what extent they are covered by the guarantees established in the ECHR and in the Charter:[66] in Calzolari's words, 'the relation between criminal and competition law is not a matter of "if", but of "how much": namely, how much protection should be ensured to undertakings involved in competition proceedings compared to the full catalogue of criminal procedural guarantees'.[67] In any case, it is submitted that competition fines are subject to the legality principle in regard to the need for determination and foreseeability.[68]

B. The Import of Turnover-Based Fines Into Hard-Core Criminal Law

Irrespective of whether or not turnover-based *administrative* fines, such as those provided for by competition law, should be considered as 'criminal' to the effects of applying the fundamental guarantees established in the ECHR and the Charter (and in national constitutions), the Commission's proposals for new directives on the approximation of criminal law[69] entail a duty for Member States to adopt them as *criminal* sanctions, at least to the extent that their respective legal orders provide for the criminal liability of legal persons.[70]

Blurring Boundaries Between Administrative and Criminal Law. The Influence of the EU (Bruxelles, Editions de l'Université de Bruxelles, 2014); Mazzacuva (n 5); L Papadopoulos, 'Administrative Punitive Law' in P Caeiro, S Gless and V Mitsilegas (with MJ Costa, J de Snaijer and G Theodorakakou), *Elgar Encyclopedia of Crime and Criminal Justice*, (Cheltenham, Elgar Publishing, 2024); and F Mazzacuva, 'Sanctions (Types of Criminal)' in ibid.

[65] See WPJ Wils, *Principles of European Antitrust Enforcement* (Oxford, Hart Publishing, 2005) 77.

[66] See, eg, Forrester (n 22) 823 et seq.

[67] Calzolari (n 22) 250.

[68] In this direction, see the thorough analysis conducted by Mazzacuva from a multilevel perspective, who concludes: 'il collegamento del significato individual-garantistico del principio di legalità – riassumibile nell'esigenza di "prevedibilità" delle conseguenze del proprio agire – con l'istanza di colpevolezza (tanto da poter qualificare il primo come corollario della seconda) non può che comportarne la natura cogente rispetto a qualsiasi manifestazione del *ius puniendi*. Da tale premessa deriva, naturalmente, la quotazione costituzionale dei canoni di irretroattività e di determinatezza (…) anche nel diritto penale amministrativo' (Mazzacuva (n 5) 284–285).

[69] Above, n 17.

[70] Above, n 3. In fact, it would be inappropriate for a Member State that recognises legal entities' criminal liability to implement these sanctions as administrative ones. However, given the apparent indifference of the EU legislator regarding the nature of the sanctions chosen by the Member States, the question remains as to whether these instruments infringe upon either the *ultima ratio* principle (since administrative sanctions are deemed sufficient if the Member State does not criminalise legal entities) or the principle of effective protection (because criminal law is actually necessary and the EU legislator allows for the use of insufficient sanctions): see P Caeiro, 'The influence of the EU on the "blurring" between administrative and criminal law' in F Galli and A Weyembergh (eds), *Do Labels Still Matter?* (n 64) 178.

The following considerations assess whether the turnover-based fines put forward in the recent Commission's proposals comply with the guarantees established for criminal penalties in the ECHR, the Charter and, more generally, national constitutions – namely, the principles of legality and proportionality.[71]

i) Turnover-Based Fines and the Legality Principle

It is undisputed that the legality principle applies to the definition of both offences and penalties (*nulla poena sine lege certa*). The aims of such a fundamental principle are twofold: on the one hand, criminal sanctions must be established and defined by law (statutory or customary),[72] and cannot be left to the full discretion of judicial bodies, in order to avoid any arbitrariness;[73] on the other hand, the law must establish the penalties in a way that makes it possible to anticipate, at the time of the offence, the type and severity of state intervention on individual rights (freedom, property, professional or political rights) incurred by committing the prohibited conduct, which shall inform the decision over taking the risk of suffering such penalties.

In the light of the 'cap construction' described in Section II.A., the percentage of annual turnover works as a limit to which fines exceeding it must be *reduced*. Its function is not to designate the most severe sanction generally applicable to a certain class of infringements. Instead, it intends to protect *each* company's ability to pay. This means that fines are unlimited because they do not carry a maximum amount – in other words, virtually *any* amount can be imposed. It should be noted that the lack of a maximum amount – a proper limit – cannot be compensated for by consistent practice based on soft law such as the mentioned Guidelines. These Guidelines can be amended, adapted or replaced by the authorities as they deem fit, as long as they provide appropriate justification.[74] It is reasonable to speculate that, in most Member States, allowing courts to determine the maximum amount of fines in accordance with their sentencing guidelines, which can be deviated from when deemed justified, would violate the principle of legality.

In the absence of a maximum amount in the law, norm addressees cannot anticipate it when they violate the rule. As the BGH acknowledged, such a regime would not meet the legality principle standards.

[71] Whether or not fines are the most appropriate punishment for legal entities is beyond the remit of this paper: see, in that respect, the assessment by Faraldo Cabana (n 3) 264 et seq.

[72] *Dallas v The United Kingdom* App No 38395/12 (ECtHR, 11 February 2016), para 70.

[73] *Kafkaris v Cyprus* App No 21906/04 (ECtHR, 12 February 2008), para 137.

[74] The ECJ has characterised the *Guidelines* as follows: '(…) although those measures may not be regarded as rules of law which the administration is always bound to observe, they nevertheless form rules of practice from which the administration may not depart in an individual case *without giving reasons that are compatible with the principle of equal treatment* (…) (see Case C-171/00 P *Libéros v Commission* [2002] ECR I-451, paragraph 35)' (Case C-189/02 P *Dansk Rørindustri and Others v Commission* ECLI:EU:C:2005:408, para 209; emphasis added).

If we now turn to the second construction of turnover-based sanctions, which has been ultimately adopted by Directive ECN+, the first objection no longer proves valid because the fines become limited: the percentage of turnover in the year preceding the fining decision works as the upper threshold for applicable fines. However, one should bear in mind that a fine consists of the payment of an actual *amount*, a value, not a *percentage*: a percentage of an undetermined and undeterminable amount is also an undeterminable amount when the offence is committed. This construction therefore violates the legality principle (*lex certa*) as well because the addressee cannot be expected to anticipate when the fine decision will take place or what the turnover of the year that precedes it will be.[75] The situation is fundamentally different from the days fine model, where most laws provide for maximum quantitative values both for the number of days *and* the daily rate, which allows for calculating, at the time of commission, the maximum amount of the applicable fine.[76]

It is also different from proportional fines, such as those that have been maintained in the Spanish criminal code in exceptional cases.[77] Proportional fines are calculated as a multiple – set by the law – of a value ('*el tanto*') that, in principle, can be determined (or at least sufficiently estimated) at the time of perpetration, eg, the value of the drugs trafficked, the subsidies unduly received, or the damage caused by computer-related offences (Articles 264 to 264 *quater* of the Spanish Penal Code).[78] In cases where such value cannot be calculated by the court, the law provides that the fine cannot be imposed and another penalty must be chosen (natural persons), or that the proportional fine must be replaced by a fine calculated through the days fine method (legal persons).[79] This will cover most, if not all, cases where it is not possible to roughly estimate the base-value at the time of commission. In other words, it is unlikely that the court can establish *el tanto*, for sentencing purposes, in instances where the offender could not anticipate, at all, what such value would be when he/she committed the offence.

In the event that such a marginal situation arises, there is still a significant difference compared with turnover-based fines. One can argue that the base-value is directly linked to the offence, either as an undue benefit or a damage, which

[75] See F Gürtler, '§ 17' in E Göhler, F Gürtler and H Seitz (Hrsg.), *Gesetz über Ordnungswidrigkeiten*, 16th edn (München, C. H. Beck, 2012) mn. 48c. For this reason, it is not possible to agree with the CJ's finding that 'le montant de l'amende susceptible d'être imposée connaît un plafond chiffrable et absolu, calculé en fonction de chaque entreprise, pour chaque cas d'infraction, de sorte que le montant maximal de l'amende pouvant être infligée à une entreprise donnée est déterminable à l'avance' (Case C-266/06 *Degussa v Commission* ECLI:EU:C:2008:295, para 50); see also below.

[76] There are however some exceptions: cf the information provided by Faraldo Cabana (n 3) 262–263, and JL Fuentes Osorio, 'Dolorosa, pero no letal. La cuantía de la multa según la capacidad económica de la persona jurídica', (2022) 2 *InDret* 209, 214, fn. 50.

[77] cf S Cardenal Montraveta, 'La pena de multa prevista para los delitos relacionados con el consumo ilegal de drogas', (2020) 1 *InDret* 180.

[78] *Contra*, AS Dias, *Direito das Contra-Ordenações* (Coimbra, Almedina, 2018) 74 et seq, who argues that proportional administrative fines violate the principle of legality / legal certainty, in terms of foreseeability and determinability of the sanctions.

[79] ibid.

must be somehow imputable to the offender, even if they are not elements of the offence stricto sensu. The sanction (and its determination) is thus still somehow 'in the hands' of the perpetrator. The agent knows or can know that the measure of the penalty depends fundamentally, *as established by law*, on the consequences (benefit/damage) of their acts. They can therefore foresee that they will be punished in proportion to the consequences the infringements will bring, even if the imposable amount is not determinable at the time of commission. Whether this is sufficient to satisfy the legality principle in those marginal cases is another discussion.

The (then) Court of First Instance and the Court of Justice addressed the compatibility of turnover-based fines with the legality principle in the *Degussa* case, which concerned competition law infringements.[80] The reasons given in those judgments are of the utmost relevance for our topic, since they do not seem to attach any relevance to the non-criminal nature (*stricto sensu*) of the turnover-based fines impugned and thus have not resorted to the 'flexible approach' mentioned above. Consequently, the findings of the courts and the grounds on which they were based could apply, in principle, to criminal penalties, save for those that relate directly to the role played by the Commission (and its *Guidelines*) in the sanctioning system, which would have to be adapted.

Both EU courts found that competition law fines were subject to the legality principle. They also found that the determination of sanctions based on the turnover of the sanctioned enterprise in the year preceding the fining decision constituted no violation of such a principle. The main arguments on which the judgments relied were the following: (i) the legality principle does not require that the wording of the provisions be so precise that the consequences are foreseeable with absolute certainty;[81] (ii) vague terms are admissible to a certain extent;[82] (iii) the method used by the Commission (Guidelines) is public and can be foreseen by the traders;[83] (iv) while ascertaining the infringement and determining the sanction, the Commission is bound by general legal principles, in particular the principles of equal treatment and proportionality, as developed by the EU courts in their case law.[84]

It is submitted that the first three arguments overlook the point. The issue at stake is not the use of vague words or expressions, but rather the sheer absence, or random variation, of a maximum limit of the sanction. There is a difference between vague terms with a determinable content, to be clarified by the courts within their remit,[85] and precise terms with an indeterminable content. For instance, the expression 'the penalties for such infringement will be determined

[80] Above, n 62.

[81] Case T-279/02 *Degussa v Commission* ECLI:EU:T:2006:103, para 71; Case C-266/06 *Degussa v Commission* ECLI:EU:C:2008:295, para 44.

[82] Case T-279/02 *Degussa v Commission* ECLI:EU:T:2006:103, para 72.

[83] ibid, paras 82–83.

[84] ibid, para 51.

[85] See *Del Río Prada v Spain* App No 42750/09 (ECtHR, 21 October 2013) paras 91–93, with further references.

by the court at its own discretion' is perfectly precise and therefore has a univocal meaning. However, this does not make it compatible with the legality principle because, in that case, the penalties are not established by law. The lack of a *legal* maximum limit for fines cannot be filled in by the 'well established and published case-law of the Court', or by the Commission's *Guidelines*, because it is not for the judicial or administrative/political bodies to determine the maximum abstract limit of a sanction subject to the legality principle. The fact that the sanctioning method is public and can be foreseen by the addressees is thus immaterial.

Indeed, if this kind of sanction is implemented in the Member States' criminal law, there are usually guidelines, even with legal status that the courts should follow while setting *criminal* penalties. However, such instruments can only help the adjudicator determine the actual fine to be imposed: they cannot replace a framework with clear minimum and maximum limits.

As for the last argument, the legality principle has an autonomous stand, and its function cannot be properly ensured either by the 'practice' of the institutions or by general legal principles such as equal treatment or proportionality – otherwise it would be redundant and would not deserve separate consideration in the several instruments on human and fundamental rights.

The EU courts' judgments affirming the compatibility of turnover-based fines with the legality principle are therefore not convincing, especially when the latter should apply with its full stringency, given the criminal law nature of the proposed fines.

ii) Turnover-Based Fines and the Proportionality Principle

Offences carry different degrees of seriousness, depending on multiple factors – mostly, the social harm they cause. It is clear that sanctions must be proportionate to the violations (cardinal and ordinal proportionality),[86] which are imposed, *inter alia*, by Article 49(3) of the Charter,[87] and, indirectly, by the principle of equal treatment. Consequently, proportionality requires a system of gradable sanctions that can translate the different intensity of the reproach underlying each sanction, which in turn calls for an *objective scale* in which the penalties are organised in an order of magnitude between a minimum and a maximum threshold (years of imprisonment, day fines, money amounts). Even when the penalties embody an 'absolute' value that cannot be graded, such as the death penalty or

[86] See P Asp, *The Substantive Criminal Law Competence of the EU* (Stockholm, Jure, 2012) 199 et seq.

[87] 'Hence, Article 49 applies to the adoption of EU legislation providing for criminal sanctions, the interpretation of EU criminal law by the CJEU and the national courts, the implementation and enforcement of EU law by the Member States as well as the evaluation of national criminal law in the light of its compliance with EU law' (E Billis and N Knust, 'Proportionality (Principle of)' in P Caeiro, S Gless and V Mitsilegas (with MJ Costa, J de Snaijer and G Theodorakakou), *Elgar Encyclopedia of Crime and Criminal Justice* (n 64); see also Case C-384/17 *Dooel Uvoz-Izvoz Skopje Link Logistik N&N v Budapest Rendőrfőkapitánya* ECLI:EU:C:2018:494, Opinion of the AG Bobek, para 32); and Gilliams (n 35) 439 et seq, who proposes a proportionality test for competition fines.

life imprisonment,[88] they are still on a scale because they are seen as the gravest sanctions (as compared to imprisonment, temporary imprisonment, fines or other limitations of rights).

The *Guidelines* adopted by the European Commission govern that the fine is determined on the basis of a certain percentage of the 'value of sales' in the market concerned by the infringement in the last full business year when it took place.[89] This basic amount can be increased specifically 'for deterrence' for 'undertakings which have a particularly large turnover beyond the sales of goods or services to which the infringement relates'.[90] However, in the 'cap construction', there is no actual maximum limit and therefore no framework within which each infringement can meet the appropriate level of punishment. As the BGH noted,[91] it is impossible to know which sanction will apply to the gravest infringement. Moreover, in the absence of a scale, it is also impossible to assess whether a given (and to this effect aleatory) *amount* is proportionate to the offence committed (severe enough and not excessive), not only in view of the gravity of the infringement itself (absolute proportionality), but also in comparison with the penalties applied to other kinds of offences (relative heterologous proportionality) or to other offences of the same kind (relative homologous proportionality).

In a nutshell, the absence of an objective maximum limit for fines and the resulting impossibility of having a sanctioning scale run counter to the purpose of gradable sanctions and the very rationality of the system.[92]

Are things any different if the turnover percentage is regarded as the *upper limit* of fines instead of an external cap? Such construction allows for the establishment of a framework within which sanctions can be organised rationally, as well as for comparison between them. However, none of the proportionality principle functions can be properly fulfilled. The fine – the actual payable amount – does not bear any objective connection with the offence (unlike, eg, the number of days'

[88] It should be noted that the same legal system can provide for several modes of the death penalty or life imprisonment (eg, with or without tariff/parole) – in which case they become just another instance of gradable penalties.

[89] GL 2006: '13. In determining the basic amount of the fine to be imposed, the Commission will take the value of the undertaking's sales of goods or services to which the infringement directly or indirectly relates in the relevant geographical area within the EEA. It will normally take the sales made by the undertaking during the last full business year of its participation in the infringement (hereafter "value of sales") (…) 19. The basic amount of the fine will be related to a proportion of the value of sales, depending on the degree of gravity of the infringement, multiplied by the number of years of infringement'. (…) 21. As a general rule, the proportion of the value of sales taken into account will be set at a level of up to 30% of the value of sales'.

[90] As pointed out by Gilliams (n 35) 442–443, this 'increase for deterrence' is hardly reconcilable with proportionality to the infringement. Indeed, it seems that in this instance *prospective* proportionality encroaches upon *retrospective* proportionality (on these concepts, see, eg, T Elholm, 'The Emotional Component of Proportionality' in E Billis, N Knust and JP Rui (eds), *Proportionality in Crime Control and Criminal Justice* (Oxford, Hart Publishing, 2021) 80.

[91] See above.

[92] Highlighting the connection between proportionality and rationality, even within the realm of symbolic law, and exploring novel approaches to put the 'emotional' element embedded therein in a 'reasonable proportion' with other interests, Elholm (n 90) 79 et seq.

fine in the classic system), as it is a proportion of the *current economic capacity* of the undertaking. Serious offences can result in small fines if the annual turnover in the year preceding the fining decision is exceptionally low, whereas minor infringements can be punished with fines of several million euro if the turnover is particularly high.

By referring to an exclusively subjective standard, this model obliterates the relationship between the sanction and the gravity of the offence/guilt of the offender (cardinal proportionality):[93] the fine is not calculated within a given objective framework that expresses social blame, but exclusively in terms of what the offender (presumably) can pay at the time of sentencing. It is as if imprisonment sentences were calculated, in each case, as a percentage of the remaining lifetime each sentenced person has until they reach the average life expectancy threshold.

The subjective nature of penalties undermines both relative homologous proportionality and equal treatment. Even if similar offences committed by different perpetrators are punished with the same percentage of annual turnover (eg, 6%), economic factors can distort the proportion. Variables such as the size of the enterprise (smaller enterprises suffer more from the impact) or the type of economic activity (enterprises with narrow profit margins are more affected[94]) play a significant role.

It can be argued against this reasoning that the calculation of the daily rate in the traditional system also considers the economic situation of the convicted person at the time of sentencing, not at the time of the offence. However, the situation is different in all respects. Firstly, the sanction primarily consists of a number of days fine, which reflects the gravity of the offence and ensures uniform treatment for similar offences with a similar degree of guilt. Secondly, the determination of the daily rate does not aim to preserve the convicted person's ability to pay or maintain productive power. Instead, its goal is to deduct an amount from the convicted person's income each day to ensure that *all convicts* reach the 'minimum existential level appropriate to their socio-economic conditions' during the specified sentence duration[95] (thereby contributing to warranting equal treatment). Achieving this goal requires basing the calculation on the convicted person's economic situation at the time of sentencing.

Finally, the introduction of a turnover-based fines system, regardless of the specific construction adopted, raises additional concerns in terms of relative heterologous proportionality, even within EU criminal law. It is impossible to ensure that fines imposed through this method will be proportionate in comparison to

[93] Upholding the need to establish a relationship between any fine and the offence, Fuentes Osorio (n 76) 209; more generally on the requisite proportionality between the seriousness of the offence and the severity of the applicable sanctions, see FLC Pinto, 'O ilícito de mera ordenação social e a erosão do princípio da subsidiariedade da intervenção penal' (1997) 7 *Revista Portuguesa de Ciência Criminal* 73.

[94] See Biermann (n 40) mn. 53.

[95] JF Dias, *Direito Penal Português. As Consequências Jurídicas do Crime* (Lisboa, Aequitas, 1993) 119.

those applied for other offences under the classic system. The two models cannot be easily reconciled because they follow structurally different logics. Consequently, it is possible that less serious offences (eg, violations of restrictive measures) will be punished more harshly under the new method than more serious offences, such as slavery or trafficking in human beings. It is simply not possible to establish an order that encompasses both systems in rational terms, as they operate in parallel scales.

iii) Other Issues Raised by the Proposals: Competence and Coherence

In addition to the issues discussed above, there are other reasons why the EU should refrain from establishing criminal turnover-based fines.

Those fines are not common among Member States, which poses two problems. It is debatable whether the introduction of a sanctioning model that is entirely new to many Member States aligns with the 'minimum rules' clause that limits the EU's competence in this field, which sits uneasily with *innovation*. At the very least, such a radical innovation (also in relation to current EU criminal law) is at odds with the principle of horizontal and vertical coherence that the EU should adhere to,[96] potentially leading to unnecessary contradictions and disruptions in domestic legal systems and within EU criminal law itself.

IV. Towards a New Model of Turnover-based Fines?

A. Writing on Water: The Adjustments Introduced by the Council in the Commission's Proposals

In the preceding sections, I have analysed the proposals put forth by the Commission, which provided a backdrop for papers presented at conferences in Porto (April 2023),[97] Turin (May 2023)[98] and Madrid (December 2023).[99] In those papers, I argued that the Commission's proposals for turnover-based criminal fines were inherently flawed, and possibly contravene the Treaties and fundamental principles of criminal law. I criticised the imposition of a fining method unfamiliar to the criminal law of most Member States as a 'minimum rule'.[100] Drawing

[96] See European Criminal Policy Initiative, *A Manifesto on European Criminal Policy*, (2009) 12 *Zeitschrift für Internationale Strafrechtsdogmatik* 707, 709 and 714.

[97] 'International Conference on European Criminal Law: From the legal foundations to its impact on national legal orders', Lusíada University (Porto), 28 April 2023.

[98] 'Proportionality of Criminal Penalties in EU Law', University of Turin, 11–12 May 2023.

[99] 'Nuevos Retos del Derecho Penal Europeo y Internacional. Congreso internacional de las secciones española y portuguesa de la Asociación Internacional de Derecho Penal', Spanish and Portuguese Groups of the AIDP, 30 November – 1 December 2023.

[100] A parallel argument has been made against the introduction, by the EU legislator, of mandatory jurisdictional grounds that are not common to many Member States: see P Caeiro, 'Commentary on

from previous research on competition law fines,[101] I also suggested some changes to mitigate the most glaring flaws of this method should the proposals proceed, particularly regarding the principles of legality and foreseeability of sanctions.

It appears that the Council experienced similar concerns,[102] as evidenced by the last available versions of the *PDirEnv* and the *PDirVRM*.[103] Notably, the final versions of Articles 7(3)(a)(b) *PDirENV*[104] and 7(2)(a)(b) *PDirVRM*,[105] which are identical in this respect, include two significant improvements over the original

the "European Touch" of the Comparative Appraisal' in A Klip (ed), *Substantive Criminal Law of the European Union* (Antwerpen, Maklu, 2011) 130.

[101] P Caeiro, 'Punível com coima de até 10% de um montante qualquer' (n 21) *passim*.

[102] See Council of the European Union, Document ST 16171 2022 INIT, Proposal for a Directive of the European Parliament and of the Council on the protection of the environment through criminal law – General approach, 16.12.2022; and Council of the European Union, Document ST 10366 2023 INIT, Proposal for a Directive of the European Parliament and of the Council on the definition of criminal offences and penalties for the violation of Union restrictive measures – General approach, 12.06.2023.

[103] European Parliament Legislative Resolution of 27 February 2024 on the proposal for a directive of the European Parliament and of the Council on the protection of the environment through criminal law and replacing Directive 2008/99/EC (COM(2021)0851 – C9-0466/2021 – 2021/0422(COD)), and European Parliament legislative resolution of 12 March 2024 on the proposal for a directive of the European Parliament and of the Council on the definition of criminal offences and penalties for the violation of Union restrictive measures (COM(2022)0684 – C9-0401/2022 – 2022/0398(COD)).

[104] '3. Member States shall take the necessary measures to ensure that, at least for legal persons held liable pursuant to Article 6(1), criminal offences covered by Article 3(2) are punishable by criminal or non-criminal fines, the amount of which shall be proportionate to the gravity of the conduct and to the individual, financial and other circumstances of the legal person concerned. Member States shall take the necessary measures to ensure that the maximum level of such fines is not less than:

(a) for criminal offences covered by Article 3(2), points (a) to (l), and points (p), (s) and (t):
  (i) 5% of the total worldwide turnover of the legal person, either in the business year preceding that in which the offence was committed, or in the business year preceding that of the decision to impose the fine, or
  (ii) an amount corresponding to EUR 40 000 000;
(b) for criminal offences covered by Article 3(2), points (m), (n), (o), (q) and (r):
  (i) 3% of the total worldwide turnover of the legal person, either in the business year preceding that in which the offence was committed, or in the business year preceding that of the decision to impose the fine, or
  (ii) an amount corresponding to EUR 24 000 000'.

[105] '2. Member States shall take the necessary measures to ensure that a legal person held liable pursuant to Article 6 for criminal offences referred to in Article 3(1) is punishable by criminal or non-criminal fines, the amount of which shall be proportionate to the gravity of the conduct and to the individual, financial and other circumstances of the legal person concerned. Member States shall take the necessary measures to ensure that the maximum level of such fines is not less than:

(a) for criminal offences covered by Article 3(1), points (h)(iii) and (iv):
  (i) 1 % of the total worldwide turnover of the legal person, either in the business year preceding that in which the offence was committed, or in the business year preceding the decision to impose the fine, or
  (ii) an amount corresponding to EUR 8 000 000;
(b) for criminal offences covered by Article 3(1) points (a) to (g), points (h)(i) and (ii), and point (i):
  (i) 5 % of the total worldwide turnover of the legal person, either in the business year preceding that in which the offence was committed, or in the business year preceding the decision to impose the fine, or
  (ii) an amount corresponding to EUR 40 000 000'.

Commission's proposals (below, i) and ii)), while leaving one issue partly unattended (below, iii)).

i) An Option, not an Obligation

In the first place, Member States are not *obligated* to implement turnover-based fines, which are now presented as an option, alternatively to setting quantitative (minimum) maximum limits for the imposable fines. This accommodation addresses the concerns of Member States that do not provide for turnover-based fines in their legal systems.

However, the novel inclusion of explicit quantitative minimum thresholds for maximum fines prompts criticisms akin to those levelled against the same approach when applied to sentences of imprisonment.[106] It is likely to result in disproportionate punishment, compared to fines established by national laws for other offences (heterologous relative proportionality),[107] including those that are subject only to the 'minimum trias'[108] under approximation directives enacted by the EU. There is a risk that national legislators, bound by the minima imposed by the new directives, try to avoid manifest disproportionality by increasing fines applicable to other offences, unnecessarily exacerbating the punitiveness of their legal systems.

Additionally, many Member States that adopt the days fine system will likely (and rightfully) deem the reintroduction of blunt quantitative thresholds as an objectionable regression in terms of criminal policy.[109] This may lead to the creation of special rules for punishing legal entities for the specific offences contained in the directives, setting higher limits for the number of days-fine, which will only highlight their disproportionate nature compared with more serious offences (ordinal proportionality).

The double qualification method, utilising qualitative categories of penalty severity,[110] should also apply here. However, this seems to be a lost cause, as EU

[106] P Caeiro, 'Beyond Competence Issues' (n 1) 657 et seq.

[107] See above, III.B. ii). By way of example, under Portuguese law, the maximum fine applicable to legal entities for the most serious offences (eg, aggravated murder = 3000-day fine) and at the highest daily rate (10.000 euro) is 30 million euro, whereas the *PDirVRM* imposes a minimum maximum – for offences such as violation of restrictive measures … – of 40 million euro.

[108] K Ambos, *European Criminal Law* (Cambridge, Cambridge University Press, 2018) 340.

[109] See Faraldo Cabana (n 3) 262, with further references.

[110] See the original seed of a model based on qualitative categories in P Caeiro and MA Lemos, 'Content and impact of approximation: the case of terrorist offences (Council Framework Decisions of 2002 and 2008)' in F Galli and A Weyembergh (eds.), *Approximation of Substantive Criminal Law in the EU. The Way Forward* (Bruxelles, Editions de l'Université de Bruxelles, 2013) 166–167, explained in more detail in P Caeiro, 'Beyond Competence Issues' (n 1) 662 et seq; compare H Satzger, 'The Harmonisation of Criminal Sanctions in the European Union', (2019) *eucrim* 115. See also the testing and development of the model in H Satzger (Hrsg.), *Harmonisierung* (n 1) 707 et seq, *passim*, and its appraisals by A Soo, A Lott and A Kangur, *Euroopa Liidu õiguses sätestatud halduskaristuste kohaldamine Eesti õiguses* (Aruanne, Tartu Ülikool, 2020) 63, and K Nuotio, 'Supranational Criminal Law, Harmonisation and Approximation' in K Ambos and P Rackow, *The Cambridge Companion to European Criminal Law* (Cambridge, Cambridge University Press, 2023) 129.

bodies (particularly the Commission) do not seem to be concerned with disproportionate punishment or the imbalances it causes across Europe. On the contrary, the new proposals for quantitative minimum maximum thresholds indicate the EU's willingness to further pursue this flawed path.

ii) Legality and Foreseeability

The legality principle mandates that the maximum fine amount be foreseeable at the time of the offence. The current version of the proposals take some positive steps in this regard, by recognising that basing the fine on the turnover from the year preceding the fining decision could pose issues. They therefore offer Member States the option to reference either 'the business year preceding that in which the offence was committed' or 'the business year preceding the decision to impose the fine'.[111] Recitals 33 *PDirEnv* and 23 *PDirVRM* state that 'Member States should decide which of those two options they will use, when transposing this Directive'.

Nevertheless, it is regrettable that the latter option is viewed as an *alternative* to the former. The two criteria serve different purposes and should be seen as complementary: referencing the turnout of the year of the offence ensures compliance with foreseeability and the legality principle, while using the percentage of the last turnover before the fining decision aims at protecting the current financial capacity of the legal entity. Exclusively referring to the latter is not consistent with the legality principle.[112]

Interestingly, the Portuguese legislator seems to have acknowledged the problem already within the field of competition infringements. The law implementing Directive ECN+[113] amended the previous regime on the calculation of sanctions (deemed to be unconstitutional by some authors[114]) and Article 69(7) of Law

[111] Above nn 104 and 105.

[112] This has been exhaustively pointed out in the literature on competition law (see above III. B. i)) and the arguments apply *a fortiori* to criminal sanctions.

[113] Law No 17/2022 of 17 August 2022.

[114] Already in 2009, MM Pereira characterised the regime of competition sanctions as 'potentially arbitrary' and expressed 'serious doubts' about its constitutional conformity (MM Pereira, *Lei da Concorrência Anotada* (Coimbra, Coimbra Editora, 2009) 428). Over time, other authors have been more adamant about those issues, particularly regarding the violation of the legality and proportionality principles: JL Moutinho, 'Legislador português. Precisa-se. Algumas notas sobre o regime sancionatório no Regulamento Geral sobre a Protecção de Dados (Regulamento (UE) 2016/679' (2017) 4 *Forum de Proteção de Dados* 54, 54–56; AS Dias, *Direito das Contra-Ordenações* (n 78) 58 et seq, 77 (AS Dias and RS Pereira, *Direito das Contra-Ordenações*, 2nd edn (Coimbra, Almedina, 2023) 72 et seq, 92–93); in detail, P Caeiro, 'Punível com coima de até 10% de um montante qualquer' (n 21) 2443–2469.

Contra, JF Dias and FN Loureiro, 'Artigo 69.º – Determinação da Medida da Coima' in ML Porto, JL da Cruz Vilaça, C Cunha, M Gorjão-Henriques, G Anastácio (coord), *Lei da Concorrência. Comentário Conimbricense* (Coimbra, Almedina, 2013) 701; and PS Mendes, *O Sancionamento das Práticas Restritivas da Concorrência* (Coimbra, Almedina, 2022) 89 et seq. While critiquing my approach, the latter author fails to engage with the arguments that led me (among the other authors whom he neglects to mention) to conclude that the law in force at the time was unconstitutional. Instead, Mendes merely observes that I do not provide an interpretation that would salvage the law's constitutional validity and, based on this, dismisses my conclusion as 'inadmissible', asserting that it

No 19/2012 of 08 May 2012 now provides that 'from the application of the rule contained in paragraphs 4 and 5 [which refers the maximum limit of the fine to the annual turnover in the business year preceding the decision to impose the fine], a maximum fine amount cannot result that exceeds what would result from referencing the value corresponding to the economic year prior to the infringement'. While the terms may seem somewhat inverted, the result remains the same: the fine cannot exceed *either* limit.

Finally, the proliferation of options for Member States to choose from is also open to criticism as it undermines the harmonising effect that directives are supposed to achieve.[115]

iii) Protection of the Capacity to Pay

Similarly to Directive ECN+, but unlike Regulation (EC) No 1/2003 and the instruments inspired by it, the *PDirEnv* and the *PDirVRM* do not impose on Member States the duty to cap fines at a certain percentage of the annual turnover of the legal persons *in the year preceding the fining decision* to protect their capacity to pay.

This omission may not be problematic if Member States either adopt the turnover-based method and, albeit objectionably,[116] refer the upper limit to the annual turnover in the year preceding the fining decision, or implement the maximum quantitative limits through the system of days fine. In the former, the annual percentage serves as both the upper limit of the sanction and a cap protecting the current financial capacity of the legal entity, whereas in the latter the daily rate performs a similar[117] function of limiting the fine amount to the legal person's capacity to pay.

However, it can become problematic if Member States opt for turnover-based fines and refer the upper limit to the year in which the offence was committed, as required by the legality principle, or if they introduce a fixed quantitative limit. In

would 'completely destroy the Portuguese sanction regime for competition infringements'. Mendes concludes by simply restating, with no further justification, the constitutional conformity of the provision at stake. Such reasoning is untenable, as it effectively makes the unconstitutionality of a provision contingent upon its impact on the sanctioning system. It suggests that the integrity of the competition legal regime should take precedence over the fundamental principles enshrined in the Constitution. Moreover, it is worth noting that the Portuguese legislator evidently shared concerns about the constitutional validity of the sanctioning system then in force, leading to legislative changes in 2022, as outlined in the text.

[115] The EU legislator should refrain from including optional clauses and suggestions in instruments intended to establish binding minima: see P Caeiro, 'Commentary on the "European Touch" of the Comparative Appraisal' (n 100) 130; and L Foffani, V Mitsilegas and P Caeiro, 'Strengthening the fight against economic and financial crime within the EU', (2020) 12 *eucrim*, https://doi.org/10.30709/eucrim-2020-022.

[116] Above IV.A. ii).

[117] The difference lies in the strict nature of a legally imposed cap compared to the calculation of daily rates within a legal framework, which allows for considerable judicial discretion.

those cases, a cap is necessary to tailor the fine to the current financial condition of the legal person – a provision lacking in the proposals. Unlike in competition law, *criminal* penalties for legal entities usually include judicial winding up. Fines should therefore not function as a means to indirectly drive enterprises out of business but should instead be applied in a manner that preserves their operational capacity. Establishing a cap on fines as a percentage of the annual turnover in the *year preceding the fining decision* would be sensible. Such a cap would serve its original purpose of safeguarding the viability of enterprises. The absence of such a provision in the proposals reinforces the perception that EU criminal law is primarily driven by unbridled punitiveness.[118]

B. Reform Instead of Revolution: Turnover-Based Fines can be Effective, Foreseeable, Coherent, and Proportionate

There are good reasons to uphold the principle of equivalent punishment that underlies the provision of a certain number of days' fine for a specific crime, without distinguishing between natural persons and legal entities. This principle, which honours the notion of criminal law based on the act (*Tatstrafrecht*) rather than the agent (*Täterstrafrecht*), also explains the legal ratio between the duration of applicable imprisonment sentences and days' fines applicable to the latter.[119]

Nevertheless, if one concludes that such a method cannot effectively prevent and punish offences committed by the wealthiest legal persons, then it is not theoretically (or indeed politically) impossible to devise alternative sanctioning models. Yet, in doing so, it would be prudent to avoid establishing within the same legal system two disparate models with entirely different structures. Such a 'schizophrenic' approach is bound to create imbalances and undermine ordinal proportionality. It may be more beneficial, therefore, to reconsider the entire concept and, after careful deliberation, decide whether it is advantageous to overhaul the punishment of legal persons entirely and apply it uniformly across the legal system for all offences. The following considerations present some ideas towards a potential new model.

It is submitted that the most appropriate way to ensure legal certainty, proportionality and effectiveness is to keep the traditional framework of days fine, with minimum and maximum thresholds.[120] This framework offers a scale – a finite

[118] AM Rodrigues, 'Fundamental rights and punishment: Is there an EU perspective?' (2019) 10 *New Journal of European Criminal Law* 17.

[119] In this direction, see also N Brandão, 'O regime sancionatório das pessoas colectivas na revisão do Código Penal' (2008) 8 *Revista do CEJ* 45, fn 16 and 17; possibly in the opposite direction, Faraldo Cabana (n 3) 256, who criticises the link between the multiplying factor included in fines applicable to legal persons and the length of imprisonment sentences applicable to individuals, considering it 'a hardly justifiable parallel'.

[120] *Contra*, Faraldo Cabana (n 3) 262 et seq, argues that proportional fines (viz., fines that are a multiple of the damage caused, the gain obtained, the object of the offence, and so forth) are more suitable for

number of days – in which the seriousness and duration of the offence, the guilt of the offender and other relevant factors can be appropriately weighed. Crucially, days fines adhere to *proportionality*, both cardinal and ordinal, by offering a wholly *objective* scale – an endeavour that is left unattended when fines are calculated solely as percentages of individual turnovers.[121]

Moreover, while the EU should generally avoid disturbing the coherence of Member States' criminal law without good reason,[122] it should exercise particular caution when innovating in the field of criminal *sanctions*, given the sensitivity of national systems in this regard – perhaps even more so than when introducing new offence definitions.[123]

Secondly, the days fine method does not necessarily result in a weak or ineffective penal response when it comes to punishing large enterprises. In these instances, the economic power of the offender challenges the deterrent effect of fines bound by quantitative limits concerning the number of days and daily rate. Since the problem arises from the *individual circumstances of the offender*, it should not be solved by blindly increasing the penal weight of the elements related to the *criminal act* (number of days-fine, astronomical quantitative thresholds[124]), which leads to irrational exasperation of the system's overall punitiveness. Instead, addressing this issue requires innovation in the calculation of the *daily rate* and adapting it to reflect a different reality. Rather than relying solely on a quantitative scale, it would be appropriate to refer the daily amount to the annual turnover of the business year (or the average of the two or three years[125]) *preceding the time of commission*, or any subjective standard that allows for calculating the maximum amount of the fine at that point in time.[126]

To determine the fine, the chosen reference (annual turnover, average turnover in a number of years, and so forth) would be divided by 365 to calculate the 'daily turnover'. Referring to this daily value at the time of the offence (unlike fines for individuals) is imposed by the legality principle. By multiplying the 'daily

punishing legal entities. However, the shortcomings of the days fine system pointed out by the author do not relate to the system *itself* but rather to the actual values provided for by several laws for the daily rate, which are deemed too high or too low, depending on the case.

[121] Above, III.B. ii).

[122] Asp (n 86) 208.

[123] European Criminal Policy Initiative (n 1) 432; P Caeiro, 'Constitution and Development of the European Union's Penal Jurisdiction: Responsibility, Self-reference and Attribution' (2021) 27 *European Law Journal* 459.

[124] See also Biermann (n 40) 51: 'Eine sehr hohe absolut bezifferte Obergrenze würde vor allem für kleine Unternehmen ein Problem der Verhältnismäßigkeit darstellen'.

[125] cf the Opinion of the Committee on Civil Liberties, Justice and Home Affairs for the Committee on Legal Affairs on the proposal for a directive of the European Parliament and of the Council on the protection of the environment through criminal law (COM(2021)0851 – C9-0466/2021 – 2021/0422(COD))2021/0422(COD), 6.02.2023, 52–53, Amendments Nos 114 and 117.

[126] Although it affords less certainty, the law could also refer to *the last year of commission* because the legal person can make a rough estimate of the turnover of the business year(s) in which the offence is actually committed. Wils' objections mentioned above (n 28) do not apply here: firstly, because the fine is not calculated as a percentage of the turnover; secondly, because the fine is not conceived as a function of economic harm or illegal gain (see below).

turnover' for the maximum number of applicable days-fine for the offence, the legal person can precisely anticipate the maximum *amount* of the fine it could face for committing the offence.[127] Indeed, this method could potentially lead to fines becoming unduly burdensome if the financial capacity of the legal person significantly diminishes by the time of sentencing. Hence, the establishment of a safeguard clause (a proper cap) is needed to avoid it.[128]

Calculating the daily rate based on legal persons' turnover rather than relying on a quantitative scale can impact the decision over the maximum number of applicable days-fine (the 'abstract' framework). While this number is a political choice, it should be approached with caution. For instance, Regulation (EC) No 1/2003 currently allows for fines of up to 10% of annual turnover, which, under the proposed model, would translate to roughly 37-day fines. Even if, at this stage, only the objective harm or danger caused by the offence is considered, it would hardly be reasonable to establish a legal maximum for the number of days' fine that equates to several years of the undertaking's economic activity.[129]

The purpose of the fine would be to deprive the legal entity of a value proportionate to its economic activity, encompassing not only profit but also overall worth, for a specified period. Unlike competition law, where fines aim to address market influence, the criminal offences at stake in the directives do not bear direct market implications. Moreover, the other argument supporting turnover-based fines in competition law – the lack of effective mechanisms for confiscating proceeds of administrative infringements – does not apply to criminal law, where confiscation of proceeds is a well-developed tool, in both domestic and EU law, and should be kept separate from fine calculations.[130]

Finally, to prevent fines from exceeding the legal person's financial capacity, the law should set a cap at a certain percentage (eg, 10% or 15%) of the annual turnover in the *business year preceding the sentencing decision*, mirroring the original concept in competition law.

There may be instances where the annual turnover of the legal person has significantly increased between the time of commission and the imposition of the

[127] Fuentes Osorio (n 76) 212-213, also presents a method based on the days fine system, albeit with two significant differences. Firstly, he suggests that the daily rate should correspond to a percentage (25%–40%) of the legal entity's annual *net income* ('*ingresos netos*') rather than its overall turnover. However, using net income as a basis can be problematic since it can be negative. For instance, large companies like Tesla may experience net losses for a decade. Secondly, the author proposes referring to the net income of the *year preceding the fining decision*. This method aligns with the legality principle if the calculation remains *within* a certain legal maximum limit, as provided for in Article 50(4) of the Spanish Penal Code (1,8 million euro per year: 360-day fine x 5.000 euro). If, in contrast, it seeks to replace the maximum legal threshold with a percentage of a value that is entirely indeterminable at the time of commission, it becomes vulnerable to the criticisms outlined in Section III.

[128] See below.

[129] As could occur, eg, in Portuguese law due to the ratio established by Article 90º-B of the Portuguese Penal Code, where one month of imprisonment corresponds to a 10-day fine for legal persons. Under the proposed system, this would amount to fining the legal person for a sum equivalent to eight years of turnover.

[130] In the same direction, Faraldo Cabana (n 3) 263.

fine. This evolution could result in the fine amount having a weaker deterrent effect than intended because it is calculated on the basis of a lower turnover. However, this is the inherent cost of upholding fundamental principles such as the legality principle, which serves to protect basic individual guarantees *at the expense* of the state and the maximisation of its endeavours.

V. Conclusion

The European Union, along with its courts, does not seem to encounter any legitimacy issues with turnover-based administrative fines that lack a maximum limit or have an indeterminable maximum limit at the time of the infringement. The Commission initially proposed three directives to introduce this method into criminal law. If adopted, Member States would be compelled to implement fines in their legal systems, with a maximum limit set as a percentage of turnover in the year prior to the fining decision. However, during the legislative procedure, the Council (with the acquiescence of Parliament) significantly modified the proposals in two aspects: on the one hand, the implementation of such a model will be optional; on the other hand, the reference turnover may be that of the year of the offence.

While the adopted sanctioning method remains subject to various criticisms, the introduced modifications mitigate some of the most serious problems raised by turnover-based fines, particularly regarding the mandatory nature of their implementation and respect for the legality principle. However, the issues concerning proportionality, both cardinal and, especially, ordinal, are not only unresolved but probably further intensified with the potential introduction of two sanctioning methods based on different principles within the same legal system.

The reluctance of Member States to adopt turnover-based fines in *criminal* law is noteworthy and warrants reflection, especially considering that turnover-based *administrative* fines in other branches of domestic legal systems also implicate fundamental guarantees, such as the legality principle and proportionality. Ultimately, it is conceivable for a Member State to establish sanctions under the same name (fines) in different branches of its legal system (eg, administrative and criminal), with comparable preventive and punitive aims, potential impact on fundamental rights, and qualification for the purposes of the ECHR – yet restrict compliance with the principle of legality solely for those formally categorised as criminal.

This possibility reveals, not without irony, one of the known entropies arising from the blur between administrative and criminal law. The 'flexible approach', which modulates the applicability of criminal law guarantees to procedures and sanctions of a different nature, presupposes that the latter have a lesser impact on fundamental rights than criminal law – an assumption that, as argued, is subject to debate.

Yes, turnover-based fines are unknown to the criminal law of most Member States (and, as it is, to many criminal law scholars). Yes, the sanctioning model currently in force in competition law, which the Commission tried to transplant, *qua tale*, to the criminal law of Member States makes turnover-based fines deservedly unloved. But this does not mean that there are no alternatives that might better reconcile the various conflicting interests, leaning more towards the protection of fundamental rights and respect for the basic principles of criminal law, such as legality and proportionality. The submitted method is certainly not perfect, in the sense that there may be cases in which the economic growth of the legal entity between the infringement and the sentence would advise for fines higher than those established on the basis of the turnover at the time of the offence. But one must bear in mind that the model currently in force in competition law is not foolproof against ineffective fines either. It suffices that the turnover of the year before the fining decision is exceptionally low due to anomalous circumstances, despite the significant wealth and financial power of the legal entity.

If ineffectiveness in marginal situations represents a constant potential cost, it is therefore (especially) preferable to implement a system that is generally fair rather than one that is generally unfair.

10

Proportionality of Criminal Penalties and EU Judicial Cooperation

EMANUELA PISTOIA

I. Introduction

Proportionality of criminal penalties has been an issue in connection with the European Arrest Warrant (EAW) for years. The Council, the European Parliament and the Commission have all dealt with it repeatedly and it did happen that some national judicial authorities took action to halt disproportionate surrender requests. Over the years, without any common measure ever being taken but the collection of practices in the Handbook on how to issue and execute an EAW, through its several editions from 2008 to 2023, the discussion on the matter waned. However, in the context of a comprehensive analysis of the meaning and impact of the principle of proportionality of penalties in EU law, a review of this topic is appropriate, especially if completed with more recent case-law of the European Court of Justice on the direct effect of Article 49(3) of the Charter. The purpose of this chapter is both to recapitulate the main points of the discussion and to review them from the perspective of the fundamentals of judicial cooperation in criminal matters within the Union, i.e. mutual recognition, mutual trust and fundamental rights protection under the Charter.[1]

Proportionality has come into the limelight with regard to penalties deemed too severe for an offence, not the other way round: too light a sentence is preferable to impunity, which the execution of an EAW has the mission to rule out; moreover, the surrender of someone who resides in another Member State or has fled there is inevitably perceived as part of the sentence, with the effect of aggravating it as a matter of fact.

EAWs have been blamed as disproportionate when issued for trivial cases. Behind this clearly stated censure there are two different concerns, which might

[1] On a different note, the principle of proportionality is also believed to lie behind the two-step test that governs the relation between mutual trust and fundamental rights in the judicial cooperation in criminal matters: A Nato, 'Mandato di arresto europeo e principio di proporzionalità nella sentenza *Puig Gordi*' (2023) 18 *Studi sull'integrazione europea* 345.

not necessarily coexist in every situation. One is strictly about the issuing of an EAW, insofar as the removal of individuals from the Member State where they are located and their surrender to the judicial authorities of another member State, including the restriction to liberty that this requires, is perceived as disproportionate to the gravity of the offence in the circumstances of the case.[2] Such a concern would surely not arise for serious offences,[3] yet the blame concentrates on the choice to issue an EAW to prosecute an individual accused for a minor offence or to execute a person sentenced for it. Otherwise, beyond the issuing of an EAW, what is deemed excessive can be the custodial sentence handed down for the offence in connection with which the EAW is issued, either because of its very impact on the right to personal liberty or for its length. In the first instance, the proportionality assessment focuses on the action taken by the judicial authority of another Member State, i.e. the very issuing of an EAW. In the second instance, the authentic target is the criminal legislation of the issuing Member State.

In the following pages, the two different legal issues will be dealt with separately, with the purpose to clearly identify the legal bases of their solutions and the bodies responsible for implementing them. In the first instance, a proportionality test is constantly recommended: therefore, its content and conditions will be explored. In the second instance, the nature of the benchmarks to be used in the application of Article 49(3) of the Charter will be discussed. The drawing of a full picture of the matter will lead to an assessment of the current role of the principle of proportionality of penalties in the functioning of the EAW.

The last part of the analysis will focus on the current sharing of responsibility between the issuing and executing authorities in the application of the principle of proportionality of penalties in connection with EAWs. The question as to whether Member States may, or should, ever disregard their obligation to execute an EAW if the latter is deemed to constitute a disproportionate action or if it leads to a disproportionate penalty or to a disproportionate sentence will be explored.

[2] See generally G Di Chiara, 'The Protection on the Right of Freedom on the European Union Level: the European Arrest Warrant and Non-custodial Pre Trial Measures. The Guideline of the Principle of Proportionality: an Interpretive Perspective in S Ruggeri (ed), *Transnational Inquiries and the Protection of Fundamental Rights in Criminal Proceedings. A Study in Memory of Vittorio Grevi and Giovanni Tranchina* (Heidelberg New York Dordrecht London, Springer, 2013) 246–248; S Haggenmüller, 'The Principle of proportionality and the European Arrest Warrant' (2013) 3 *Oñati Socio-legal Series* [online] 95; J Russell, A Tinsley, 'The European Arrest Warrant' (2013) 92 *Criminal Justice Matters* 10, 10–11; V Mitsilegas, *EU Criminal Law After Lisbon. Rights, Trust and the Transformation of Justice in Europe* (Oxford, Hart Publishing, 2016) 142–146; E Xanthopoulou, *Fundamental Rights and Mutual Trust in the Area of Freedom, Security and Justice* (London, Bloomsbury 2020); C Cantone, 'The principle of proportionality and the EAW: uneasy bedfellows?' (19 May 2022) *European Law Blog*; P. Bárd, S Carrera, M Stefan, *The Judicialization of the European Arrest Warrant. Rule of Law and Fundamental Rights as Preconditions for Merited Mutual Trust* (2023) *CEPS* 30. See also W van Ballegoij, *The Nature of Mutual Trust in European Law* (Cambridge Antwerp, Intersentia, 2015) 238–243, where further nuances are provided.

[3] Russell and Tinsley (n 2) 11.

II. The Mainstream Understanding of 'Proportionality of EAWs' as Referred to in the Issuing of EAWs

The political institutions of the European Union (Council, European Parliament, Commission) have addressed proportionality of EAWs in a number of documents: the Handbook on how to issue and execute an European arrest warrant (hereinafter 'the Handbook');[4] the 2009 Council's Final Report on the Fourth Round of mutual evaluations on the EAW;[5] the European Parliament's resolution of 27 February 2014 with recommendations to the Commission on the review of the European Arrest Warrant (reiterated in the European Parliament Resolution of 13 December 2016 on the situation of fundamental rights in the European Union in 2015);[6] and the 2020 Commission's Report to the European Parliament and the Council on the implementation of Council Framework Decision of 13 June 2002 on the European Arrest Warrant and the surrender procedures between Member States.[7] In all of them, it clearly emerges that the concerns on proportionality mainly affect the usage of the EAW.

In the Charter, the legal basis of these concerns is identified in Article 52(1): an EAW brings about several limitations on the exercise of the rights and freedoms recognised by the Charter, such as the right to liberty, and often the right to personal and family life, etc. Article 52(1) of the Charter requires that, subject to the principle of proportionality, limitations on the rights envisaged in the Charter are allowed only if they are necessary and genuinely meet objectives of general interest recognised by the Union or the need to protect the rights and freedoms of others. Also, the European Court of Human Rights constantly underlines that limitations to a certain fundamental right should still respect the essence of that right.

By contrast, Article 49(3) of the Charter is not applicable as it requires proportionality with regard to the severity of penalties. Indeed, actions pertaining to judicial cooperation (i.e. issuing an EAW, surrender in execution of an EAW, but the same applies to the transmission of a custodial sentence along with the certificate, the transmission of a final decision requiring a financial penalty to be paid, etc.) are not penalties.

[4] The European Handbook on how to issue a European arrest warrant ('EAW') was first issued by the Council on 8 May 2008. As a follow-up of the Final Report on the Fourth Round of mutual evaluations on the EAW, the revised version published on 17 December 2010 was amended with regard to the criteria to apply when issuing an EAW, including the principle of proportionality. Through its revised editions (the last having been published on 15 December 2023: C/2023/1270, OJ C, 15.12.2023), it has constantly dealt with the role of the executing State in ensuring proportionality).

[5] Final report on the fourth round of mutual evaluations – The practical application of the European Arrest Warrant and corresponding surrender procedures between Member States, 29 May 2009.

[6] Para 43.

[7] COM (2020)270 final, para 3.4.

In the legal literature, this perspective has been referred to as 'prospective proportionality', namely the opportunity to issue an EAW against the background of the impact of an EAW on the right to freedom and on the right to private and family right of the person to be surrendered.[8]

The Member State where trivial cases in connection with EAWs first became the subject of debate, including hitting the headlines, was the United Kingdom, where the sudden leap of extradition cases, indeed EAWs, was referred to the obligation of other Member States' judicial authorities to prosecute.[9] The responsibility to abide by proportionality was therefore easily placed upon the issuing authority as the one to take the choice of applying the EAW in the specific case. However, as late as 2014, an amendment of the Extradition Act of 2003 added breach of proportionality as a ground for refusal to execute a European Arrest Warrant. This was blamed as 'a significant challenge to the system of mutual recognition based on mutual trust'.[10]

In recent years, the Court of Justice has repeatedly acknowledged that assessment of proportionality in the usage of an EAW is the responsibility of the issuing Member State.[11] With regard to Member States where the competence to issue a EAW belongs to an authority that is not a court, the decision to issue a EAW must be capable of judicial review: the Court specified that such judicial review should include the proportionality to issue an arrest warrant.[12]

The Court of Justice also pointed out that the proportionality assessment is encompassed in the protection of procedural safeguards and fundamental rights that the issuing Member State is expected to provide in order for the executing judicial authority to take the course of actions envisaged in the EAW Framework Decision.[13] From the Court's perspective, along with the protection of procedural safeguards and fundamental rights, due regard to proportionality at the issuing stage is essential for mutual trust to function properly.

[8] See especially Haggenmüller (n 2) 101; Cantone (n 2).

[9] A Hirsch, 'Door thief, piglet rustler, pudding snatcher: British courts despair at extradition requests' (20 October 2008) *The Guardian*. On the Polish side (as the EAWs which raised issues in the country came from Poland), see T Ostropolski, 'The Principle of Proportionality under the European Arrest Warrant with an Excursus on Poland' (2014) 5 *New Journal of European Criminal Law* 167. See also Xanthopoulou (n 2) 115–120.

[10] Mitsilegas, *EU Criminal Law* (n 2) 146.

[11] Joined Cases C-508/18 and C-82/19 PPU *OG and PI (Public Prosecutor's Offices in Lübeck and Zwickau)* ECLI:EU:C:2019:456, paras 71 and 75; Case C-509/18 *PF (Prosecutor General of Lithuania)* ECLI:EU:C:2019:457, para 49; Joined Cases C-566/19 PPU and C-626/19 PPU *JR and YC* ECLI:EU:C:2019:1077, paras 63, 68 and 70; Case C-625/19 PPU *XD (Swedish Public Prosecutor's Office)* ECLI:EU:C:2019:1078, paras 40–42; Case C-414/20 PPU *MM (Spetsializirana prokuratura)* ECLI:EU:C:2021:4, paras 64 and 65. See A H Ochnio, 'Why Is a Redefinition of the Autonomous Concept of an "Issuing Judicial Authority" in European Arrest Warrant Proceedings Needed?' (2020) 5 *European papers* 1305, 1315–1318.

[12] *OG and PI (Public Prosecutor's Offices in Lübeck and Zwickau)*, para 75; *PF (Prosecutor General of Lithuania)* para 53; *JR and YC* paras 62–63, 68 and 70; *MM (Spetsializirana prokuratura)* para 65; *XD (Swedish Public Prosecutor's Office)*, 41–42.

[13] *OG and PI (Public Prosecutor's Offices in Lübeck and Zwickau)*, para 70; *XD (Swedish Public Prosecutor's Office)*, para 40.

III. The Shaping of a Prior Proportionality Check under the Responsibility of the Issuing Judicial Authorities

To sum up, 'prior proportionality check' soon became a mantra in Union circles, with the three political institutions and the Member States showing full agreement on the responsibility of the issuing Member State in abiding by proportionality.

One of the prerequisites for issuing a warrant is that custodial sentences or detention orders established for offences to which the EAW should apply have a certain minimum duration: 12 months for EAWs issued for the purpose of prosecution; 4 months where a sentence has been passed or a detention order has been made.[14] If surrender without verification of double criminality is required, a higher threshold applies: a maximum period of at least three years.[15]

These standards match those established in the European Convention on Extradition signed in the framework of the Council of Europe on 13 December 1957,[16] with the intent of ensuring judicial economy (*de minimis non curat praetor*).[17] Their repetition in the Framework Decision is due to the latter's purpose to replace the system of multilateral extradition built upon the European Convention in relations between Member States.[18] Yet they end up working as a minimum threshold to help ensure proportionality.[19] However, meeting these thresholds may easily prove to be insufficient in terms of proportionality required to limit impingement on fundamental rights:[20] in what way could a sentence of a few months justify removing someone from their State of residence, including most likely freezing their family and personal relationships and placing them in a prison premise where few people, if anyone, can speak their language? In this perspective, the following approach to the proportionality check imposed on the issuing State is fully understandable: 'a check additional to the verification of whether or not the required threshold is met, based on the appropriateness of issuing an EAW in the light of the circumstances of the case'.[21]

[14] Council Framework Decision 2002/584/JHA on the European arrest warrant and the surrender procedures between Member States [2002] OJ L190/1, Article 2(1).

[15] *Ivi*, Article 2(2).

[16] Article 2(2). This provision obviously does not set up a minimum threshold applicable when double criminality is ruled out.

[17] R Blekxtoon, 'Commentary on an Article by Article Basis' in R Blekxtoon (ed), *Handbook on the European Arrest Warrant* (The Hague, TMC Asser Press, 2005) 227. See also S Peers, *EU Justice and Home Affairs Law* vol 2 4th edn (Oxford, Oxford University Press, 2016) 63.

[18] Framework Decision 2002/584/JHA, recitals 7 and 10.

[19] T Marguery, 'Confiance mutuelle, reconnaissance mutuelle et crise de valeurs: la difficile équation entre justice pénale européenne et diversité nationale' (2020) 5 *European Papers* 1271, 1286.

[20] K Weis, 'Introduction to the ruling of the Higher Regional Court of Stuttgart of 25 February 2010 – The proportionality of a European Arrest Warrant' (2010) 1 *New Journal of European Criminal Law* 145, 145 ft 3.

[21] Final report on the fourth round of mutual evaluations, para 3.9, 15. An analysis on the proportionality test to be placed under the responsibility of the issuing judicial authorities is in Xanthopoulou (n 2) 118–120.

Interestingly, in the first edition of the Handbook, the principle of proportionality as a criterion to apply when issuing an EAW was not introduced in relation to trivial cases. In 2008, the Handbook mentioned proportionality in terms of 'weighing the usefulness of the EAW in the specific case against the measure to be applied and its consequences'.[22] The idea was to make use of EAWs only if preventive detention was deemed proportionate, adequate and applicable and, if it was, provided that another coercive non-custodial measure was unavailable.

However, the seriousness of the offence already took centre stage through the fourth round of mutual evaluations on the EAW, whose results are described in the Final Report of 2009. In this Report, the proportionality test is all about weighing the seriousness of the offence on the one hand and the consequences of the execution of the EAW for the individual and dependants on the other hand, with an eye on the possibility of achieving the objective of combating impunity by other less disruptive means and a cost/benefit analysis of the execution of the EAW.[23] In subsequent editions of the Handbook, the Commission further elaborated the concept of seriousness of the offence by distinguishing the harm or danger it has caused and 'the likely penalty imposed if the person is found guilty of the alleged offence'.[24]

The European Parliament Resolution of 2014 defined the proportionality check as comprising an assessment of the impact of the EAW on the rights of the suspected or accused persons, including their right to private and family life.[25] A different nuance of the same concern surfaces in the subsequent editions of the Handbook: the possibility (or likelihood) of the suspect being detained is listed amongst the factors to be weighed up.[26] The Handbook has consistently made a point about alternative measures that the issuing authority should consider in the framework of the proportionality test. The 2010 edition mentioned 'instruments of mutual legal assistance'; videoconferencing (for suspects); and, by means of a summons, the use of the Schengen Information System to establish the place of residence of a suspect or the use of the mutual recognition of financial penalties.[27] The 2017 and 2023 editions made a distinction between measures to be considered at the pre-trial stage of criminal proceedings and measures to be considered at the post-trial stage.[28] The former includes issuing a European Investigation Order for a suspect to be heard via a video link in another Member State; issuing a European Supervision Order for a non-custodial supervision measure; issuing an alert in SIS for the purpose of establishing the place of residence or domicile of

[22] Handbook, edition 2008, para 3.

[23] Final report on the fourth round of mutual evaluations, para 3.9, 15.

[24] Handbook, edition 2017, para 2.4, 14.

[25] European Parliament resolution of 27 February 2014 with recommendations to the Commission on the review of the European Arrest Warrant (2013/2019/INL), para 7 b) and Annex.

[26] Handbook, edition 2010, para 3, p 14; 2017 and 2023 editions, para 2.4, 14 and 19 respectively.

[27] Handbook, edition 2010, para 3, 14–15.

[28] Handbook, editions 2017 and 2023, para 2.5, 15–16 and 19–20 respectively.

a suspect, under Article 34 of the SIS II Decision; requiring a suspect located in the executing Member State to appear before a relevant authority responsible for criminal proceedings in the issuing Member State; inviting a person to attend the criminal procedure voluntarily. Measures applicable post-trial are transferring a custodial sentence to the Member State of residence of the convicted person to be executed by that Member State and transferring an alternative sentence (for example, community service) or a probation order to the Member State of residence of the convicted person to be executed by that Member State. In its 2014 Resolution, the European Parliament was on the same wavelength by calling on Member States and their judicial authorities to exhaust all possible alternative mechanisms before issuing an EAW.[29]

Remaining on the factors to weigh up when assessing proportionality, the Parliament also required considering whether the case was trial-ready,[30] while the Handbook adds the interests of the victims of the offence.[31]

To conclude, by requiring that EAWs be replaced by different measures not only do the conditions included in the proportionality check mirror the classic necessity test, but they also cover *stricto sensu* proportionality.[32]

IV. Executing Member States which Distance Themselves from the Domestic Legislation of Issuing Member States and their Non-Involvement in the Application of Article 49(3) of the Charter

More rarely, judicial authorities have found it troublesome to execute an EAW because their domestic legislation established considerably less severe penalties for the corresponding offence. Their reluctance to order the surrender of the accused or sentenced person has lain in their determination to refrain from lending support to the application of a disproportionate penalty.[33]

There are a few reported cases, the best known probably being the Oberlandesgericht Stuttgart (Higher Regional Court Stuttgart)'s decision of 25 February 2010, which did scrutinise the proportionality of the penalty applied

[29] European Parliament resolution of 27 February 2014 with recommendations to the Commission on the review of the European Arrest Warrant, para 3.

[30] *Ivi*, para 7 b).

[31] Handbook, editions 2017 and 2023, para. 2.4, 14 and 19 respectively.

[32] On the classic dual test incorporated in the principle of proportionality, plus *stricto sensu* proportionality, see T Tridimas, *The General Principles of EU Law*, (Oxford, Oxford University Press, 2007) 139. A three-step test on proportionality is put forward in R Alexy, 'Proportionality and Rationality' in V C Jackson and M Tushnet (eds), *Proportionality. New Frontiers, New Challenges* (Cambridge, Cambridge University Press, 2018) 14. On the principle of proportionality in EU law see generally also P Craig, *EU Administrative Law* 3rd edn (Oxford, Oxford University Press, 2018) chapters 19–20.

[33] This is known as 'retrospective proportionality': Haggenmüller (n 2) 100–101; Cantone (n 2).

by the issuing judicial authority.[34] Another critical point of the decision is that, by relying on the previous German case-law on extradition, the Stuttgart Court took advantage of a *national* scale of assessement for the proportionality of the penalty imposed in the national legislation of the issuing State.

In more detail, the Stuttgart Court ruled that, should the foreign judgment be deemed 'severely serious' or 'excessively serious' in light of the German 'legal sensitivity', the executing judge should still carry out extradition. Should the sentence be deemed 'intolerably serious' or 'disproportionate in a unjustified manner', execution should be refused. In the wake of extradition cases, the threshold set up to allow refusal to execute an EAW was therefore quite high; such was the balance struck between the principle of proportionality in criminal penalties and favouring judicial cooperation with other member States emerging from the applicability of extradition treaties and the EAW in the specific case. In other words, the German judicial authorities deemed that application of the principle of proportionality of penalties was placed under their responsibility even when they acted as executing bodies. Germany's commitment to judicial cooperation with other Member States required shifting the balance towards surrender of a person to be surrendered despite uneasiness, yet with limitations. Indeed, refusing to execute an EAW as issued in connection with an intolerably disproportionate penalty was deemed possible.

Legal commentators underlined that the proportionality test should rather counterpoise the gravity of the offence in connection with which the EAW was issued to the consequences of the latter upon the person concerned and also its costs for the two criminal justice systems involved.[35] This remark is mirrored in the political institutions' documents dealt with in the previous sections. In support, one could also try and take a formal point of view and argue that the executing Member State is not bound by Article 49(3) of the Charter while taking a decision on the surrender of a person or on the execution of other mutual recognition tools because surrender does not constitute implementation of any EU obligations on penalties.

However, looking at the ECJ case-law, in principle nothing prevents the application of Article 49(3) while implementing rules on the EAW: in the *KL* judgment, Articles 2(4) and 4(1) of Framework Decision 2002/584 were interpreted in the light of Article 49(3).[36] Yet on that occasion the Court clearly stated that 'in the system established by Framework Decision 2002/584, it is for the judicial authorities of the issuing Member State to ensure compliance with the principle of

[34] In *New Journal of European Criminal Law*, n. 2/2010. See Weis (n 20) 145; J Voegel, JR Spencer, 'Proportionality and the European Arrest Warrant' (2010) 6 *Criminal Law Review* 474; P Pérez Fernández, 'La Orden europea de detención y entrega y el principio de proporcionalidad de las penas. Comentario a la sentencia del Tribunal Superior de Justicia de Stuttgart, de 25 de febrero de 2010 (asunto número 1246/09)' (13 Mayo 2013) *Revista general de Derecho Penal* (www.iustel.com); L Romano, 'Principio di proporzionalità e mandato d'arresto europeo: verso un nuovo motivo di rifiuto? Nota a OLG Stuttgart, Beschl. v. 25.2.2010 – 1 Ausl (24) 1246/09' (2013) *Diritto penale contemporaneo* 250.

[35] L Romano (n 34) fn. 29.

[36] Case C-168/21 *KL* ECLI:EU:C:2022:558, para 64.

proportionality of criminal offences and penalties',[37] particularly it is 'not for the executing judicial authority, when assessing that condition [of double criminality], to assess the sentence handed down in the issuing Member State in the light of Article 49(3) of the Charter'.[38] Hence, the critical point does not lie in considering Article 49(3) as a possible standard of application of EAWs, but in the identification of the executing judicial authorities as those in charge of the related assessment. The reason is the very structure of the EAW's procedure, particularly its being inspired by the principle of mutual recognition. Indeed, two out of three arguments put forward by the Court of Justice in *KL* are mutual recognition classics: in the system established by Framework Decision 2002/584, 'observance of the rights of the person whose surrender is sought falls primarily within the responsibility of the issuing Member State';[39] lack of proportionality of the sentence handed down in the issuing State is not a self-standing ground for refusal.[40]

Back to the decision of the Stuttgart Court, another critical point is that the assessment of the sentence in connection with which the EAW had been issued relied on domestic standards, despite invoking them in the framework of Article 49(3) of the Charter. Not only does this approach appear in striking contradiction with the principle of mutual recognition, which requires no assessment whatsoever of the criminal legislation and the criminal justice system of the issuing Member State, but also, by acknowledging the casting of a critical eye on the criminal legislation of the issuing Member State on the basis of that of the executing Member State, this approach marks the end of mutual trust.

Interestingly, the Court of Justice has developed a series of common criteria to evalutate proportionality of penalties, so that a *European* concept of proportionality in this area is now on the table.[41] Moreover, by its judgment in case C-205/20, *NE*, the Court overruled its previous stand on the lack of direct effect of State's obligation to establish proportionate penalties.[42] Indeed, as in previous cases the question referred to the Court dealt with the obligation to establish proportionate penalties set out in a directive. However, the Court took care to explain (which was not necessary in order to provide an answer to the referring judge) that, even in the absence of specific obligations in harmonisation directives, Member States are still bound to establish proportionate penalties on the basis of Article 49(3) of the Charter, provided that they are implementing EU law.[43] This clearly gives the green light to the extension of the doctrine of direct effect of the obligation on proportionate penalties to Article 49(3).

[37] *Ivi*, para 65.
[38] *Ivi*, para 68.
[39] *Ivi*, para 65.
[40] *Ivi*, para 66.
[41] Case C-537/16 *Garlsson* ECLI:EU:C:2018:193, paras 48–61; Case C-544/19 *Ecotex Bulgaria* ECLI:EU:C:2021:803, paras 89–111; Case C-35/20 *A* ECLI:EU:C:2021:813, paras 84–92; Case C-77/20 *KM* ECLI:EU:C:2021:112, paras 36–59.
[42] Case C-205/20 *NE Bezirkshauptmannschaft Hartberg-Fürstenfeld* ECLI:EU:C:2022:168, [2022], 29.
[43] *NE*, para 31. M Lanotte, 'La proporzionalità della sanzione: un principio ritrovato? Note a margine della sentenza *NE*' (2023) 5 *I Post di AISDUE* 367; F Viganò, 'La proporzionalità della pena tra diritto costituzionale italiano e diritto dell'Unione europea: sull'effetto diretto dell'art. 49, paragrafo 3, della Carta alla luce della recentissima sentenza della Corte di giustizia' (2022) *Sistema penale* 15.

Such a stand paves the way for an unprecedented role of control for national judges over domestic criminal legislations, which they can exercise whenever they are implementing Union law (Article 51(1) of the Charter). This role involves relying on common standards of review, which considerably weakens the objection on mutual trust impairment. Hence, the question arises as to whether the newly emerged doctrine of direct effect of the principle of proportionality of penalties may open a crack in the fabric of mutual recognition.

Indeed, the doctrine of the direct effect of a Charter provision can perfectly combine with the 'division of labour' between Member States – or, rather, between national judicial authorities – in the implementation of the Charter, which is a byproduct of the principle of mutual recognition in terms of compliance of the related legal tools with fundamental rights. The principle of mutual recognition is not intended to entangle any backsliding in the protection of fundamental rights: Article 1(3) of Framework Decision 2002/584/JHA (and mirroring provisions in other mutual recognition acts) is all but ambiguous. Instead, mutual recognition relies on strict sharing of responsibility between the national judicial authorities on the matter: those entrusted with issuing an EAW are to assess whether seeking the surrender of those on trial or found guilty in their own Member State, who either reside elsewhere in the Union or have fled there, is proportionate and brings about no breaches to the Charter; those required to execute an EAW are to carry our their obligation to surrender a person smoothly and efficiently, which includes trusting in that assessment fully. Hence, the direct effect of Article 49(3) of the Charter is an important addition to the toolkit of the issuing national authorities, but there is no reason to regard it as a game-changer for the role of executing national authorities.

V. Charter-Checking the Role of Executing Member States

In a nutshell, at the EU level no scope for executing judicial authorities in assessment of direct or indirect proportionality was ever contemplated: neither in the case-law of the Court of Justice, nor in the various documents dealt with in previous sections. Specifically, lack of proportionality was never deemed a ground of refusal.

However, awareness that executing Member States could well happen to face disproportionate EAWs has also come to light. In its 2014 Resolution, the European Parliament requested the Commission to submit, within a year, a legislative proposal based on Article 82 TFEU aimed at adding a new mandatory refusal ground 'where there are substantial grounds to believe that the execution of the measure would be incompatible with the executing Member State's obligations in accordance with Article 6 of the TEU and the Charter, notably Article 52(1) thereof with its reference to the principle of proportionality'.[44] The European Parliament also urged the Commission to introduce a proportionality test.[45] Such recommendations were reiterated in 2016, along with the recommendation to introduce a fundamental rights exception.[46]

The Commission never followed these recommendations by Parliament. In the current legal framework, in the case of concerns regarding the proportionality of a certain EAW, the Handbook encourages the issuing and executing judicial authorities to engage in a dialogue that could lead to the withdrawal of the EAW.[47] The Handbook itself underlines that this only applies in exceptional circumstances.

All the above shows that the refusal to acknowledge any role of executing judicial authorities is all but satisfactory, yet it is believed to be the only solution that is consistent with the principle of mutual recognition of judicial decisions as currently implemented in the Framework Decision 2002/584/JHA. In the following pages, I will discuss the applicability of the *Aranyosi* doctrine in proportionality cases, to reconsider whether and to what extent executing national authorities can play a constructive role in rebalancing issuing national authorities. It is known that executing judicial authorities are entrusted with compliance of an EAW with fundamental rights only as long as they are embedded in the mandatory or optional grounds of refusal laid down in the Framework Decision 2002/584/JHA, or in pursuance with the *Aranyosi* doctrine. The latter is the interpretation of a State's unchanged obligation to respect fundamental rights, reiterated in Article 1(3) of Framework Decision 2002/584/JHA, when mutual recognition is at stake, i.e. when mutual trust is due despite the apparent low level of protection of a certain fundamental right in the issuing State. Under the *Aranyosi* doctrine, mutual recognition becomes recessive compared with the protection of fundamental rights if two conditions are met: there is a context of systemic or generalised deficiencies that concern a certain fundamental right in the issuing Member State (or deficiencies which affect certain groups of people, or certain places), so that there is evidence of a real risk that a breach of that right in the specific case could occur; there is evidence that the individual concerned will be exposed to this risk. The assessment is entirely in the hands of the executing authorities, which are never entitled to refuse execution indefinitively but only to postpone it until surrender proves safe in terms of protection of fundamental rights.[48]

[44] European Parliament resolution of 27 February 2014 with recommendations to the Commission on the review of the European Arrest Warrant, para 7 d).

[45] European Parliament resolution of 27 February 2014 with recommendations to the Commission on the review of the European Arrest Warrant, para 7 b).

[46] European Parliament resolution of 13 December 2016 on the situation of fundamental rights in the European Union in 2015, para 43.

[47] Handbook, edition 2017, para 5.7; Handbook, edition 2023, para 5.8.

[48] Joined Cases C 404/15 and C 659/15 PPU *Aranyosi and Căldăraru* ECLI:EU:C:2016:198, para 98. See generally G Anagnostaras, 'Mutual confidence is not blind trust! Fundamental rights protection and the execution of the European arrest warrant: *Aranyosi and Căldăraru*' (2016) 53 *Common Market Law Review* 1675; E Bribosia, A Weyembergh, 'Arrêt Aranyosi et Căldăraru: imposition de certaines limites

Starting from disproportionate EAWs whithin the terms illustrated in Sections 1 and 2, in contexts where prosecution in the issuing State is obligatory, the issuing of an EAW in connection with trivial offences may well have a disproportionate impact on fundamental rights of the person to be surrendered with no possibility to refuse on the part of the judicial authority entrusted with executing the EAW. On average, fundamental rights being disproportionately affected in trivial cases are the right to personal liberty (Article 6) and the right to private and family life (Article 7), whose derogation is in principle allowed for the prosecution of criminal offences. However, lack of proportionality may prove in breach with Article 52(1) of the Charter. Yet in this provision proportionality is a principle, not a fundamental right: it is doubtful that the *Aranyosi* doctrine could ever apply.

Turning to EAWs issued with regard to disproportionate sentences in breach of Article 49(3) of the Charter, the feasibility of the *Aranyosi* test is far from obvious. *Aranyosi*'s step two, on the actual existence of the risk that a certain right will be breached after surrender (or as a consequence thereof), is indeed quite clear: it appears viable especially with regard to EAWs issued for the purpose of execution of sentences or detention orders. Instead, step one is unclear as to what should be understood by a systemic or generalised breach of Article 49(3) of the Charter. To refer such a breach to all the penalties laid down in the issuing Member State would make the *Aranyosi* test entirely utopian. Moreover, this would be a restrictive application of *Aranyosi*, which is certainly consistent with its nature of exception to the obligation to give execution to EAWs; yet understanding of the *Aranyosi* doctrine cannot even be such as to make it *de facto* inapplicable. Furthermore, the *Aranyosi* test is by itself a restrictive interpretation of the obligation of Article 1(3) of Framework Decision 2002/584/JHA, given the mutual trust amongst the Member States and the landmark role of mutual recognition of judicial decisions and sentences. Another way to understand the requirement of a systemic or generalised breach is therefore preferable. The idea is to link it to the existence of a statutory provision in the issuing Member State: should the penalty laid down for a certain offence be unreasonably severe pursuant to the Court's case-law on Article 49(3) of the Charter, a systemic and generalised breach of this provision in the issuing State should be acknowledged. Too severe a statutory penalty for a certain offence does not necessarily lead to a disproportionate sentence, as the trial judge may consider a number of circumstances in favour of

à la confiance mutuelle dans la coopération judiciaire pénale' (2016) *Journal de droit européen* 225; S Gáspár-Szilágyi, 'Joined Cases Aranyosi and Căldăraru: Converging Human Rights Standards, Mutual Trust and a New Ground for Postponing a European Arrest Warrant' (2016) 24 *European Journal of Crime, Criminal Law and Criminal Justice* 197; N Lazzerini, 'Gli obblighi in materia di protezione dei diritti fondamentali come limite all'esecuzione del mandato di arresto europeo: la sentenza *Aranyosi e Căldăraru*' (2016) *Diritti umani e diritto internazionale* 445; P Zinonos, 'The curious case of *Pál Aranyosi*: precarious balance or manual on the consolidation of mutual trust and fundamental rights?' (2018) 30 *Revue européenne de droit public / European Review of Public Law / Europäische Zeitschrift des öffentlichen Rechts* 2018 417; A Klip, 'The European Arrest Warrant, from Mutual Recognition to Mutual Supervision?' (2022) 12 *European Criminal Law Review* 82.

the accused person. Consequently, in principle the executing national authorities could take responsibility to ensure respect of the right to proportionate sentences.

Provided that this approach is deemed persuasive, what is still doubtful is whether the right to proportionate penalties laid down in Article 49(3) of the Charter is among those capable of calling for the refusal to execute an EAW (should the two-tier test prove successful). This doubt is justified by the meticulous explanations provided by the Court of Justice before implementing the *Aranyosi* test, as though the latter could justify the stopping of the EAW procedure only with regard to certain fundamental rights, or only in certain circumstances.[49] In the *Aranyosi* judgment itself, after reiterating that 'limitations of the principles of mutual recognition and mutual trust between Member States can be made "in exceptional circumstances"',[50] the Court apparently did not identify such circumstances simply in the serious risk of a prospective breach of a fundamental right; instead, it stressed that the prohibition in Article 4 of the Charter 'is closely linked to respect for human dignity, the subject of Article 1 of the Charter'[51] and that the right laid down in Article 4 therein is absolute.[52] In a similar fashion, in cases concerning the right to a fair trial established in Article 47 of the Charter, the Court underlined that the latter is 'a right which is of cardinal importance as a guarantee that all the rights which individuals derive from EU law will be protected and that the values common to the Member States set out in Article 2 TEU, in particular the value of the rule of law, will be safeguarded'.[53] In case *LM*, paragraph 47 leaves no doubt on the need for a fundamental right to meet a certain threshold of relevance in order for its prospective breach to be capable of bringing the EAW mechanism to a standstill. However, recently the Court seems to have taken a different path: the judgment in case *GN (Motif de refus fondé sur l'intérêt supérieur de l'enfant)* paid no comparable attention to a supposedly special character of the right to one's private and family life and the best interest of children (Article 7 and 24, paras. 2 and 3), whose prospective breach was discussed.[54] The Court limited itself to pointing out that '[t]he mutual enjoyment by parent and child of each other's company

[49] On a different note, the view has been put forward that, in Aranyosi (as well as in a similar case), the Court of Justice has been open to a ground of refusal based on a prospective breach of fundamental rights because the underlying criminal offences were not amongst the most serious offences: J Ouwerkerk, 'Balancing Mutual Trust and Fundamental Rights Protection in the Context of the European Arrest Warrant. What Role for the Gravity of the Underlying Offence in the CEU Case-law?' (2018) 26 European Journal of Crime, Criminal Law and Criminal Justice 103.

[50] Aranyosi and Căldăraru, para 82.

[51] Ivi, para 85; Case C-128/18 Dorobantu ECLI:EU:C:2019:857, 62.

[52] Aranyosi and Căldăraru, para 86; Dorobantu, para 62.

[53] Case C-216/18 PPU LM ECLI:EU:C:2018:586, para 48. But see V Mitsilegas, 'Joined Cases C-404/15 and C-659/15 PPU – Pál Aranyosi and Robert Căldăraru v Generalstaatsanwaltschaft Bremen. Resetting the Parameters of Mutual Trust: From Aranyosi to LM' in V Mitsilegas, A Di Martino, L Mancano (eds), The Court of Justice and European Criminal Law (Oxford, Hart Publishing, 2019) 436, who regards LM as 'opening the door for an across-the-board fundamental rights benchmark in the operation of mutual recognition in criminal matters'.

[54] Case C-261/22 GN (Motif de refus fondé sur l'intérêt supérieur de l'enfant) ECLI:EU:C:2023:1017.

constitutes a fundamental element of family life',[55] which may indeed lead to the conclusion that not every breach of one's family life could meet the threshold. Yet this is undoubtedly a far softer approach to the possibility to refuse surrender in execution of an EAW, with the effect of opening the way for the *Aranyosi* test to arouse suspicion of breaches of fundamental rights in general.

Should the Court take a different view on the applicability of the *Aranyosi* test to prospective breaches of Article 49(3) of the Charter, no refusal to surrender could be justified. This conclusion would also apply if an accused person was to be surrendered in execution of an EAW upon the condition of being returned to the executing State in order to serve the sentence or order issued against him in the issuing State (Article 5(3) of Framework Decision 2002/584/JHA). This situation is particularly delicate because the executing Member State would end up giving execution to a disproportionate sentence directly, not merely to a warrant aimed at the execution of a disproportionate sentence in the issuing Member State (i.e. indirect execution of a disproportionate sentence). In case *KL*, the Court underlined that, when the condition of double criminality of the act applies, a Member State could not refuse execution if there is no exact match between the constituent elements of the offence in the two Member States concerned, or between the name given to or the classification of the offence under the national law of the respective States.[56] Even more so this should apply with regard to a disproportionate sentence.

VI. Concluding Remarks

Despite occasional criticism and a widespread sensation of uneasiness, government and Commission officials, national judges and academics have constantly stood against refusal of execution of an EAW by reason of lack of proportionality of a sentence in relation to the offence for which the EAW was issued. The arguments in support are the essence of mutual recognition of judicial decisions and sentences and the structure of mutual recognition tools (such as the EAW), which are based on the obligation to execute warrants and orders issued by the judicial authority of another Member State with the sole exception of mandatory or optional grounds for refusal, which are to be interpreted restrictively. Instead, disproportion regarding a sentence handed down in the issuing Member State is not among the grounds for mandatory and optional non-execution of a EAW set out in Articles 3, 4 and 4a of Framework Decision 2002/584. The same applies to other mutual recognition tools. Consequently, it is for the issuing judicial authority to make sure that the trial behind an EAW, the EAW itself and the follow-up of its execution are compliant with fundamental rights. Accordingly, it is for the

[55] Ivi, 42.
[56] *KL*, 35.

issuing judicial authorities to ensure that an EAW is not disproportionate in the specific case and that it does not disregard proportionality of criminal penalties in breach of Article 49(3) of the Charter. In principle, executing judicial authorities should not have a say on the matter as this would be in contrast with the concept of mutual trust and mutual recognition as designed by the Court of Justice over the years; however, the above analysis showed that they could play a role as a last resort, on ground of the *Aranyosi* doctrine, only in connection with Article 49(3) of the Charter.

Concerning the role of the issuing authorities in verifying proportionality, the adoption of clear and common rules has been widely called for.[57] Indeed, despite the wide consensus on the appropriateness of a prior proportionality check, a certain degree of difference in the practice of Member States was reported even lately. The 2020 Commission's Report stated that a small number of member States still do not provide discretion for their issuing judicial authorities to assess whether issuing an EAW is proportionate in the light of the circumstances of the case.[58] It also provided details on the scope to assess proportionality: sometimes States lay down a higher threshold than that established in Article 2 of Framework Decision 2002/584/JHA; sometimes it is required that a term of four months still remains to be served or that the EAW is issued in the interest of justice. However, these provisions mark a step forward in comparison with ten years earlier: the 2009 Council's Final Report stated that at that time, while the opportunity of a proportionality test at the level of the issuing authorities was already widely shared amongst national delegations, only in some States was it applied on a regular basis. Moreover, practice varied a great deal in terms of circumstances to take into consideration and assessment criteria. Accordingly, by way of conclusion, it can be acknowledged that the Commission's soft power, along with the soft power of dialogue amongst national judicial authorities and national officers, helped to minimise proportionality issues, against the background of the Commission's reluctance to start enforcement actions against non-compliant Member States.

As repeatedly clarified in the previous sections, the Union's political institutions have been dealing with proportionality in the EAW in connection with the very issuing of a warrant in the specific case. The above remark concerns this aspect only.

Instead, entrusting the issuing judicial authority with the responsibility to ensure that the offence or the sentence behind an EAW complies with Article 49(3) of the Charter does not appear appropriate. A construction in which the principle of proportionality of penalties is subject to the same regime as other fundamental rights has clearly an Achilles' heel: it appears unlikely that the issuing judicial authority could question either the sentence passed by a trial bench in its own

[57] On the Commission's decision to continue with a soft-law approach see W van Ballegooij, *European Arrest Warrant. European Implementation Assessment* (European Parliamentary Research Service, 2020) 14–17.

[58] Para 3.4.1.

judicial system or the penalty laid down in its own domestic legislation. Perhaps the requirement that a European arrest warrant be distinct from a national arrest warrant could be a game-changer.[59] The fact remains that it is unlikely that domestic legislation could allow such an assessment, which is objectively odd in the economy of national criminal justice. Therefore, in principle proportionality of criminal penalties in EU judicial cooperation apparently can be enforced only by executing judicial authorities.

[59] Case C-241/15 *Bob-Dogi* ECLI:EU:C:2016:385.

11

The EU-UK Extradition Arrangement and the Principle of Proportionality: Some Hints from the Practice of EU Institutions and Italian and UK Legislation and Case-Law on the EAW

ALESSANDRO ROSANÒ

I. Introduction

On 30 December 2020, the European Union (EU) and the United Kingdom (UK) concluded the Trade and Cooperation Agreement (TCA), designed to govern their future relationship following the UK's decision to leave the bloc. The TCA, which has been provisionally applied since 1 January 2021 and entered into force on 1 May 2021, covers several areas of future cooperation between the EU and the UK,[1] including law enforcement and judicial cooperation in criminal matters, to which Part Three is devoted.

Title VII of Part Three (Articles 596–632) establishes an extradition arrangement based on the issuance of arrest warrants, that is, judicial decisions rendered by courts or prosecutors of the EU Member States or the UK. These features alone reveal an attempt made by the EU and the UK to preserve the status quo on extradition through a mechanism similar to the European Arrest Warrant (EAW) and therefore based on relations between judicial authorities rather than between governments.[2]

[1] For an introduction on the TCA, P Birkinshaw, 'Brexit and the Trade and Cooperation Agreement: Endgame or Prolegomenon?' (2021) 2 *European Public Law* 229; F Fabbrini (ed), *The Law and Politics of Brexit. Volume III: The Framework of New EU-UK Relations* (Oxford, Oxford University Press, 2021); G Adinolfi, A Malatesta, M Vellano (eds), *L'accordo sugli scambi commerciali e la cooperazione tra l'Unione europea e il Regno Unito* (Torino, Giappichelli, 2022).

[2] A Kramer, R Dickson, 'The Changing Landscape of EU-UK Policing and Justice Cooperation' (2020) 1 *European Papers* 479.

The mechanism envisaged by the TCA is similar to the EAW for other reasons. In both cases, warrants may be issued for acts punishable by the law of the issuing State by a custodial sentence or a detention order for a maximum period of at least twelve months or, if a sentence has been passed or a detention order has been made, for custodial sentences or detention orders of at least four months.[3] Moreover, there is a perfect coincidence between the grounds for mandatory non-execution.[4] Furthermore, in the TCA, like the Framework Decision (FD) on the EAW, there is no ground for refusal relating to the protection of the requested person's fundamental rights, the rights of the requested person are regulated in a very similar way,[5] similar arrangements are made for the exchange of information between the judicial authorities of the two States[6] and the certificates which must accompany the warrants, models of which are annexed to the FD and the TCA, are almost identical.[7]

As for the differences between the FD on the EAW and the extradition regime governed by the TCA, it should be noted that the former provides for the waiver of the requirement of double criminality with regard to thirty-two categories of offence, whereas in the TCA the overcoming of this condition works on an optional basis and is subject to reciprocity between the Member States of the EU and the UK.[8] It should also be noted that the TCA provides for the possibility of reintroducing, on a reciprocal basis, the traditional exceptions to surrender arising from the political nature of the offence and the nationality of the surrendering person.[9]

Last but not least, the provisions relating to the principle of proportionality should be highlighted. Article 597 of the TCA provides that cooperation by means of an arrest warrant must be necessary and proportionate, taking into account the rights of the requested person and the interests of the victim, the seriousness of the act, the likely penalty that would be imposed and the possibility for a State to take less coercive measures than surrendering the requested person, in particular to avoid unnecessarily long periods of pre-trial detention. Article 613(1) emphasises that the executing judicial authority shall decide on surrender in accordance with the terms and conditions laid down in the relevant provision, in particular the principle of proportionality as set out in Article 597.

This is a significant difference, given that the FD on the EAW does not mention the principle of proportionality in relation to the issuance and execution

[3] Art 2(1) of Council Framework Decision 2002/584/JHA on the European arrest warrant and the surrender procedures between Member States [2002] OJ L190/1 and Art 599(1) of the TCA.

[4] Art 3 of Council Framework Decision 2002/584/JHA and Art 600 of the TCA.

[5] Art 11 of Council Framework Decision 2002/584/JHA and Art 609 of the TCA.

[6] Art 15(2) of Council Framework Decision 2002/584/JHA and Art 613(2) of the TCA.

[7] S Montaldo, 'La cooperazione giudiziaria in materia penale' in G. Adinolfi, A. Malatesta, M. Vellano (eds), *L'accordo sugli scambi commerciali e la cooperazione tra l'Unione europea e il Regno Unito* (n 1), 226.

[8] Art 2(2) of Council Framework Decision 2002/584/JHA and Art 599(4)(5) of the TCA.

[9] Art 602 and Art 603 of the TCA.

of EAWs.[10] The TCA, on the other hand, which is inspired by British legislation in this respect,[11] provides for a proportionality check.

This chapter is therefore devoted to the role of the principle of proportionality within the extradition arrangement set out by the TCA. To understand the scope of the principle, it analyses the way in which the proportionality issue has been addressed in relation to the EAW. It considers some of the provisions of the FD on the EAW, placing them in relation to other EU acts applying the principle of mutual recognition to judicial cooperation in criminal matters (section 2); it then examines how the issue has been addressed by the EU institutions (section 3). The chapter then reviews the relationship between proportionality and the EAW in Italian legislation and the case law of the Italian Supreme Court of Cassation (section 4) and in the UK legal system (section 5). The aim is to identify the key points that allow an understanding of how the principle of proportionality can be interpreted and operate in relation to the extradition arrangement set out by the TCA (section 6). The conclusion summarises the reasoning carried out in this chapter (section 7).

II. The Principle of Proportionality and the EAW: What FD 2002/584/JHA Provides (and does not Provide) for

The number of issued EAWs has increased significantly over the years.[12] In 2014, almost 15,000 EAWs were issued, in 2015 and 2016 more than 16,000, in 2018 more than 17,000, in 2019 more than 20,000, and in 2020 just under 16,000.[13] The success of this instrument, which is used in particular by some EU Member States such as Poland, Germany, France, and Romania, is therefore undeniable.[14]

Such high numbers spontaneously lead one to wonder whether the use of the EAW is consistent with the principle of proportionality. The cases in which an EAW has been issued for the theft of two tyres or one piglet,[15] or even

[10] Recital 7 simply states that the FD does not go beyond what is necessary to achieve its objectives, in accordance with the principle of proportionality.

[11] See the Extradition Act 2003, as reformed in 2014. This will be discussed *infra*.

[12] For the following data, see https://e-justice.europa.eu/90/EN/european_arrest_warrant.

[13] The exceptionally high number of EAWs issued in 2019 can be traced back to the fact that the 2379 warrants issued by Germany had to be reissued after the Court of Justice (see Joined cases 508/18 and 82/19 PPU *OG (Parquet de Lübeck)* ECLI:EU:C:2019:456) ruled that German prosecutors could not be considered as issuing judicial authorities, thus forcing Germany to quickly pass a reform whereby warrants are now issued by courts (Commission Staff Working Document, *Statistics on the practical operation of the European arrest warrant – 2019*, SWD(2021) 227 final, 4–5).

[14] See Commission Staff Working Document (n 13), 40–41.

[15] Council, 'Proposed subject for discussion at the experts' meeting on the application of the Framework Decision on the European arrest warrant on 17 July 2007 – the proportionality principle', 10975/07, 3.

ten chickens,[16] are well known, as are the remarks of those scholars according to whom an EAW "can be issued for any case of theft: whether it is on the scale of the Great Train Robbery, or a piece of minor shoplifting".[17]

The fact that the FD on the EAW does not mention *expressis verbis* the application of a proportionality check for the purposes of issuing warrants certainly contributes to this state of affairs. The only element that seems to be of value in this respect is that Article 2 of the FD, in which the scope of application of the EAW is defined, provides that EAWs may be issued for acts that are punishable under the law of the issuing Member State by a custodial sentence or a detention order for a maximum period of at least twelve months or, where a sentence has been passed or a detention order has been made, for sentences of at least four months. It should therefore be inferred that it would be disproportionate to issue an EAW for acts punishable by a custodial sentence or a detention order for a maximum period of less than 12 months or, where a sentence has been passed or a detention order has been made, for sentences of less than four months.

Other acts relating to judicial cooperation in criminal matters that apply the principle of mutual recognition make no reference to a verification of proportionality: one can think of FD 2005/214 on the mutual recognition of financial penalties, FD 2008/909 on the transfer of sentenced persons, FD 2008/947 on the application of the principle of mutual recognition to judgments and probation decisions with a view to the supervision of probation measures and alternative sanctions, and FD 2009/829 on the European Supervision Order (ESO), that is, on the application of the principle of mutual recognition to decisions on supervision measures as an alternative to provisional detention.

It is important to remember, however, that the acts now being recalled are nevertheless sources of secondary EU law, which must therefore respect the sources of primary law. These include the principle of proportionality, which is reaffirmed in Article 5(4) TEU.

However, the results of legislation adopted in recent years are quite different. One example is Directive 2014/41 on the European Investigation Order in criminal matters (EIO). According to Article 6(1)(a), the issuing authority may only issue an EIO if it considers it necessary and proportionate for the purpose of the proceedings, taking into account the rights of the suspected or accused person. The same applies to Regulation 2018/1805 on the recognition of freezing and confiscation orders. As provided for under Article 1(3), when issuing a freezing or confiscation order, the issuing authorities must ensure compliance with the principles of necessity and proportionality. Finally, reference can be made to the Regulation 2023/1543 on *e-evidence*, which provides that the European Production Order and the European Preservation Order shall be, inter alia, necessary and proportionate.[18]

[16] *Sandru v Government of Romania*, 28 October 2009, [2009] EWHC 2879 (Admin).

[17] J Vogel, JR Spencer, 'Proportionality and the European Arrest Warrant' (2010) 6 *Crim LR* 581.

[18] Artt. 5(2) and 6(2) of the Regulation.

III. Proportionality and the EAW: How the European Institutions have Dealt with the Issue

A. The Council

In 2009, the Council argued that the issue of proportionality of EAWs should be addressed as a matter of priority, as this would allow for a control beyond the thresholds laid down in Article 2 of the FD, assessing the appropriateness of the measure in the light of the circumstances of the concrete case. To that end, account should have been taken of the seriousness of the offence, the possibility of achieving the objective pursued by less coercive means and a cost-benefit analysis of the execution of the EAW. In this respect, it has been pointed out that, although some Member States have provided for the application of a proportionality test for the purposes of issuing EAWs, practice is inconsistent.[19]

The Council also drew up a European manual on how to issue an EAW, which states that this instrument should be used efficiently, effectively, and proportionately as a tool for preventing and combating crime, while respecting the human rights of suspects and convicted persons, with a view to prosecuting the most serious and harmful forms of crime, justifying its use and the enforcement of sentences.[20]

In outlining the criteria to be taken into account when issuing an EAW, the principle of proportionality is also mentioned. In this regard, it is argued that given the seriousness of the consequences of the execution of an EAW in terms of restrictions on the liberty of the requested person, the competent authorities should take proportionality into account before deciding to issue the warrant by assessing a number of factors, including in particular the seriousness of the offence, the possibility of detaining the suspect and the likely penalty imposed if the requested person was found guilty of the offence of which they were accused. Other factors include ensuring the effective protection of the public and taking into account the interests of the victims. Alternatives to the EAW could be considered, such as the use of mutual legal assistance instruments, videoconferencing of suspects, the Schengen Information System to locate the residence of a suspect, or the FD on financial penalties.[21]

B. The European Commission

In 2011, the European Commission noted that trust between the Member States in the application of the EAW had been undermined by the systematic issue of EAWs

[19] Council, 'Final report on the fourth round of mutual evaluations – The practical application of the European Arrest Warrant and corresponding surrender procedures between Member States', 8302/4/09, p. 15.

[20] Council, 'Revised version of the European handbook on how to issue a European Arrest Warrant', 17195/1/10, p. 4.

[21] ibid, 14–15.

in relation to minor offences and that a proportionality test was needed. Judicial authorities should therefore apply this test consistently and use the EAW only if the request for surrender is proportionate to all the circumstances of the case, taking into account the guidance provided by the Council handbook. Training of judicial authorities would be key to ensure consistency in the application of the test.[22] The European Commission referred, inter alia, to the factors identified in the Council handbook for assessing proportionality.[23]

The European Commission subsequently produced a handbook on the issuing and execution of an EAW, which states that the EAW must always be proportionate to the objective pursued.[24] The issuing judicial authorities are required to assess whether, in the specific case, the issuing of an EAW is a justified measure, taking into account a number of factors, such as the seriousness of the offence, the penalty that is likely to be imposed if the requested person is found guilty of the alleged offence, the likelihood that the person will be detained in the issuing Member State after surrender, the interests of the victims and the possibility of using other judicial cooperation measures. With regard to the latter, the possibility of resorting to the EIO, the transfer of sentenced persons, the recognition of probation decisions and alternative sanctions, the ESO, and the recognition of financial penalties should be considered.[25]

Finally, there is the question of the role of the executing Member State. In line with the principle of mutual recognition, the FD on the EAW does not provide for the possibility for the executing Member State to assess the proportionality of the EAW. However, if serious doubts arise in the executing Member State as to the proportionality of the EAW received, the issuing and executing judicial authorities should, in exceptional cases, communicate directly. In such cases, it may be preferable to withdraw the EAW and use other measures. Eurojust or the EJN contact points may also be consulted.[26]

Furthermore, the European Commission clarified that Article 2(1) of the FD has been correctly transposed by most Member States. However, a small minority have not explicitly empowered their competent issuing judicial authorities to assess the proportionality of an EAW in light of the specifics of each case.[27]

[22] Report from the Commission to the European Parliament and the Council on the implementation since 2007 of the Council Framework Decision of 13 June 2002 on the European arrest warrant and the surrender procedures between Member States, COM(2011) 175 final, 7–8.

[23] ibid.

[24] Commission Notice – Handbook on how to issue and execute a European arrest warrant (C/2023/1270), 18 (reference is made to the most recent version of the handbook).

[25] ibid, p. 19.

[26] ibid, p. 57.

[27] Report from the Commission to the European Parliament and the Council on the implementation of Council Framework Decision of 13 June 2002 on the European arrest warrant and the surrender procedures between Member States, COM(2020) 270, 9.

C. The European Parliament

In 2014, the European Parliament adopted a resolution highlighting a number of issues that would justify a review of the FD by the European Commission.[28]

Among other things, the European Parliament underlined the existence of problems related to the lack of precision in the definition of the list of serious offences related to the EAW and the inclusion of offences whose seriousness is not provided for in the criminal codes of all the Member States and which may not comply with the principle of proportionality.[29] Furthermore, the disproportionate use of the EAW for minor offences or in circumstances where less intrusive alternatives could be used has been criticised as leading to unjustified arrests, excessive periods in detention, and disproportionate interference with the fundamental rights of suspects and accused persons.[30]

The European Parliament therefore called on the European Commission to submit legislative proposals on the basis of Article 82 TFEU in order to provide for, inter alia, a proportionality check taking into account factors such as the seriousness of the offence, the impact on the rights of the requested person, the economic implications and the availability of an appropriate and less intrusive measure,[31] and a ground for mandatory non-execution where there are important reasons to believe that the execution of the EAW would be incompatible with the EU's legal obligations regarding the protection of fundamental rights, also taking into account 52(1) of the Charter of Fundamental Rights on the principle of proportionality.[32]

D. The European Court of Justice

The issue of the relationship between the principle of proportionality and the EAW has been addressed repeatedly by the European Court of Justice (ECJ) in its case law. Without claiming to be exhaustive, the following are the most important passages.

In *Lanigan*, the ECJ addressed the legal conundrum concerning the retention of the requested person in custody after the time limit for surrender had expired. The ECJ held that the executing judicial authority may decide to keep the person in custody provided that the procedure for executing the EAW has been

[28] European Parliament resolution of 27 February 2014 with recommendations to the Commission on the review of the European Arrest Warrant (2013/2109(INL)).

[29] ibid, para F(iv).

[30] ibid, para F(v).

[31] ibid, para 7(b).

[32] ibid, para 7(d).

conducted with sufficient diligence and that the duration of the custody is therefore not excessive.[33] In doing so, the executing judicial authority must take into account all relevant elements, such as any inaction on the part of the authorities of the Member States concerned, the contribution of the requested person to that duration, the sentence imposed or likely to be imposed and the risk of that person absconding.[34]

In *JZ*, the ECJ was asked to clarify whether, with regard to the obligation of the issuing Member State to deduct the period of custody served in the executing Member State under Article 26 of the FD on the EAW, measures applied by the executing Member State consisting of a nine-hour night-time curfew, combined with monitoring of the person concerned by means of an electronic tag, an obligation to report daily or several times a week to a police station at specified times, and a prohibition on applying for the issue of valid travel documents, should also be regarded as relevant. The ECJ emphasised that the purpose of the provision is to ensure that the requested person does not have to serve a custodial sentence the total duration of which in the executing and the issuing Member State exceeds the duration of the custodial sentence to which that person has been sentenced in the issuing Member State. This is consistent with the obligation to protect the fundamental rights of the requested person, preserving their right to liberty under Article 6 of the Charter of Fundamental Rights, and the practical effect of the principle of proportionality under Article 49(3) of the Charter. Given, however, that the measures in question, having regard to their nature, duration, effects, and the manner of implementation, are not so restrictive as to entail an effect of deprivation of liberty comparable to that arising from imprisonment, they cannot be classified as custody. The specific circumstances must in any event be established by the referring court.[35]

Later, in the *Vilkas* case, Advocate General Bobek, addressing the question of whether the FD allows for a new surrender date to be agreed more than once, argued, in the light of the Court's judgment in *Lanigan* and the case law of the European Court of Human Rights, that the executing judicial authority must carry out a concrete assessment of the situation, taking into account elements such as the likely or actual sentence, the risk of absconding, the actions of the competent authorities and the requested person's contribution to the duration.[36] This approach has been confirmed by the ECJ, which has emphasised that the surrender procedure should be carried out with due diligence and therefore the duration of the custody should not be excessive.[37]

[33] Case C-237/15 PPU *Lanigan* ECLI:EU:C:2015:474, paras 57–58.
[34] ibid, para 59.
[35] Case C-294/16 *JZ* ECLI:EU:C:2016:610, paras 42–43, 58.
[36] Opinion of AG Bobek in Case C-640/15 *Vilkas* ECLI:EU:C:2016:826, paras 48, 54.
[37] Case C-640/15 *Vilkas* ECLI:EU:C:2017:39, para 43.

Furthermore, it should be recalled that the ECJ has made it clear that the EAW entails a dual level of protection of the procedural and fundamental rights of the requested person, inasmuch as the judicial protection afforded at the first level, when a national decision such as a national arrest warrant is adopted, is supplemented by that which must be guaranteed at the second level, when the EAW is issued. In so far as issuing the EAW may affect the right to liberty, this protection implies that at least at one of the two levels a decision must be taken that satisfies the requirements of effective judicial protection. Compliance with these requirements thus makes it possible to reassure the executing judicial authority that the decision to issue an EAW for the purpose of prosecution is based on national proceedings subject to judicial review, and that the person against whom that national arrest warrant has been issued has benefited from all the safeguards inherent in the adoption of that type of decision, in particular those deriving from fundamental rights. More specifically, the second level of protection of the rights of the requested person implies that the judicial authority competent to issue an EAW must, in particular, verify that the conditions necessary for such an issuance are met and examine its proportionality, taking into account the particularities of each case. The issuing judicial authority must be able to exercise this function objectively, taking into account, inter alia, all incriminating and exculpatory elements. Where the law of the issuing Member State confers jurisdiction to issue an EAW on an authority which, although participating in the administration of justice in that Member State, is not itself a court, the decision to issue that EAW, and in particular the proportionality of that decision, must be subject to judicial review in that Member State which fully satisfies the requirements of effective judicial protection.[38]

Finally, one should remember *Procureur général près la cour d'appel d'Angers*, where it was held that it was for the issuing judicial authority to ensure that the principle of proportionality was respected and that any disproportionality of the penalty imposed in the issuing Member State was not one of the grounds for non-execution listed in the FD.[39]

In light of the above, then, it seems clear that the verification of proportionality requires an assessment of the specific circumstances of the individual case and that, at the same time, such an assessment is reserved for the issuing judicial authority alone, whereas the executing judicial authority cannot make any objections in this respect.

[38] Joined cases C-508/18 and C-82/19 PPU *OG (Parquet de Lübeck)* ECLI:EU:C:2019:456, paras 67–75. See also Case C-414/20 PPU *MM* ECLI:EU:C:2021:4, para 64, Case C-489/19 PPU *NJ (Parquet de Vienne)* ECLI:EU:C:2019:849, para 49 and Case C-509/18 *PF (Prosecutor General of Lithuania)* ECLI:EU:C:2019:457, para 49.

[39] Case C-168/21 *Procureur général près la cour d'appel d'Angers* ECLI:EU:C:2022:558, paras 65–66.

IV. The Principle of Proportionality and the EAW: The Italian Legal System and the Case Law of the Court of Cassation

As far as the Italian legal system is concerned, the FD on the EAW was transposed by Law 69/2005, which does not provide for any proportionality test with regard to the issuance of EAWs. The only element that could be emphasised in this respect is that, under Article 28(1)(b), an EAW *in executivis* is issued by the public prosecutor provided that it concerns an offence punishable by a sentence of not less than one year and there is no stay of execution. In line with what has already been said in relation to Article 2(1) of the FD, an EAW issued for offences punishable by a custodial sentence of less than one year should be regarded as disproportionate, although the consequences of issuing an EAW in such a case remain unclear.

In this regard, it should be noted that the Italian Ministry of Justice has adopted a manual on the issuance of EAWs,[40] which also addresses the issue of proportionality. In this regard, it is stated that the issuing authority must, inter alia, assess the elements available in the specific case. Among other things, this involves taking account of the limits of reasonableness and proportionality on which the common action of the EU in the field of judicial cooperation is based, by carrying out a twofold assessment. At the domestic level, account must be taken of the seriousness of the offence, the personality of the offender, the length of the sentence, and the duration of the pre-trial measure. At the international level, it should be borne in mind that the issuing of an EAW gives rise to a complex actividty of international cooperation between police bodies and judicial authorities and that the execution of an EAW entails arrest and detention in another State for a long period of time.[41]

The absence of provisions dealing with the issue of proportionality has been confirmed by the Court of Cassation's case law,[42] which, however, has expressly referred to the approach outlined in the aforementioned manual with regard to the assessment of the relevant elements, both at the national and international level.[43] Nevertheless, the Court of Cassation has clarified that the manual is an

[40] For the text, see https://www.giustizia.it/resources/cms/documents/Vademecum_mandato_arresto_europeo.pdf.

[41] Ministry of Justice's Handbook, paras 3.1, 3.5–3.6.

[42] For what concerns the execution in Italy of an EAW issued by foreign authorities, see *ex multis* Italian Court of Cassation, 25 January 2008, ruling No 4053 and 25 March 2016, ruling No 12671. Furthermore, the Court of Cassation held that, for the purposes of the execution of an EAW, the different sanctioning treatment provided for in the foreign legal system is not relevant, since any difference in the sanctioning treatment may be relevant only if it is wholly unreasonable and manifestly contrary to the general principle of legality and proportionality of penalties (Italian Court of Cassation, 18 November 2010, ruling No 40842; 15 December 2011, ruling No 46573, and 15 April 2022, ruling No 14938).

[43] Italian Court of Cassation, 2 April 2012, ruling No 12321, 29 February 2016, ruling No 8209 and 31 August 2016, ruling No 35879.

administrative act with no regulatory value, and as such it should therefore be regarded as a recommendation, aimed at limiting potential problems at the issuing stage.[44]

An interesting aspect concerns the relationship between the EAW and EIO in the light of the principle of proportionality. According to the Court of Cassation, an EAW issued solely for the purpose of subjecting the requested person to investigative measures, such as interrogation and questioning, cannot be executed because it would be used for investigative purposes, which is not provided for in the FD.[45] In some cases, the Court has acknowledged that the surrender in execution of an EAW for the purpose of prosecution is lawful if the EAW specifies that the measure is also for the purpose of permitting a joint examination[46] or interrogation[47] or for the performance of the interrogation and formal recognition of the requested person.[48]

In its judgments, however, the Court has ruled on cases in which the investigative acts to be carried out were specified. In the case of unspecified acts and in the absence of a specific statement of reasons, an EAW is not the right instrument, since EU law does not provide for an EAW for purely investigative purposes, but only for the purpose of prosecution or in relation to the execution of a sentence already passed. The inadmissibility of an EAW for purely investigative and indeterminate purposes is also confirmed by Directive 2014/41 on the EIO. Recital 25 of the Directive states that an EIO may be issued for the temporary transfer of a person to the issuing Member State or for the purpose of conducting a hearing by videoconference. However, where such a person is to be transferred to another Member State for the purposes of criminal proceedings, including to appear before a court for trial, an EAW should be issued. Recital 26 adds that, in order to ensure the proportionate use of the EAW, the issuing authority should consider whether an EIO is an effective and proportionate means of conducting criminal proceedings, and in particular whether issuing an EIO for the purpose of hearing a person under investigation or a defendant by videoconference may constitute a valid alternative. Thus, an EAW may not be issued solely for investigative purposes in isolation from prosecution in the issuing Member State, as alternative means of judicial cooperation in criminal matters are provided for the pursuit of legitimate investigative purposes. If the reasons for the investigation are unclear, it is necessary to request additional information from the issuing authority in order to understand which investigative acts are to be carried out with the presence of the requested person and whether their presence is indispensable for the continuation of the proceedings or for the prosecution.[49]

[44] Italian Court of Cassation, 29 February 2016, ruling No 8209 and 31 August 2016, ruling No 35879.

[45] Italian Court of Cassation, 17 April 2007, ruling No 15970.

[46] Italian Court of Cassation, 18 December 2013, ruling No 51511.

[47] Italian Court of Cassation, 11 October 2016, ruling No 43386.

[48] Italian Court of Cassation, 20 December 2010, ruling No 45043.

[49] Italian Court of Cassation, 15 April 2022, ruling No 14937.

Finally, it should be noted that the Court of Cassation has had the opportunity to emphasise that the TCA has established a surrender system that differs from the one designed by the FD on the EAW, since the principle of proportionality is the subject of a specific provision. This principle is crucial as it forms an integral part of the rules governing the decision on surrender and requires that the criteria mentioned above in section 1 be taken into account.[50]

V. The Principle of Proportionality and the EAW: The UK Legal System and Case Law

In the UK, the origins of a form of proportionality check applied to extradition can be traced back to the 1989 Extradition Act. Section 11(3) provided that the competent court should have released the requested person if the offence for which that person was being prosecuted was trivial in nature. Furthermore, the requested person should have been released because of the time that had elapsed since the offence was alleged to have been committed or since the person had unlawfully absconded, or because the charge against them had not been brought in good faith in the interests of justice and their repatriation would therefore be unjust or oppressive.

The Extradition Act of 2003 made no provision in this respect, and this led the British courts to emphasise that if trivial offences were severely punished in the EAW's issuing Member State, the EAW could not be challenged in the UK on the basis of the principle of proportionality,[51] and any challenges would have to be made in the issuing Member State.[52]

Gradually, the defence of the requested persons began to focus on bringing claims based on a possible violation of Article 8 ECHR relating to the right to respect for private and family life, deeming the interference by the EAW to be excessive. This issue had already arisen with regard to extraditions to third States in *Norris*, prompting the UK Supreme Court to acknowledge that it is only where there is a very compelling feature, or combination of features, that the interference with family life resulting from extradition is not proportionate to the aim that extradition serves.[53]

In relation to the EAW, the UK Supreme Court held in *HH* that there is a constant and weighty public interest in extradition and that the public interest will always carry great weight. However, that weight varies according to the nature

[50] Italian Court of Cassation, 16 September 2021, ruling No 34466.

[51] *Assange v Swedish Prosecution Authority* (Nos. 1 & 2) [2012] 2 AC 471, paras 89–90.

[52] *Sandru v Government of Romania*, 28 October 2009, [2009] EWHC 2879 (Admin), para 15.

[53] *Norris v Government of the United Sates of America* (No 2) [2010] UKSC 9, [2010] 2 AC 487, paras 51 and 56.

and seriousness of the offences. As a result, it is likely that the public interest will outweigh Article 8 unless the interference is exceptionally severe.[54]

At the regulatory level, the 2014 reform of the Extradition Act 2003 brought about a significant change. Indeed, section 21A now provides that if the judge is required to proceed under this section, the judge must decide whether extradition would be compatible with the ECHR and whether extradition would be disproportionate. In relation to the latter, the judge must take into account some specified matters, namely the seriousness of the conduct alleged to constitute the extradition offence, the likely penalty that would be imposed if the requested person were found guilty of the extradition offence, and the possibility of the competent foreign authorities taking measures that would be less coercive than the extradition. Should the judge deem that the extradition would be disproportionate, the requested person's discharge must be ordered.

General guidance was issued by the Lord Chief Justice of England and Wales to assist judges in carrying out the proportionality check provided under section 21A. The Lord Chief Justice emphasised that where the conduct alleged to constitute the offence falls within some specific categories – for example, minor theft, minor financial offences, minor road traffic, driving and related offences, minor public order offences – the judge should generally find that extradition would be disproportionate, unless there are exceptional circumstances. Exceptional circumstances include a vulnerable victim, an offence committed against someone because of their disability, gender-identity, race, religion or belief, or sexual orientation, significant premeditation, multiple offences, extradition also sought for another offence and criminal record.[55]

The proportionality check was first applied in *Miraszewski*, which concerned the surrender of two Polish nationals to Poland in execution of an EAW. The England and Wales High Court (EWHC) provided some clarification on the meaning of the three criteria to be taken into consideration when applying the proportionality check under section 21A. In relation to the seriousness of the conduct, the EWHC held that it should be assessed in the light of domestic standards, provided that the court respects the views of the issuing Member State if they are offered. The maximum penalty for the offence must be taken into account; but the focus must be on the conduct, namely the nature and quality of the alleged acts, the requested person's culpability for those acts and the harm caused to the victim.[56] With regard to the likely penalty, the competent court should consider whether it would be proportionate to order the surrender of a requested person who is not likely to receive a custodial sentence in the issuing Member State. If the competent court cannot rely on information provided by the issuing judicial authority, it should draw inferences from the content of the EAW and apply

[54] *HH v Deputy Prosecutor of the Italian Republic, Genoa* [2012] UKSC 25.
[55] Lord Chief Justice of England and Wales, *Criminal Practice Directions 2023*, paras 12.2.2–12.2.4.
[56] *Miraszewski & Others v Poland* [2014] EWHC 4261 (Admin), para 36.

domestic sentencing practice as a measure of the likelihood. In any case, the likelihood of a non-custodial penalty does not preclude the competent court from deciding that the surrender would be proportionate. In this regard, the EWHC refers to an offence against the environment, which may be unlikely to attract a sentence of immediate custody; however, there is a significant public interest in the prosecution of this kind of offence.[57] Finally, it is necessary to consider whether less coercive measures could be adopted, taking into account, for example, that the presence of the requested person may be required in pre-trial proceedings. In this case, a video link, telephone or mutual legal assistance might be a viable solution. In any event, the burden of proof is on the requested person.[58] This kind of approach has been confirmed in subsequent case law.[59]

VI. Some Critical Remarks

In light of what results from the practice of the EU institutions, as well as the Italian and UK legal system and case law, it can be said that there are three elements to be taken into account when assessing the proportionality of an EAW: the seriousness of the conduct, the likely penalty and the possibility of resorting to less coercive measures. The same elements are mentioned in Article 597 of the TCA; it therefore seems that the existing law can provide guidance in interpreting this provision.

Some questions may arise, however, with regard to the possibility of resorting to less coercive measures. In order to understand the issue at hand, it is worth recalling what the European Commission made clear in its handbook. In fact, there may be situations where, instead of the EAW, it is preferable to resort to the EIO, the transfer of prisoners, the recognition of probation decisions and alternative sanctions, the ESO, or the recognition of financial penalties.

However, taking into account the legal framework provided by the TCA, one may wonder whether it is actually possible to resort to measures other than extradition. When considering a case where investigations need to be carried out abroad, it must be borne in mind that the UK no longer participates in the EIO. Instead, the TCA provides for the application of the Council of Europe's European Convention on Mutual Assistance in Criminal Matters, concluded in 1959, and its Additional Protocols, concluded in 1978 and 2001, which provide for the use of letters rogatory to carry out investigative measures and transmit

[57] ibid, paras 37–39.
[58] ibid, para 41.
[59] See for instance *Krol v Regional Court Poznan (Poland)* [2015] EWHC 2573 (Admin); *Gerulskis & Anor v The Prosecutor General's Office of the Republic of Lithuania* [2020] EWHC 1645 (Admin); *Saptelei v Hunedoara Law Court of Romania (Rev 1)* [2021] EWHC 506 (Admin); *Ziembinski v Regional Court of Plock (Poland)* [2022] EWHC 693 (Admin).

evidence or documents, and regulate, for example, the handing over of procedural documents and court decisions, the appearance of witnesses, experts and prosecuted persons, and the transmission of extracts from criminal records. The TCA thus provides an alternative that may prove to be less coercive than extradition. However, one may wonder whether it is really possible to compare the two situations. In fact, the Convention and the Additional Protocols outline a form of intergovernmental cooperation, i.e. cooperation takes place between the governments of the Contracting Parties, which enjoy political discretion in deciding whether to cooperate with each other. This seems to be confirmed by the definition of the competent authority under Article 634 of the TCA: it is identified as any authority competent to send or receive requests for mutual assistance in accordance with the provisions of the Convention and its Additional Protocols and as defined by the States in their respective declarations addressed to the Secretary General of the Council of Europe. The competent authority is therefore not necessarily a judicial authority. Instead, the EIO is a mechanism of judicial cooperation, meaning cooperation between authorities that participate in the administration of justice, which perform a technical assessment, and the same holds true with respect to the EAW and the extradition arrangement provided by the TCA. So, do the European Convention on Mutual Assistance in Criminal Matters and its Additional Protocols actually provide for less coercive measures? Yes, they do, but do they provide for a viable alternative in the fight against impunity? It should be remembered that, according to Article 597 of the TCA, the assessment of proportionality must take into account not only the rights of the requested person, but also the interests of the victim. Given the structural differences between intergovernmental cooperation and judicial cooperation, it is likely that the answer to this question is no, and that as a result the judicial authorities of the EU Member States and the UK will be more inclined to make use of the extradition arrangement.

Moreover, the TCA does not stipulate anything with regard to the transfer of prisoners, the recognition of probation decisions and alternative sanctions, the recognition of decisions on alternative measures to pre-trial detention (i.e. an instrument that would replace the ESO) or the recognition of financial penalties. Thus, focusing exclusively on the TCA legal framework, it should be noted that no less coercive measures than extradition are available.

With regard to the transfer of prisoners and the recognition of probation decisions and alternative sanctions, reference can be made to the 1983 Strasbourg Convention and the 1964 Strasbourg Convention, both concluded within the framework of the Council of Europe. Again, however, the cooperation envisaged by these Conventions is intergovernmental in nature and, therefore, if one assesses them in terms of effectiveness – that is to say, ability to achieve the desired objective and fight against impunity – they might be seen as a step or two backwards when compared to forms of judicial cooperation. With regard to the 1964 Convention, it should also be borne in mind that the United Kingdom is not a party to it.

Finally, for what concerns the recognition of decisions on alternatives to pre-trial detention and financial penalties, there are currently no alternatives to which recourse can be made.

Thus, there are some cases where neither the TCA nor other international agreements provide for measures alternative to extradition (the recognition of decisions on alternatives to pre-trial detention and financial penalties). As a consequence, it would not be possible to resort to any measure other than extradition.

In one case (the recognition of probation decisions and alternative sanctions), the TCA does not address the issue and the UK is not a Contracting Party to the only European treaty that does. Therefore, even in this case, it would not be possible to resort to any measure other than extradition.

There is no provision in the TCA dealing with the transfer of sentenced persons. It is possible to apply the 1983 Strasbourg Convention, but this provides for an intergovernmental cooperation, which is not as effective as judicial cooperation (meaning the extradition arrangement).

The only case in which the TCA provides for an alternative to extradition is mutual legal assistance, but again the form of cooperation provided for is of an intergovernmental – i.e. political – nature.

VII. Conclusion

The principle of proportionality occupies an important place in the extradition regime established by the TCA. Under Article 597, cooperation by means of an arrest warrant must be necessary and proportionate, taking into account the rights of the requested person and the interests of the victim, the seriousness of the offence, the likely penalty, and the possibility that a State might take less coercive measures than surrendering the requested person.

Although the FD on the EAW does not devote any provision to a proportionality check, the subject has been addressed at length by EU institutions and at the national level, as confirmed by the cases of the Italian and UK legal systems. In particular, criteria such as the seriousness of the offence, the likely penalty and the possibility of resorting to less coercive measures have been highlighted by national courts and used to assess the proportionality of EAWs. It therefore seems logical to apply existing law to the interpretation of Article 597 of the TCA in order to carry out the proportionality check provided for therein.

However, as regards the possibility of resorting to less coercive measures, it should be borne in mind that the TCA either does not provide for an alternative measure or obliges the Contracting Parties to resort to forms of intergovernmental cooperation which are not as effective as judicial cooperation. There is therefore a risk that the EU Member States and the UK will always have recourse to the extradition arrangement for lack of alternatives or because there are no viable alternatives, depending on the case. It would therefore seem desirable for the EU and the UK to return to negotiations in the coming years and to lay down rules on these aspects. This would, of course, require the political will on the part of the EU to establish a more comprehensive system of judicial cooperation mechanisms with a third country, and on the part of the UK to abandon the cherry-picking that characterised the TCA negotiations.

12

The Proportionality of Criminal Sanctions and *Ne Bis In Idem*

ARACELI TURMO

I. Introduction

The proportionality of criminal sanctions and *ne bis in idem* may be understood as serving, at least in part, a similar goal: to avoid imposing excessive punishment on a person sentenced for a criminal offence. However, there is little case-law from the European Court of Justice (ECJ) on the relationship between the two. Moreover, while the corresponding provision of the Charter of Fundamental Rights, Article 50, is now a systematic feature of every judgment applying *ne bis in idem*, the same cannot be said of the other principle. There are, however, many instances of discussion of the relationship between *ne bis in idem* and other facets of 'proportionality'. Other contributions to this volume have noted the polysemy of the term in the legal order of the European Union.[1] The same observations need to be borne in mind when examining the relationship between proportionality and *ne bis in idem*. This chapter explores the interaction between the two principles as they appear in the case-law of the ECJ. As these sources show, they are essentially complementary (III), but nevertheless distinct (II). Much would be gained, including for the implementation and clarification of the guarantees offered by *ne bis in idem*, by greater explicit reliance on Article 49(3) (IV).

II. Two Distinct Principles

Neither the EU Charter nor the European Convention on Human Rights (ECHR) contain explicit provisions establishing a specific relationship between the proportionality of criminal penalties and *ne bis in idem*. They are presented as two entirely distinct principles, an impression which is reinforced in EU law by the

[1] See, in particular, the contribution of Jacob Öberg to this volume.

fact that proportionality is included in the Charter provision on the principle of legality, and in the ECHR by the absence of any specific provision guaranteeing it. However, the case-law of the ECJ does contain a significant number of examples which connect the two principles in a more or less explicit way.

Article 49(3) of the Charter provides that 'the severity of penalties must not be disproportionate to the criminal offence.' The Charter establishes a relationship between this right and the principle of legality of criminal offences and penalties, which is set out in the first two paragraphs of the same provision. *Ne bis in idem*, on the other hand, is guaranteed by a separate provision, Article 50: 'No one shall be liable to be tried or punished again in criminal proceedings for an offence for which he or she has already been finally acquitted or convicted within the Union in accordance with the law.' This encourages us to think of the two principles as entirely separate. The Explanatory Notes to the Charter[2] do not establish any connection between the two. The European Convention on Human Rights is not particularly helpful in this matter, since although it contains a provision guaranteeing *ne bis in idem* in Article 4 of Protocol 7,[3] it does not explicitly guarantee the proportionality of criminal offences or penalties. The case-law does provide some limited protection in the sense that, although the Court has held that Member States have a wide margin of appreciation as to the appropriate nature and severity of penalties, a manifestly disproportionate penalty may be contrary to Article 3.[4] However, the principle of legality protected by Article 7 of the Convention[5] is not linked to proportionality as it is in the Charter.[6]

[2] Explanations Relating to the Charter of Fundamental Rights [2007] OJ C303/17.

[3] Article 4 (1) of Protocol No 7 to the European Convention for the Protection of Human Rights and Fundamental Freedoms (Strasbourg, 22 November 1984): 'No one shall be liable to be tried or punished again in criminal proceedings under the jurisdiction of the same State for an offence for which he has already been finally acquitted or convicted in accordance with the law and penal procedure of that State'.

[4] See the Guide on Article 3 of the ECHR (Council of Europe – European Court of Human Rights, 2022, https://www.echr.coe.int/documents/d/echr/Guide_Art_3_ENG), paras 72 *et seq.*: 'the Court accepts that while, in principle, matters of appropriate sentencing largely fall outside the scope of the Convention, a grossly disproportionate sentence could amount to ill-treatment contrary to Article 3 at the moment of its imposition. This requires a strict test and violations are only found on rare occasions: see *Babar Ahmad and Others v the United Kingdom* App. Nos 24027/07, 11949/08, 36742/08, 66911/09, 67354/09 (ECtHR, 10 April 2012), para 237; *Harkins and Edwards v the United Kingdom* App. Nos. 9146/07 and 32650/07 (ECtHR, 17 January 2012), para 133'.

[5] Article 7(1) of the ECHR: 'No one shall be held guilty of any criminal offence on account of any act or omission which did not constitute a criminal offence under national or international law at the time when it was committed. Nor shall a heavier penalty be imposed than the one that was applicable at the time the criminal offence was committed.'

[6] See para 51 of the Guide on Article 7 of the ECHR (Council of Europe,/ European Court of Human Rights, 2022, https://www.echr.coe.int/documents/d/echr/Guide_Art_7_ENG). The Court merely satisfies itself that no heavier penalty is imposed than that which was applicable at the time of commission of the offence. Issues relating to the appropriateness of a penalty, the length of the prison sentence or the type of penalty suited to any given offence do not fall within the scope of Article 7 of the Convention or the Court's competences: *Hummatov v. Azerbaijan* App. Nos 9852/03 and 13413/04 (ECtHR, 29 November 2007); *Hakkar v. France* App. No. 43580/04 (ECtHR, 7 April 2009), *Vinter and Others v the United Kingdom* App. Nos. 66069/09, 130/10 and 3896/10 (ECtHR, 9 July 2013), para 105).

Thus, the main impression one derives from the core texts of European law is that the principles of proportionality of criminal penalties and of *ne bis in idem* are entirely distinct. Basic definitions of the content of the two principles also seem to indicate that they relate to different aspects of the criminal justice system and protect different interests of individuals and of society as a whole. A further issue of definition, of course, concerns the concept of proportionality itself and its polysemic and polymorphous nature in EU law.

The principle of proportionality, set out in Article 49(3) of the Charter, is described in the Explanatory Notes to the Charter as a 'general principle' 'enshrined in the common constitutional traditions of the Member States and in the case-law of the Court of Justice'. This seems to indicate that any interpretation of this provision must take into account the case-law on the broader requirement of proportionality. Indeed, proportionality is a very well-established general principle of EU law. However, its functions in the legal order are diverse. The general principle of proportionality, as one of the core constitutional principles of EU law, limits the actions of the EU, as well as those of the Member States, through the two-pronged tests of suitability and necessity.[7] The principle of proportionality has also been interpreted to mean that penalties must be sufficient to match the severity of an offence, in particular in the *Greek Maize*[8] test. These interpretations of proportionality do not appear to be closely linked with the protection guaranteed by *ne bis in idem*.

The *Greek Maize* paradigm establishes that, in the absence of any EU law provisions that lay down specific penalties for an infringement, Member States must take all measures necessary to ensure the application and effectiveness of EU law. To determine if the sanctions provided for under domestic law meet these requirements, the Court examines whether they are equivalent to those provided for similar infringements of domestic law and whether they are 'effective, proportionate and dissuasive'.[9] The term 'proportionate' is understood here in a repressive light: the penalty must be sufficiently serious in relation to the infringement of EU law. It precludes insufficiently effective measures that are disproportionate to the offence committed. This is an integral aspect of proportionality as traditionally understood in EU law, but is unlikely to be part of the interpretation of Article 49(3) due to its nature as a fundamental right.

[7] V Mitsilegas and E Billis, 'Article 49 – Principles of Legality and Proportionality of Criminal Offences and Penalties', in S Peers, T Hervey, J Kenner and A Ward (eds), *The EU Charter of Fundamental Rights. A Commentary*, 2nd edn (Oxford, Hart Publishing, 2021) 1498–1499.

[8] Case 68/88 *Commission v Hellenic Republic* ECLI:EU:C:1989:339, [1989] ECR 2965.

[9] On this judgment and its long-standing legacy in EU criminal law, see in particular: F Giuffrida, 'Effectiveness, Dissuasiveness, Proportionality of Sanctions and Assimilation Principle: The Long-Lasting Legacy of the Greek Maize Case' and R Sicurella, 'The Greek Maize Case/ From Sincere Cooperation to Criminal Law Integration in the EU' in V Mitsilegas, A Di Martino and L Mancano (eds), *The Court of Justice and European criminal law: leading cases in a contextual analysis* (Oxford, Hart Publishing, 2019) 107–121 and 122–136, respectively.

As a fundamental right, the proportionality of criminal penalties is intended to protect individuals from excessive punishment, and the wording of the provision leaves little room for a more repressive interpretation. Under such an understanding of the principle, Article 49(3) and *ne bis in idem* appear more similar. They share similar objectives in the overall functioning of the judicial system, as they both seek to prevent disproportionate punishment of offenders by the criminal justice system. The polysemic or multifaceted nature of proportionality therefore creates complexity, since different facets of the principle may be invoked to justify increasing or decreasing the severity of the response to a set of actions. However, even considering the more protective role of proportionality, its relationship with *ne bis in idem* is not straightforward. While both may sometimes be applied to a single situation, they remain distinct norms. Indeed, while proportionality can sometimes be used to determine the appropriate level of protection of *ne bis in idem*,[10] the reverse is not true.

This position is set out in the Opinion of Advocate General Wahl in *Powszechny Zakład Ubezpieczeń na Życie*.[11] The preliminary reference asked whether a national competition authority is precluded from imposing a fine on an undertaking for anti-competitive conduct in a single decision on the basis of both national and EU law. As a first step in his reasoning, the Advocate General explained his understanding of *ne bis in idem* and, in particular, that '*ne bis in idem* does *not* constitute a yardstick against which the proportionality of a (criminal) sanction is to be measured in a particular procedure'.[12] The rationale of avoiding double prosecution or punishment is different from that of the principle of proportionality of criminal sanctions. In this case, for example, *ne bis in idem* was not applicable. The issue was, rather, whether one action (an anti-competitive conduct) could be characterised as constituting more than one offence and whether a single procedure could lead to several sanctions (here the measures on the basis of both national and EU law, combined in a single decision). *Ne bis in idem* should not be extended to cover any situation where the penalties could be considered disproportionate, nor should the inapplicability of *ne bis in idem* be considered an obstacle to the verification of the proportionality of the penalty imposed on the offender. In such a case, where *ne bis in idem* does not apply, the main question raised by the concurrent application of national and EU law is that of the overall requirement of proportionality,[13] as confirmed by the Court of Justice in its ruling.[14]

[10] In particular, under a third facet of proportionality, as a component of the test set out in Article 52(1) of the Charter: see below, section 3.

[11] Opinion of AG Wahl in Case C-617/17 Powszechny Zakład Ubezpieczeń na Życie v Prezes Urzędu Ochrony Konkurencji i Konsumentów ECLI:EU:C:2018:976.

[12] ibid, para 22.

[13] ibid, paras 54–55.

[14] Case C-617/17 Powszechny Zakład Ubezpieczeń na Życie v Prezes Urzędu Ochrony Konkurencji i Konsumentów ECLI:EU:C:2019:283.

The opinion illustrates a phenomenon often noted in this volume: the Advocate General and the Court refer to Article 50 of the Charter, but not to Article 49(3). It is therefore not clear whether they are referring to the specific manifestation of proportionality enshrined in that provision, or whether they intend to refer to the more general requirement of proportionality. As we will show, the case-law provides numerous examples of connections between certain facets of proportionality and *ne bis in idem*, showing how they can function as complementary principles contributing to the protection of related legal interests.

III. Two Complementary Norms

The connections between *ne bis in idem* and the proportionality of criminal penalties are easily perceived. By preventing the imposition of further prosecutions or penalties on individuals for acts that have already been prosecuted, *ne bis in idem* evidently contributes to the proportionality of criminal penalties. The accumulation of prosecutions and criminal penalties for one action (or set of actions) would likely lead to disproportionate punishment, considering that one of the aims of the decision reached in the first criminal proceedings must have been to set an appropriate sentence, matching the seriousness of the offence (or offences). Similar general goals of justice and fairness in the law are at stake under both principles. The potential complementarity between the two is made apparent in the case-law applying the 'set-off' principle, often described as a manifestation of the principle of proportionality. However, the connection between this principle and Article 49(3) is not entirely clear.

The idea that *ne bis in idem* contributes to ensuring proportionality in criminal justice and that the two principles are related is widespread.[15] References to the two principles will typically establish a hierarchy between them: either presenting *ne bis in idem* as an expression or a guarantee of a more general requirement of proportionality, or presenting proportionality as offering a lesser degree of protection than *ne bis in idem*,[16] albeit in a wider range of situations. In other situations, which we will examine in the next section, proportionality appears at a later stage in the reasoning, as one of the conditions for finding certain restrictions on *ne bis in idem* acceptable. However, most of this case-law refers to either the general principle of proportionality or to a more specific iteration not specifically related

[15] The U.S. Supreme Court has held that, although double jeopardy does not apply across state borders, in determining whether a penalty is disproportionate, a court must look at criteria such as '[…] (iii) the sentences imposed for the same crime in other jurisdiction' (*Solem v. Helm*, 463 U.S. 277, at 286).

[16] B van Bockel, 'The Interpretation and Application for the Ne Bis In Idem Principle in the EU Area of Freedom, Security and Justice' in S Iglesias Sánchez and M González Pascual (eds), *Fundamental Rights in the EU Area of Freedom, Security and Justice* (Cambridge, Cambridge University Press, 2021) 356–357.

to criminal justice. References to Article 49(3) of the Charter remain extremely rare, even in situations in which they might have seemed entirely appropriate.

In his Opinion in *Bourquain*,[17] Advocate General Ruiz-Jarabo Colomer stressed the solidity of the protection guaranteed by the principle of *ne bis in idem*, writing that; 'The *ne bis in idem* rule acquires true legislative weight with the creation of a subjective right to be prosecuted only once for the same acts, thus being set on solid foundations, which help to offset the weakness of some institutions, like limitation, *res judicata* or the numerous proportionality theories, which cannot be satisfactorily resolved only by recourse to the mutual trust between States.' In other words, all of these principles help to serve the same interest of the individual in a fair trial and in safeguards against the excessive power of public authorities to enforce criminal law.

According to the Advocate General, *ne bis in idem* provides better protection due to its recognition as a subjective right. It could be argued that the aim of Article 49(3) of the Charter is precisely to guarantee the proportionality of penalties as an autonomous fundamental right, and that this is the core distinction between the general principle of proportionality and the right protected by this provision. The fact that the Advocate General did not refer to Article 49(3) reflects the more general practice of the European Court of Justice, which has not yet used it to its full potential, preferring instead to refer to proportionality as a general principle rather than to the specific iteration protected by Article 49(3).

A similar view is expressed by Advocate General Bot in his Opinion in the *Gaetano Mantello*:[18] *ne bis in idem* 'is inherent in the concept of the rule of law. Once society has exercised its legitimate right to punish the perpetrator of an offence contrary to its rules, it has exhausted its right to prosecute and therefore has no further authority to punish a person already convicted of that offence. This principle is therefore inseparable from the principles of *res judicata* and of proportionality of penalties, according to which the sanction must be proportionate to the seriousness of the acts in respect of which the prosecution has been brought.' Once again, we find the idea that all three principles actually contribute in practice to the same objective: to prevent a person from suffering disproportionate sanctions by being prosecuted or punished more than once for a given set of actions.

The affinity between the two principles is also visible in the case-law on a principle which is often presented as deriving from the principle of proportionality, but which is also closely connected to *ne bis in idem*: the 'set-off' principle – *Anrechnungsprinzip* in German, or *imputation* in French. This principle, or the more general concept of proportionality, is sometimes cited as a substitute for *ne bis in idem* when the latter is not applicable. Although it cannot prevent another

[17] Opinion of AG Ruiz-Jarabo Colomer in Case C-297/07 *Staatsanwaltschaft Regensburg v Klaus Bourquain* ECLI:EU:C:2008:206, [2008] ECR I-9425, para 49.

[18] Opinion of AG Bot in Case C-261/09 *Gaetano Mantello* ECLI:EU:C:2010:501, [2010] ECR I-11477, para 27.

set of proceedings from taking place, it does require the authority imposing a second penalty on an offender to take into account the sanctions that have already been imposed for the same set of facts. One might question the existence of 'set-off' or 'imputation' as an autonomous principle of EU law, but the expression is regularly used in the case-law, although parties and Advocates General sometimes rely directly on the principle of proportionality. This function of proportionality is also apparent in provisions unrelated to *ne bis in idem*, such as Framework Decision 2008/675,[19] which aims to establish the conditions under which, in the course of criminal proceedings in a Member State against a person, previous convictions handed down against them for different facts in other Member States must be taken into account. Recital 9 of the Framework Decision indicates that Member States may, in certain cases, decide not to take into account previous foreign convictions if this would limit the discretion of the judge in imposing a sentence, but that they must ensure that their courts can otherwise take them into account if they consider that the result would be 'disproportionately harsh'.

In *Könecke*,[20] the question arose as to the imposition of a fine by the Commission where fines had already been imposed for the same facts in national criminal proceedings. The Advocate General wrote that, in principle, the two parallel proceedings may coexist since they pursued different objectives and resulted from the division of powers between the EEC and the Member States.[21] However, in determining the later penalty, the earlier penalties should be taken into account 'as a special application of the principle of proportionality' and *not* as an application of *ne bis in idem*,[22] given the non-criminal nature of the European penalty in question. Although claims based on such reasoning are rarely successful, they regularly appear in the case-law and confirm that 'set-off', as a facet of proportionality, offers a similar kind of protection against double punishment as *ne bis in idem*.

Könecke is based on the famous *Walt Wilhelm* precedent.[23] In this case, the Court of Justice ruled that concurrent sanctions adopted by the Commission and national authorities in cartel matters were possible, but that 'a general requirement of natural justice' demanded that any previous punitive decision must be taken into account in determining the later penalty.[24] This was soon confirmed by the

[19] Framework Decision 2008/675/JHA of 24 July 2008 on taking account of convictions in the Member States of the European Union in the course of new criminal proceedings [2008] OJ L220/32.

[20] Case 117/83 *Karl Könecke GmbH & Co. KG, Fleischwarenfabrik v Bundesanstalt für landwirtschaftliche Marktordnung* ECLI:EU:C:1984:288, [1984] ECR 3317.

[21] Opinion of AG Verloren van Themaat in Case 117/83 *Könecke* ECLI:EU:C:1984:221, [1984] ECR 3317.

[22] ibid.

[23] Case 14/68 Walt Wilhelm and others v Bundeskartellamt ECLI:EU:C:1969:4, [1969] ECR 1. On this judgment and the case-law of the European Court of Justice on ne bis in idem in competition law, more generally, see inter *alia* R Nazzini, 'Parallel Proceedings in EU Competition Law' in B van Bockel (ed.), *Ne Bis in Idem in EU Law* (Cambridge, Cambridge University Press, 2016) 131–166 and 157 *et seq*.

[24] ibid, para 11.

case-law,[25] although the same does not apply to penalties imposed by the competition authorities of third countries.[26] For instance, in *SGL Carbon v Commission*,[27] a corporation argued that the Commission should have taken into account the fine imposed in the United States for the same actions when setting the amount of the fine to be paid under EU law. The corporation argued that *ne bis in idem* was applicable but, even if it was not, proportionality should lead to the same solution.[28] However, Advocate General Geelhoed argued that there was no need for the Commission to set off fines imposed in a third country due to the absence of any reciprocity or territorial overlap.[29] The Court confirmed this stance, thereby ruling that the Commission had no duty to take into account fines imposed previously in third countries, although it may choose to do so.[30]

In a situation more akin to that in *Walt Wilhelm*, the applicants in *Printeos*[31] argued that by failing to take into account the fine already imposed by the Spanish competition authority when adopting its own decision, the Commission had violated the principle of proportionality, which is 'relevant even where the *ne bis in idem* principle is not applicable'.[32] The General Court distinguished the case from *Walt Wilhelm*, but left open the question whether the principle of fairness could apply in a situation where Article 101 TFEU and the corresponding national competition law are applied in parallel.[33]

The set-off principle also appears in Article 26(1) of the Framework Decision on the European Arrest Warrant[34] and in Article 56 of the Convention Implementing the Schengen Agreement (CISA).[35] In the latter instrument, the set-off principle is included in the chapter on the application of the *ne bis in idem* principle, which indicates their close affinity. 'Set-off' is understood to have a broader scope

[25] Case 7/72 *Boehringer Mannheim GmbH v Commission* ECLI:EU:C:1972:125, [1972] ECR 1281, para 3. See also, in particular, the judgments of the Court of First Instance in Cases T-141/89 *Tréfileurope Sales SARL v Commission* ECLI:EU:T:1995:62, [1995] ECR II-791, para 191; T-149/89 *Sotralentz SA v Commission* ECLI:EU:T:1995:69, [1995] ECR II-1127, para 29; T-224/00 *Archer Daniels Midland Company and Archer Daniels Midland Ingredients Ltd v Commission* ECLI:EU:T:2003:195, [2003] ECR II-2597, para 87.

[26] See, for example: Case T-322/01 *Roquette Frères SA v Commission* ECLI:EU:T:2006:267, [2006] ECR II-3137, para 288; Case C-397/03 P *Archer Daniels Midland Co. and Archer Daniels Midland Ingredients Ltd v Commission* ECLI:EU:C:2006:328, [2006] ECR I-4429, para 52.

[27] Case C-308/04 P *SGL Carbon AG v Commission* ECLI:EU:C:2006:433, [2006] ECR I-5977.

[28] Opinion of AG Geelhoed in Case C-308/04 P *SGL Carbon AG v Commission* ECLI:EU:C:2006:54, [2006] ECR I-5983, paras 40–41.

[29] ibid, para 50.

[30] Case C-308/04 P *SGL Carbon AG v Commission*, para 36.

[31] Case T-466/17 *Printeos, SA and others v European Commission* ECLI:EU:T:2019:671.

[32] ibid, para 147.

[33] ibid, para 158.

[34] Council Framework Decision 2002/584/JHA on the European arrest warrant and the surrender procedures between Member States [2002] OJ L190/1. Article 26(1) concerns issuing Member State's obligation to deduct periods of detention served in the executing Member State.

[35] Convention implementing the Schengen Agreement of 14 June 1985 between the Governments of the States of the Benelux Economic Union, the Federal Republic of Germany and the French Republic on the gradual abolition of checks at their common borders [2000] OJ L239/19.

however, offering a more limited protection, but available in cases where the conditions for *ne bis in idem* are not met.[36] This provision does not protect against further prosecution *per se*, but requires national authorities to take into account the penalties imposed in the first place and to deduct them from any further penalties. Within the CISA, this provision is clearly intended to offer some protection from the disproportionate punishment that could result from two or more sets of proceedings for the same acts, when the situation does not meet the criteria set out in Article 54 for *ne bis in idem*.

As Advocate General Sharpston once observed, Article 56 is clearly irrelevant where Article 54 applies, since the question of taking into account previous penalties cannot arise if the court hearing the second set of proceedings is prevented from prosecuting and sentencing the accused.[37] Indeed, *ne bis in idem* takes precedence over the prohibition of double punishment.[38] Where only the 'idem' requirement is met, i.e. the acts at issue in both sets of proceedings are the same, but other criteria are not met, Article 56 provides some relief. Advocate General Sharpston and the Commission in *Norma Kraaijenbrink* were both of the view that Article 56 is a manifestation of a general principle of set-off, which is also protected in other contexts in EU law and which requires that previous penalties be taken into account if further sanctions are imposed on the same offender for the same acts.[39] According to the Advocate General, this principle can be construed as a general principle of criminal law in all Member States and, by extension, as 'a general principle of Community law arising from the requirements of natural justice and the principle of proportionality in criminal justice'.[40]

Whether or not the set-off or 'imputation' principle is recognised by the Court of Justice as an autonomous principle of EU law or whether it should be seen as an expression of the general principle of proportionality, this case-law is an excellent illustration of the complementary nature of these two concepts in EU criminal law. Proportionality, related to the value of fairness, can provide some protection against double punishment in cases where *ne bis in idem* is not applicable. However, an important element is missing from this case-law: Article 49(3) has not yet been invoked in the context of the principle of set-off. Yet, at least in the context of the CISA, references to proportionality must be understood as an expression of the requirement of proportionality of criminal penalties.

[36] For a broader discussion of the relationship between Arts 54 and 56 CISA and the distinction between *ne bis in idem* and the prohibition of double punishment, see B van Bockel, *Ne Bis in Idem in EU Law: A Conceptual and Jurisprudential Analysis* (Amsterdam, Ipskamp Drukkers, 2009) 221 *et seq*.

[37] Opinion of AG Sharpston in Case C-367/05 *Norma Kraaijenbrink* ECLI:EU:C:2006:760, [2006] ECR I-6619, para 54. On the same provision, see the Opinion of AG Sharptston in Case C-288/05 *Criminal proceedings against Jürgen Kretzinger* ECLI:EU:C:2006:759, [2006] ECR I-6445, paras 64–70.

[38] van Bockel (n 36) 250.

[39] Opinion of AG Sharpston in Case C-367/05 *Norma Kraaijenbrink*, paras 56 and 58. The Court did not rule on this aspect of the preliminary reference.

[40] ibid, para 60.

IV. Double Proceedings: The Potential for an Increased Use of Article 49(3)

Double proceedings, especially when they are perceived as creating a limitation of *ne bis in idem*, are a perfect illustration of the connection between the two principles and also of the polysemic nature of 'proportionality' in EU law. The idea that exceptions or limitations placed on *ne bis in idem* must be evaluated in terms of proportionality is common. For example, it could be argued that exceptions to the principle are justified due to the seriousness of an offence or to the importance of the public interest to be protected.[41] Conversely, the principle of proportionality of criminal penalties might also be invoked to argue that such exceptions must be restricted to avoid excessive punishment. The case-law allowing the double prosecution of specific offences in the Member States, which has attracted so much attention over the past decade,[42] provides a good illustration of the potential for a more extensive use of Article 49(3) of the Charter in conjunction with Article 50 of the Charter. This is because this line of case-law contains two different manifestations of proportionality: firstly, under the test set out to allow limitations on *ne bis in idem*, and secondly, as an additional hurdle that the rule in question must pass in order to be compatible with EU fundamental rights standards.

Proportionality checks under Article 52(1) of the Charter constitute a specific facet of the principle, unrelated to the proportionality of criminal penalties guaranteed under Article 49(3) of the Charter. Due to the phrasing of Article 52(1), this type of test appears in all of the case-law on restrictions to fundamental rights, including *ne bis in idem*, and is in no way specific to criminal law. An interesting example is the case-law regarding the limitations on the scope of *ne bis in idem* in the CISA. In *Spasic*,[43] the Court of Justice ruled that the execution condition set out in Article 54 of the CISA was proportionate within the meaning of Article 52(1) and was therefore compatible with Article 50 of the Charter, since it 'does not go beyond what is necessary to prevent, in a cross-border context, the impunity of persons definitively convicted and sentenced in the European Union'.[44] Similarly, a recent judgment ruled on the proportionality of the restrictions on *ne bis in idem* entailed by the Declarations made on the basis of Article 55 of the CISA.[45]

[41] UK Law Commission, *Double Jeopardy*, Consultation Paper no 156, 1999, https://www.lawcom.gov.uk/app/uploads/2015/04/CP156.pdf, 37–39.

[42] See, *inter alia*: G Lo Schiavo, 'The Principle of Ne Bis In Idem and the Application of Criminal Sanctions: Of Scope and Restrictions' (2018) 14 *EuConst* 644; M Luchtmann, 'The ECJ's Recent Case-Law on Ne Bis in Idem: Implications for Law Enforcement in a Shared Legal Order' (2018) 55 *CML Rev* 1717; A Turmo, 'Ne Bis In Idem in European Law: A Difficult Exercise in Constitutional Pluralism' (2020) 5 *European Papers* 1341; P Wattel, 'Ne Bis In Idem and Tax Offences in EU Law and ECHR Law' in B van Bockel (ed), *Ne Bis in Idem in EU Law* (Cambridge, Cambridge University Press, 2016) 167.

[43] Case C-129/14 PPU *Zoran Spasic* ECLI:EU:C:2014:586.

[44] ibid, para 72.

[45] Case C-365/21 *Generalstaatsanwaltschaft Bamberg (Exception to the principle ne bis in idem)* ECLI:EU:C:2023:326.

The Court held that the possibility provided for by that provision of the CISA was appropriate for attaining the general interest objective of enabling a Member State to punish damage to its security or other equally important interests, and that the conditions under which such declarations were made satisfied the requirement of necessity. Article 55 thus meets the proportionality requirement set out in Article 52(1) of the Charter.[46] The concept of proportionality referred to in these two judgments is clearly distinct from the proportionality of criminal penalties. They clearly use the term in the context of the evaluation of a restriction placed on one fundamental right, *ne bis in idem*, instead of looking at proportionality as a specific right itself.

Cases that involve dual proceedings within a Member State raise the question of the impact that not applying *ne bis in idem* has on the proportionality of the sanctions. In *Bonda*,[47] the question referred focus on whether the national administrative proceedings after incorrect declarations in an application for agricultural aid were of a criminal nature, so as to give rise to the application of *ne bis in idem* in the subsequent criminal proceedings for fraud. Although the Court of Justice answered the question without giving any additional indications, Advocate General Kokott went further and examined the consequences of the inapplicability of *ne bis in idem*. In her Opinion, she suggested that this finding 'must not lead to the person concerned being disproportionately burdened' by an excessively severe criminal penalty in the second proceedings.[48] This was a consequence of the principle of proportionality, which was applicable because the national sanctions were taken in order to comply with EU law and were thus within the scope of its general principles.[49]

The Opinion does not explicitly cite the principle of proportionality of criminal penalties, but it is based on the idea that the general principle of proportionality applies to criminal sanctions imposed by the Member States within the scope of EU law. According to the Advocate General, the principle can usefully be relied on by offenders to argue for a reduced sentence in a new set of criminal proceedings where an administrative sanction has already been imposed on them for the same facts. It is unfortunate that the Court did not rule on this point in this case, but the position seems congruent with the established case-law on the set-off principle. Although the reasons for the inapplicability of *ne bis in idem* may be different, in all these situations the same general principles lead to a similar requirement that the overall punishment remain proportionate and, therefore, that any further sanctions imposed after the conclusion of the first proceedings must take into account the first sentence.

[46] ibid, paras 59–66. Interestingly, Advocate General Szpunar had a very different understanding of the legal issues at hand and proposed that the Court should find the provision incompatible with Articles 50 and 52(1) of the Charter (Opinion of AG Szpunar in Case C-365/12 *Generalstaatsanwaltschaft Bamberg (Exception to the principle ne bis in idem)* ECLI:EU:C:2022:823).

[47] Case C-489/10 *Łukasz Marcin Bonda* ECLI:EU:C:2012:319.

[48] Opinion of AG Kokott in Case C-489/10 *Bonda* ECLI:EU:C:2011:845, para 78.

[49] ibid, para 18 and footnote 74.

Interestingly, in *Åkerberg Fransson*,[50] the proportionality of the sanction was challenged in the opposite way. The Court did not settle whether the combination of tax and criminal proceedings and penalties at the national level was contrary to *ne bis in idem*, since it left the issue of whether the former were of a criminal nature under the *Bonda* criteria to the referring court. It did rule that, *if* they were not, the *ne bis in idem* principle guaranteed under EU law did not preclude the combination of penalties. However, it noted that such a combination could be considered contrary to *domestic* fundamental rights standards, 'as long as the remaining penalties are effective, proportionate and dissuasive'.[51] Although the Court did not address the issue of the possible disproportionality of the overall penalty, we find an interesting reference to the *Greek Maize* test to remind domestic authorities of the need to adequately punish tax evasion. This judgment illustrates another facet of the idea of proportionality of penalties, understood as a principle expressing a value of fairness and justice in the criminal justice system.

The Opinion of Advocate General Sánchez-Bordona in *Volkswagen*[52] illustrates how the two functions of proportionality can interact with *ne bis in idem* in judicial reasoning. The case concerned the convergence of penalties and proceedings against a single conglomerate in two Member States, with insufficient coordination. The Advocate General started by acknowledging the proportionality test as part of the conditions enshrined in Article 52(1) of the Charter for limiting the enjoyment of a fundamental right such as ne bis in idem.[53] Later, as part of the necessity test carried out under this provision, he presented the question of the proportionality of the total penalties imposed in relation to the seriousness of the offence: the total penalty may be considered necessary if it remains proportionate to the offence committed, in the sense that its seriousness justifies the sanctions resulting from the duplication.[54] This is an interesting example of the potential clarification that would result from an explicit reliance on Article 49(3) of the Charter. Clearly, the second occurrence of proportionality is an expression of the principle set out in this provision, and the lack of an explicit reference to it may cause confusion between that standard and the test established under Article 52(1) of the Charter.

In our view, this potential is clear from the case-law on double proceedings. The ECJ case law has now firmly established that the protection granted by *ne bis in idem* may, under certain circumstances, be restricted by the combination of an administrative penalty of a criminal nature and a criminal penalty for a single offence. This case law always shows the two distinct roles played by proportionality with regard to limitations of *ne bis in idem*: firstly, in the form of the check

[50] Case C-617/10 *Åklagaren v Hans Åkerberg Fransson* ECLI:EU:C:2013:105.

[51] ibid, para 36.

[52] Opinion of AG Sánchez-Bordona in Case C-27/22 *Volkswagen Group Italia S.p.A., Volkswagen Aktiengesellschaft v Autorità Garante della Concorrenza e del Mercato* ECLI:EU:C:2023:265.

[53] ibid, paras 90 *et seq.*

[54] Paras 97–100.

applied on any restriction to a fundamental right protected under the Charter, and secondly, in the form of principle of proportionality of criminal penalties. As the Court ruled in *Menci*,[55] 'the duplication of penalties of a criminal nature requires rules allowing it to be guaranteed that the severity of all of the penalties imposed corresponds with the seriousness of the offence concerned, that requirement resulting not only from Article 52(1) of the Charter, but also from the principle of proportionality of penalties set out in Article 49(3) thereof. Those rules must provide for the obligation for the competent authorities [...] to ensure that the severity of all of the penalties imposed does not exceed the seriousness of the offence identified.'[56] Interestingly, the Advocate General had not mentioned Article 49(3) of the Charter at all in that case, but had relied on Article 52(1).[57]

Following this extract from *Menci*, the Court's position is that the exception it is creates to the protection of *ne bis in idem* must be limited to what is compatible with both of these iterations of proportionality: the Charter's limitation on restrictions to fundamental rights and the more specific limitation placed on the severity of criminal punishment. The judgment thus provides an excellent illustration of both the potential overlap between *ne bis in idem* and proportionality, and the distinction between different manifestations of the concept of proportionality in this context. Proportionality is being relied upon as a further form of protection from excessive punishment, even as *ne bis in idem* is restricted. The same paragraph appears in the later *Garrlson Real Estate* judgment.[58] Nevertheless, although later judgments reiterate the importance of ensuring that the overall sum of the penalties is not disproportionate in such situations, the reference to Article 49(3) has disappeared and only Article 52(1) remains.[59] Even when it was specifically interrogated on the requirement resulting from this case law by a national court that cites both provisions, the Court replied without specifically referring to Article 49(3).[60]

V. Concluding Remarks

The lack of consistency in the case law, specifically regarding the use of Article 49(3) of the Charter, is unfortunate. Explicit references to this provision,

[55] Case C-524/15 *Menci* ECLI:EU:C:2018:197.

[56] ibid, para 55.

[57] Opinion of AG Campos Sánchez-Bordona in Case C-524/15 *Menci* ECLI:EU:C:2017:667, in particular para 122.

[58] Case C-537/16 *Garlsson Real Estate SA and others v Consob* ECLI:EU:C:2018:193, para 56.

[59] On the combination of proceedings in competition law, see the ECJ judgments in Cases C-117/20 *bpost SA v Autorité belge de la concurrence*, ECLI:EU:C:2022:202; and C-151/20 *Bundeswettbewerbsbehörde v Nordzucker AG and others*, ECLI:EU:C:2022:203.

[60] Case C-570/20 *Criminal proceedings against BV* ECLI:EU:C:2022:348, paras 49–54.

rather than to the principle of proportionality, would clarify the difference between the different facets of proportionality. In judgments where proportionality is used both in the meaning referred to in Article 49(3) and within the examination of a restriction imposed on a different right, this precision in language is indispensable. One must be able to identify the passages where the ECJ is referring to proportionality as a specific fundamental right, enshrined in Article 49(3), and which must be protected even when the protection granted under *ne bis in idem* itself is restricted. This would enable litigants and domestic courts to take better account of the overall impact of the penalties imposed, since the implementation of the existing case law currently pays disappointingly little attention to ensuring the proportionality of the overall punishment.[61]

[61] G Lasagni and S Mirandola, 'The European *Ne Bis In Idem* at the Crossroads of Administrative and Criminal Law' (2019) 2 *Eucrim* 126.

PART C

The Impact of the Supranational Principle of Proportionality of Criminal Penalties on Domestic Legal Orders

13

Domestic Sanctions and the *Greek Maize* Obligation to Impose Effective, Proportionate and Dissuasive Penalties: Empowering National Courts

STEFANO MONTALDO

I. Introduction

The multilevel model of implementation on which the legal order of the Union is based requires the Member States to play a frontline role in implementing EU law. National authorities have a share of responsibility for upholding EU interests and must therefore take any appropriate measure to achieve them. This duty stems from the overarching principle of loyal cooperation and includes the adoption of domestic sanctions aimed to tackle violations of the expected pattern of compliance.

When fulfilling the obligation to deter departures from EU law by means of national sanctions, the Member States are expected to abide by the so-called *Greek Maize* paradigm, whereby such measures have to be aligned to the requirements of effectiveness, dissuasiveness and proportionality. Overall, these threefold criteria orient the national authorities' legal and policy options: while infringements to EU law cannot be granted impunity to the detriment of the effectiveness of relevant EU provisions, the resort to coercive powers must be confined within the limits set by the principle of proportionality.

This chapter builds on this premise to delve into the implications of the *Greek Maize* formula for the Member States, with a focus on proportionality. From this viewpoint, the European Union dimension of proportionality is multi-perspective in nature. On the one hand, it combines domestic constitutional considerations and the quest for a specific European outlook; on the other hand, it calls for judicial scrutiny by national courts, although under the leading interpretative guidance of the Court of Justice. In this blurred context, the core question is to what extent – and how – the EU legal order can impose proportionality considerations on the national legislators and courts: the just exercise of *jus puniendi* is a daily challenge that requires the 'constitutional framework' of EU remedies to be exploited in full, for the benefit of individual rights and the protection of EU interests.

Bearing in mind this articulated scenario, this chapter tries to put some common denominators in order by focusing on the role, substance and implications of proportionality of penalties in the specific context of the implementation of EU law by the Member States. Section II outlines the evolution of this principle over the decades and introduces proportionality as a component of the *Greek Maize* threefold obligation to adopt effective, proportionate and dissuasive sanctions to tackle violations of EU law at the national level. The analysis moves on to discuss into greater detail the content of the *Greek Maize* proportionality requirement, considering the main trends in the Luxembourg case-law (Section III). Section IV addresses the recent Court's decision to acknowledge that the principle of proportionality of sanctions enjoys direct effect, as it provides for a clear and unconditional negative obligation to refrain from imposing disproportionate penalties. The stance taken by the Court empowers national courts, which are now entitled to autonomously set aside domestic provisions leading to a breach of the principle in question. This move ahead is raising debate with respect to the risk of a violation of the principles of legality, separation of powers and equality. Section V discusses these objections, aiming to demonstrate that the existing remedies available in the EU legal order provide relief to such concerns. The concluding remarks revolve around a core argument, namely the increasingly central role of national courts not only with respect to the proportionality scrutiny, but also in relation to the more precise determination of the inherent limits of the remedy of disapplication.

II. The Proportionality of Penalties in the Context of the *Greek Maize* Formula

By virtue of the duty of loyal cooperation enshrined in Article 4(3) TEU, national authorities are under a duty to take all measures necessary to ensure the fulfilment of the obligations arising out of the Treaties and of EU secondary law, as well as to refrain from jeopardising the attainment of the Union's objectives. In this context, the enforcement of European Union law envisages an articulated policy chain encompassing three subsequent stages, namely monitoring, investigating and sanctioning.[1] It follows that the penalisation of breaches of either EU law or national laws implementing it is a key component of the EU multi-level model

[1] J Vervaele, 'Shared Governance and Enforcement of European Law: From Comitology to a Multi-level Agency Structure?' in C Joerges and E Vos (eds), *EU Committees: Social Regulation, Law and Politics* (Oxford, Hart Publishing, 1999) 131.

of compliance, where the domestic authorities play a key role.[2] This is even more true for the exercise of *jus puniendi*. The abstract normative options of the type and severity of sanctions to their actual determination have been traditionally perceived as an expression of the *noyau dur* of national sovereignty.[3]

In line with this deeply held assumption, until the early 1980s, the Community offered leeway to national authorities on their choice of measures for enforcing EC law and, with a few exceptions,[4] refrained from imposing specific harmonised sanctioning standards. This approach was also reflected in the case-law of the Court of Justice. Accordingly, in *Amsterdam Bulb*, the ECJ took the stance that, in the absence of Community rules, loyal cooperation 'allows the Member States to choose the measures which they consider appropriate, including sanctions which may even be criminal in nature', without further specific limits.[5]

Yet, in 1989, the *Greek Maize* case ignited a gradual paradigm shift. The Court placed two major constraints on the national authorities' margin of manoeuvre when enforcing EC law by means of domestic sanctioning regimes.[6] First, the ECJ established the principle of assimilation, according to which the Member States must ensure that comparable violations of EC and national law[7] are penalised under analogous substantive and procedural conditions.[8] As clarified by the Court in its subsequent case-law, this principle extends to the obligation to punish violations of EC law 'by instituting criminal proceedings'.[9] Second, while the choice of penalties remains in the discretion of the national authorities, the Court contended that the relevant domestic measures must comply with three cumulative criteria: effectiveness, proportionality, and dissuasiveness.

This further obligation mirrored the auspices of the European Commission in the infringement proceedings against Greece.[10] The Guardian of the Treaties

[2] On the idea of multilevel dynamic of compliance see E Thomann and F Sager (eds), *Innovative approaches to EU multilevel implementation: Moving beyond legal compliance* (London, Routledge, 2020).

[3] See the introductory reflections put forward by M Poelemans, *La sanction dans l'ordre juridique communautaire: contribution à l'Etude du système répressif de l'Union européenne* (Bruxelles, Bruylant, 2004).

[4] The main example is the enforcement of competition law, where in any case the EU enjoys exclusive competence.

[5] Case 50/76 *Amsterdam Bulb* ECLI:EU:C:1977:13, para 32. In the same paragraph, the Court also clarified that such measures 'may even be criminal in nature'.

[6] Case 68/88, *Commission v Greece (Greek Maize)* ECLI:EU:C:1989:339, para 24.

[7] Comparability refers to the 'similar nature and importance' of the violations at issue, in light of their constituent elements. More recent case-law of the Court seems to suggest that also external factors such as the 'difficulty involved in their detection' should be taken into consideration when assessing comparability. See case C-574/15 *Scialdone* ECLI:EU:C:2018:295, para 57.

[8] At para 25 of the *Greek Maize* ruling, the Court also laid down an obligation for the competent domestic authorities 'to proceed, with respect to infringements of Community law, with the same diligence as that which they bring to bear in implementing corresponding national laws'. It has been rightfully pointed out that this further aspect of the *Greek Maize* ruling has been generally neglected both in the practice of the EU institutions – including the Court – and by scholars: A Klip, *European Criminal Law. An Integrative Approach* (Antwerp, Intersentia 2016), 81–82.

[9] Case C-2/88 *Imm Zwartveld* ECLI:EU:C:1990:440, para. 17.

[10] The Court went even beyond the expectations of the Commission. In its fourth submission to the Court, the Commission advocated for the acknowledgment of the principle of assimilation alone. The threefold criteria constituted an unelicited elaboration of the Court of Justice.

had been pressing for stricter scrutiny over domestic enforcement options, with a view to (at least partially) bridge the 'European enforcement gap' stemming from the almost total absence of direct EC *jus puniendi*. This is the reason why, in the aftermath of the ruling, the Commission issued a notice to outline its view on the systemic importance of the stance taken by the Court.[11] In particular, it magnified the cross-cut nature of the requirements in question and pointed at their structural implications in all EC policy fields in which the response to violations of Community law and to national provisions implementing it was entrusted to the Member States.

This context provides an explanation of the immediate follow up to *Greek Maize*. Whilst the principle of assimilation was confined within the realm of primary law and was mainly conceptualised in relation to the protection of the EU financial interests,[12] the 'effective, proportionate and dissuasive' formula soon became a regular refrain in EU secondary law. Strongly backed by the Commission, the '*Greek Maize* mantra' started to be incorporated as a matter of routine in EU secondary law.[13]

At the same time, the institutional narrative of securing the attainment of EU objectives by means of stricter boundaries to the discretion of the national authorities has attracted two main objections. On the one hand, some commentators have pointed at the risk of fostering effectiveness at the expense of competing proportionality considerations.[14] On the other hand, the threefold obligation in question has been depicted as 'relatively clear in the abstract yet often vague in their specifics',[15] from the viewpoint of both national legislatures – tasked with the duty to identify appropriate measures to implement EU law – and of judicial authorities charged with the *ex post* scrutiny over domestic sanctioning regimes. These concerns are amplified by the inherent multilevel nature of the integration process in which the EU's attempt to develop a common and autonomous understanding face fragmented views of proportionality, effectiveness and dissuasiveness.

This is why, over the decades, the Court of Justice has tried to fine-grain the components of the *Greek Maize* formula, also with a view to orient the national legislators' activity and to provide a more stable and sounder basis for judicial

[11] European Commission notice concerning the judgment of the Court of Justice of 21 September 1989 in case 68/88 [1990] OJ C1 147/3.

[12] In particular, as from the Treaty of Amsterdam, Article 209a(1) TEC, later re-numbered in Article 280 TEC and eventually replaced by Article 325 TFEU.

[13] On this point, see the contribution of L Grossio to this book. Article 325(1) TFEU, instead, more vaguely refers the obligation to enact 'deterrent' measures – therefore not necessarily sanctions – to secure effective protection of the EU budgetary interests.

[14] F Giuffrida, 'Effectiveness, Dissuasiveness, Proportionality of Sanctions and Assimilation Principle: The Long-Lasting Legacy, in V Mitsilegas, A Di Martino and L Mancano (eds), *The Court of Justice and European Criminal Law. Leading Cases in a Contextual Analysis* (Oxford, Hart Publishing, 2021) 107.

[15] M Dougan, 'From the velvet glove to the iron fist: Criminal sanctions for the enforcement of Union law', in M Cremona (ed), *Compliance and Enforcement in EU Law* (Oxford, Oxford University Press, 2012) 84.

review. The following section provides an overview of the Court's approach, with greater focus on the gradual – although still largely blurred – determination of the boundaries of the principle of proportionality of penalties.

III. Fine-Graining the *Greek Maize* Formula: The Role of the Court of Justice

The *Greek Maize* effectiveness requirement can be considered a specification of the homonymous general principle binding the Union and the Member States to direct their activities towards the achievement of the objectives set forth by the Treaties. This systemic reading is regularly referred to by the Court, even though its most refined illustrations with respect to sanctions are to be traced in the opinions of various Advocates General. The first in time was Advocate General van Gerven. In his Opinion in *Hansen*, he described effectiveness as the obligation on the part of the Member States to 'endeavour to attain and implement objectives of the relevant provisions of Community law', via sanctions imposed on natural or legal persons.[16] Years later, in *Berlusconi*,[17] Advocate General Kokott stressed the importance of the normative conditions – both substantive and procedural – surrounding the pre-determination of a (in that case criminal) penalty. Thus, she added that penalties are effective when 'they are framed in such a way that they do not make it practically impossible or excessively difficult to impose the penalty provided for (and, therefore, to attain the objectives pursued by Community law)'.[18]

Conversely, dissuasiveness has been rarely addressed in the Court's case-law as such. Scholarly definitions connect this requirement to the individual perspective of the natural or legal person facing obligations deriving from EU law. The prospect of a dissuasive penalty would 'neutralise the incentives' to depart from such obligations and to obstruct the attainment of EU goals.[19] In this respect, the criterion at issue should not be assessed only *in abstracto*. It rather needs an *ad hoc* evaluation of the circumstances of a case. These encompass considerations on the close link between deterrence and the degree of likelihood of a sanction being actually and entirely served.

Lastly, an extensive body of Luxembourg case-law contributes to the determination of the substance of the requirement of proportionality. As it is renowned,

[16] Case 148/77 *Hansen* ECLI:EU:C:1978:173, para 8.

[17] Joined cases C-387/02, C-391/02 and C-403/02 *Berlusconi and Others* ECLI:EU:C:2005:270, para 88. See also Advocate General Jarabo Colomer's opinion in the so-called environmental crimes case: case C-176/03 *Commission v Council* ECLI:EU:C:2005:311.

[18] Opinion of AG Kokott in *Berlusconi and Others*, cit., para 88.

[19] *Ibid.*, para 89. The reach of the dissuasiveness criterion has sometimes been stretched to include orienting a person's behaviour to given values protected and/or promoted by the EU or the national legal orders: K Nuotio, 'A legitimacy-based approach to EU criminal law: Maybe we are getting there, after all' (2020) 11 *New Journal of European Criminal Law*, 24.

proportionality generally requires that a measure is suitable and necessary to attain a given legitimate interest and that it does not cause excessive disadvantages *in concreto*. In the case of sanctions, the appropriateness of national measures is closely connected to the aim of ensuring compliance with the obligations stemming from EU law and, ultimately, of preserving the objectives pursued by the Union. Moreover, in light of the necessity and proportionality *stricto sensu* criteria, the severity of the sanction must be commensurate with the seriousness of the offence and must not go beyond what is necessary in order to attain the objectives legitimately pursued by the domestic legislation at issue.[20]

It follows that the definition of proportionality of sanctions encompasses two complementary dimensions that reflect different lines of reasoning for determining whether this requirement has been met. On the one hand, it is concerned with a retrospective dimension, requiring the alignment of a present response (the sanction) to the features of a past event (the violation of national provisions implementing EU law). This relationship entails a twofold assessment of the severity of the sanction and of the seriousness of the infringement. On the other hand, the conceptual structure of proportionality of sanctions is also prospective. It entails a "means to end"[21] relationship, questioning if and to what extent a given measure is appropriate to the objectives that it pursues. Both perspectives need to be considered when assessing the legitimacy of a sanction, from its normative pre-determination to its actual imposition.

In this context, the Court regularly recalls that, in the absence of EU harmonisation, the Member States are in principle free to 'choose the penalties which seem to them appropriate' to punish violations of EU law, provided that they 'exercise that power in accordance with European Union law and its general principles'.[22] The Court is therefore concerned with avoiding the measures involved exceeding the limits of what is appropriate to attain the objectives that the Union pursues by means of the secondary legislation that the Member State was expected to implement. This is an important aspect, as it marks a clear difference from the review of domestic sanctions derogating from EU law. In the latter category, the measures under scrutiny pursue domestic ends, which might conflict with a provision of EU law, and therefore need to be justified on grounds of overriding requirements in the public interest.[23] Conversely, in *Greek Maize* cases the role of essentially national objectives is *per se* marginal, provided that the Member States are under a duty to achieve common Union goals by means of their own legislation. At the same time, the Luxembourg case-law is not immune

[20] *Ex multis*, see case C-64/18 *Maksimovic* ECLI:EU:C:2019:723, para. 39 and case-law referred to therein.

[21] A Duff, 'Proportionality and the Criminal Law: Proportionality of What to What?', in E Billis, N Knust and JP Rui (eds), *Proportionality in Crime Control and Criminal Justice* (Oxford, Hart Publishing, 2021), 29.

[22] *Ex multis*, case C-188/09 *Profaktor Kulesza* ECLI:EU:C:2010:454, para 29.

[23] When reviewing national measures based on express derogations established in the Treaties or in EU secondary law or which stem from the exercise of the Member States' retained powers, the

from considerations regarding the domestic context that might have influenced the exercise of the national legislature's discretion. In particular, the Court seems to be inclined to pay due consideration for national cultural, social and economic factors to lead to a given perception of the degree of wrongfulness of a conduct, and to the ensuing options in terms of the type and severity of sanctions.[24]

The ECJ usually combines this purely prospective approach, oriented to the aims of a sanction, with a retrospective analysis of whether severity of the measure and the seriousness of the infringement are actually aligned. Accordingly, the case-law clarifies that 'in order to assess whether a penalty is consistent with the principle of proportionality, account must be taken of, *inter alia*, the nature and the degree of seriousness of the infringement which that penalty seeks to sanction, and of the means of establishing the amount of that penalty'.[25] The Court considers a constellation of factors, depending on the type of sanction and on the violation concerned. As a common denominator to the highly fragmented case-law, penalties that are not tailor-made to the breach they are intended to punish are usually subject to strict scrutiny. In a similar way, national provisions imposing the same penalty for a set of actions displaying an ascending scale of seriousness usually do not pass the proportionality test.[26] Another recurring element of the ECJ case-law is the scant support for absolute or automatic criteria for determining the nature and the quantum of a penalty, insofar as they remove any reasonable possibility of tailoring the sanction to the infringement. This is the case of minimum mandatory penalty thresholds and automatic penalty increases or multipliers.

Overall, even though some recurring patterns can be identified, and the methodology and assessment criteria used by the Court of Justice are generally established, it is not possible to rely on a one-size-fits-all standard of review.

This is also due to the fact that the components of the *Greek Maize* formula cannot be considered in isolation. First, they are mutually intertwined and impact each other, their respective balance, and – eventually – the assessment of the compatibility of the domestic sanctions with Union law. Second, the fulfilment of one requirement does not secure the attainment of the others. For instance, a proportionate measure might be plainly ineffective, thereby raising issues of

Court is concerned with the different objective of avoiding national sanctioning regimes hampering the full effectiveness of EU law. See e.g., for derogations and national retained powers respectively, case 203/80 *Casati* ECLI:EU:C:1981:261, para 27, and case C-35/20 *A (franchissement defrontières en navire de plaisance)* ECLI:EU:C:2021:813. Only in a few cases, the Court has used a more nuanced formula, whereby it seems to uphold a lighter proportionality scrutiny: 'a penalty must not be so disproportionate to the gravity of the infringement that it becomes an obstacle to the freedoms enshrined in the Treaty'. E.g. case C-322/16 *Global Starnet Ltd* ECLI:EU:C:2017:985, para 60. Lastly, the Court recalls that 'the national authorities should not impose penalties for disregard of a provision which is incompatible with [EU] law'. Case 8/77 *Sagulo* ECLI:EU:C:1977:131, para 6.

[24] Case C-262/99 *Louloudakis* ECLI:EU:C:2001:407; case C-156/04, *Commission v Greece* ECLI:EU:C:2007:316.

[25] Case C-712/17 *EN.SA.* ECLI:EU:C:2019:374, para 40.

[26] Case C-210/10 *Marton Urbán* ECLI:EU:C:2012:64.

non-compliance with EU law and urging the option for another – more effective but still proportionate – sanction. Third, compliance with the *Greek Maize* criteria is largely dependent on a variety of external factors, such as the policy domain at issue, the objectives pursued by the EU, as well as the features of the national legal order concerned. These elements make it unreasonable – where not impossible – to identify in absolute terms what (kind and severity) of measure should be considered proportionate to an abstractly defined infringement of EU law. In the same way, from a reverse perspective, the pre-determination of a fixed ascending scale of seriousness would be a useless and naive exercise.[27]

These considerations make the role of the national courts particularly important, since the ECJ often leaves to the referring court and to the competent national authorities the task of determining if a sanction is ultimately (dis) proportionate.[28]

IV. A Turning Point: The Acknowledgement of the Direct Effect of the Prohibition on Imposing Disproportionate Penalties

Precisely with respect to the role of national courts, 2022 marked a turning point in the Luxembourg case-law. In its preliminary ruling in *NE v Bezirkshauptmannschaft Hartberg-Fürstenfeld*,[29] the Grand Chamber of the Court of Justice declared that the proportionality criterion embedded in the Greek Maize formula is endowed with direct effects. In doing so, the Court expressly departed from its settled precedents. In particular, just a few years before, in *Link Logistic*,[30] the Court had denied the direct effect of the proportionality criterion on grounds of its inherent ambiguity. According to the Fifth Chamber, by its nature, an obligation to set up proportionate penalties is neither clear and precise nor unconditional, because it requires transposition in domestic law and thus gives the national legislatures a broad margin of discretion.

These arguments echoed the traditional approach that the more limited the room for *manoeuvre* entrusted to the national authorities, the higher the probability of establishing direct effects. As *Link Logistic* demonstrates, this was

[27] These arguments echo another categorisation of proportionality of sanctions into cardinal and ordinal. The former predefines the absolute measure (the *quantum*) of which is proportionate to a given offence and is therefore deserved by the offender. The latter conveys the idea of attaching a higher degree of severity to more serious crimes; A von Hirsch, 'Proportionality in the philosophy of punishment' (1992) *Crime and Justice*, 55.

[28] E.g. case C-487/14 *Total Waste Recycling* ECLI:EU:C:2015:780, para 55.

[29] Case C-205/20 *NE v Bezirkshauptmannschaft Hartberg-Fürstenfeld* ECLI:EU:C:2022:168. For a comment see S Montaldo, 'Handle with care! The direct effect of the requirement of proportionality of sanctions and the remedy of disapplication: *NE* v. *Bezirkshauptmannschaft Hartberg-Fürstenfeld*' (2022) 59 *CMLRev*, 863.

[30] Case C-384/17 *Dooel Uvoz-Izvoz Skopje Link Logistic* ECLI:EU:C:2018:810.

perceived to be true *a fortiori* where a Directive was concerned, because the extent of the discretion entrusted to the national legislatures amplifies the variety of implementation choices at the disposal of the Member States.

This reasoning paved the way for criticism, on two main grounds.

First, by relying on the fact that the duty to adopt 'effective, proportionate and dissuasive' sanctions compellingly needed to be complemented by national measures, *Link Logistic* upheld a misleading approach to the analysis of the conditions for the direct effect to occur. It excluded the criterion of sufficient precision on the grounds of an inherent characteristic of any Directive, namely the imposition of an obligation of result leaving the Member States free to determine the means to achieve it. In *NE v Bezirkshauptmannschaft Hartberg-Fürstenfeld*, the Grand Chamber openly departed from this argument. It recalled its case-law, according to which the core element to be assessed is the inherent quality of the duty of implementation, namely if it is worded in unequivocal terms and clearly identifies the result to be achieved.[31]

Second, the Fifth Chamber did not consider that Luxembourg case-law has markedly mitigated the incidence of Member States' discretion on the determination of direct effects. The ECJ has drawn a conceptual dividing line between the features of a provision of EU law and the discretion enjoyed by the Member States when transposing or enforcing it. The latter element is external to the substance of the obligation deriving from EU law in question and to the unequivocal nature of its wording. It follows that it 'does not alter the precise and unconditional nature' of such obligation.[32] Not necessarily, at least.

In this respect, *NE v Bezirkshauptmannschaft Hartberg-Fürstenfeld* marks another important departure from *Link Logistic*. There, the Court's legal reasoning revolved around the assumption that proportionality entails a positive obligation to design appropriate sanctioning regimes in the national legal orders. The Grand Chamber reversed the perspective and contended that the requirement imposes 'a prohibition on adopting disproportionate penalties'.[33] This approach allowed the ECJ to rely on its longstanding case-law, according to which prohibitions or obligations to refrain from doing something, where not qualified by any condition, are 'complete, legally perfect and consequently capable of producing direct effects'.[34] In addition, it placed the Court on a rather obligatory argumentative pathway: it would have been difficult to justify a different approach to the prohibition on imposing disproportionate sanctions compared to, for instance, the principle of non-discrimination or the prohibition on imposing quantitative restrictions and measures having equivalent effect – negative obligations which the Court has deemed to be directly effective since its early case-law.

[31] E.g. case C-194/08 *Gassmayr* ECLI:EU:C:2010:386, para 45; case C-387/19, *RTS infra and Aannemingsbedriif Norré-Behaegel* ECLI:EU:C:2021:13, para 46.

[32] Case C-282/10 *Maribel Dominguez v Centre informatique du Centre Ouest Atlantique* ECLI:EU:C:2012:33, para 35.

[33] See NE, cit., paras 24 and 26.

[34] Case 28/67 Firma Molkerei-Zentrale Westfalen/Lippe GmbH ECLI:EU:C:1968:17, 153.

It follows that the margin of *manoeuvre* entrusted to the Member States extends only to the set of proportionate measures available to the national legislatures, from which they can select the one that best fits their political priorities.

Interestingly enough, the Court took the opportunity of *NE v Bezirkshauptmannschaft Hartberg-Fürstenfeld* to outline a further forward-looking implication of its ruling: in an *obiter dictum*, it affirmed that the proportionality requirement embedded in the *Greek Maize* formula 'merely reiterates' Article 49(3) of the Charter, concerning the principle of proportionality of offences and (criminal) penalties, which is 'imperative in nature'.[35]

Acknowledging the direct effects of a provision of EU law has two main implications. First, it empowers the protection of individuals, who are entitled to invoke the provision concerned against the Member States. Second, provides that it is not possible to resort to consistent interpretation,[36] it equips the national administrative authorities and courts with the autonomous power to set aside – in an individual case – domestic rules that conflict with the directly effective provision of EU law in question.

Although a well-established practical implication of primacy and direct effect, disapplication still raises a debate, which is even more heated in the case of conflicts between domestic sanctioning regimes and the prohibition to impose disproportionate penalties. The concerns in question revolve around the operational and systemic hurdles that disapplication brings with itself. These can be grouped in four main arguments, which the next Section addresses briefly.

V. The National Authorities' Power to Autonomously Set Aside Domestic Provisions Leading to the Imposition of Disproportionate Penalties: General Principles and Disapplication Locking Swords?

First, the referring court in *NE* sought for clarifications on how to handle the remedy of disapplication, namely whether the relevant domestic provisions were to be set aside in their entirety or to the sole extent that would have made the sanctioning regime proportionate. The referring court's doubt touched the essence of the theory and practice of disapplication. In fact, the necessary pre-condition for the decentralised operation of the duty to set aside conflicting national provisions to work is a clear delimitation of the object of disapplication itself. The actual scope of this remedy largely depends on the nature and the substance of the obligation incumbent upon the Member States. To this respect, the Court has

[35] The ECJ conditions the direct effect of the provisions of the Charter to their imperative nature and unconditional character. E.g. case C-414/16 Vera Egenberger v Evangelisches Werk für Diakonie ECLI:EU:C:2018:257, paras 75–76.

[36] Ex multis, case C-282/10, Maribel Dominguez, cit.

consistently held that, in principle, the legal boundaries of disapplication coincide with the declaration of incompatibility with EU law.[37] It follows that the national authorities are required to set aside only those rules which conflict with the EU footprint, whereas no disapplication is needed for situations that are not precluded by EU law.

Any choice to extend the scope of this remedy pertains to the national authorities alone and must not lead to further incompatibility with other EU rules or undermine other objectives pursued by the Treaties and secondary legislation. A duty to set aside disproportionate sanctions would therefore hardly amount to an obligation to entirely disapply the national provisions at issue. If the specific features of the domestic rules concerned and if the conflict with EU law allows it, priority should be granted to the selective disapplication of those precise normative elements that make a sanction disproportionate. If this was not the case, the primacy of EU law would lead to the paradoxical consequence of a legal void that automatically and entirely prevents the Member States from preserving the effectiveness of EU law itself at an even minimum level of intensity.[38]

Crucially, shielding EU law from the dangerous consequences of a legal vacuum caused by blind disapplication – for instance in terms of plain lack of protection of certain EU interests – raises the delicate problem of balancing EU legality with the unwanted and excessive consequences of the remedies that are aimed at preserving EU law itself. In the specific context of penalties, a vacuum would provide leeway to unduly frustrate the EU-wide interest to avoid impunity in a borderless legal space, where effective law enforcement is key to secure the fully-fledged implementation of EU policies.

In *NE*, partial disapplication was indeed an available avenue, since the severe sanctions imposed by Austrian law were the outcome of a series of overlapping rules, such as an automatic multiplier and a fixed and not scalable amount for each violation occurred. The domestic law in question was a textbook example of some normative approaches that the Luxembourg case-law regularly considers to be incompatible with a proportionate exercise of *jus puniendi* and the scope of disapplication was delimited accordingly, with no surprises and within the limits of a physiologic interpretative activity. In other words, the Court of Justice's task was a relatively easy one.

However, and clearly enough, this might not always be the case. On the one hand, selective disapplication could simply be not possible, thereby raising a dilemma between maintaining disproportionate penalties in force until they are amended by the national legislator and prioritising individual rights at the expense of impunity and poorly effective implementation of EU law. On the other hand, it could require the national court overcoming the limits of its hermeneutic powers and making critical steps into the realm of the legislator, by re-designing *ex novo* the domestic sanctioning regime.

[37] *Ex multis*, case C-226/97 *Lemmens* ECLI:EU:C:1998:296.
[38] M Dougan, 'Primacy and the remedy of disapplication' (2019) 56 *CMLRev*, 1459.

These situations reflect a second concern raised by *NE v Bezirkshauptmannschaft Hartberg-Fürstenfeld*, that is to say avoiding harms to the principles of legality and separation of powers, *a fortiori*, in the sensitive field of punitive powers. This is probably the most recurring criticism to the ECJ approach. In its ruling, the Court of Justice dismisses this objection, raised by two intervening governments in the oral hearing.[39] On the one hand, setting aside domestic provisions would entail a more lenient treatment for the person involved. On the other hand, the revised version of the Austrian sanction, modelled by means of selective disapplication, is still entirely based on pre-existing domestic rules. The remedy in question merely imposes a duty to curb those specific provisions that are at the root of the conflict with EU law. By aligning the national sanctioning regime to EU law, the referring court does not craft new legislation, rather it relies on normative choices that the national legislator had made previously. As outlined above, this argument fits the evident dissonances of Austrian legislation and the rather obligatory pathway towards their alignment with the requirement of proportionality. It follows that the Court's argument could be less convincing where more blurred normative scenarios were at issue or where multiple options are available to the national judicial authorities. In such situations, the competent courts could be asked to make discretionary choices that stretch the inherent limits of judicial interpretation or that re-shape national law significantly. This is indeed a serious concern which, however, does not amount to dismantling the ECJ position. In fact, should similar cases occur, a national court would still have viable options in its toolbox. In particular, it could resort to judicial dialogue through a preliminary reference, to seek more detailed guidance from the Court of Justice. Judicial dialogue could also entail reliance on national constitutional adjudication, to seek for a domestic and wide-ranging way out of the conflict with EU law.

The resort to the national hierarchy of judicial remedies or to direct constitutional adjudication would also be in line with the remarkable complexity of the law of sanctions. Apart from plainly disproportionate implementation choices on the nature and/or the *quantum* of a measure, sanctions are usually the result of an articulated set of criteria, very often combining several factors with a view to aligning the penalty to the seriousness of the violation and to other elements, such as the reiteration of infringements or further mitigating or aggravating circumstances. Moreover, sanctions often take the shape of a series of cumulative measures, such as pecuniary fines, seizure, confiscation, and revocation of administrative decisions granting authorisations or benefits. The criteria for determining a sanction, the imposition of various cumulative measures and also the changes which the sanction originally imposed might undergo during its enforcement – e.g. the imposition of an additional interest due to a payment delay, the replacement of a pecuniary fine with a custodial sentence, or the regime of statute of limitations – can derive from the combination of the national law specifically adopted to implement

[39] Case C-205/20, *NE v Bezirkshauptmannschaft Hartberg-Fürstenfeld* cit., paras 47 ff.

or complement an act of EU secondary law and more general provisions that set the overarching legal framework for administrative or criminal sanctions in the legal order concerned. This specificity of the law of *Greek Maize* sanctions likely – but not necessarily – favours the possibility of selective disapplication, but at the same time requires the national courts and the ECJ itself to be as detailed as possible in pointing out the elements of national law that conflict with the proportionality requirement. At the same time, the variety of factors that influence the concrete manifestation of a sanction (and of its enforcement) could make disapplication a practically clueless instrument and calls for either a general stance from the relevant constitutional court or a rapid legislative reform.

In any event, where the features of domestic legislation would bring the competent national courts to plainly exceed the limits of their institutional mandate, the protection of the principles of legality and of separation of powers – the latter being a core component of the rule of law and therefore a cornerstone of the EU integration process – could lead to reliance on the renowned *MAS* case-law,[40] where the Court of Justice itself acknowledged that the autonomous duty of disapplication cannot affect the general principles recognised by the EU legal order.

Third, some commentators have pointed at the lack of a clear and shared European outlook on the structure of the proportionality review and on how the assessment of proportionality should be conducted.[41] By declaring the direct effects of the requirement in question, the Court deemed to impose its own – and largely undefined – view of this principle on the national authorities. The side effect would then be the de facto replacement of rooted domestic proportionality schemes with a unilateral and uniform EU approach, crucially affected by poor conceptual elaboration, unclear choice between the models of prospective and retrospective proportionality and little consideration for constitutional traditions. In my view, although fascinating, this argument should be considered the other way around. The ECJ approach to proportionality scrutiny is indeed blurred, for the very simple reason that – as the Court itself reiterates on every occasion – the judges sitting in Kirchberg are not best placed to tackle domestic proportionality issues. This assessment is regularly left to the national courts, which benefit from a comprehensive set of factual and legal elements necessary to perform this task. As recently recalled by Advocate General Emiliou, 'the Court has rarely ruled specifically on the proportionality of a given penalty set out in national law. Unless the reasonable or excessive nature of a penalty is clear-cut, the Court entrusts responsibility for reviewing proportionality to the referring courts, providing them with useful guidance to enable them to carry out that review'.[42]

[40] Case C-42/17 *MAS ad MB* ECLI:EU:C:2017:936.

[41] M Lanotte, 'La proporzionalità della sanzione: un principio ritrovato? Note a margine della sentenza NE' (2023) *I post di AISDUE*, 367.

[42] See AG Emiliou's opinion delivered in case C-40/21, *Agenția Națională de Integritate* ECLI:EU:C:2022:873, para 38.

Even though elements of judicial harmonisation of the dividing line between proportionate and disproportionate measures can be traced in the abundant Luxembourg case-law, these have to do with *icto oculi* excesses of coercive powers.

The fourth and last concern calls into question the principle of equality before the law, enshrined in Article 20 of the Charter.[43] The remedy of disapplication inherently entails a certain lapse of time within which the solution to the incompatibility between national and EU law is based on *ad hoc* choices of the authorities required to settle a dispute. This means that, on the very same legal problem, the practical outcomes can be as diversified within the spectrum 'full disapplication/denial of disapplication' as the number of cases brought before national judges and courts. Autonomously setting aside allegedly incompatible domestic provisions is in itself the result of an interpretative decision, which might not be plainly straightforward. Several factors may lead the domestic authorities tasked with solving an incompatibility with EU law to adopt diverging solutions, with varied implications for the individuals concerned. It follows that, in comparable situations, the national judicial authorities could impose different sanctions. While at first sight differential treatment could be problematic in terms of equality – once again, *a fortiori* in the area of sanctions – the multifaceted consequences of the autonomous power of disapplication shall not be considered in their static dimension. Instead, diachronically, every domestic legal order is fully equipped with appropriate tools to ensure that any uncertainty is short-lived:[44] certainty and equality can be achieved progressively through the set of hierarchical judicial remedies, leading apex courts to secure general operational guidance and interpretative consistency.

While a last word from domestic supreme courts or even a preliminary reference to the Court of Justice are the physiologic ways out of this conundrum, the related *in itinere* legal uncertainty is inherently connected to the way disapplication works, by virtue of the systemic structure of the multilevel EU legal order. If we were to uphold criticism based on considerations of (temporary) inconsistency, we would necessarily need to challenge disapplication as such, a spillover which would force the entire reconsideration of the current shape of the EU legal order.

At the same time, temporarily inevitable as it can be, such an instability needs to be kept to the bare minimum to allow the national institutions to reach a satisfactory way out, to avoid harm to the individuals concerned and to the credibility of the legal system as a whole. This is why, under the general theory of disapplication, this remedy does not override the Member States' duty to fully align their legal orders to EU law. It is hence up to the national legislatures or to the other authorities entrusted with the necessary power to delete or amend the

[43] Case C-205/20, NE v Bezirkshauptmannschaft Hartberg-Fürstenfeld cit., paras 54–56.

[44] This would not be the case in the event of final decisions conflicting with EU law, with respect to which there would not be room for adjustments, due to the Court's approach to *res judicata* and the underlying interest for legal certainty. See for instance case C-234/17 *XC* ECLI:EU:C:2018:853.

provisions concerned, to the extent that they depart from EU law. Even though the practice shows that the actual responsiveness of legislatures and public administrations can be questioned, the convergence of EU driven remedies – judicial dialogue and disapplication on the frontline – and of national ones, should avoid that the uncertainty deriving from an incompatibility between EU and domestic law would turn from a 'temporary normal' to a 'new normal'.

VI. Concluding Remarks

Compliance of national sanctioning regimes with proportionality has been a recurring concern in domestic litigation and has eventually been brought before the Court of Justice through preliminary rulings on an overwhelming number of occasions. Judicial dialogue has thus offered the Court an opportunity to elaborate on a European way toward sanction proportionality. Although the determination of a specific proportionality paradigm is yet to come, the abundant Luxembourg case-law has identified a series of minimum common denominators, such as the (dis)proportionality alert placed on fixed penalties applying to different violations and on automatic multipliers. In general, however, the case-law shows no clearly pre-determined patterns: the Court swings between retrospective and prospective proportionality schemes and prefers to point at specific normative elements and their (lack of) compliance with the composite tripartite proportionality assessment. In fact, factors such as the inextricable link between proportionality and the other components of the *Greek Maize* formula, the basically unlimited case-by-case variability of legal and factual circumstances and the inherent complexities of the law of sanctions make it particularly difficult to identify blanket standards about the measures that are considered to comply with this requirement. This is why the Court still relies on the role of national courts, which it usually declares to be best placed to perform a meaningful proportionality assessment, tailored to the features of a case. This approach fuels judicial dialogue and might contribute to the gradual elaboration of increasingly shared standards in the long run. In this context, two further actors might play a crucial role. On the one hand, national supreme and constitutional courts could contribute to developing an increasingly common understanding of the proportionality of sanctions, by virtue of the qualified role that the constitutional traditions common to the Member States play in the EU legal order. On the other hand, the EU legislature can direct the national implementation choices to certain types or levels of sanctions, thereby preventing proportionality concerns at the national level. This twofold trend could be backed by the recent acknowledgement of the direct effects of the proportionality requirement embedded in the *Greek Maize* formula and enshrined – with respect to criminal law – in Article 49(3) of the Charter.

The stance taken by the Court of Justice empowers lower courts in two complementary ways. First, it equips any national court with the tool of disapplication, to bridge conflicts between national and EU legal orders. Admittedly, this remedy raises debate in relation to the risk of judicial activism affecting the principle of legality and separation of powers. However, as the analysis developed above has tried to demonstrate, the Court's main concern in *NE v Bezirkshauptmannschaft Hartberg-Fürstenfeld* was to avoid loopholes in the system of EU remedies, to the detriment of the final addressees of disproportionate sanctions. From this viewpoint, disapplication becomes a crucial tool towards avoiding abusive exercises of *jus puniendi* under the aegis of the need to implement EU law. Any controversial situation where this remedy would require too intrusive judicial reconsiderations of the applicable sanctioning regime could be handled through the system of hierarchical judicial remedies available in every Member State. Similarly, any substantial and concrete risk of violation of key components of the rule of law such as the principle of separation of powers could be solved by resorting to the *MAS* case-law and to the related limits to disapplication.

Second, national courts face the increasingly pressing quest for a clear determination of the outer borders of disapplication. While expanding the scope of this remedy through declaring the direct effect of the prohibition on imposing disproportionate penalties, the Court has indirectly shed light on the importance of the limits thereof. In fact, disapplication in an individual case can be effective as it can be potentially problematic. On the one hand, as already recalled, it could hamper general principles of law; on the other hand, it could paradoxically be a source of further conflicts with EU law, since setting aside a domestic provision could lead to a legal vacuum depriving the effectiveness of EU law of any defence. In both cases, domestic judicial authorities are required to take this remedy and its inherent limits seriously, with the crucial interpretative support of the Court of Justice and – hopefully – the timely intervention of national legislators. While in *Simmenthal* the Court of Justice depicted disapplication as an all-encompassing remedy,[45] drawing the precise limits to its scope will likely be a crucial step in the coming season of EU multilevel adjudication.

[45] Case 106/77 Amministrazione delle Finanze dello Stato v Simmenthal ECLI:EU:C:1978:49, paras 21–22.

14

The Influence of Proportionality of Penalties Derived from EU Law on Domestic Criminal Legislation and Sentencing

MARCO PELISSERO

I. Overview: The Principle of Proportionality in the Italian Criminal System before and after Article 49 of the Charter

In Italian case-law, the principle of proportionality of penalties derived from EU law is gaining importance. In the current primary law framework, this principle is codified in Article 49 of the Charter, which stipulates that 'the severity of penalties must not be disproportionate to the criminal offence'. However, this principle was already enshrined in several framework decisions, following the *Greek Maize* judgment of the Court of Justice,[1] and now it is also present in the directives on substantive criminal law, since these sources always require that 'Member States shall ensure that the criminal offences [...] are punishable by effective, proportionate and dissuasive criminal sanctions' (sometimes criminal or non-criminal sanctions).[2]

The impact of these provisions on the Italian criminal system must be reconstructed on the basis of the importance of the principle of proportionality in our legal system, which predates the adoption of the Charter of Fundamental Rights.

If we look at the historical development of criminal law, this principle represents the secular precipitate of the retributive function of the penalty, which acts

[1] Case C-68/88 Commission v Greece ECLI:EU:C:1989:339.

[2] For example, Art 5 and 8 of Directive (EU) 2018/1673 of the European Parliament and of the Council on combating money laundering by criminal law [2018] OJ L 284/22; Art 15 of Directive (EU) 2017/541 of the European Parliament and of the Council on combating terrorism and replacing Council Framework Decision 2002/475/JHA and amending Council Decision 2005/671/JHA [2017] OJ L88/6; Artt 5 and 7 of Directive 2008/99/EC of the European Parliament and of the Council on the protection of the environment through criminal law [2008] OJ L328/28.

as a limit to the preventive instances of the punitive power: a guarantee for the members of society. Effectively, this guarantee has a twofold dimension.

Proportionality acts first of all as a limit to the choice of incrimination. I am referring to the proportionality of the criminal response in relation to other possible sanctions: the principle of proportionality in the broad sense also implies a judgment on the subsidiarity of the criminal response; if a legal interest can be protected by other means, these must be privileged over penalties. In this sense, the principle of proportionality is a criminal policy principle on the merits (*Strafwürdigkeit*) and necessity (*Strafbedürfnis*) of punishment, which limits the legal incrimination options.

This dimension of the principle of proportionality suffers the greatest discrepancy between the assessments expressed by the doctrine and the choices made by the legislator, which are often irrational (symbolic penal law, penal populism): one need only think of the use of penal control in relation to illegal immigration (in Italy, the mere fact that a non-EU citizen enters or remains illegally on the territory of the State is a criminal offence);[3] or the choice made in 2006 by the Italian legislature to equate hard drugs and soft drugs in criminal law. Parliament is currently debating the approval of a bill[4] that would apply Italian criminal law to acts of surrogacy (which is a crime in Italy: Article 12 of Law 40/2004), even when the act is committed in a territory where this practice is regulated: if the bill becomes law, the Italian judge will be able (or rather, will be required) to initiate criminal proceedings against the couple of commissioning parents who have carried out surrogacy in the States where the act is regulated in a lawful manner.

In many cases, the EU directives aim to introduce new criminal offences into national legislation, for example, in the fight against international terrorism (Directive (EU) 2017/541 of the European Parliament and of the Council on combating terrorism and replacing Council Framework Decision 2002/475/JHA and amending Council Decision 2005/671/JHA [2017] OJ L88/6). Sometimes the directive only asks for penalties, criminal or non-criminal, as long as they are effective, proportionate and dissuasive; in Italy, however, directives are often implemented through the introduction of new crimes and misdemeanors. EU law can thus contribute to an irrational and excessive extension of criminal protection (*overcriminalisation*).

Once the legislator has opted for the criminal sanction, the second dimension of the principle of proportionality intervenes as a guarantee of the punitive response, on two levels:

(a) the legal determination of the penalty, which means that the penalties provided for by the law must be proportionate to the offence: the principle of proportionality is addressed to the legislator;
(b) the determination of the sentence, which means the judge must quantify and enforce penalties that are proportionate to the seriousness of the offence: in this sense, the principle of proportionality is addressed to the judge.

[3] The offence is punished by a fine from 500 to 10.000 euro (Art. 10-*bis* of the Consolidate Test Immigration Law 25 July 1989, No 286, inserted by Law 15 July 2009, No 94).

[4] Bill No 887 approved by the Chamber of Deputies and forwarded to the Senate for approval (26 July 2023).

In the Italian penalty system, there is no rule that expressly provides for the principle of proportionality: neither with regard to penalties nor with regard to security measures. It is, however, a principle that scholarship and case-law consider to be constitutional in nature and that is enshrined in the following articles of the Italian Constitution:

- Article 3, which provides for the principle of equality from which the Constitutional Court has also inferred the principle of reasonableness;
- Article 27(1), which provides that 'criminal responsibility is personal': one is liable for one's own act committed culpably and with a penalty proportionate to the offence committed
- Article 27(3), which provides that penalties may not consist of treatment contrary to the sense of humanity and must aim at the re-education of the convicted person: a disproportionate penalty is dysfunctional to the re-educational function, as the convicted person will feel that the penalty is an abuse of punitive power, thus compromising any re-education program.

In this context, Article 49(3) of the Charter reinforces the principle of proportionality of punishments, which is already established as a constitutional principle. In fact, Article 49 can serve as 'interposed norm' for the judgement of constitutional legitimacy on the basis of Articles 11 and 117 of the Italian Constitution. The argument of the interposed norm was developed by the Constitutional Court in the so-called 'twin judgments' in relation to the European Convention on Human Rights standards.[5] Article 11 of the Constitution states that 'Italy [...] consents, on equal terms with other States, to the limitations of sovereignty necessary for an order that ensures peace and justice among nations' and according to Article 117 therein, 'Legislative power is exercised by the State and the Regions in compliance with the Constitution, as well as the constraints deriving from the EU order and international obligations'. These two constitutional norms require respect for the supranational rules binding on Italy, such as the norms of the EU legal order, including the Charter, which has the same legal value as the EU Treaties and contains norms that are directly binding on the Italian legal system; a law that provides for disproportionate penalties therefore violates Article 49(3) of the Charter and, consequently, Articles 11 and 117 of the Italian Constitution.

II. The Principle of Proportionality of Penalties in the Constitutional Legitimacy of the Statutory Limits of Penalties

The principle of proportionality has become an important tool used by the Constitutional Court to assess the legitimacy of statutory penalties in relation to specific offences. From the principle of equality, the Constitutional Court

[5] Constitutional Court rulings Nos 248/2007 and 249/2007.

has developed the principle of reasonableness, which is a more flexible criterion employed by the Italian Constitutional Court to review constitutional legitimacy. Normally, the Court does not intervene in the determination of the quantum of punishment provided for specific crimes because penalties are fixed by law and the Court cannot intervene in the 'political' choices of the legislature. However, the Court has intervened in some cases to review the 'manifest unreasonableness' of the penalty treatment. Some arguments that have the principle of proportionality at their core are outlined below.

a) The Constitutional Court often uses the *tertium comparationis* argument to examine the constitutional legitimacy of penalties: a penalty provided for one offence is compared with the penalty provided for another offence that protects a similar interest; if the comparison between the penalties provided for the two offences reveals a disparity in the treatment of the penalty that appears manifestly unreasonable, the Court declares the penalty unlawful.[6] More recently, however, the Constitutional Court has abandoned the *tertium comparationis* argument and developed an intrinsic test of reasonableness: that is, it has directly assessed the proportionality of the penalty in relation to the fact of the offence, in some cases going so far as to declare the criminal sanction constitutionally illegitimate when the penalty envisaged appeared manifestly disproportionate to the disvalue of the fact. At the same time, the Constitutional Court identifies the penalty that, taking into account the overall systemic context, appears to be the most appropriate to ensure compliance with the constitutional principles, while leaving the legislature free to identify a different penalty treatment in the future, provided that it is in line with constitutional principles.[7]
b) The principle of proportionality applies not only to penalties in the strict sense, but to all punitive sanctions, even if they are not designated as 'penalties' by law. For punitive sanctions, which are formally non-criminal, the Constitutional Court bases itself on Article 3 of the Constitution, and not on Article 27(3) therein, since that provision does not apply to administrative sanctions but refers to criminal penalties in the formal sense.[8]
c) Fixed penalties tend to contravene the constitutional principle of proportionality because they do not allow the judge to adapt the penalty to the concrete facts.[9] The same principle has been extended to punitive administrative sanctions: if they are fixed, they are unconstitutional.[10]
d) The relationship between the offender and the offence in sentencing is conditioned by the principle of proportionality: the assessment of the offender's personality influences the determination of the penalty, but it cannot be

[6] See, for example, Constitutional Court ruling No 241/1994.
[7] Constitutional Court ruling No 236/2016.
[8] Constitutional Court ruling No 185/2021.
[9] Constitutional Court decision No 50/1980 and, more recently, ruling No 222/2018.
[10] Constitutional Court ruling No 88/2019.

so 'heavy' as to prejudice the objective assessment of the seriousness of the incident. On several occasions,[11] the Constitutional Court has declared unconstitutional the provisions of Article 69 (4) of the Criminal Code, which gave greater weight to the assessment of the aggravating circumstance of repeated recidivism than to mitigating circumstances, which the Court cannot consider to be predominant. If the circumstance of repeated recidivism coincides with another mitigating circumstance that is relevant to the lesser gravity of the offence, the impossibility for the latter to prevail obliges the court to impose a sentence that is disproportionate to the value of the offence.

In many of these areas, Article 49(3) of the Charter has been recalled by the Constitutional Court as a supplementary source for the constitutional principle of proportionality of punishment: we can say that the EU source has had a marginal function, to the point that in some cases the Constitutional Court, having already assessed the penal provision on the basis of the constitutional rules establishing the principle of proportionality, has declared the profile of censure based on Article 49 of the Charter absorbed.[12]

However, the reference to the Charter has made it possible to consider the principle of proportionality of the penalty in an EU dimension, which, on the other hand, has had a more significant impact on the concrete commensuration of the penalty by the judge.

III. The Principle of Proportionality and the Powers of the Criminal Judge

In the Italian criminal system, the judge, unless the law provides otherwise, must determine the penalty *in concreto* within the minimum and maximum limits set by law for each individual offence.[13] Within these statutory limits, the principle of proportionality constitutes a fundamental criterion for the application of the penalty to the specific case, since Article 133 of the Criminal Code requires the judge to take into account first of all the seriousness of the offence. This limitation of the judge's sentencing within the limits provided for by law, constitutes an application of the principle of legality, which concerns not only the constituent elements of the offence, but also the penalty.

This limitation of the quantification of the penalty within the limits set by the law seems to be undermined precisely by the reference to the principle of proportionality of the penalty from the EU source, which allows the judge

[11] See, for example, rulings Nos 251/2012, 105/2014, 106/2014 74/2016, 205/2017 and 143/2021.
[12] See, for example, Constitutional Court ruling No 22/2018.
[13] Article 132 of the Italian Criminal Code.

to deviate from the legal limits if the punishment set by the law is considered disproportionate to the crime. This is the real novelty of the effect recognised in Article 49(3) of the Charter, which has freed itself from its ancillary role in relation to the constitutional principle of proportionality of punishment to become the main criterion of assessment for the judge of cognition. There are two areas in which the principle of proportionality has had an impact from the European Union's point of view:

(A) in the assessment of *ne bis in idem*;
(B) in the determination of the penalty.

A. The Principle of Proportionality in the Context of *Ne Bis in Idem*

Following the *Grande Stevens* ruling of the Grande Chambre of the European Court of Human Rights (ECtHR),[14] which had interpreted the *ne bis in idem* rule in procedural terms[15] by extending it to the relationship between formally criminal sanctions and punitive administrative sanctions, to be considered 'criminal matters' in the application of the conventional guarantees, the ECtHR in *A. and B. v. Norway*[16] gave a substantive reading of the *ne bis in idem* guarantee. The so-called dual-track system, namely, when the law provides for criminal and administrative sanctions, is allowed if certain requirements are met, including – and this is the important point for my observations – the overall assessment of the proportionality of the sanctioning response. It is necessary that 'the sanction imposed in the proceedings which become final first is taken into account in those which become final last, so as to prevent that the individual concerned is in the end made to bear an excessive burden, this latter risk being least likely to be present where there is in place an offsetting mechanism designed to ensure that the overall amount of any penalties imposed is proportionate'.[17]

The conclusions reached by the ECtHR are echoed in the case-law of the Court of Justice in the context of matters of EU competence, to which the *ne bis in idem* principle under Article 50 of the Charter also applies.[18]

The assessment of proportionality gives the judge a wide discretionary power to establish a violation of the *ne bis in idem* principle. If the other conditions required by the ECtHR are met (sufficiently close connection in substance and in time, consisting in dual proceedings with different purposes, their foreseeability;

[14] *Grande Stevens v Italy* App Nos 18640/10, 18647/10, 18663/10, 18668/10 e 18698/10 (ECtHR, 4 March 2014).
[15] Article 4 of Protocol No 7 to the European Convention for the Protection of Human Rights and Fundamental Freedoms (Strasbourg, 22 November 1984).
[16] *A. and B. v Norway* App Nos 24130/11 and 29758/11 (ECTHR, 15 November 2016).
[17] See para 132 of the grounds.
[18] Case C-537/16 Garlsson Real Estate and Others ECLI:EU:C:2018:193.

economy of evidence), the assessment of proportionality is decisive for evaluating the legitimacy of double penalties. This assessment has two possible outcomes:

- If the double penalty results in a proportionate penalty burden, there is no infringement of the *ne bis in idem* principle;
- if, on the other hand, the Court considers that the overall penalty burden is excessive, the *ne bis in idem* principle requires the disapplication of the rule sanctioning the second offence.

This conclusion was confirmed by an important judgment of the Court of Cassation:[19] here, the principle of proportionality of the penalty had a 'strong effect', which also justified the possibility of derogating from the principle of legality in relation to the penalties. In what sense?

In relation to an offence such as market manipulation, the Court of Cassation considers inadequate the offsetting mechanism provided for in Article 187-*terdecies* of the Consolidated Law on Financial Intermediation,[20] which requires the criminal court to quantify the financial penalty by taking into account any administrative sanction already imposed by the Italian Securities and Exchange Commission (the Italian acronym is Consob). Similarly, Consob, if it intervenes after the criminal court, must take into account the pecuniary penalty imposed by the latter. This compensation mechanism is not sufficient to ensure compliance with the principle of proportionality as it only concerns the financial penalty, whereas the offence of market manipulation is also punishable by imprisonment.

This does not pose a problem in cases where the criminal court first pronounces a conviction: Consob will have to take this into account when applying the administrative penalty, using the compensation mechanism provided for in Article 187-*terdecies* of the Consolidated Law on Finance.

The problem arises when Consob is the first to pronounce a ruling and applies an administrative fine that the criminal court considers to be wholly or partially proportionate to the gravity of the offence. In such a case:

a) the criminal court may dismiss the criminal proceedings in their entirety, thereby recognising *ne bis in idem as applicable to that case*, if it considers that the administrative fine complies with the canon of proportionality of the response to the two offences, criminal and administrative: the Court of Cassation considers this case to be 'an exceptional hypothesis';[21]
b) outside this limiting hypothesis, the criminal court may, by assessing the administrative penalty already definitively imposed, redetermine the applicable term of imprisonment, disapplying *in mitius* the minimum sentences: in other words, even if Italian criminal law provides for a minimum penalty

[19] See Court of Cassation, Section V, ruling No 5679/2019, precisely on a matter falling under the scope of EU law (market manipulation).
[20] Decree Law No 58/1998.
[21] See Court of Cassation, Section V, ruling No 5679/2019.

limit (for the offence of market manipulation, it is one year's imprisonment: Art. 185 of the Consolidated Law on Financial Intermediation), the criminal court may apply a lower penalty, with only one limit: compliance with the minimum limit of 15 days imprisonment, which is the absolute *minimum* of imprisonment for criminal offences under the Italian Criminal Code.

The argument developed by the Court of Cassation is of fundamental importance, because the principle of proportionality of punishment, which has been substantially developed in the jurisprudence of the ECtHR in interpreting the principle of *ne bis in idem*, is also applied by the Court of Justice and in the context of matters of EU competence under Article 49(3) of the Charter.

The conclusion reached by the Court of Cassation is characterised by two elements:

(a) firstly, the disapplication of domestic provisions can only produce effects *in bonam partem*;
(b) secondly, the need to ensure the principle of proportionality of the penalty with respect to the concrete fact prevails over the principle of the legality of the penalty.

The *minimum* penalty is set by law and serves the purpose of general prevention, but the assessment of the law is made by considering only the penalty provided for the offence; on the other hand, if we are in the presence of an accumulation of penalties (criminal and administrative), the *minimum* may become disproportionate *in concreto* by reason of the penalty already applied in a first proceeding, and the judge may apply a penalty lower than the legal minimum.

B. The Principle of Proportionality and the Determination of the Sentence

In cases where the judge has to ensure that the *ne bis in idem* principle is respected, a derogation from the principle of legality is justified because of a penal system that provides for a dual track, the cumulation of which may undermine the person's right to a proportionate penalty.

More radical, on the other hand, are the effects that could be produced by the recent ruling of the Court of Justice in 2022[22] on the relationship between the power of the judge to impose a proportionate sentence and the principle of the legality of punishment.

In this judgment, which refers to the Austrian system, the Court of Justice recognises that the proportionality of the penalty, as laid down in EU law, is directly applicable, since it is unconditional and characterised by sufficient precision.

[22] Case C-205/20 *Bezirkshauptmannschaft Hartberg-Fürstenfeld* (Effet direct) ECLI:EU:C:2022:168.

The argument is developed by the Court of Justice in relation to Directive 2014/67/EU on the posting of workers in the framework of the provision of services, which provides in Article 20 that penalties must be effective, proportionate and dissuasive. The proportionality of the penalty provided for in the directive is further confirmed in Article 49(3) of the Charter: 'that principle of proportionality, which Article 20 […] merely refers to, is imperative'. Therefore, even without the express mention in the Directive, the principle of proportionality of the penalty would have been mandatory under Article 49(3) of the Charter. The case concerned an Austrian administrative but substantially criminal fine.

According to the Court, the principle of proportionality enables an intervention to be made, *in bonam partem*, in the quantification of the penalty:

- if the judge considers that the penalty provided for by the law is excessive and disproportionate, they are entitled to apply a lower penalty than that provided for by the law, thus partially disapplying the 'legal' penalty in order to ensure compliance with the principle of proportionality;
- this intervention can be made directly by the judge, without waiting for the prior repeal of such legislation by the legislature or the Constitutional Court;
- this conclusion is not contrary to the principle of certainty of the penalty, which under Art. 49(1) of the Charter requires the law to clearly define not only the offences but also the penalties that punish them. On the other hand, the principle of retroactivity of more favourable legislation, which operates *in bonam partem*, is also compatible with the guarantee of *nullum crimen sine lege*; the principle of proportionality only has the effect of enabling the court to mitigate the severity of the penalty;
- the fact that, in a case such as that at issue in the main proceedings, the penalty imposed is less severe than the penalty provided for by the applicable national legislation as a result of its partial disapplication on account of that requirement cannot be regarded as infringing the principles of legal certainty, legality and proportionality of criminal offences and penalties, and non-retroactivity of criminal law.[23]

The ruling is disruptive because its effect on the principle of legality is even stronger than in relation to the *ne bis in idem* rule. In both cases, the principle of proportionality operates in favour of the offender, but the two cases are different: in relation to *ne bis in idem*, the court's assessment is conditioned by a penalty previously definitively imposed on the person and it is necessary to ensure that there is no duplication of the penalty for the same act; in the case most recently considered by the Court of Justice in 2022, the effect of the direct application of the principle of proportionality with the disapplication, even partial, of the penalty

[23] See para 51 of the grounds.

provided in the domestic legal framework is independent of a previous penalty imposed for the same act. In the latter case, it seems to me that the decision of the Court of Justice comes into conflict with the principle of the legality of punishment, because it attributes criminal judges a broad power to depart from the minimum limits laid down by law. The final result is therefore very different from the centralised control exercised by the Constitutional Court.

IV. The Possible Effects of the Ruling of the Court of Justice

The question then arises as to what the consequences of the Court's decision might be.

First of all, it must be made clear that the effect of the decision concerns only punitive sanctions that relate to matters falling within the competence of the EU. Secondly, the decision has an impact on 'criminal matters' in a broad sense, including both criminal matters in the strict sense and punitive administrative sanctions according to the *Engel* criteria (the judgment under analysis actually referred to a case involving Austrian administrative sanctions).

Although the ruling of the Court of Justice concerns a directive providing for the principle of proportionality of penalties, its implications go far beyond the cases covered by the directive or any piece of secondary law providing for the principle of proportionality of penalties. In any event, the Court clearly refers to Article 49(3) of the Charter, which has the legal force of the Treaties and also direct effects. This means that, although all the directives adopted under Article 83 TFEU contain the principle of the proportionality of penalties (or rather the triptych of effective, proportionate and dissuasive penalties), Article 49(3) of the Charter would still apply even if it were not mentioned in a Directive. However, the reasoning of the Court of Justice remains focused on the principle of proportionality in Article 20 of the Directive rather than on Article 49(3) of the Charter.

It is not at all clear to what extent the judge's assessment of the application of the principle of proportionality can be affected, since the Court of Justice states that the judge must disapply only those parts of the national legislation that appear incompatible with the principle of proportionality:

(a) can the judge apply a penalty lower than the minimum set by law? In other words, it is as if these offences and administrative offences did not have a minimum penalty, even though the law lays down a minimum penalty;
(b) if the judge can apply a penalty below the statutory minimum, can the judge also go below the general minimum prescribed by the Criminal Code for individual penalties? The Italian Supreme Court has ruled this out in relation to *ne bis in idem*, and I believe that this limit should be respected in all cases;

(c) if there is more than one penalty applied in a single proceeding (this circumstance does not pose a problem of compliance with the prohibition of *ne bis in idem*), could the court consider some penalties proportionate and others disproportionate? For example, to consider the custodial penalty disproportionate and apply only the pecuniary penalty; or to apply only the pecuniary penalty without applying confiscation, attributing to this the nature of a penalty;
(d) could the court find the penalty entirely disproportionate and disapply it? This seems to me to be an impossible solution, since it would imply the trial court finding an offence without imposing a penalty;
(e) moreover, given that the principle of proportionality of penalties enjoys a constitutional foundation, at the domestic level even before being part of EU law, is there a disparity in treatment between matters falling under the scope of EU law, for which the disapplication of the minimum would operate, and other areas in which the reasoning of the Court of Justice cannot be followed? Furthermore, in matters outside the fields of EU competence, could the criminal court, applying the constitutional principle of proportionality, reach the same conclusion as the Court of Justice?

All of these questions seem to me to show the system in a state of great uncertainty.

The Court of Justice argues that this antinomy between the legality of the penalty and the principle of proportionality can be tolerated by reason of the fact that the disapplication of the legal penalty has an *in bonam partem* effect. That is to say, it is the opposite case to *Taricco*,[24] in which the disapplication of the limitation regulation (Article 161 of the Criminal Code), in order to ensure the effective protection of the European Union's financial interests, would have had effects *in malam partem*. While it is true that the two cases have different effects, I believe that the ruling of the Court of Justice is incompatible with two principles: the principle of equality and the principle of precision.

With regard to the principle of equality, it is not convincing to give the individual criminal judges the power to disapply, even in part, the penalty: criminal judges do not exercise a centralised control, as the Constitutional Court does, but a diffuse power, the exercise of which may lead to unequal treatment. In the Italian system, the purpose of maximum sentences is to limit the judge's discretionary power and they cannot be departed from except in the cases provided for by law.

Nor is the juxtaposition drawn by the Court between the application of a lower penalty, in order to guarantee the principle of proportionality, and the retroactive application of the more favourable penalty, convincing, since we are dealing with two different situations: in the first case, it is the discretionary power of the judge in the assessment of the specific case that affects the penalty; in the second case, it is instead a different assessment made by the legislator, introducing a more favourable discipline, that justifies its retroactive application.

[24] Case C-105/14 *Taricco and Others* ECLI:EU:C:2015:555.

The principle of precision requires that the law must be clear, which means the necessity to respect the principle of foreseeability. It seems to me that the Court of Justice's ruling contains a limitation that the Constitutional Court[25] had already found in the so-called 'Taricco criteria' that the Luxembourg Court had hastily identified: the lack of sufficient determinacy of the prerequisites in the presence of which the judge should have disapplied the rules on the interruption of the statute of limitations. In last year's judgment, the Court of Justice clarified in a few passages the verification of the sufficient precision of the prohibition of disproportionate penalties: 'although that provision leaves the Member States a certain discretion in defining the rules on penalties applicable in the event of infringements of the national provisions adopted pursuant to that directive, that discretion is limited by the prohibition, laid down by that provision in a general manner and in unequivocal terms, on imposing disproportionate penalties'.[26] This is an apodictic statement: the Court does not explain at all why the criterion is certain.

On the contrary, it is inferred that the principle of the prohibition of disproportionate penalties is far from certain, as shown by the decisions of the Italian Constitutional Court, which intervenes only in cases of manifestly disproportionate penalties: however, the Constitutional Court, whose judgments have *erga omnes* effect, exercises centralised review, while the Court of Justice defers to the widespread power of the criminal courts.

The principle of proportionality of punishment requires the judge to quantify the penalty in accordance with the limits set by law (including minimum limits), but as it is not a sufficiently precise principle, it cannot allow the judge to depart from the minimum limit. This is required by the principle of the rule of law, which also operates in the determination of penalties. Precisely because of the fact that it is not a sufficiently precise and therefore self-executing principle, the judge, if convinced that the sanctioning discipline would in any case entail the application of a disproportionate penalty, should raise the question of constitutional legitimacy and refer the case to the Constitutional Court (whose scope for intervention would in any case be limited as it can only intervene in the case of manifest unreasonableness of the minimum sentence).

This more reasonable solution is confirmed by two elements, one normative and the other of jurisprudential nature. In the field of administrative tax penalties, Article 7(4) of Legislative Decree 472/1997 provides that: 'If there are circumstances that make manifest the disproportion between the amount of the tax to which the breach refers and the penalty, the latter may be reduced by up to half of the minimum'. In this case, it is the law itself that allows a penalty lower than the minimum to be applied to ensure the principle of proportionality.

[25] Constitutional Court, ruling No 49/2015.

[26] Case C-205/20 *Bezirkshauptmannschaft Hartberg-Fürstenfeld (Effet direct)* ECLI:EU:C:2022:168, para 27.

Also, in Article 133-*bis* of the Criminal Code, the economic condition of the convicted person can have an effect on the penalty: 'The court [...] may decrease the pecuniary punishment established by law ... by up to one-third when, due to the economic and property conditions of the offender, it finds that ... the minimum measure is excessively burdensome'. In this case, too, the possibility of sentencing below the minimum is established by law.

A further argument in favour of a centralised review by the Constitutional Court of compliance with minimum sentence limits can be derived from reflection on a court case. In 2023, the Court of Florence[27] raised a question of constitutional legitimacy in relation to the absence in culpable offences of the criminal relevance of the 'natural penalty', i.e. the harm that the offender suffers as a result of the same unlawful conduct: the judge considered that the impossibility of refraining from applying the penalty determines the disproportionate nature of the criminal sanction, the subject having already suffered a natural penalty for the act committed. The case concerned the culpable conduct on the part of an uncle in the performance of repair work on a roof, which resulted in the death of his nephew. Now, the issue, which in my opinion will be declared inadmissible by the Constitutional Court (since it would be up to the legislature to regulate the matter anyway) is interesting from another point of view. The offence committed did not fall under the scope of EU law, but I wonder if it had been, would the judge have been able, following the reasoning of the Court of Justice, not to impose the sentence, considering the natural punishment suffered to be sufficient? I do not think so, because the assessment should, if anything, have been referred to the Constitutional Court; on the contrary, following the argument developed by the Court of Justice, the judge could disapply the penalty set by law, taking into account the natural penalty just suffered by the defendant and considered proportionate to the offence.

V. Conclusion

The framework outlined reveals a complex relationship between EU law provisions on criminal matters and the Italian criminal system. Issues do not arise in the context of the constitutional review of manifestly disproportionate punishments, where the European Union's sources on the principle of proportionality become argumentum *ad abundantiam* with respect to the constitutional foundation of the principle; the problem concerns, conversely, the direct incidence of the principle of proportionality in the application of the penalty.

The importance assumed by the principle of proportionality of punishment, well established in the case-law of the Italian Constitutional Court and the Court of Cassation, has led to the progressive attribution to the individual criminal judge

[27] Court of Florence, Order 20 February 2023, in www.giurisprudenzapenale.com, 14 March 2023.

of widespread powers in the quantification of punishment above and beyond the limits of the law: it is a power always exercised *in bonam partem*, since in the *Taricco* case the Constitutional Court clearly excluded *in malam partem* effects deriving from the disapplication of internal rules that were in conflict with binding EU provisions. When this power is exercised to ensure compliance with the *ne bis in idem* guarantee, the sacrifice of the principle of legality is justified in a system that provides for double administrative and criminal penalties for the same wrongdoing. Outside this sphere, giving the criminal judge the power to disapply, in whole or in part, the penalties provided for by law means introducing an element of uncertainty that undermines the rule of law in criminal matters, which in our legal system safeguards not only the principle of certainty for the citizens, but also the principle of the separation of powers, which gives Parliament the power to provide for penalties.[28] On this point, I believe that only the intervention of the Constitutional Court is possible, which would assess, on a case-by-case basis, whether the minimum sentence envisaged is manifestly unreasonable.

If anything, the Court's decision has led to two other proposals that relate to the process of harmonising national legal systems and the reform of Italian criminal law. As far as the process of harmonising penalties in the Member States is concerned, Article 83 TFEU gives 'light' indications on the content of the directives in criminal matters, which must indicate 'minimum rules concerning the definition of offenses and penalties'. Directives never give rules on minimum penalty, but on maximum limits, which are sometimes an anchor on minimum limits (maximum penalty of at least …). Directives and the Court of Justice, therefore, do not seem to appreciate the significance of minimum limits from a perspective of harmonisation of criminal laws. This is a very different perspective from the one followed by a part of Italian doctrine, which considers not so much the maximum, but the minimum penalty, as an index of the seriousness of the crime.

The second suggestion concerns the Italian criminal system. If, according to the Court of Justice, the principle of proportionality of penalties allows the judge to go below the edict limits, what is the more general sense of a penal system that uses minimum limits in penalty? One could imagine a system that goes in one of two possible directions: either it provides that the judge may apply a penalty lower than the minimum, and also indicates to the judge the criteria for sentence reduction if the minimum appears disproportionate, or it moves more drastically towards a system, like the French one, that does not use minimums. In either case, the evaluation of proportionality would be left to the legislator.

[28] Constitutional Court ruling No 230/2012.

15

Tax Penalties and Proportionality: The Search for Consistency

Open Questions for the Coming Years

STEFANO MARIA RONCO

I. Introduction

In recent years, there has been an expansion in the powers of Member States' tax authorities to impose criminal and administrative tax sanctions with a view to increase taxpayers' compliance and to tackle tax evasion. However, this trend has not been accompanied by a commensurate strengthening of sanction-related rights under domestic law.

In response to this tendency, the ECJ has increasingly been called upon to clarify the scope of EU principles regarding punitive sanctions. In this respect, the recent case-law highlights a growing recognition of the principle of proportionality, as set out in Article 49(3) of the Charter, in matters relating to punitive tax sanctions.

II. The Relationship between Administrative and Criminal Penalties: From the Dual-Track Enforcement System to the Application of the *Ne Bis in Idem* Principle

The integration of criminal sanctions alongside administrative financial sanctions constitutes a common feature of many EU countries' punitive systems.[1]

[1] For a comparative overview see the IBFD Yearbook on Taxpayers' Rights 2022, Chapter 7, 143 ss., available at https://www.ibfd.org/sites/default/files/2023-05/optr-yearbook-2022_for-release-120523.pdf. See also J Kokott, P Pistone, R Miller, 'Public International Law and Tax Law: Taxpayers' Rights' (2021) 50 *Georgetown Journal of International Law* 381; P Baker, P Pistone, 'General Report', in *The Practical Protection of Taxpayers' Fundamental Rights* vol 100B (The Hague, Sdu Uitgevers, 2015) 15–99. For an EU-centred perspective see, in particular, R Seer, AL Wilms (eds), *Surcharges and Penalties in Tax Law, EATLP Annual Meeting, European Association of Tax Law Professors, Milan, Italy, 28–30 May 2015* (Amsterdam, IBFD, 2016).

Traditionally, the coherence and rationality of the comprehensive punitive framework were maintained by applying the principle of specialty, both substantively and procedurally, through the operation of the dual-track enforcement system for the imposition of administrative sanctions pending criminal proceedings.

This model, crafted to regulate the application of *vis punitiva* in the presence of parallel sanctioning structures, sought to maintain consistency between the two punitive systems, while respecting the principle of *ne bis in idem*.[2]

However, the regulatory framework originally conceived to provide certainty in the application of punitive sanctions has gradually been undermined by the evolving case-law of the ECJ and ECtHR.

It is widely recognised that, on a broad interpretation of the concept of 'criminal charge' in accordance with the Engel criteria,[3] administrative financial sanctions, irrespective of their classification as administrative penalties under domestic law, bear a substantial similarity to criminal sanctions in view of their punitive nature and high degree of severity.[4]

This stream of case-law led supranational courts to adopt a substantive approach, suggesting a potential reconsideration of the dual-track enforcement system prevalent in many countries. In essence, this case-law implied that the imposition of both administrative and criminal sanctions constituted double jeopardy and violated the application of the ne bis in idem principle.

However, subsequent jurisprudence has significantly deviated from such an understanding of the *ne bis in idem* principle, asserting that the simultaneous presence of cumulative administrative and criminal sanctions does not necessarily infringe upon the double jeopardy clause.[5] More specifically, both the ECtHR

[2] In general, at the EU level the *ne bis in idem* principle prohibits duplication of proceedings and penalties of a criminal nature for the same acts and against the same person (as affirmed in the ECJ judgment in Case C-617/10 *Åkerberg Fransson* ECLI:EU:C:2013:105, paras 33–37) either within the same Member State or in several Member States if the person has exercised their right to freedom of movement (see, in this respect, the ECJ judgment in Case C-467/04 *Gasparini and Others* ECLI:EU:C:2006:610). Moreover, the *ne bis in idem* principle is also enshrined in Art. 4 of Protocol No 7 to the ECHR, and consistently applied in the ECtHR case-law.

[3] See the judgment of the ECtHR in *Engel and Others v The Netherlands* Series A no 22 (1976).

[4] It is well established that the ECJ, following the guidance of the ECtHR, has consistently confirmed that three criteria are relevant in the context of this assessment: (i) the legal classification of the offence under national law, (ii) the intrinsic nature of the offence, and (iii) the degree of severity of the penalty. In particular, the first criterion, based on the legal classification under national law, is not in itself sufficient to determine that a certain offence is not 'criminal' in nature if the other two criteria demonstrate that it is so in substance. With regard to the second criterion, the ECJ has clarified that the clear punitive (and not merely deterrent) purpose of the sanction is decisive in determining the intrinsic criminal nature of the offence (i.e. the sanction must not be limited to repairing damage or preventing any economic gain from the unlawful conduct). As regards the third criterion, the severity is usually measured by the maximum potential penalty that can be imposed on the wrongdoer.

[5] Following, in particular, the reasoning put forward in the ECtHR judgment in *A and B. v. Norway* App nos 24130/11 and 29758/11 (ECtHR, 15 November 2016). This line of reasoning has also been upheld by the ECJ; in this respect see, *ex multis*, the ECJ judgment in Case C-524/15 *Menci* ECLI:EU:C:2018:197.

and the ECJ have more recently maintained that the duplication of criminal proceedings and penalties, as well as administrative proceedings and penalties of a criminal nature for the same act, constitutes a limitation of the *ne bis in idem* principle which may be justified from the perspective of fundamental rights,[6] provided that specific conditions are met.[7]

Given this context, the need to ensure that the severity of all penalties imposed is commensurate with the gravity of the respective offence is paramount. This is a crucial element in ensuring that the cumulative punishment resulting from the simultaneous imposition of administrative and criminal sanctions does not constitute disproportionate treatment and that it is limited to what is strictly necessary.

III. The Role of the Principle of Proportionality in Tax Matters and the Complexity of Ensuring Predictability in the Application of Punitive Sanctions

Although the application of the principle of proportionality is theoretically straightforward, it poses complex challenges in practice.

As a starting point, two fundamental dimensions of the principle of proportionality come into play in the field of tax penalties.[8]

A first concept of proportionality, which is of a general nature, links proportionality to the nature and severity of the sanction, the latter designed to protect the legal interest underpinning the punitive provision. In this respect, proportionality in punitive tax matters serves as a guiding principle for the legislator in deciding whether violations are serious enough to justify the application of criminal provisions. Thus, serious tax offences should be punished with criminal law remedies,[9]

[6] See para 40 of the *Menci* judgment, in which the ECJ stated that 'the Court ruled that a limitation to the *ne bis in idem* principle guaranteed by Article 50 of the Charter may be justified on the basis of Article 52(1) thereof'.

[7] In particular, and limiting the analysis only to the ECJ case-law, the Court has stated in the *Menci* (as reiterated in other decisions such as, notably, Case C-537/16 *Garlsson Real Estate and Others* ECLI:EU:C:2018:193) that Art. 50 of the Charter does not preclude national legislation whereby criminal proceedings may be brought against a person, even though that person has already been made the subject of a final administrative penalty of a criminal nature in relation to the same acts, on condition that: (1) the legislation pursues an objective of general interest that justifies such a duplication of proceedings and penalties, it being necessary for those proceedings and penalties to pursue additional objectives; (2) it provides rules ensuring coordination that limits the additional disadvantage resulting from the legislation to only what is strictly necessary; and (3) it provides for rules that make it possible to ensure that the severity of all of the penalties imposed is limited to what is strictly necessary in relation to the seriousness of the offence concerned.

[8] In general, see F Viganò, *La proporzionalità della pena. Profili di diritto penale e costituzionale* (Torino, Giappichelli, 2021). See also S Montaldo, 'Handle With Care! The Direct Effect of the Requirement of Proportionality of Sanctions and the Remedy of Disapplication: NE v. Bezirkshauptmannschaft Hartberg-Fürstenfeld' in (2023) 60 *CML Rev* 863, 874–875.

[9] A custodial sentence is the traditional type of punishment, usually accompanied by confiscation of the proceeds of tax evasion in several EU countries.

while less serious offences should only be reprimanded with administrative penalties imposed by means of financial charges.

However, a shift in public opinion's perception of the risks of tax evasion and, more generally, increased budgetary needs have led to a proliferation of tax punitive sanctions in many EU countries, with a view to promoting compliance and ensuring the effective punishment of tax violations. It is therefore debatable whether the punitive tax framework of EU Member States still ensures that punishments for illicit tax activities are proportionate and do not lead to a disproportionate treatment in given cases.

For these reasons, another concept of proportionality has become increasingly important. This declination of proportionality applies at the jurisdictional level and from an *ex-post* perspective, as judges are requested to review whether the imposition of penalties is actually proportionate to the disvalue of the conduct of the wrongdoer.

In this respect, courts have become increasingly instrumental in ensuring that the cumulative punishment resulting from the application of administrative and criminal tax sanctions is not disproportionate on a case-by-case basis.

Previously, domestic courts had been reluctant to engage in proportionality review, as this could be seen as an attitude that disregards the principle of separation of powers between the legislative and judicial branches. Thus, the courts have traditionally refrained from interfering with the discretionary choices made by the legislator in punitive matters.

Recently, however, the situation has changed. This change of perspective is well testified by the ECJ landmark ruling in *NE*,[10] which emphasised that the principle of the primacy of EU law should be interpreted as imposing on national authorities an obligation to disapply national legislation contrary to the requirement of proportionality of penalties, to the extent necessary to enable the imposition of proportionate penalties.[11]

The ECJ also noted that any ambiguity as to the legal rules applicable to the offences in question, deriving from the duty to disapply punitive laws which are contrary to the application of the principle of proportionality, cannot be regarded as a justification for not applying the penalty in question. Although such a jurisdictional review may entail the disregard of certain elements of the national legislation on penalties, the protection of the principle of proportionality – in conjunction with that of equality before the law, set out in Article 20 of the Charter – requires that comparable unlawful conduct should not be treated differently and that different unlawful conduct should not be treated in the same way from a punitive perspective, unless such different treatment is objectively justified.

Following the guidance of the ECJ, a shift in perspective is now also taking place at the domestic level: as a series of decisions underlines, domestic constitutional

[10] Case C-205/20 Bezirkshauptmannschaft Hartberg-Fürstenfeld (Effet direct) ECLI:EU:C:2022:168.
[11] For an in-depth analysis of this judgment see, *ex multis*, Montaldo (n 8).

courts are indeed becoming more inclined to carry out a full review of proportionality of administrative and criminal sanctions, paving the way for a more intense level of scrutiny of domestic punitive measures through the lens of proportionality.[12] It should be emphasised that this jurisprudential trend has become increasingly relevant, especially in punitive tax measures. In fact, the duty to ensure a punishment that is in line with the principle of proportionality has emerged from several decisions of domestic courts that have mitigated the harshness of the punishment imposed on the taxpayer, or have completely disregarded national penalty provisions, resulting in the imposition of disproportionate penalties.[13]

Notably, the activism that characterises this recent approach is not without ambiguities. One significant conceptual challenge, which deserves further discussion, concerns the intersection of the guarantees set out in Articles 49(3) and 50 of the Charter. It is debatable whether the case-law interpreting *ne bis in idem* – which asserts that the simultaneous pursuit of administrative and criminal proceedings, as well as sanctions, in respect of the same facts which share a 'close connection in space and time', does not contravene the double jeopardy principle – has effectively merged the review of *ne bis in idem* with that of proportionality.

An insightful examination of the *ne bis in idem* case-law reveals a blurred distinction between Article 49(3) and 50 of the Charter. In practice, the application of *ne bis in idem* is intertwined with the review of the proportionality of penalties pursuant to Article 52(1) Charter, which raises the concern that the protective scope of *ne bis in idem* may gradually narrow over time.

In a broader context, the standard of review established in *NE* places a remarkable burden on the courts. They are tasked with scrutinising domestic punitive laws on a case-by-case basis, interpreting them through the broad lens of proportionality and equality before the law, as required by Articles 20 and 49(3) of the Charter.

While the direct effect of the proportionality principle allows individuals to challenge Member States that have incorrectly implemented it, ensuring consistency in this complex environment is a challenge in consideration of the inherently casuistic nature of the courts' approach. That may overlook the importance of predictability in punitive treatment. Domestic judges find themselves adjudicating cases by balancing domestic, constitutional, and EU-based rules, with the potential risk that the principle of legality in tax penalties, as enshrined in many national constitutions, is not adequately upheld.[14]

[12] The judgment n. 95 of the Italian Constitutional Court of 14 April 2022 is an example that demonstrates the growing relevance of the principle of proportionality in assessing the legality of administrative penalties.

[13] Judgement n. 46 of the Italian Constitutional Court of 17 March 2023 is interesting in this respect, as it is one of the first cases in which the Italian Constitutional Court has clearly stated that administrative tax sanctions cannot lead to disproportionate punishment and shall be assessed in light of the principle of proportionality as enshrined in Article 49(3) of the Charter.

[14] For a critical account see, *ex multis*, R Rudoni, 'Sul doppio binario punitivo in materia tributaria. *Ne bis in idem*, coordinamento procedimentale e proporzionalità del cumulo sanzionatorio' in (2019) 4 *Diritto pubblico comparato ed europeo* 1015.

In this context, interpreting: (i) the *ne bis in idem* principle as not precluding the initiation of two simultaneous sets of proceedings based on the same facts, leading to the possible imposition of two sets of sanctions; and (ii) the principle of proportionality as directly enforceable, thereby allowing individuals to challenge national legislation before national courts for failure to comply with the requirement of proportionality of sanctions, could significantly increase the challenges faced by courts, particularly in tax matters.

In practice, due to the prevalence of a dual-track enforcement system in many EU countries, taxpayers often face cumulative tax penalties, both of a criminal and administrative nature, for the same illicit conduct.[15] Moreover, as mentioned above, it is not uncommon to observe situations in which the combined punishment imposed on a taxpayer may be disproportionate given the specific circumstances of the case. In view of the above, the obligation placed on courts to ensure the application of the fundamental rights set out in Articles 49(3) and 50 of the Charter seems particularly demanding and adds a further layer of complexity to the proper adjudication of tax cases.

The preliminary ruling in the case *BV*[16] provides, *inter alia*, useful insights into the complexities inherent in the standard of review of tax-related sanctions of a criminal and administrative nature in the light of the principles of *ne bis in idem* and of proportionality.

In this case, BV, a sole trader, worked as an accountant and was subject to VAT. Following a tax audit, criminal proceedings were initiated for tax evasion – VAT and income tax – and the taxpayer was convicted. The taxpayer claimed that his criminal conviction was contrary to the principle of *ne bis in idem* enshrined in Article 50 of the Charter, on the ground that he had already been the subject of a tax adjustment procedure in respect of the same acts, which had resulted in the imposition of a final tax penalty of 40% of the tax evaded.[17]

The taxpayer argued that the French legal system did not satisfy the requirements that a duplication of prosecution and penalties of a criminal nature must comply with. In particular, the French rules lacked clarity and foreseeability and, in particular, did not satisfy the requirements of necessity and proportionality of the duplication of penalties.

In BV, the ECJ initially reaffirmed its stance, stating that the simultaneous occurrence of administrative and criminal proceedings related to the same facts, which are linked by a 'close connection in space and time' and which involve so-called indirect penalties, does not violate the *ne bis in idem* principle. However, the ECJ also clarified that in order for national law to be compatible with EU law, it must lay down clear and precise rules to ensure that, where a fine and a custodial

[15] As can be inferred from the IBFD Yearbook on Taxpayers' Rights 2022, Chapter 7, 144.

[16] Case C-570/20 *Criminal proceedings against BV* ECLI:EU:C:2022:348.

[17] For an analysis of the judgment see L Lonardo, 'The reasonable foreseeability of criminal proceedings for tax evasion: Case BV (C-570/20)' in EULawLive, 13 May 2022 (available at https://eulawlive.com/).

sentence are imposed concurrently, the total penalties imposed do not exceed the gravity of the offence established.

In this context, in line with the *Garlsson* case-law,[18] the ECJ emphasised the significance of the principle of proportionality and indirectly urged domestic courts to address situations in which the national legislator has not provided a comprehensive framework to ensure that the cumulation of penalties does not result in a disproportionate punishment.

In essence, through this judgment, the ECJ aims to ensure that a comprehensive assessment of both criminal and administrative penalties associated with the relevant illicit conduct is made when imposing punishment. Without such consideration, the objective of the *ne bis in idem* principle would be undermined, as the mere existence of a 'close connection in space and time' would not provide a substantive mechanism to prevent the disproportionate duplication of penalties.[19]

This decision has two implications. First, it confirms, in line with the *Menci* case-law, that the legitimacy of concurrent tax sanctions under the *ne bis in idem* principle depends fundamentally on a proportionality assessment. In essence, if there is a mechanism in place whereby cumulative punitive sanctions are aggregated, the simultaneous imposition of punitive measures through parallel proceedings is considered irrelevant from a *ne bis idem* perspective to the extent that a proportionate overall punitive response in ensured.

Secondly, the merging of the *ne bis in idem* review within a proportionality assessment may overlook the distinct nature inherent in criminal and administrative tax sanctions, notwithstanding the fact that these sanctions overall retain punitive nature under the Engel criteria.

In essence, while the proportionality principle ensures that, from a substantive perspective, the severity of the offence is reflected in the gravity of all the penalties imposed, this outcome diminishes the significance of certain substantive and procedural rules. This is even though these rules, such as those relating to the burden of proof, the cross-utilisation of evidentiary material from criminal proceedings in administrative proceedings and vice versa, and the principle of *res judicata*, are not uniformly regulated at both the criminal and administrative levels, as different procedural guarantees apply.

In other words, if the main objective of proportionality is simply to ensure that the final sanction, whether criminal or administrative, is not excessive, certain specific safeguards that apply differently in administrative and criminal proceedings become less relevant from a judicial perspective. Consequently, a broad application of the principle of proportionality, in adherence to the guidance of the case-law of the ECJ, while capable of achieving proportionate outcomes in terms of substance,

[18] Case C-537/16 *Garlsson Real Estate and Others* ECLI:EU:C:2018:193.

[19] Nevertheless, it is crucial to emphasise that the guidelines offered by the ECJ in this regard are still quite general. In the regrettable absence of explicit and precise regulations established by the legislator, the responsibility therefore falls solely on domestic courts to determine what would constitute a proportionate punishment in the specific case at hand.

may undermine the procedural safeguards that traditionally define the imposition of punitive measures, particularly of a criminal nature, and may ultimately reduce the level of protection to that typically associated with administrative sanctions.

IV. Exploring Selected Aspects of the Application of the Proportionality Principle in Tax Sanctions Through the Lens of the ECJ Case-Law

Ensuring proportionality in tax matters is a multifaceted challenge for several reasons. It is thus interesting to discuss three aspects in particular, that underline areas of punitive tax law where proportionality could play an increasingly important role.

First, it is debatable if punitive measures such as confiscatory measures, now routinely imposed for criminal tax violations in addition to traditional custodial sentences in the Member States' practice, are fully proportionate. Secondly, the cumulative imposition of punitive sanctions in corporate scenarios in which the entity benefiting from the tax evasion differs from the actual perpetrator of the violation may not fully respect the principle of proportionality. Thirdly, an often overlooked aspect is that, due to the elements of complexity inherent in the application of substantive and procedural tax laws, the imposition of legitimate administrative and criminal tax sanctions is often accompanied by a variety of 'quasi' tax sanctions that meet the criteria for punitive measures under the Engel framework. It is therefore also interesting to evaluate whether and to what extent the application of the principle of proportionality could play a greater role in this area.

A. Seeking Proportionality in the Imposition of Tax Penalties within Corporate Contexts

A particular problem arises when considering the application of proportionality in cases where the entity benefiting from tax evasion differs from the actual perpetrator of the violation, as is often the case in corporate settings.

In these situations, the goal of the punitive system is twofold: on the one hand, it aims to impose financial penalties on the legal entity that has obtained economic advantages from the tax violation, since it is the ultimate beneficiary of the tax evasion. On the other hand, the relevant rules do not overlook the position of the individual – usually the legal representative of the company – who initiated the illegal conduct and thus made the tax offence possible.

From a proportionality perspective, the question at hand is whether it is proportionate to impose separate sanctions on both the legal entity benefiting from the tax violation and the natural person responsible for the violation.

The ECJ had the opportunity to evaluate the compatibility of such punitive rules from the perspective of *ne bis in idem* in only one case so far, leading to the *Orsi and Baldetti* ruling of 5 April 2017.[20]

In this judgment, the ECJ essentially interpreted the meaning of the 'same person' requirement pursuant to Article 50 of the Charter with regard to the relationship between a physical person and a legal entity, and it concluded that the requirement is not met when a tax penalty is imposed on a company with legal personality but the criminal proceedings are brought against a natural person, even if the natural person was the legal representative of the company subject to the tax penalty.

At first glance, the conclusions reached by the ECJ seem unlikely to be reversed in the immediate future. However, one aspect may put pressure on the courts to adopt more nuanced solutions with regard to the imposition of tax penalties in corporate contexts.

As a matter of fact, in most EU Member States, the rules on penalties in the corporate context have been slightly modified to introduce a quasi-criminal liability of corporate bodies for tax offences. In short, this form of tax liability adopts criteria that are autonomous from those that characterise the imposition of criminal and administrative sanctions, with the ultimate result that it can be imposed on top of existing punitive sanctions.

As the introduction of this form of quasi-criminal liability for body-corporates further blurs the line between administrative and criminal sanctions, it remains to be seen how the courts will react to ensure that the cumulative punishments resulting from the imposition of criminal, administrative, and quasi-criminal sanctions comply with the principle of proportionality.

B. The Endeavour to Establish Proportionality with Reference to Confiscation Measures in Punitive Tax Matters

It is widely known that confiscation measures are frequently applied in tax matters and are usually imposed to confiscate the proceeds of tax evasion that reach the threshold for criminal liability.

However, the application of confiscation measures raises complex issues that ultimately call into question the principle of proportionality. In practice, the relationship between confiscation rules and proportionality in punitive tax matters has not yet been addressed by the ECJ, and guidance from domestic courts, particularly constitutional courts, appears to be scarce.

The reasons for this cannot be fully investigated here. Suffice it to say that confiscation measures can take many forms, depending on the applicable law and

[20] Joined Cases C-217/15 and C-350/15 *Orsi and Baldetti* ECLI:EU:C:2017:264.

the circumstances of the case, and that there is therefore a degree of ambiguity as to whether confiscation measures should be classified as punitive in nature. Specifically, it remains unclear whether forfeiture should be considered as a type of criminal punishment to be applied in addition to a custodial sentence or a fine or, conversely, it should be qualified as a mechanism exclusively aimed at recovering the proceeds of the tax evasion and, ultimately, to fully eliminate the economic benefit derived by the taxpayer as a result of the illegal conduct.

Nevertheless, at least in those cases where confiscation is imposed on a person other than the economic beneficiary of the tax violation, it is doubtful whether forfeiture could not be interpreted as an additional type of punitive measure imposed in addition to existing criminal sanctions. If this were the case, the consequence would be that the financial burden deriving from the forfeiture of an amount equal to the proceeds of the tax offence would have to be taken into account in the proportionality assessment of the punitive treatment of the various subjects involved.[21]

C. Striving for Proportionality: Navigating the Complexities of 'Quasi-Criminal' Tax Sanctions and Addressing Other Technicalities within the Tax Penalty Framework

As noted above, the application of substantive and procedural tax laws often results in situations in which taxpayers are subject to punitive measures that do not neatly align with the definitions set out in the Engel case-law. However, given the widespread use of such measures by domestic legislators, it is only a matter of time before the ECJ is called upon to determine whether the proportionality principle applies in these circumstances. The question would then be what potential remedies are available to ensure the compatibility of these domestic 'quasi' punitive rules with Article 49(3) of the Charter.

Guidance on the application of the proportionality principle would therefore be particularly important in two scenarios that are gaining increasing practical relevance.

Firstly, the imposition of 'quasi' sanctions in value-added tax (VAT) raises concerns. This is particularly problematic in the context of the fight against VAT fraud, where severe penalties, such as the denial of VAT deduction or the obligation to pay the VAT amount in lieu of the fraudster, are imposed on taxpayers who were aware or should have been aware of an evasion committed upstream or downstream in the supply chain.

[21] Admittedly, reaching this interpretative conclusion would add a layer of complexity to the proportionality review. Judges would not only have to assess whether the confiscation meets the Engel criteria and falls within the scope of a criminal charge, but also strike a balance in the cumulative imposition of custodial and financial penalties. Moreover, as recalled in the previous paragraph, this assessment may extend to the consideration of other penalties imposed on corporate entities in relation to the same set of circumstances.

In this respect, the ECJ has already provided important guidance by emphasising that the right to deduct VAT should not be denied if the taxable person, even if not acting in good faith, has completely eliminated the risk of any loss of tax revenue. In other words, the denial of VAT deduction is contrary to the principle of proportionality if the taxable person has already deducted an amount of VAT equal to that paid to the Treasury and there is no loss of revenue for the Member State. The denial of VAT deduction constitutes a 'quasi-sanction' which is not justified by the seriousness of the taxpayer's illegal behaviour.[22]

Nevertheless, the recognition of an increasingly important role for the principle of proportionality would be valuable in assessing the legality of certain penalties that appear excessively severe in the fight against VAT fraud schemes. In this context, the ECJ is increasingly called upon to scrutinise domestic legislation in this respect; however, inconsistencies in its case-law are beginning to emerge, demonstrating the difficulty for the ECJ to provide clear guidance on the interpretation of proportionality when faced with the application of different domestic punitive rules and specific fact patterns.[23] Ultimately, in such circumstances, the interplay with different legal rules and a broad set of fact patterns may hamper consistency in the case-law of the ECJ. It therefore remains to be seen whether the ECJ will indeed be able to ensure a consistent approach in its case-law on proportionality in the context of VAT, which could then be relied upon by domestic courts when setting aside disproportionate domestic financial penalties.

Secondly, aside from VAT penalties, guidelines on the relevance of the principle of proportionality would be important with reference to the growing body of sanctions imposed to punish failure to comply with disclosure requirements under various tax rules.[24]

In this respect, the goal of combating certain tax planning practices that have historically diverted revenues through sophisticated mechanisms exploiting different regulations in different countries has required the introduction of stringent penalties. These penalties aim to pre-emptively penalise behaviours that fall short of tax evasion, but represent a risk of tax revenue loss to the

[22] See the ECJ judgment in Case C-272/13 *Equoland* ECLI:EU:C:2014:2091, para 41. See also Case C-712/17 *EN.SA Srl*, ECLI:EU:C:2019:374, paras 34–36, commented by M Greggi, 'Neutrality and Proportionality in VAT: Making Sense of an (Apparent) Conflict' in (2020) 48 *Intertax* 122.

[23] See the ECJ's findings in Case C-418/22 *SA CEZAM* ECLI:EU:C:2023:418, paras 39–41, which draw a distinct conclusion regarding the application of the principle of proportionality to VAT penalties in circumstances essentially analogous to those examined in Case C-712/17 *EN.SA Srl*, ECLI:EU:C:2019:374, paras 39–45.

[24] A case in point is the Council Directive (EU) 2018/822 amending Directive 2011/16/EU as regards mandatory automatic exchange of information in the field of taxation in relation to reportable cross-border arrangements [2018] OJ L139/1 (the so-called 'DAC-6 Directive') which imposes sweeping notification obligations also onto professionals and the ensuing litigation that have has also been brought to the attention of the ECJ (Case C-694/20 *Orde van Vlaamse Balies* ECLI:EU:C:2022:963). See, in this regard, M Greggi, 'Shades of Transparency: DAC6 and the Client Attorney Privilege' in (2023) 32 *EC Tax Review* 67.

Treasury, by making it more difficult for the tax authorities to carry out their audit activities.[25]

However, the implementation of severe penalties for non-compliance with disclosure requirements raises challenges in terms of the application of proportionality, as in certain cases the imposition of such penalties could lead to disproportionate punishments that cannot be justified given the lack of harm caused by the offender to the tax revenue of the Treasury.[26]

V. Balancing Proportionality with the Protection of EU Financial Interest: A Complex Exercise

It would be inadequate to assess the significance of the proportionality principle in the field of tax penalties without addressing, although briefly, the controversial issue of the protection of the financial interests of the Union.

It is widely recognised that EU law, in particular Article 325(1) and (2) TFEU interpreted in the light of the *Taricco* case-law,[27] requires Member States to ensure that serious fraud is punishable by criminal penalties which are, in particular, effective and dissuasive. Moreover, these measures must be consistent with those taken by Member States to combat equally serious cases of fraud affecting their own financial interests. The imperative to effectively combat VAT fraud may require Member States to specifically punish the most serious fraud violations with criminal sanctions in order to ensure that EU financial interests are protected in an effective and dissuasive manner.

Essentially, the foundational concept underlying punitive sanctions in the *Taricco* judgment revolves around deterrence and effectiveness in ensuring seamless tax collection: in other words, harsher penalties amount to a means of reinforcing taxpayers' compliance and discouraging them from engaging in VAT evasion schemes.

[25] This distinction is well known in punitive law: in particular, criminal law distinguishes between 'crimes of danger' and 'crimes of event' as types of violations can be sanctioned by punitive provisions (cfr. A Di Amato, *Italian Law on Business Crime* (London-The Hague, Kluwer Law International, 2001) 11).

[26] Other elements should be considered as well, which cannot be analysed here in detail. In particular, pre-emptive punitive penalties that punish failure to comply with disclosure obligations call into question the possible role of the principle of proportionality on the application of the *nemo tenetur se detegere* principle in sanction-related matters. *Nemo tenetur* is acknowledged in many EU countries, through specific procedures to identify a point in time when it becomes likely that a penalty or a criminal charge might arise. In most of these jurisdictions, the tax authorities issue warnings to protect *nemo tenetur*, and restrictions on the use of information supplied by the taxpayer in a subsequent penalty or criminal proceeding are enforced. However, the extent to which taxpayers have the right to invoke *nemo tenetur* as a ground for refusing to provide accounting and other information to the tax authority, and the extent to which criminal penalties can be imposed to sanction taxpayers who fail to comply with a disclosure requirement by invoking the *nemo tenetur* principle, is a matter of debate.

[27] See the ECJ judgment in Case C-105/14 *Taricco* ECLI:EU:C:2015:555 and the subsequent judgment in Case C-42/17, *M.A.S. and M.B.* ECLI:EU:C:2017:936.

Against this backdrop, it is undeniable that the growing importance of proportionality can act as a counterbalance, ensuring that punitive treatment results from a balanced judgment that does not automatically prioritise the financial interests of the EU over rights related to sanctions; while imposing severe penalties for fraud remains legitimate, financial interests cannot justify disproportionate sanctions.

In this context, the ECJ's potential reliance on Article 49(3) of the Charter may add a crucial element of clarity and provides a robust foundation and justification for reviewing the legality of the punitive measures implemented by Member States with the aim of safeguarding the EU financial interests.

In essence, the reference to Article 49(3) of the EU Charter by the ECJ would unquestionably signal that respect for the principle of proportionality in tax-related matters should not be considered – as several previous judgments have suggested – merely as a corollary of general tax principles, such as neutrality in VAT, or fundamental freedoms in direct taxation,[28] but as a taxpayer's protection in its own right, that provides autonomous guarantees specifically to sanction-related matters.

VI. Brief Conclusive Remarks

In light of the considerations outlined in the previous paragraphs, two main considerations could conclusively be drawn. On the one hand, the application of the principle of proportionality of penalties in the tax domain constitutes an urgent need; on the other hand, it is extremely difficult to define a coherent framework that takes into account the competing objectives and specificity of punitive tax law as a whole.

In this respect, however, the ECJ is currently acquiring an ever-increasing role in matters concerning tax sanctions. The reference to Article 49(3) of the Charter in the recent ECJ case-law is a step in this direction, and this situation will undoubtedly place the ECJ at the forefront of the 'quest' for proportionality in tax-related sanctions.

[28] In this respect, reference may be made to Case C-788/19 *Commission v Spain (Obligation d'information en matière fiscale)* ECLI:EU:C:2022:55, paras 58–63, in which the ECJ stated that the imposition of a proportional fine of 150% of the tax due, calculated on amounts corresponding to the value of the rights or assets held abroad by the taxpayer, applied to those who did not comply or complied late, constituted a disproportionate restriction on the free movement of capital, since it applied automatically and could not be varied, and was higher than the rates of the tax, is a disproportionate restriction on the free movement of capital because it applies automatically, it cannot be varied and it is much higher than the penalty rates normally applicable for late declaration of taxable income in a purely domestic situation. For a general comment of this decision see the Opinion Statement ECJ-TF 2/2022 on the ECJ decision of 27 January 2022 in Case C-788/19, European Commission v Kingdom of Spain (Form 720) of the CFE ECJ Task Force of May 2022 (available at https://taxadviserseurope.org/project/opinion-statement-ecj-tf-2-2022-on-the-ECJ-decision-in-case-c-788-19-european-commission-v-kingdom-of-spain-form-720-on-the-lack-of-proportionality-of-the-consequences-derived-from-the-failure-to/).

However, the ECJ's approach, grounded in a case-by-case methodology, has inherent shortcomings that elicit careful consideration.

A primary concern, as recalled above, pertains to the intricate structure of the tax punitive framework, featuring diverse sanctions with distinct objectives and functions. Moreover, Member States are each guided by distinct legal systems and domestic traditions in punitive matters, which introduce significant variability. Consequently, the potential for misunderstandings and inconsistencies is high, vividly illustrated by the *Taricco* saga.

In this context, in other terms, ensuring sustained consistency in applying the principle of proportionality poses a formidable challenge for the ECJ, as the escalating number of cases brought before the ECJ heightens the risk of proliferating inconsistencies and contradictions over time.[29]

Considering these issues, it is asserted that introducing a set of minimum standards and guidelines – whether through secondary legislation or, in the absence of the latter, in the form of soft-law guidelines – would constitute a pivotal aspect in fortifying the application of the principle of proportionality in the realm of tax punitive sanctions.

As emphasised above, there is an urgent need for clarification of the scope of the proportionality principle to enhance the predictability of punitive rules, especially in the realm of VAT-related sanctions. However, other facets of punitive tax law, including confiscation measures and situations involving corporate bodies, would also greatly benefit from such clarity.

Without these clarifications, there is a risk that the ECJ's case-by-case approach may inadvertently create more uncertainties over time. This could ultimately lead to persistent conflicts between domestic and supranational courts, heightening unpredictability in decision-making and challenging established principles, such as the principle of legality, which is of paramount relevance both in many Member States and at the EU level.[30]

[29] In that respect paradoxically, the ECJ could become a victim of its own success. It is therefore crucial for the ECJ to steer clear of the situation it currently faces regarding VAT: it is well known that the surge in VAT-related cases in the docket of the ECJ has complicated its judicial review process and hampered its ability to furnish clarifications to domestic courts in the preliminary reference procedure.

[30] As recently recalled in Joined Cases C-885/19 P and C-898/19 P *Fiat Chrysler Finance Europe v Commission* ECLI:EU:C:2022:859; Joined Cases C-451/21 P and C-454/21 P *Luxembourg v Commission* ECLI:EU:C:2023:948 and Case C-457/21 P *Commission v Amazon.com and Others* ECLI:EU:C:2023:985.

16

Proportionality of the Penalty of Confiscation

Focus on French and Spanish Criminal Law

CHLOÉ FAUCHON

I. Introduction

In criminal law, the main penalties are the deprivation of liberty and fines, which are provided for in all national criminal legislations. However, there are some other penalties that exist and are regulated as complementary penalties. This is the case of confiscation,[1] which can be defined as the forced alienation of the convicted person's patrimonial assets for the benefit of the State or, more rarely, for the benefit of another person, such as the victim.[2] Our chapter will focus on this penalty and, more specifically on its proportionality. Indeed, as any sanction, confiscation must be proportionate to the severity of the offence. However, in the European Union framework, this obligation may not be respected. To study that, this chapter will analyse more particularly French and Spanish law.

Many international conventions contemplate the penalty of confiscation (for example, the Council of Europe Convention on Laundering, Search, Seizure and Confiscation of the Proceeds from Crime of 1990, the United Nations' International Convention for the Suppression of the Financing of Terrorism of 1999, the United Nations' Convention against Corruption of 2003 …). This has led many states to include this penalty in their criminal legislation. Despite the existence of a Council of Europe Convention,[3] the European Union decided to go further and

[1] Some authors question the nature of confiscation as a penalty as it can be imposed without a criminal conviction. This debate is beyond the scope of our presentation, and we will qualify confiscation as a penalty without further question.

[2] O Décima, S Detraz, E Verny, *Droit pénal général*, 5th ed (Paris, Librairie Générale de Droit et de Jurisprudence, 2022) 337.

[3] Convention on Laundering, Search, Seizure and Confiscation of the Proceeds from Crime (Strasbourg, 8 November 1990).

to oblige the Member States to include confiscation as a criminal measure in their legislation. With Framework Decision 2001/500/JHA and Framework Decision 2005/212/JHA,[4] the European Union adopted its first instruments on confiscation.

However, these instruments did not contemplate all the problems on confiscation (for instance, they did not contain any definition) and in 2014 the Union adopted a more general and comprehensive instrument: Directive 2014/42/EU on the freezing and confiscation of instrumentalities and proceeds of crime. In this Directive, the European Union defines confiscation as "a final deprivation of property ordered by a court in relation to a criminal offence".[5] Different types of confiscation are then envisaged: confiscation of instrumentalities and proceeds, value confiscation (Art. 4), extended confiscation (Art. 5) and confiscation from a third party (Art. 6). Moreover, this penalty applies to many offences, as Article 3 mentions several framework decisions and directives harmonising offences and penalties (for instance, Framework Decision 2002/475/JHA on terrorism or Directive 2011/36/EU on trafficking in human beings) that also cover more than one harmonised offence. The confiscation regime established by the European Union is therefore very broad, both in terms of the measures it can lead to and the offences for which it can be imposed.

According to the binding nature of directives, Member States are obliged to comply with European Union rules. In this perspective, in the case of a directive, Member States must adopt national legislation to adapt to European rules. Article 288 of the Treaty on the Functioning of the European Union reads that a Directive "shall be binding, as to the result to be achieved, upon each Member State to which it is addressed, but *shall leave to the national authorities the choice of form and methods*" (emphasis added). In the case of Directive 2014/42/EU, this means that Member States had to amend their national law in order to introduce confiscation as provided for in the Directive. In France, the adoption of this EU Directive did not lead to any amendment in the applicable national legislative framework. Indeed, the French law on confiscation was already quite extensive and has provided for value confiscation and confiscation from third parties since 2012 or 2013.[6] On the contrary, in Spain, the national legislator had to amend the legislation to comply with the European rules, through the adoption of Organic Law 1/2015.[7]

Confiscation is therefore widely envisaged in national legislation, in response to the European Union's commitment. The adoption of value confiscation or extended

[4] Council Framework Decision 2001/500/JHA on money laundering, the identification, tracing, freezing, seizing and confiscation of instrumentalities and the proceeds of crime [2001] OJ L182/1; Council Framework Decision 2005/212/JHA on Confiscation of Crime-Related Proceeds, Instrumentalities and Property [2005] OJ L68/49.

[5] Art. 2(4).

[6] L Ascenci, 'Les saisies et confiscations en matière pénale après la loi du 9 juillet 2010: l'édifice parachevé ?' (2015) 5 *Actualité Juridique Pénal* 228.

[7] NJ de la Mata Barranco, 'Las distintas modalidades de decomiso después de la Ley Orgánica 1/2015, de 30 de marzo' (2017) *La ley penal: revista de derecho penal, procesal y penitenciario* 764.

confiscation has been criticized in Spain, and more than in France,[8] as a way to criminalise unlawful accumulation of wealth and disregard the core principles of criminal law, such as *ultima ratio* or proportionality.[9] Indeed, the criminal law must be strictly limited as it can interfere with the most fundamental rights.[10] In this respect, criminal law is surrounded by many crucial principles. One of the most famous is the principle of legality, according to which no one can be punished except in accordance with a previous law, that is, only the law can define a crime and prescribe a penalty. The Charter of Fundamental Rights (Charter) enshrines this principle in its Article 49(1). This article is a very important provision for criminal law, as it also lays down the principle of proportionality of penalties in paragraph 3.

Indeed, Article 49(3) states that "the severity of penalties must not be disproportionate to the criminal offence". As the European Convention on Human Rights (ECHR) does not contain any reference to the principle of proportionality of sanctions, this consecration in a European instrument is innovative. Moreover, it is necessary, because this consecration makes the principle of proportionality of penalties, which is very important in the Rule of Law, mandatory in every Member State, even if the principle is not enshrined in constitutional or legal domestic texts. The inclusion of a provision on the principle of proportionality in the Charter can be seen as a consequence of its high value in national constitutional systems.[11] In France, for example, the *Conseil constitutionnel* took it from Article 8 of the Declaration of the Rights of Man and of the Citizen of 1789, a text of constitutional value. In Spain, no constitutional provision explicitly requires the proportionality of penalties. However, the doctrine has found some constitutional grounds for this principle: in particular, Article 15 of the Constitution, on the prohibition of inhuman and degrading penalties, and Article 9(3) of the Constitution, on the prohibition of arbitrariness on the part of the authorities.[12] In addition, the *Tribunal Supremo* reiterated that the principle of proportionality is linked to Article 25 of the Constitution, enshrining the principle of legality, and "should be considered as the guiding line of every court ruling, and more specifically of the judicial individualisation of penalties which should operate regarding the level of culpability and the seriousness of the offence".[13]

Moreover, the requirement of proportionality of penalties has long been enshrined by the ECJ.[14] The Court controls the proportionality of sanctions

[8] On the contrary, for a positive view of the adoption of value confiscation in France, see E Camous, 'La confiscation en valeur Une peine en devenir' (2017) 7–8 *Droit pénal* 5.

[9] de la Mata Barranco (n 7).

[10] M Muñoz de Morales Romero, *Derecho penal europeo* (Valencia, Tirant lo Blanch, 2020) 20.

[11] D Rebut, 'Article 49' in F Picod, C Rizcallah, S Van Drooghenbroeck (eds), *Charte des droits fondamentaux de l'Union européenne. Commentaire article par article*, 2nd ed. (Bruxelles, Bruylant, 2020) 1996.

[12] A Giraldi, 'La proporcionalidad de la pena en el ordenamiento español: elaboración doctrinal y evolución jurisprudencial' (2018) *La ley penal: revista de derecho penal, procesal y penitenciario*.

[13] 16 October 2014, 658/2014.

[14] For instance, Case C-157/79 *Stanislaus Pieck* ECLI:EU:C:1980:179.

provided by Member States and censures them if they are disproportionate to the seriousness of the offence, especially if they impede a right or freedom secured by EU law.[15] The enshrinement of this principle in the Charter was therefore a logical consequence of the Court's case-law. The proportionality of penalties is thus a well-established principle of European law. But, as we have already seen with confiscation, the European Union also requires Member States to provide for extensive penalties, with respect to the type. Consequently, we may wonder about the strategy and coherence of European policies that simultaneously demand the proportionality of penalties and the adoption of extensive sanctions. This controversy, based on similar domestic standards, also exists in national legal orders. Indeed, as we have mentioned, constitutional provisions guarantee the principle of proportionality of penalties. Meanwhile, criminal legislation provides for broad confiscation sanctions, as required by the European Union. The paradox between, on the one hand, the enshrinement of the principle of proportionality of penalties and, on the other hand, the demand for extended confiscation sanctions, is the starting point of our analysis, which will focus on French and Spanish criminal law.

In France, confiscation is regulated by Article 131-21 of the Criminal Code. This is a relatively comprehensive article, which begins by stating that "the complementary penalty of confiscation can be pronounced in the cases the law or regulation lays down, and also for all crimes or offences punished by at least one year of imprisonment, with the exception of the press offences". This provision then goes on to list all the modalities of confiscation: of the instruments or proceeds of the offence, of the value, of any goods in the possession of the convicted person and of which he cannot explain the origin, etc. The penalty is therefore extensive, both in terms of the offences to which it applies and in terms of the goods to which it may apply. The same conclusion can be drawn with reference to Spanish law: Articles 127 to 127 *octies* present provisions quite similar to the French ones. This is logical, since both are subject to European law, which provides for an extensive penalty of confiscation, no matter if there is proportionality or not (II).

However, confiscation has not been declared unconstitutional by the Spanish *Tribunal Constitucional* or the French *Conseil constitutionnel.* Nor has it been condemned by the European Court of Human Rights (ECtHR). National and European courts are trying to strike a balance between the effectiveness and usefulness of this penalty and the rights of the defendant trough the requirement of proportionality of sanctions. It is difficult to strike this balance. Therefore, the ECtHR has adopted many judgements on the penalty of confiscation. Similarly, the French criminal courts also control this penalty and verify the proportionality of the confiscation measure, taking into account the seriousness of the offence and the property confiscated (III). This control by the French criminal courts, which does not exist as such in Spanish criminal courts, is welcomed. Indeed, on the contrary, the European Union seems to require more extended confiscation sanctions, without any interest in the principle of proportionality.

[15] Case 8/77 *Sagulo and Others* ECLI:EU:C:1977:131; Case C-157/79 *Stanislaus Pieck*, paras 19–20.

II. Extensive Confiscation Sanctions under EU Law

First of all, it should be noted that confiscation applies to many offences. Article 3 of the directive lays down a list of harmonised offences for which confiscation can be ordered. There are two groups of offences. The first one is composed of nine out of ten of the "areas of crime" enumerated in Article 83(1) TFEU: terrorism, trafficking in human beings and sexual exploitation of women and children, illicit drug trafficking, money laundering, corruption, counterfeiting of means of payment, computer crime and organised crime. As it includes organised crime, it may include other offences as soon as they are committed by a criminal organisation within the meaning of Framework Decision 2008/841/JHA. The second group consists of offences that may exist in the future: Article 3 states that new instruments may explicitly provide that this Directive applies to the criminal offences harmonised therein.

The list of European "areas of crime" is quite long and covers many different types of criminal activity. Although confiscation is therefore applicable to many offences, the Spanish legislator has decided to extend its scope of application even further. In fact, the Spanish Criminal Code expressly provides for confiscation in the case of property offences where there is criminal continuity or recidivism, fraudulent insolvency, offences against intellectual or industrial property, money laundering, offences against Social Security and the Treasury, offences against workers' rights and embezzlement. It is worth recalling that EU provisions on substantive criminal law are only minimum rules, so national legislators can always go further. The French legislator has also extended the scope of application of confiscation beyond what is provided for in the Directive. Indeed, Article 131-21(1) of the French Criminal Code states that "the complementary penalty of confiscation can be pronounced in the cases laid down by the law or regulation, and also for all crimes or offences punished by at least one year of imprisonment, with the exception of press offences". It means that almost all offences, except the lightest ones, can lead to confiscation. Its scope of application is therefore very wide.

Moreover, the forms of confiscation are particularly extensive; in addition to "normal" confiscation (Art. 4(1)), four other types are envisaged: extended confiscation (Art. 5), non-conviction-based confiscation (Art. 4(2)), value confiscation (Art. 4(1)) and confiscation from a third party (Art. 6). It is interesting to examine each of these and see in which way they may amount to disproportionate penalties.[16] First, extended confiscation applies to a good which is not the proceeds or instrumentality of the offence, but which may be derived from criminal conduct, because the owner has been convicted of a criminal offence which is liable to give rise to

[16] Their disproportionality is criticised by José Luis De La Cuesta (JL de la Cuesta, 'Extended Confiscation in Spanish Law' in M Luchtman (ed), *Of Swords and Shields: Due Process and Crime Control in Times of Globalization, Liber Amicorum Prof. Dr. J.A.E. Vervaele* (The Hague, Eleven Publishing, 2023) 34).

economic benefit and the value of the property is disproportionate to the lawful income of the convicted person. This means that it is not necessary to prove that the property at stake was derived from a specific offence; there is no causal link between the offence for which the person was convicted and the confiscated property.[17] There is a rebuttable presumption of the unlawful origin of the goods.

Although extended confiscation is an "extremely efficient way to combat criminal organisations",[18] we may question the proportionality of this measure.[19] It is worth noting that the European legislator has attempted to comply with the principle of proportionality of criminal sanctions by limiting extended confiscation to offences punishable by a maximum term of imprisonment of at least four years.[20] The French legislator went further in the protection and limited it to offences punishable by a maximum of at least five years of imprisonment.[21] Despite this limitation, many offences are still subject to extended confiscation.

Another form of confiscation that is questionable in terms of proportionality is non-conviction-based confiscation. Article 4(2) of Directive 2014/42/EU states that "where confiscation on the basis of paragraph 1 is not possible, at least where such impossibility is the result of illness or absconding of the suspected or accused person, Member States shall take the necessary measures to enable the confiscation of instrumentalities and proceeds in cases where criminal proceedings have been initiated regarding a criminal offence which is liable to give rise, directly or indirectly, to economic benefit, and such proceedings could have led to a criminal conviction if the suspected or accused person had been able to stand trial". A final conviction is not required, so the link to the offence committed cannot be proven. Moreover, the authorities cannot determine the exact amount of proceeds obtained, because the actual offence which was committed remains uncertain. Non-conviction-based confiscation therefore presents a huge risk to be disproportionate.

Directive 2014/42/EU then also provides for value confiscation. It is not subject to the requirement that the property constituting the direct or indirect proceeds of the crime be unrecoverable. Member States must therefore adopt a broad approach to value confiscation.[22] All of the convicted person's property is at risk from this type of confiscation, as the law does not require the property to be an instrumentality or proceed of the offence, nor does it require a causal link, nor is there any need to suspect that the property confiscated is the product of an offence, as in the

[17] LF de Jorge Mesas, 'El decomiso ampliado en la Reforma del Código Penal de 2015. Ley Orgánica 1/2015, de 30 de marzo' (2016) 7 *Revista Aranzadi Doctrinal* 41.

[18] J Lelieur, 'Freezing and Confiscating Criminal Assets in the European Union' (2015) 3 *European Criminal Law Review* 300.

[19] J Boucht, 'Extended Confiscation and the Proposed Directive on Freezing and Confiscation of Criminal Proceeds in the EU: On Striking a Balance between Efficiency, Fairness and Legal Certainty' (2013) 2 *European Journal of Crime, Criminal Law and Criminal Justice* 127, 129.

[20] Art. 5(2)(e).

[21] Artt. 131-21(5) of the Criminal Code.

[22] Lelieur (n 18), 299.

case of extended confiscation. Of course, value confiscation is an adapted response to profit criminality,[23] since it allows the judge to confiscate money when a profit offence is committed, even without link between the offence and the good confiscated. For instance, the French *Cour de cassation*, in a ruling of 22 March 2017,[24] said that the judge can decide value confiscation and confiscate a good, even when it has been acquired *only partially* with the money from the offence.

The absence of the requirement of a link between the good confiscated and any offence can be criticised. Indeed, the confiscated properties may have been acquired with legal money, so their confiscation can be considered as an inadequate response to the offence committed. Fortunately, two limitations are imposed on value confiscation. The first, and most important, is that confiscation cannot exceed the value of the benefit derived from the offence committed. For instance, if drug trafficking is calculated to have generated 400 000 euros, a house valued at 500 000 euros cannot be confiscated, even if it was largely paid for with dirty money. Secondly, in order to respect the principle of proportionality, it is not possible to combine "normal" confiscation and value confiscation.

The final confiscation measure is the confiscation of property belonging to a third party. Article 6 of the Directive states that "Member States shall take the necessary measures to enable the confiscation of proceeds, or other property the value of which corresponds to proceeds, which, directly or indirectly, were transferred by a suspected or accused person to third parties, or which were acquired by third parties from a suspected or accused person, at least if those third parties knew or ought to have known that the purpose of the transfer or acquisition was to avoid confiscation, on the basis of concrete facts and circumstances, including that the transfer or acquisition was carried out free of charge or in exchange for an amount significantly lower than the market value".

The aim of this form of confiscation is to prevent attempts by some criminals to render their organisations insolvent by transferring ownership of their criminal proceeds to their relatives or legal entities. The effectiveness of third-party confiscation is not debated, but it should be noted that it is sufficient that the goods have been transferred by a "suspected or accused person" or acquired from a "suspected or accused person". Confiscation can therefore be ordered even before the person has been convicted. This change occurred between the Proposal for a Directive and its final adoption: in the proposal, it was necessary for the person who transferred the goods to have been convicted.[25] Although this requirement lowers the efficiency of confiscation, it is more respectful of the principle of proportionality.[26] Indeed, it limits the cases when confiscation can be pronounced and ensures that a final conviction exists, with a profit offence identified. In Spain, confiscation from

[23] Camous (n 8).

[24] Ruling No 16-82.051.

[25] Art. 6(1)(a).

[26] T Aguado Correa, 'La Directiva 2014/42/UE sobre embargo y decomiso en la Unión Europea: una solución de compromiso a medio camino' (2015) *Revista General de Derecho Europeo* 1, 24.

a third party is optional, contrary to other forms of confiscation; the judge can decide not to pronounce it and to leave the third party with their property, even if it is the product of an offence. This is another example of how the principle of proportionality is taken into consideration.

Finally, it is worth mentioning a recital of the Directive relating to the principle of proportionality. Indeed, recital 18 states that "when implementing this Directive, Member States may provide that, in exceptional circumstances, confiscation should not be ordered, insofar as it would, in accordance with national law, represent undue hardship for the affected person [...]. Member States should make a very restricted use of this possibility and should only be allowed to provide that confiscation shall not be ordered in cases where it would put the person concerned in a situation in which it would be very difficult for him or her to survive". Of course, the provision allowing proportionality to be taken into account is to be welcomed. However, the fact that the recital only allows judges not to order confiscation when the person cannot survive without his or her property, can be criticised,[27] since it only contemplates this option in extreme cases and not whenever the proportionality requires it.

We can see thus that the judges play a role in ascertaining the proportionality of a confiscation measure. The measure is not disproportionate or proportionate in itself, but an exam by the courts is required, regarding the severity of the offence committed and the amount of money illegally obtained. This control of the criminal courts is very well-developed in France, contrary to the situation in Spain, where no established case-law could be found.

III. The Proportionality Requirement Applied by the French Courts

In France, there was a turning point in 2016.[28] Before this date, the *Cour de cassation* ruled that judges do not have to justify the proportionality of the penalty of confiscation pronounced, as it was considered that the decision to order confiscation was left at their discretion.[29] However, on 7 December 2016, the French Court adopted two decisions that changed its case law. In the first,[30] the *Cour de cassation* obliged national judges to justify the proportionality of an extended confiscation: it is not enough to refer to the seriousness of the offence in general or to the sole

[27] ibid., 32.

[28] For an overview of the jurisprudence of the *Cour de cassation* on freezing and confiscation orders and their proportionality, see N Planchon, 'La motivation et le contrôle de proportionnalité des décisions de saisie et confiscation' in L Ascensi, P Beauvais, R Parizot (eds), *La confiscation des avoirs criminels : nouveaux enjeux juridiques* (Paris, Librairie Générale de Droit et de Jurisprudence, 2021).

[29] For instance, Ruling of 17 December 2014, No 13-86.722.

[30] No 15-85.136.

criminal experience of the convicted person, but the judges must characterise the concrete seriousness of the facts in order to justify the necessity and proportionality of the interference with the right to property. For the first time, the Court verified the proportionality of a penalty, even when it is included in the legal limits and the law does not explicitly require judges to justify the adoption of a confiscation order.[31]

The other ruling of 2016[32] is totally different, but also concerned the verification of proportionality. On a new ground, the *Cour de cassation* stated that "the principle of proportionality cannot apply to the confiscation of a good which, in its totality, is the proceed or the instrument of the offences the person was convicted of". The Court did not reject the proportionality test in general, as it had done previously, but refused to apply it to the confiscation of the instrumentalities or product of the offence. According to Olivier Violeau, this is a logical decision: it would be absurd to require a justification of the proportionality of the penalty if the convicted person would not be the owner of the confiscated goods without having committed the offence.[33] In this situation, it is sufficient to demonstrate the link between the property and the offence committed.

This case law is not isolated; the *Cour de cassation* repeated it after 2016. For instance, in a ruling of 22 March 2017,[34] the Court ruled that, because the confiscation of the proceeds of the offence referred to a good acquired partially with licit money, and so had a hybrid nature, the judges had to apply a proportionality test. Logically, the test should only take into consideration, on the one hand, the part of the good financed with licit money and, on the other hand, the seriousness of the facts and the personal situation of the convicted person.[35] Domestic courts can therefore adopt two positions. Either they decide to confiscate only illicit properties, and do not have to justify the proportionality of the measure, or they confiscate the totality of the property, including the part financed by legal means, and have to verify proportionality. In a ruling of 27 Jun 2018,[36] the *Cour de cassation* overturned a judgment in which the judges did not verify whether the freezing order, which concerned a good only partially financed by illicit money, did not constitute a disproportionate interference with the right to property. Interestingly, the *Cour de cassation* overturned the judgment according to Article 1 of the First Additional Protocol of the ECHR.

To conclude the part about French case-law, it can be said that the *Cour de cassation* does not make a proportionality exam when confiscation concerns the value of the instrumentality or the proceeds of the offence without exceeding

[31] J-H Robert, 'Les confiscations et les mesures de leur proportionnalité' (2017) 1–2 *La Semaine Juridique. Edition générale* 13.

[32] No16-80.879.

[33] O Violeau, 'Précisions sur la motivation de la proportionnalité de la peine de confiscation' (2017) *Actualité Juridique Pénal* 142.

[34] No 16-82.051.

[35] A Dadoun, 'L'intensité variable de la proportionnalité de la peine de confiscation' (2017) 7–8 *Droit pénal* 6.

[36] Ruling No 17-84.280.

its amount.[37] However, it overturns the decisions that do not allow to be sure that the value of the confiscated building does not exceed the product of the single offence.[38]

In Spain, it is worth mentioning that the Criminal Code contains a provision which is related to the principle of proportionality. Indeed, Article 128 states that no sanction of confiscation would constitute a greater restriction to fundamental rights than the benefit or advantage obtained by the convicted person from their offence. This means that confiscation can be pronounced regarding the licit properties of a convicted person without being disproportionate, if the amount confiscated is not bigger than the benefit obtained from the offence. On the other hand, when the illicit origin of the funds is demonstrated, it seems that no proportionality test is required. In a ruling of 17 November 2022,[39] the *Tribunal Supremo* stated that in order to impose confiscation, it is sufficient for the judges to establish in a rational and non-arbitrary manner that the convicted person did not use legal money for their investments. No other ruling could be found to confirm this case-law, nor to see an application of Article 128 regarding extended or value confiscation.

IV. Conclusion

Following Vittorio Manes, we can observe that, in the European Union, "an evident decrease of guarantees has accompanied the aim of economic neutralisation, implying a sincere preference for efficacy rather than protection of individual rights".[40] In other words, confiscation as required by EU law does not put an emphasis on proportionality, but instead, on the efficacy of the sanction. That is the case of Directive 2014/42/EU, which seems to mark a preference for extensive confiscation to the detriment of the principle of proportionality, although this principle is recognised in the CFR. Moreover, the Proposal for a Directive of the European Parliament and of the Council on asset recovery and confiscation of 25 May 2022[41] does not tend to limit the scope and extent of application of confiscation. For example, Article 2 extends the list of "areas of crime" for which confiscation may be ordered. Furthermore, in addition to all the forms of confiscation contemplated in the 2014 Directive, a new one is included in Article 16 (confiscation of unexplained wealth linked to criminal activities) and Article 17

[37] For instance, Ruling of 13 June 2018, No 17-83.893.

[38] For example, Ruling of 24 October 2018, No 18-80.834.

[39] Ruling No 4110/2022.

[40] V Manes, 'The Last Imperative of Criminal Policy: Nullum Crimen Sine Confiscatione' (2016) 2 *European Criminal Law Review* 146.

[41] On 12 December 2023, the European Parliament and the Council reached a provisional agreement on the draft directive (https://www.europarl.europa.eu/legislative-train/theme-promoting-our-european-way-of-life/file-revision-of-the-directive-on-the-freezing-and-confiscation-of-proceeds-of-crime).

lays down provisions to improve the effectiveness of confiscation and its execution. Fortunately, the ECtHR and the French *Cour de cassation* control the proportionality of the confiscation ordered by judges. Thanks to this control, we can hope that confiscation measures adopted by criminal judges would not be too far-reaching and would guarantee a level of proportionality. Ensuring the rights of defendants through this control is a key role for national judges, as the European Union seems to extend every time the field of application of confiscation measures. As a consequence, it would be very useful for the Spanish criminal courts to take their part in the control of proportionality.

INDEX

www.ingramcontent.com/pod-product-compliance
Ingram Content Group UK Ltd.
Pitfield, Milton Keynes, MK11 3LW, UK
UKHW020245290926
15470UKWH00002B/760

9 781509 974153